MAGICAL MIRACLE

Volume 1

By
Yuzu Mizutani

HAMBURG // LONDON // LOS ANGELES // TOKYO

Magical x Miracle Vol.1
Created by Yuzu Mizutani

Translation - Yoohae Yang
English Adaptation - Mark Ilvedson
Associate Editor - Hope Donovan
Retouch and Lettering - Jennifer Carbajal
Production Artist - Fawn Lau
Cover Design - Gary Shum

Editor - Paul Morrisey
Digital Imaging Manager - Chris Buford
Production Manager - Jennifer Miller
Managing Editor - Lindsey Johnston
VP of Production - Ron Klamert
Publisher and E.I.C. - Mike Kiley
President and C.O.O. - John Parker
C.E.O. and Chief Creative Officer - Stuart Levy

A  Manga

TOKYOPOP Inc.
5900 Wilshire Blvd. Suite 2000
Los Angeles, CA 90036

E-mail: info@TOKYOPOP.com
Come visit us online at www.TOKYOPOP.com

ISBN: 1-59816-328-0

First TOKYOPOP printing: April 2006
10 9 8 7 6 5 4 3 2 1
Printed in the USA

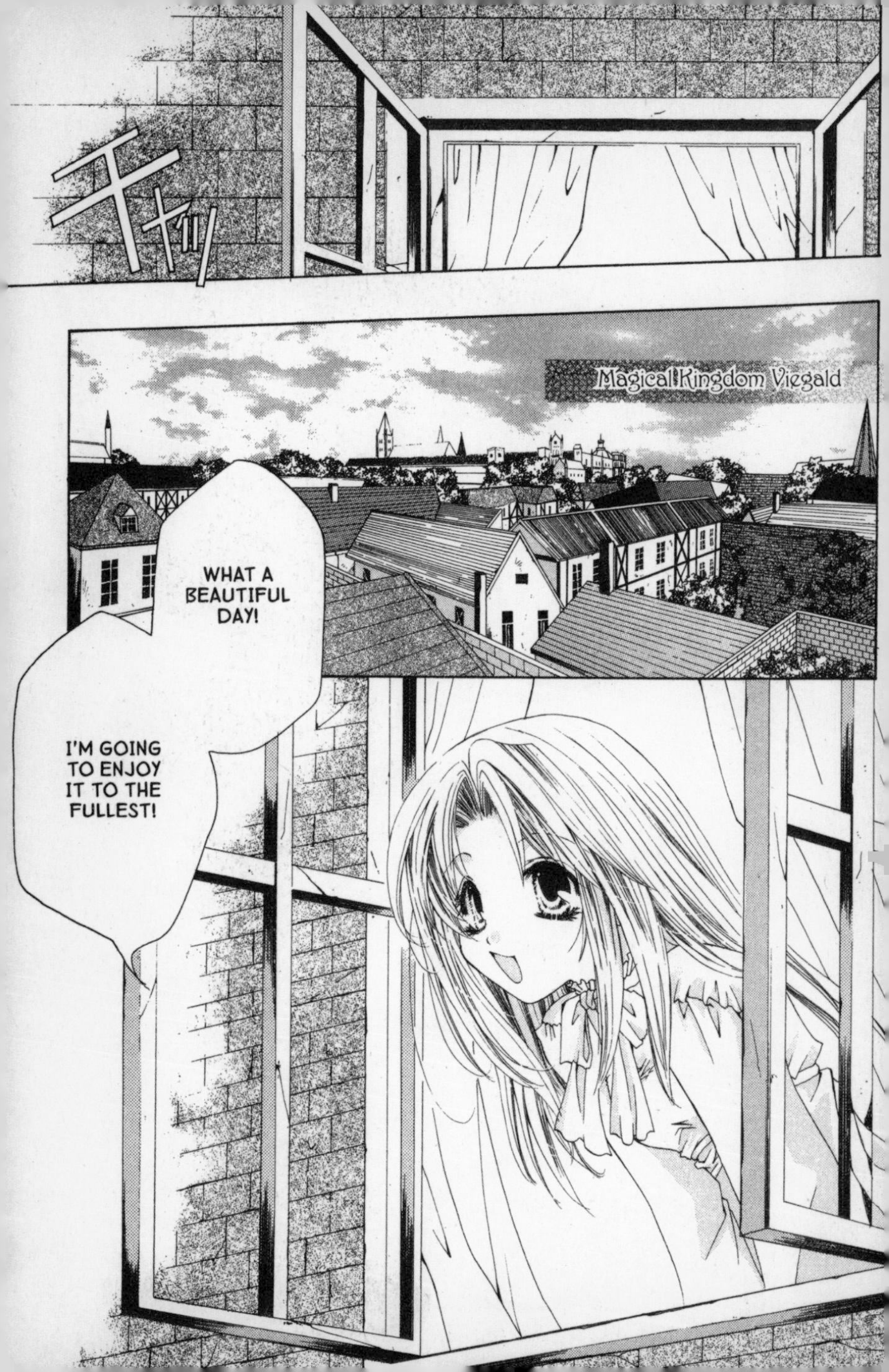
Magical Kingdom Viegald
WHAT A BEAUTIFUL DAY!
I'M GOING TO ENJOY IT TO THE FULLEST!

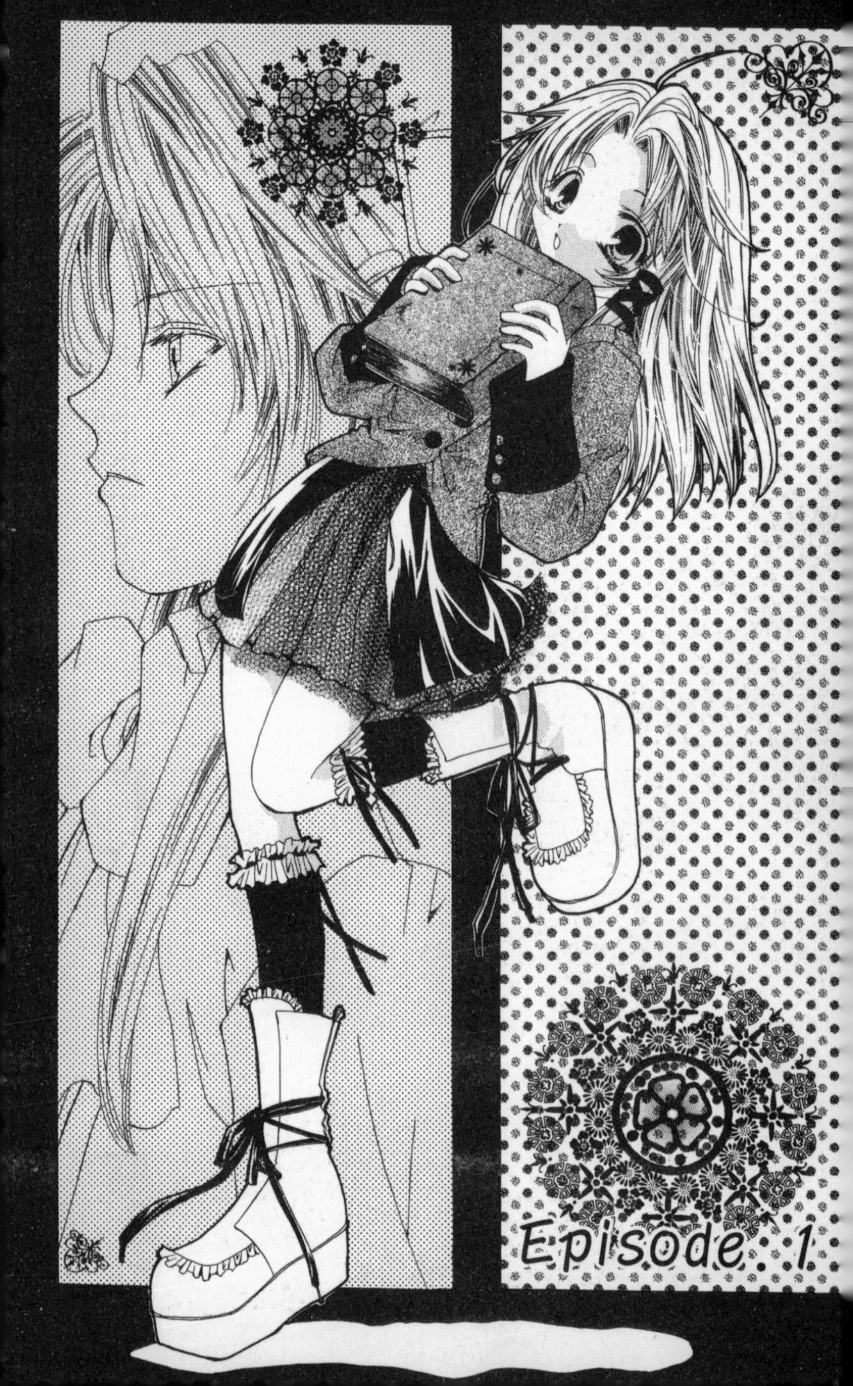
Episode. 1

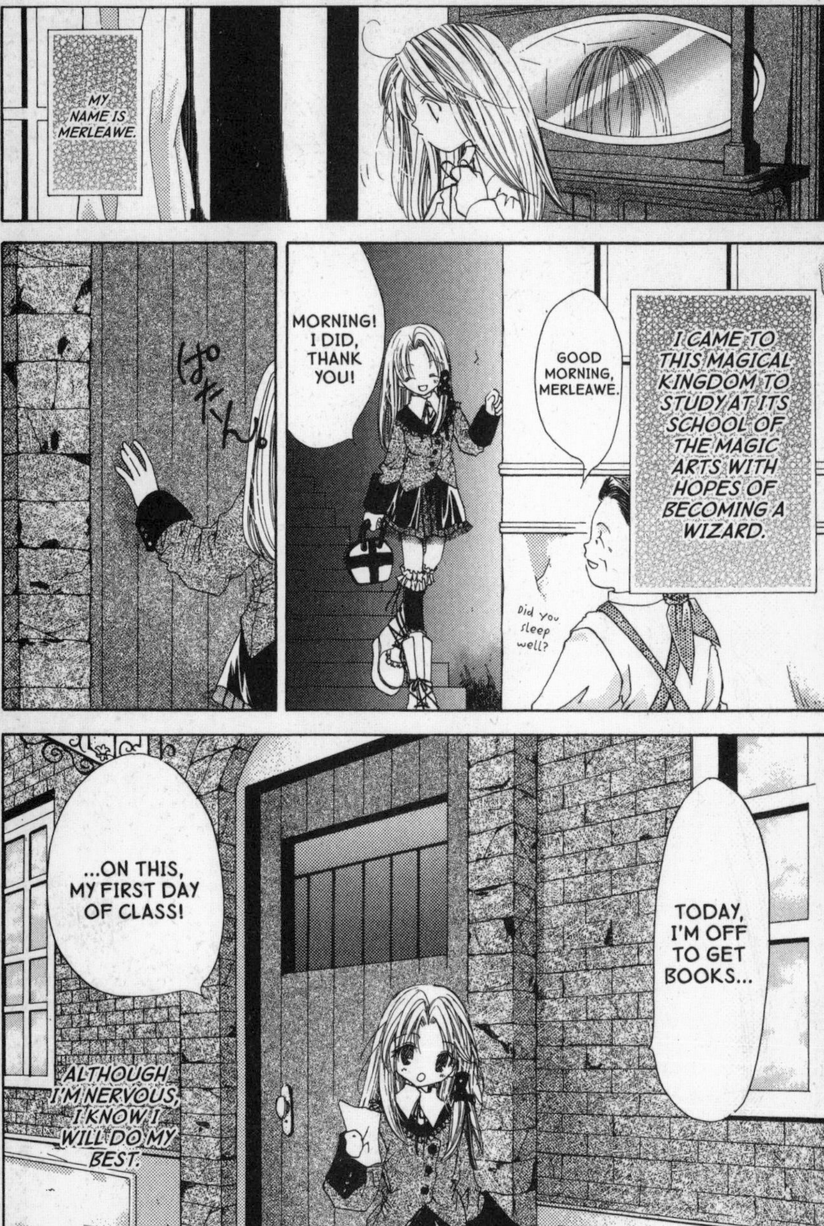
MY NAME IS MERLEAWE.
I CAME TO THIS MAGICAL KINGDOM TO STUDY AT ITS SCHOOL OF THE MAGIC ARTS WITH HOPES OF BECOMING A WIZARD.
GOOD MORNING, MERLEAWE.
Did you sleep well?
MORNING! I DID, THANK YOU!
ぱたん。
TODAY, I'M OFF TO GET BOOKS...
...ON THIS, MY FIRST DAY OF CLASS!
ALTHOUGH I'M NERVOUS, I KNOW I WILL DO MY BEST.

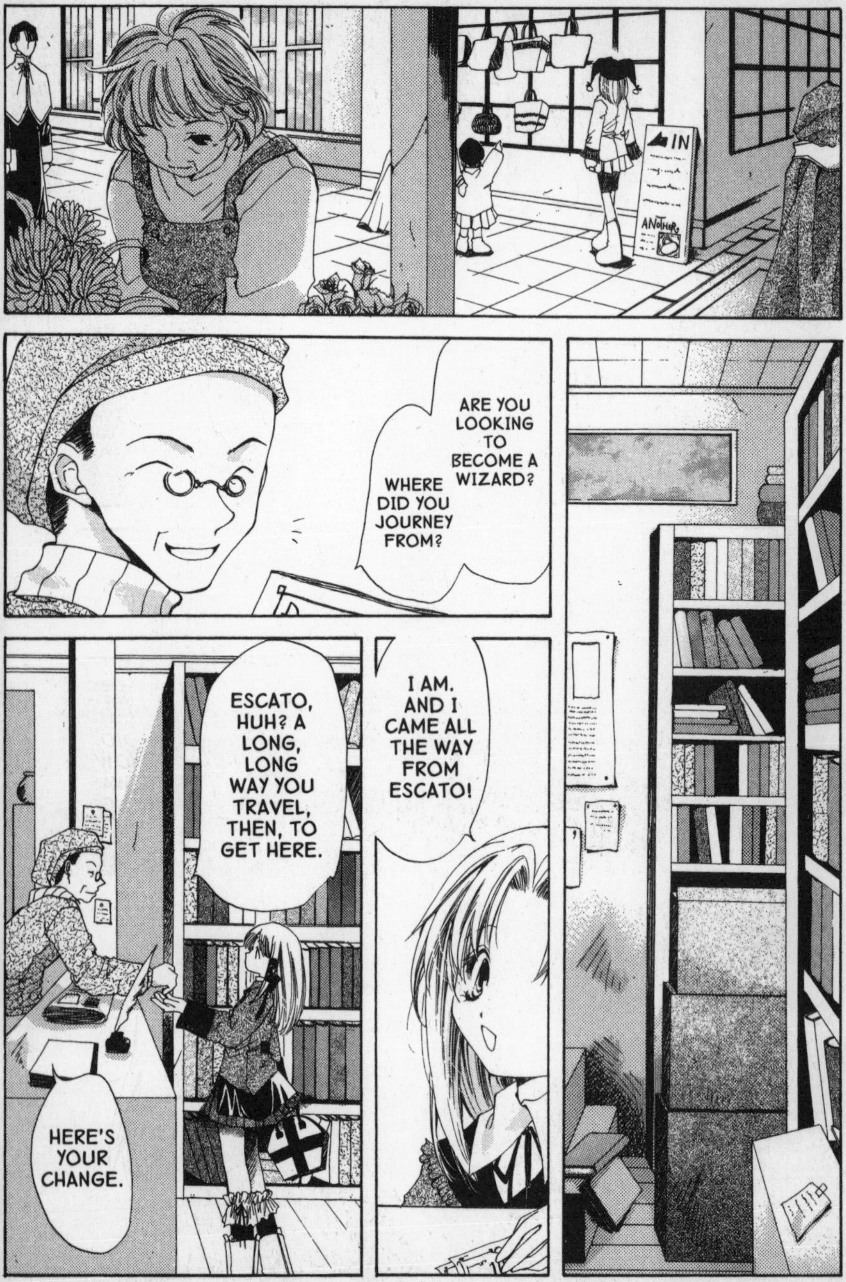

IN
ANOTHER
ARE YOU LOOKING TO BECOME A WIZARD?
WHERE DID YOU JOURNEY FROM?
I AM. AND I CAME ALL THE WAY FROM ESCATO!
ESCATO, HUH? A LONG, LONG WAY YOU TRAVEL, THEN, TO GET HERE.
HERE'S YOUR CHANGE.

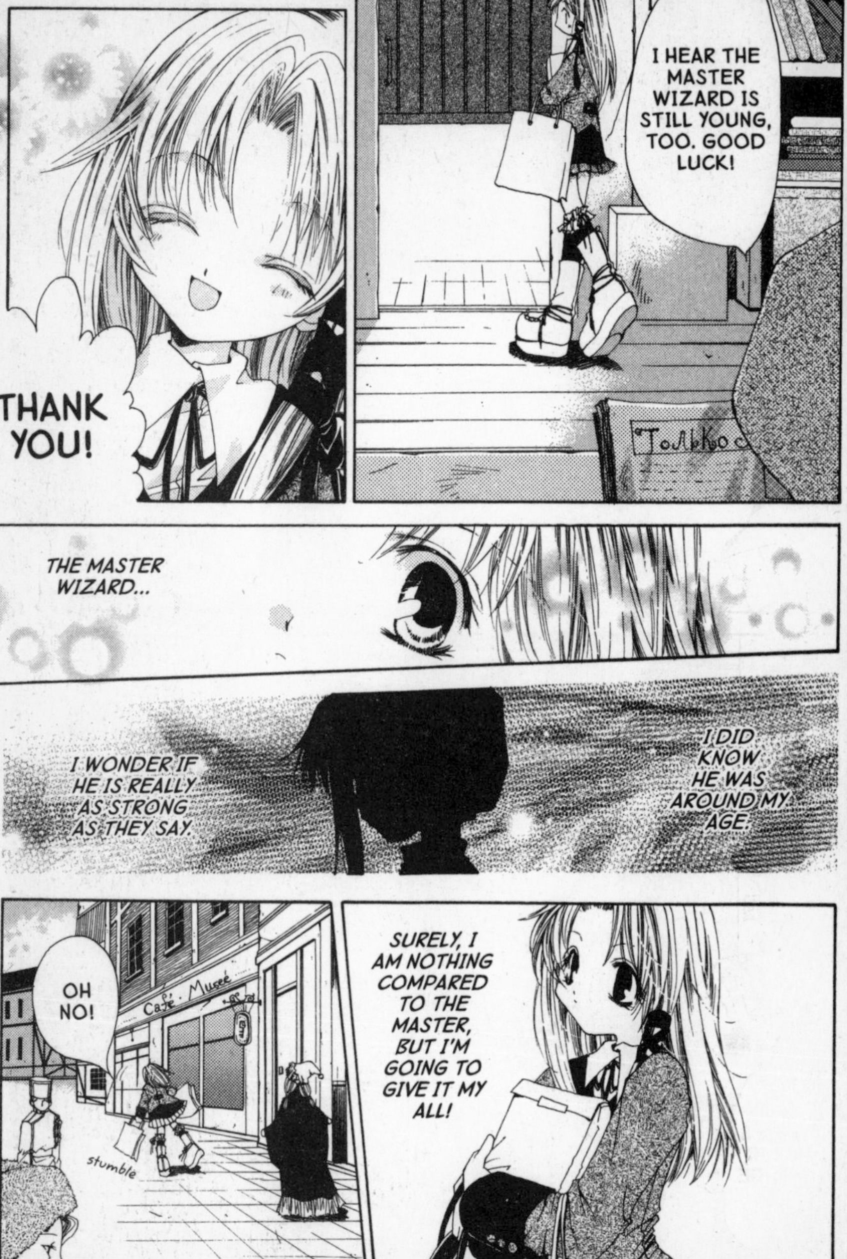

I HEAR THE MASTER WIZARD IS STILL YOUNG, TOO. GOOD LUCK!
THANK YOU!
THE MASTER WIZARD...
I DID KNOW HE WAS AROUND MY AGE.
I WONDER IF HE IS REALLY AS STRONG AS THEY SAY.
SURELY, I AM NOTHING COMPARED TO THE MASTER, BUT I'M GOING TO GIVE IT MY ALL!
OH NO!
Café · Musée
stumble

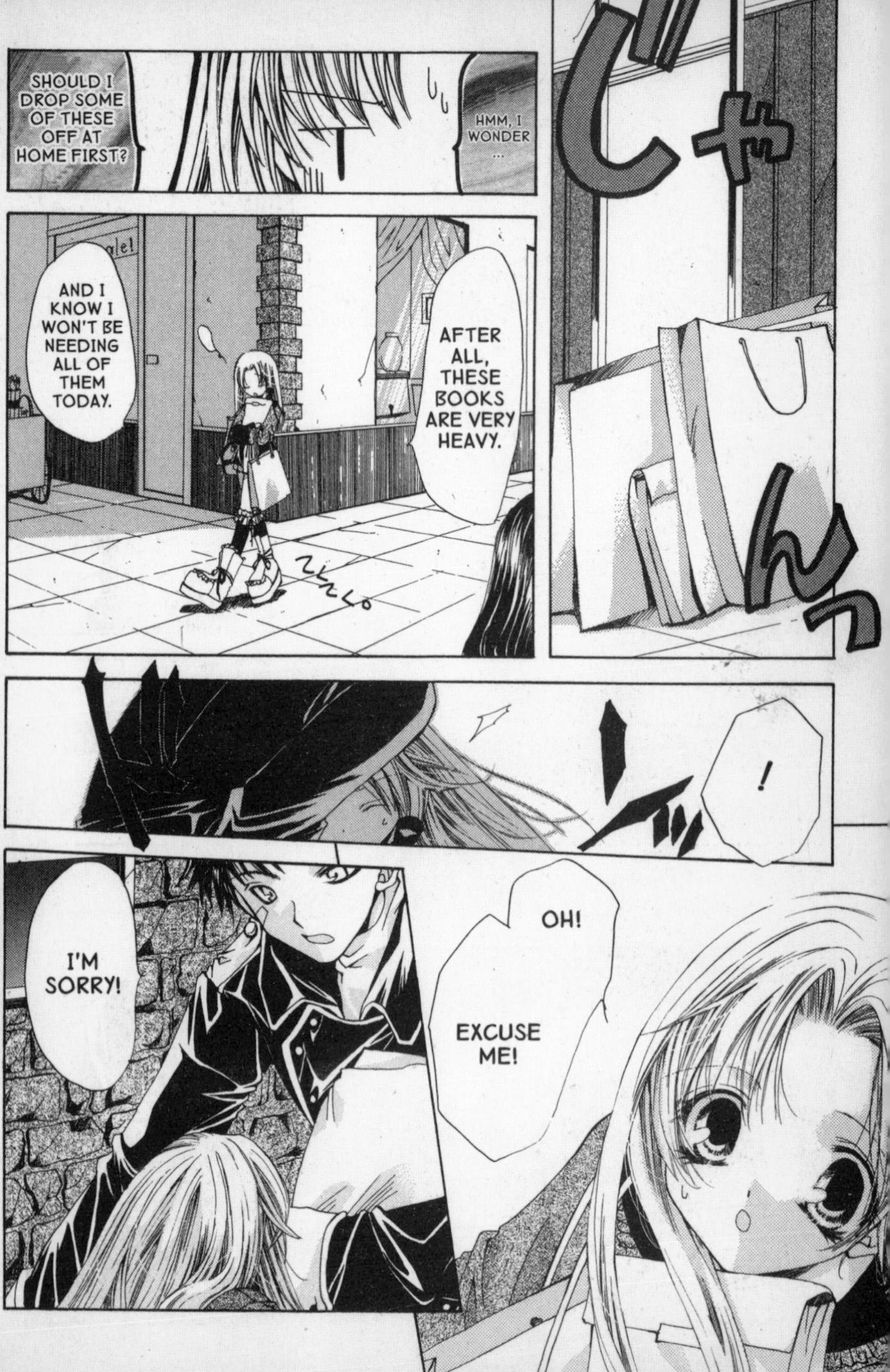
じゃ
んっ
HMM, I WONDER ...
SHOULD I DROP SOME OF THESE OFF AT HOME FIRST?
AFTER ALL, THESE BOOKS ARE VERY HEAVY.
AND I KNOW I WON'T BE NEEDING ALL OF THEM TODAY.
!
OH!
EXCUSE ME!
I'M SORRY!

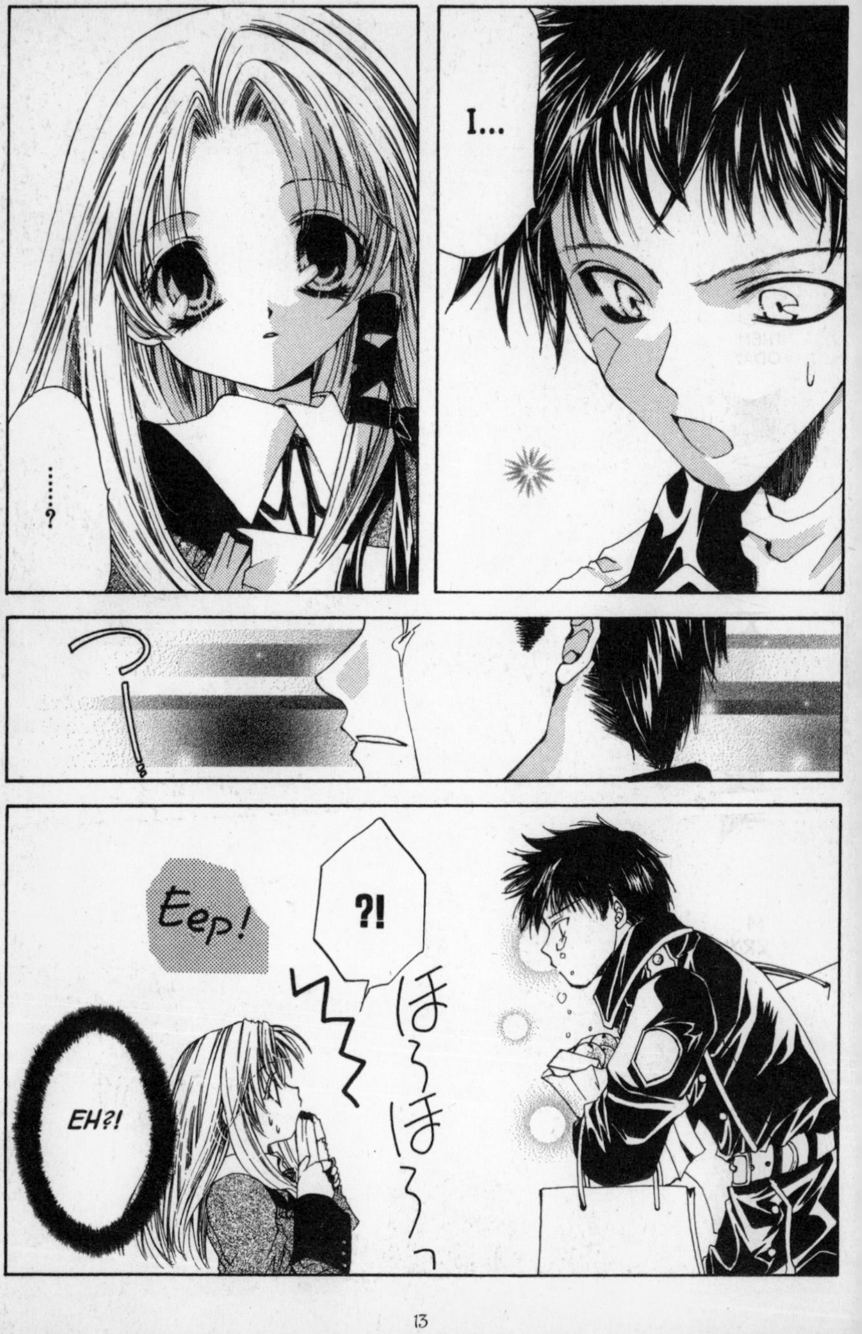
I...
......?
ほろほろっ
?!
Eep!
EH?!

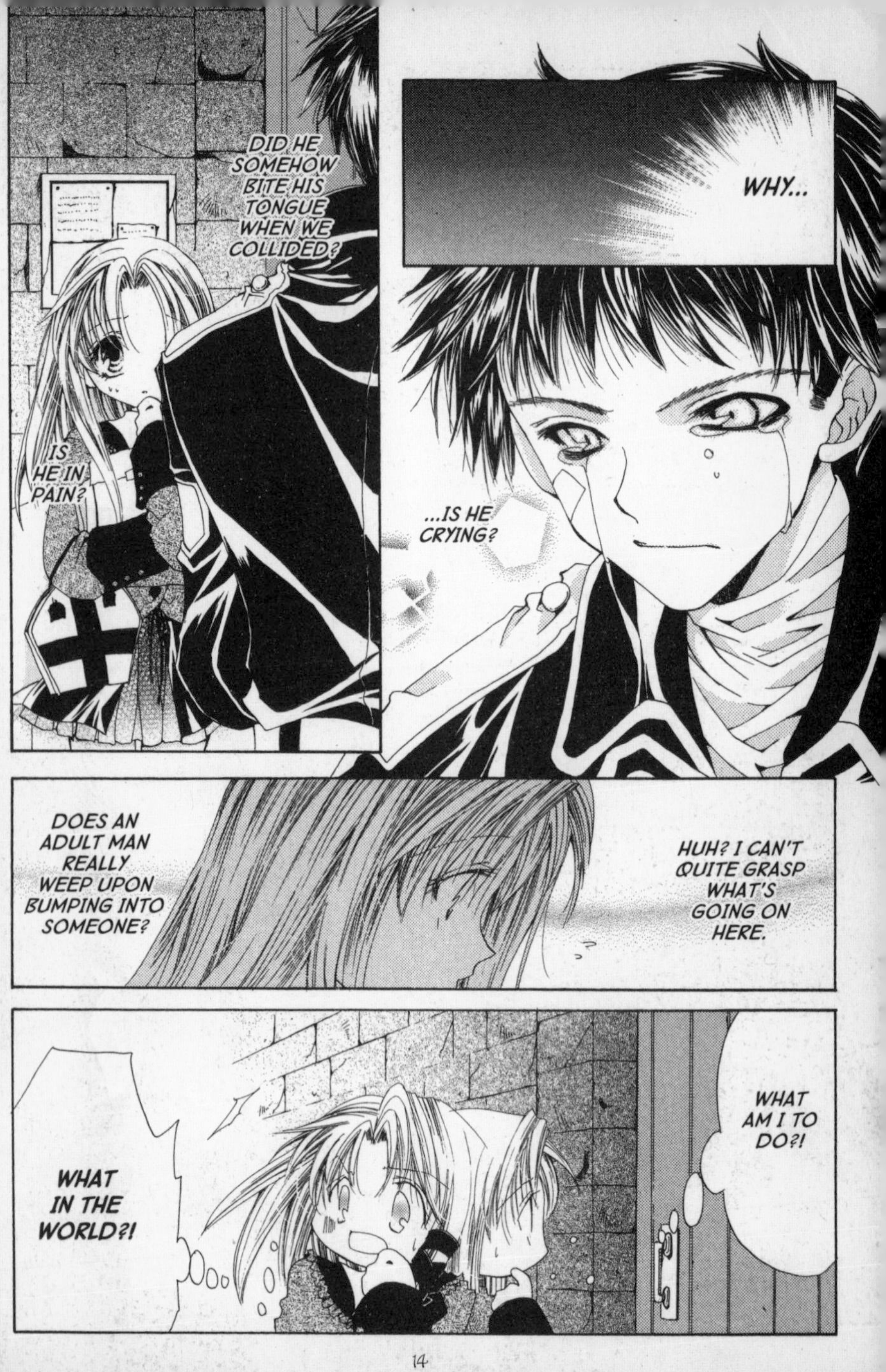
WHY...
...IS HE CRYING?
DID HE SOMEHOW BITE HIS TONGUE WHEN WE COLLIDED?
IS HE IN PAIN?
HUH? I CAN'T QUITE GRASP WHAT'S GOING ON HERE.
DOES AN ADULT MAN REALLY WEEP UPON BUMPING INTO SOMEONE?
WHAT AM I TO DO?!
WHAT IN THE WORLD?!

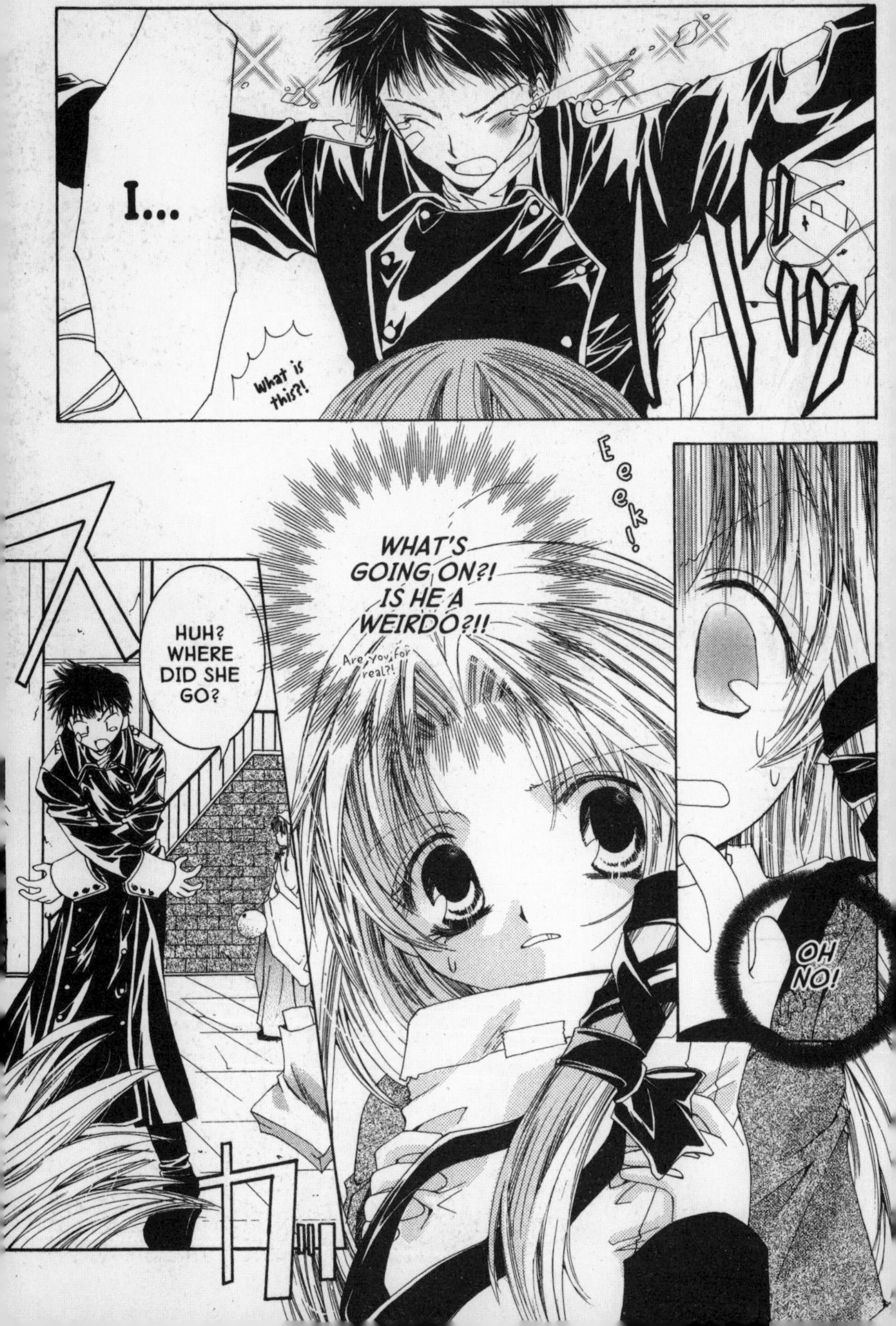
I...
what is this?!
OH NO!
Eeek!
WHAT'S GOING ON?! IS HE A WEIRDO?!!
Are you for real?!
HUH? WHERE DID SHE GO?

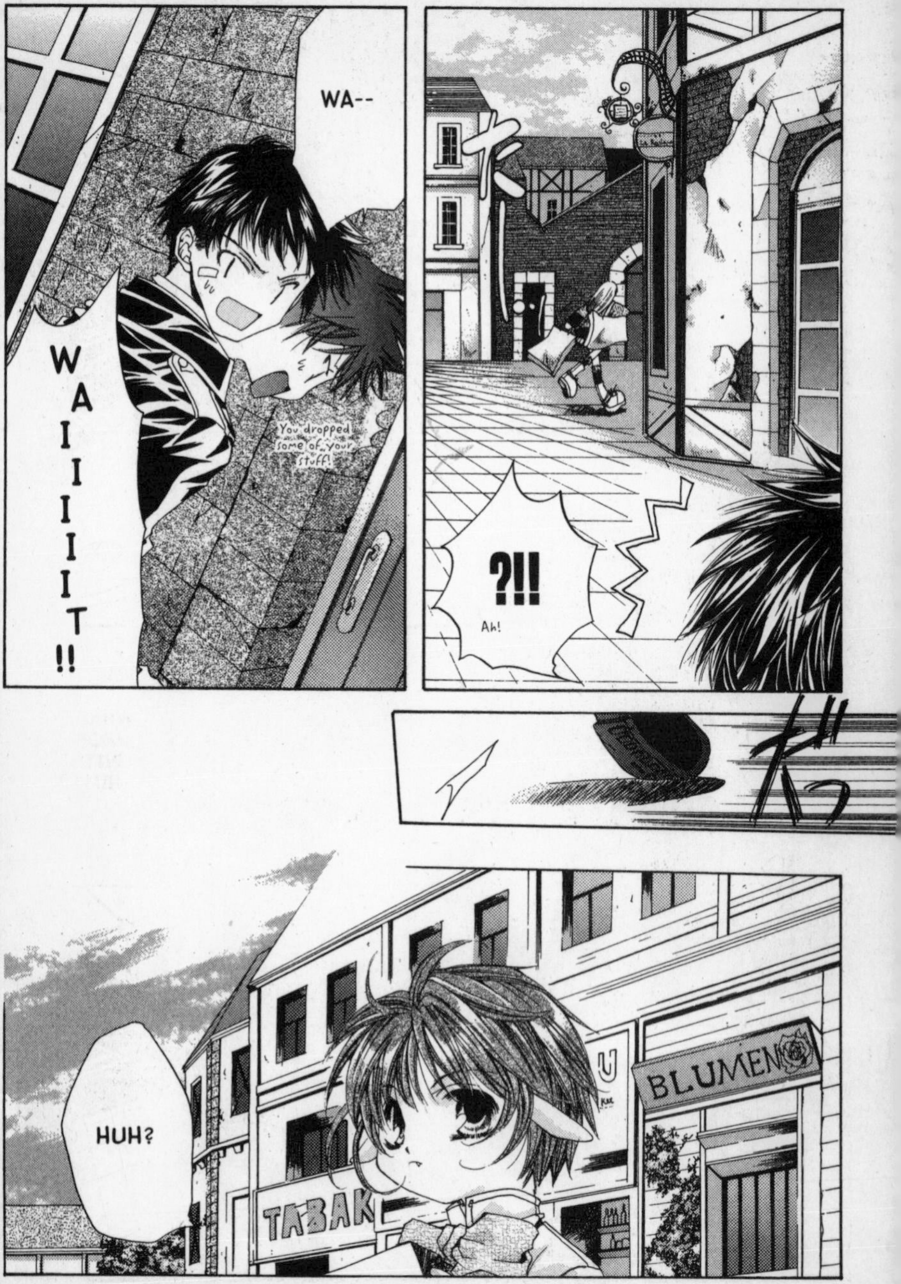
?!!
Ah!
WA--
WAIIIIIT!!
You dropped some of your stuff!
ダッ
HUH?
BLUMEN
TABAK

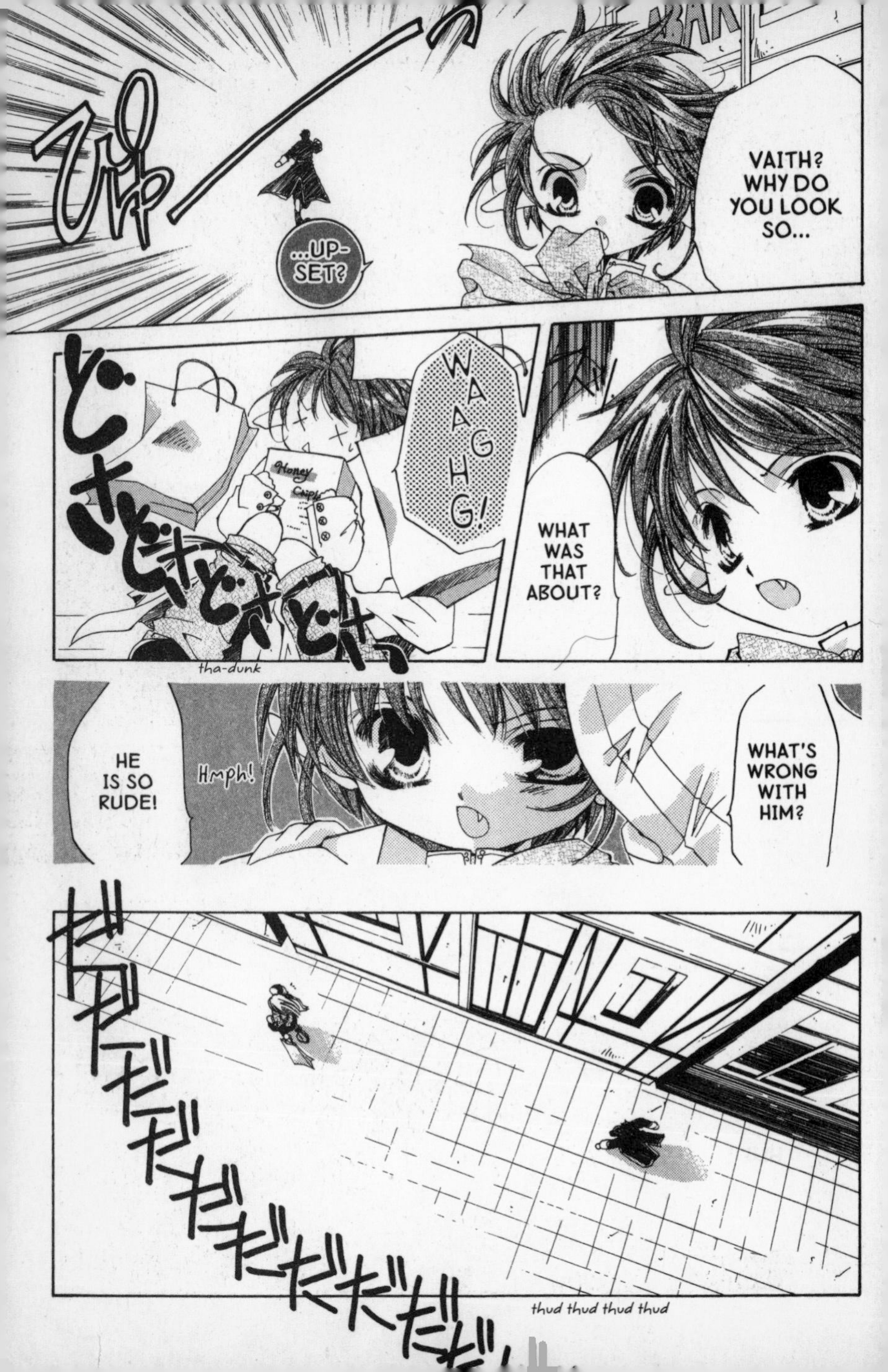
VAITH? WHY DO YOU LOOK SO...
...UP-SET?
WHAT WAS THAT ABOUT?
WAAGHG!
tha-dunk
WHAT'S WRONG WITH HIM?
Hmph!
HE IS SO RUDE!
thud thud thud thud

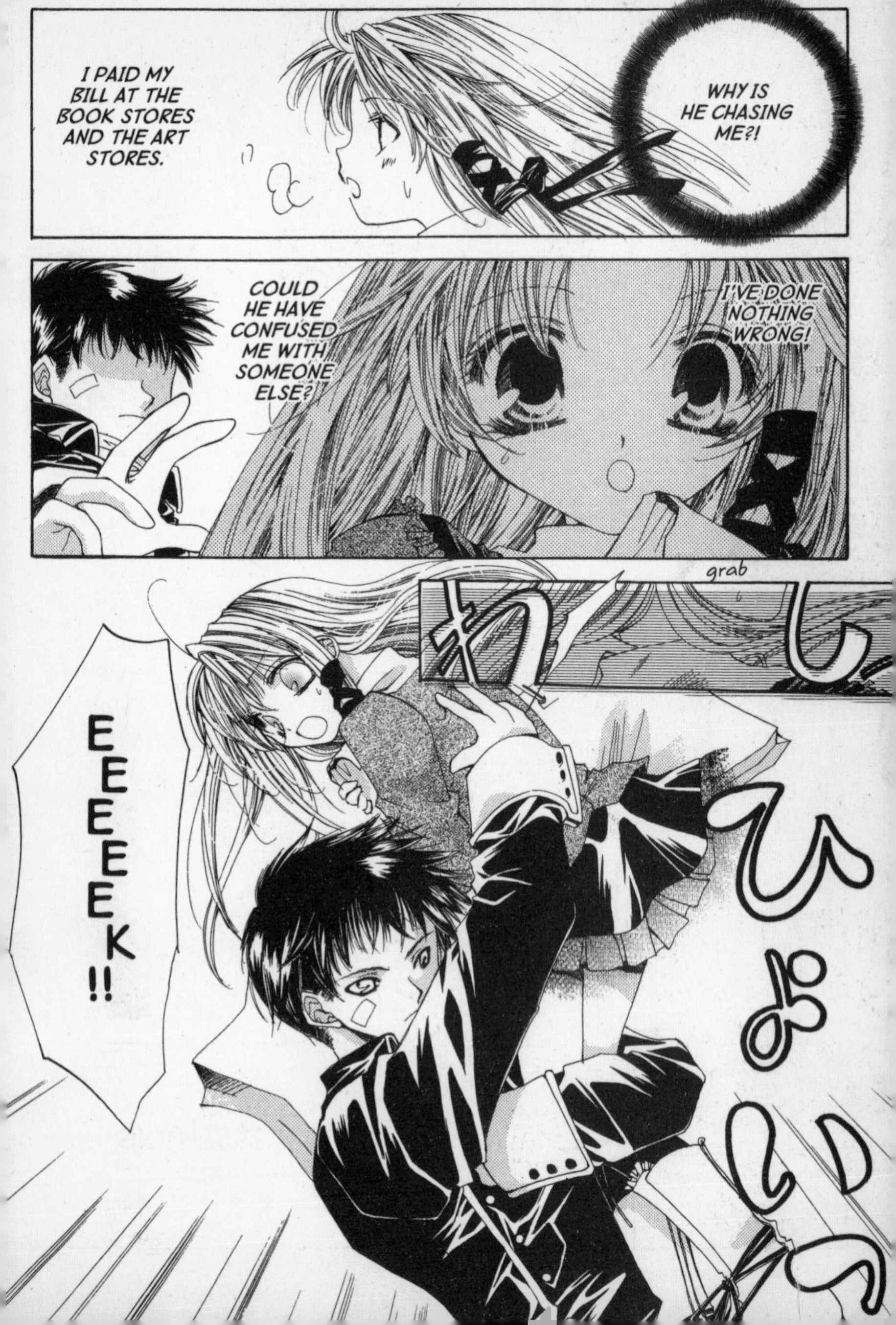
WHY IS HE CHASING ME?!
I PAID MY BILL AT THE BOOK STORES AND THE ART STORES.
I'VE DONE NOTHING WRONG!
COULD HE HAVE CONFUSED ME WITH SOMEONE ELSE?
grab
EEEEEK!!

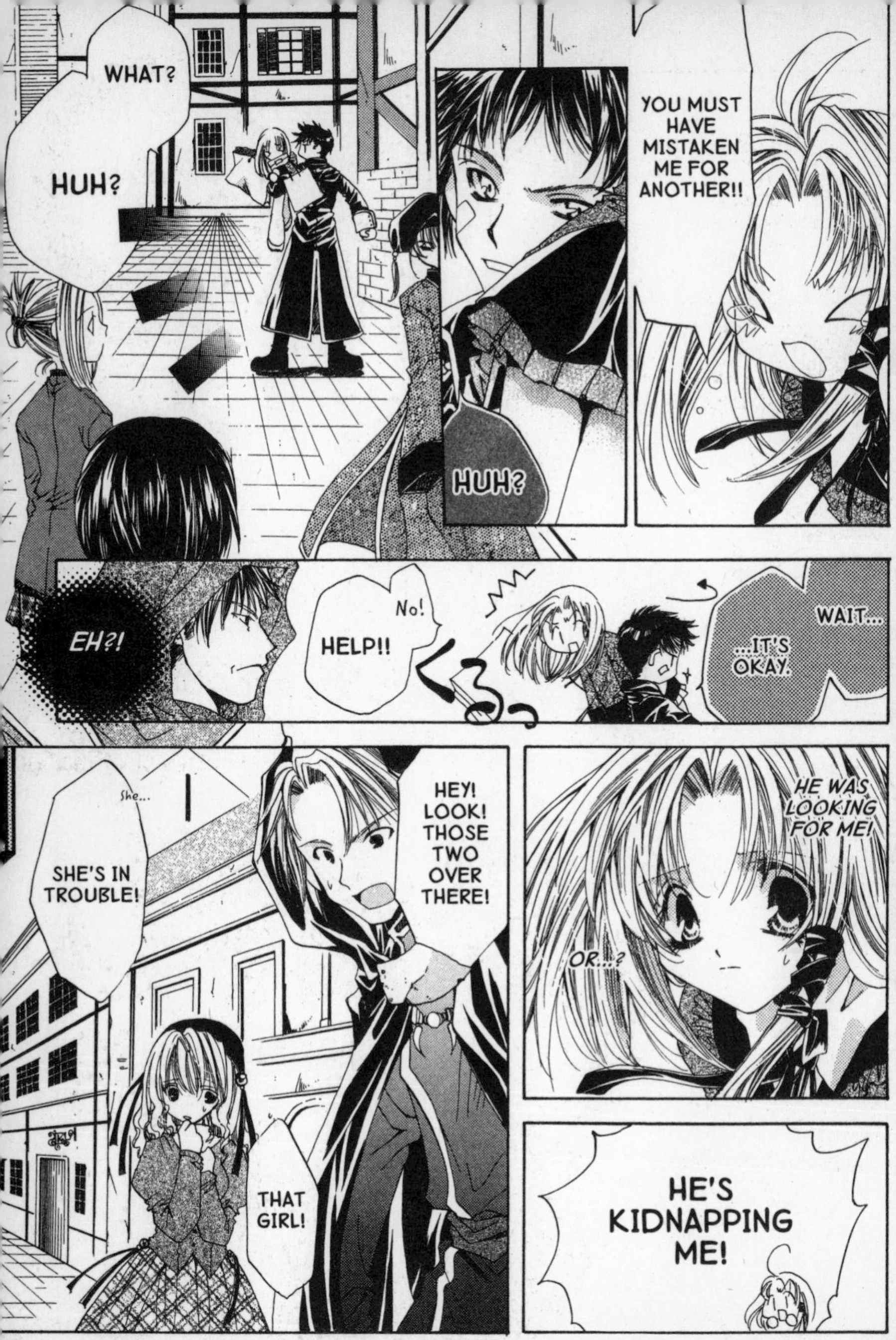
YOU MUST HAVE MISTAKEN ME FOR ANOTHER!!
HUH?
WHAT?
HUH?
WAIT...
...IT'S OKAY.
No!
HELP!!
くるっ
EH?!
HE WAS LOOKING FOR ME!
OR...?
HE'S KIDNAPPING ME!
HEY! LOOK! THOSE TWO OVER THERE!
THAT GIRL!
She...
SHE'S IN TROUBLE!

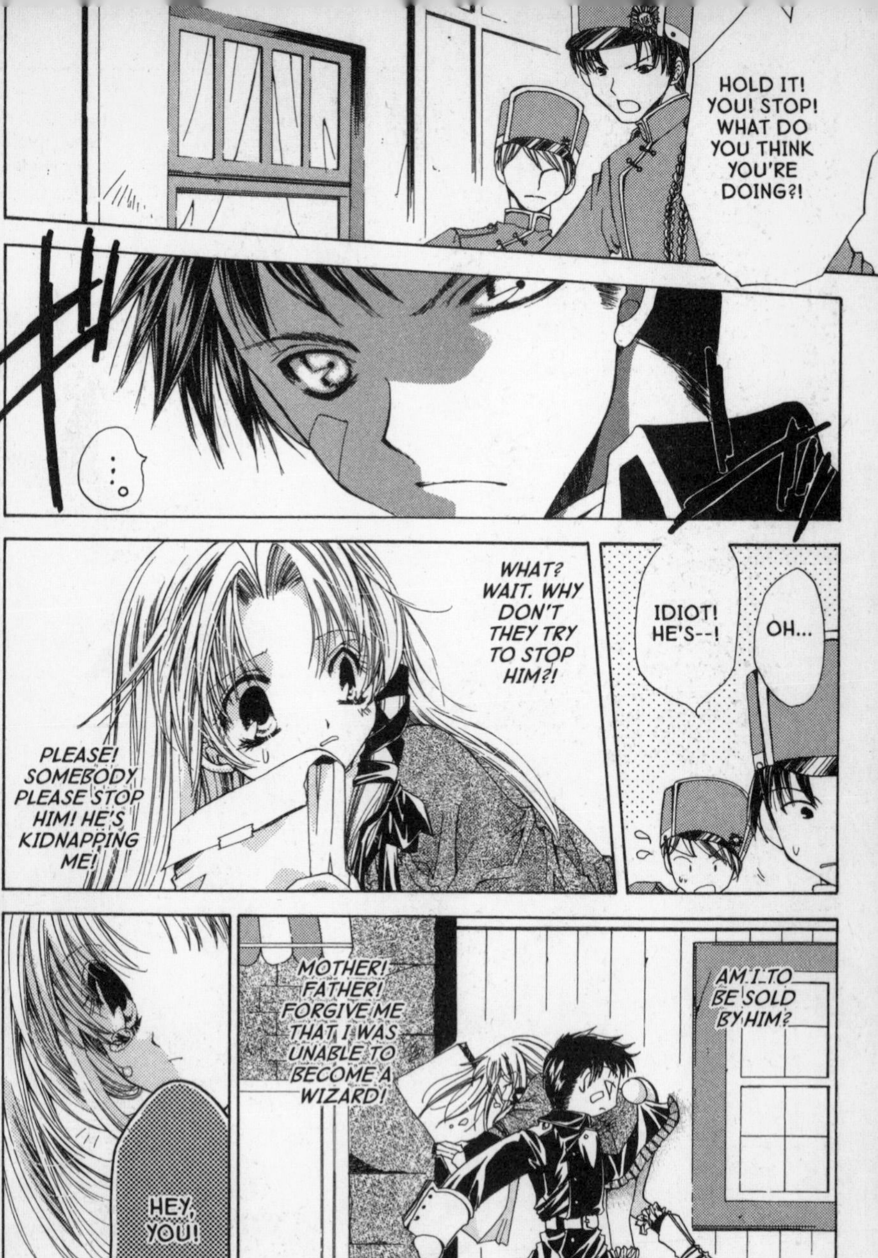

HOLD IT! YOU! STOP! WHAT DO YOU THINK YOU'RE DOING?!
...
IDIOT! HE'S--!
OH...
WHAT? WAIT. WHY DON'T THEY TRY TO STOP HIM?!
PLEASE! SOMEBODY PLEASE STOP HIM! HE'S KIDNAPPING ME!
AM I TO BE SOLD BY HIM?
MOTHER! FATHER! FORGIVE ME THAT I WAS UNABLE TO BECOME A WIZARD!
HEY, YOU!

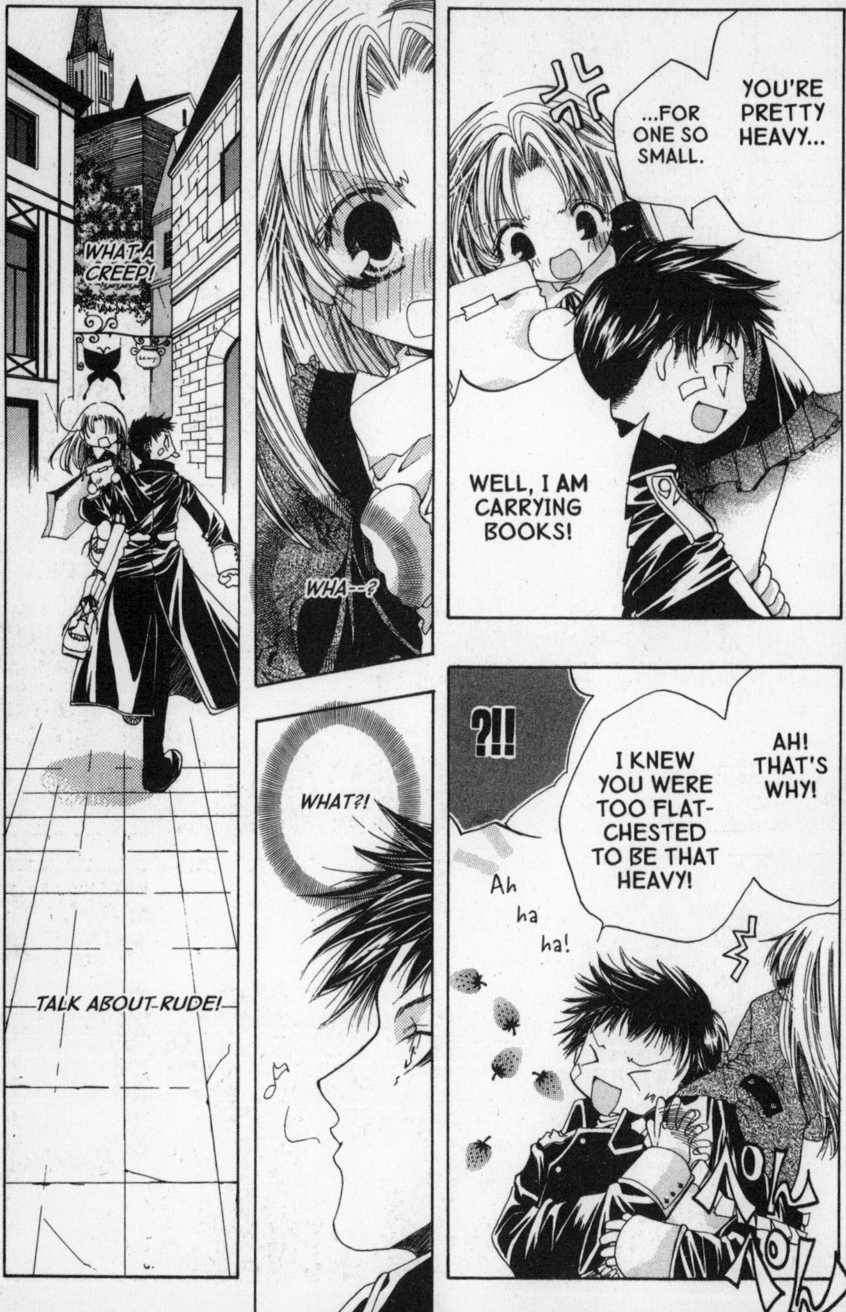
YOU'RE PRETTY HEAVY...
...FOR ONE SO SMALL.
WELL, I AM CARRYING BOOKS!
WHA--?
?!!
AH! THAT'S WHY!
I KNEW YOU WERE TOO FLAT-CHESTED TO BE THAT HEAVY!
Ah ha ha!
WHAT?!
WHAT A CREEP!
TALK ABOUT RUDE!

I SIMPLY CAN'T BELIEVE WHAT A JERK VAITH IS!

MAKING ME CARRY HIS STUFF!

ESPECIALLY WHEN THESE THINGS ARE BIGGER AND HEAVIER THAN ME!

I'M SORRY YOU HAD TO ENDURE THAT, FERN.

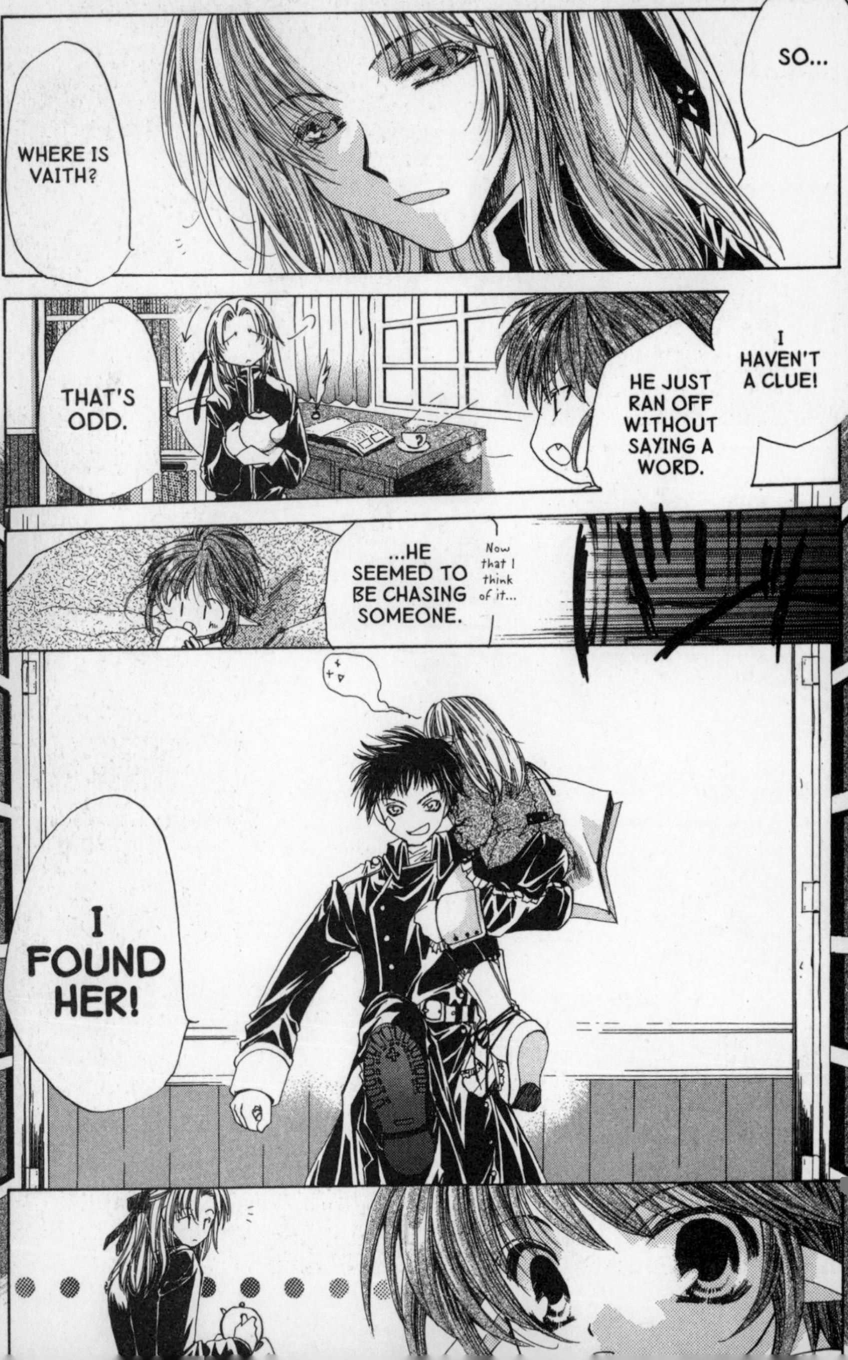
SO...
WHERE IS VAITH?
I HAVEN'T A CLUE!
HE JUST RAN OFF WITHOUT SAYING A WORD.
THAT'S ODD.
Now that I think of it...
...HE SEEMED TO BE CHASING SOMEONE.
I FOUND HER!

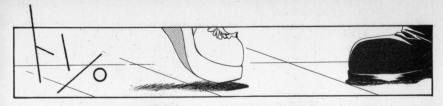

WHAT'S YOUR PROBLEM?!

WHO ARE YOU?! IS THIS A CASTLE?!

WHAT'S GOING ON?!

I'M SUPPOSED TO BE AT MY SCHOOL!

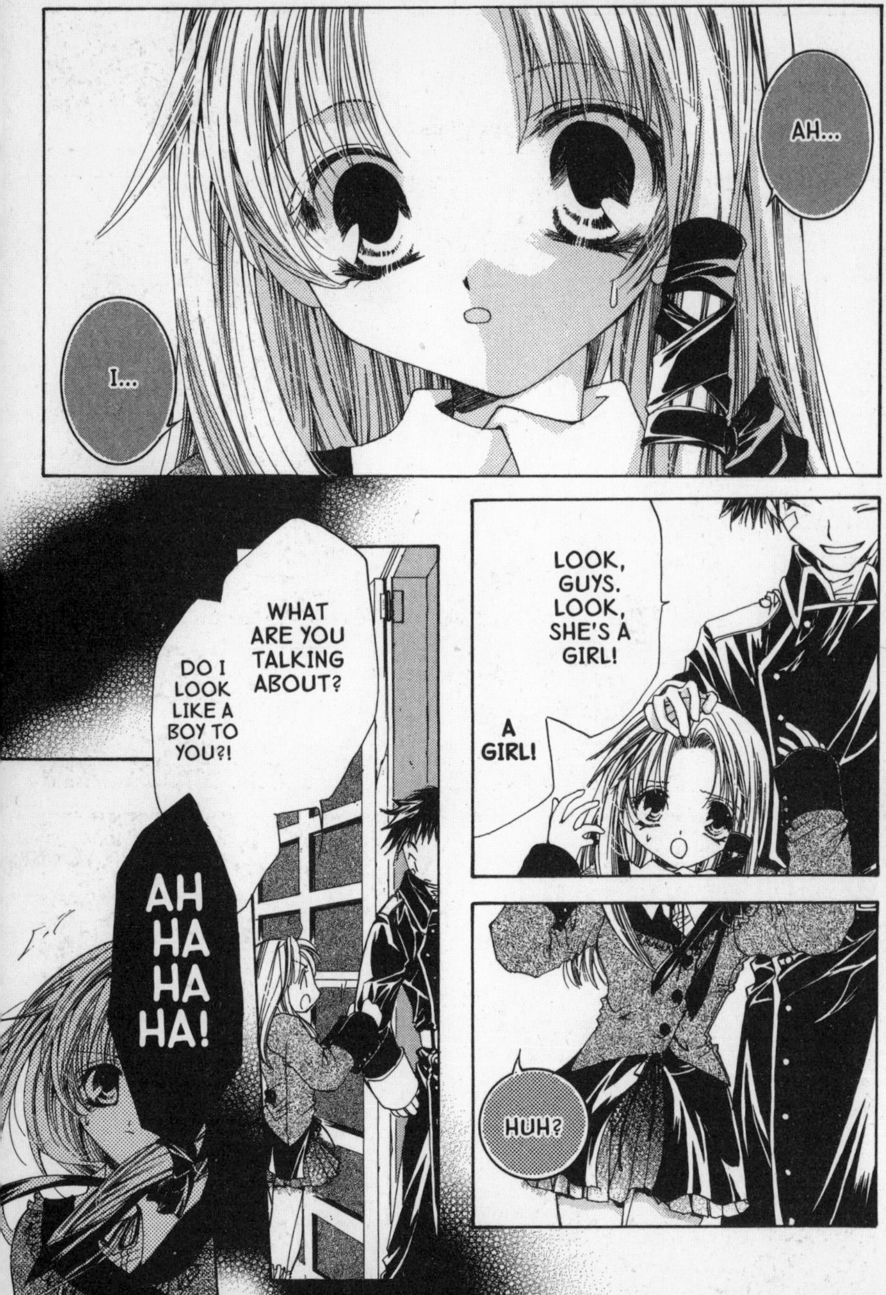
AH...
I...
LOOK, GUYS. LOOK, SHE'S A GIRL!
A GIRL!
HUH?
WHAT ARE YOU TALKING ABOUT?
DO I LOOK LIKE A BOY TO YOU?!
AH HA HA HA HA!

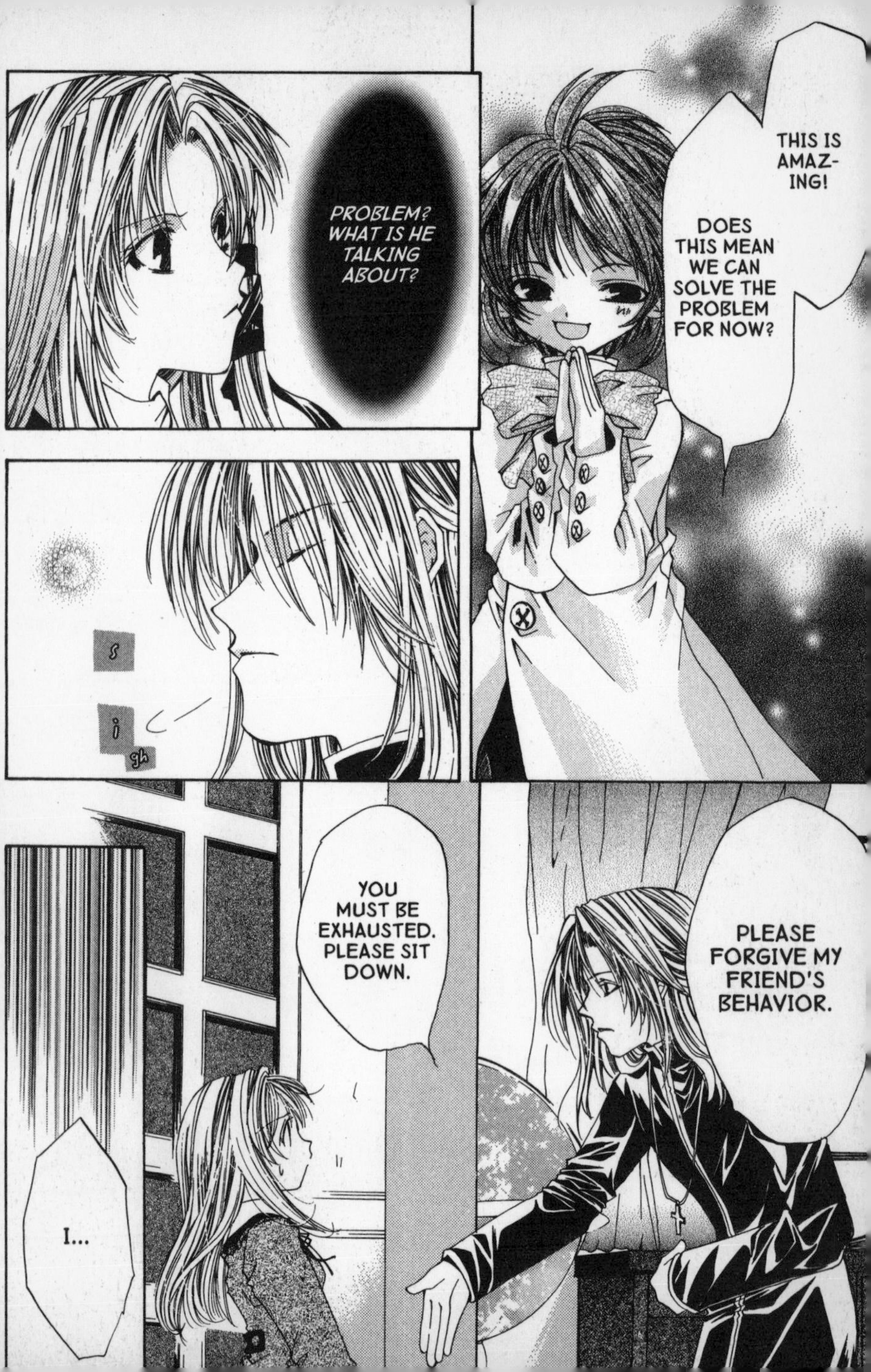
THIS IS AMAZING!
DOES THIS MEAN WE CAN SOLVE THE PROBLEM FOR NOW?
PROBLEM? WHAT IS HE TALKING ABOUT?
sigh
PLEASE FORGIVE MY FRIEND'S BEHAVIOR.
YOU MUST BE EXHAUSTED. PLEASE SIT DOWN.
I...

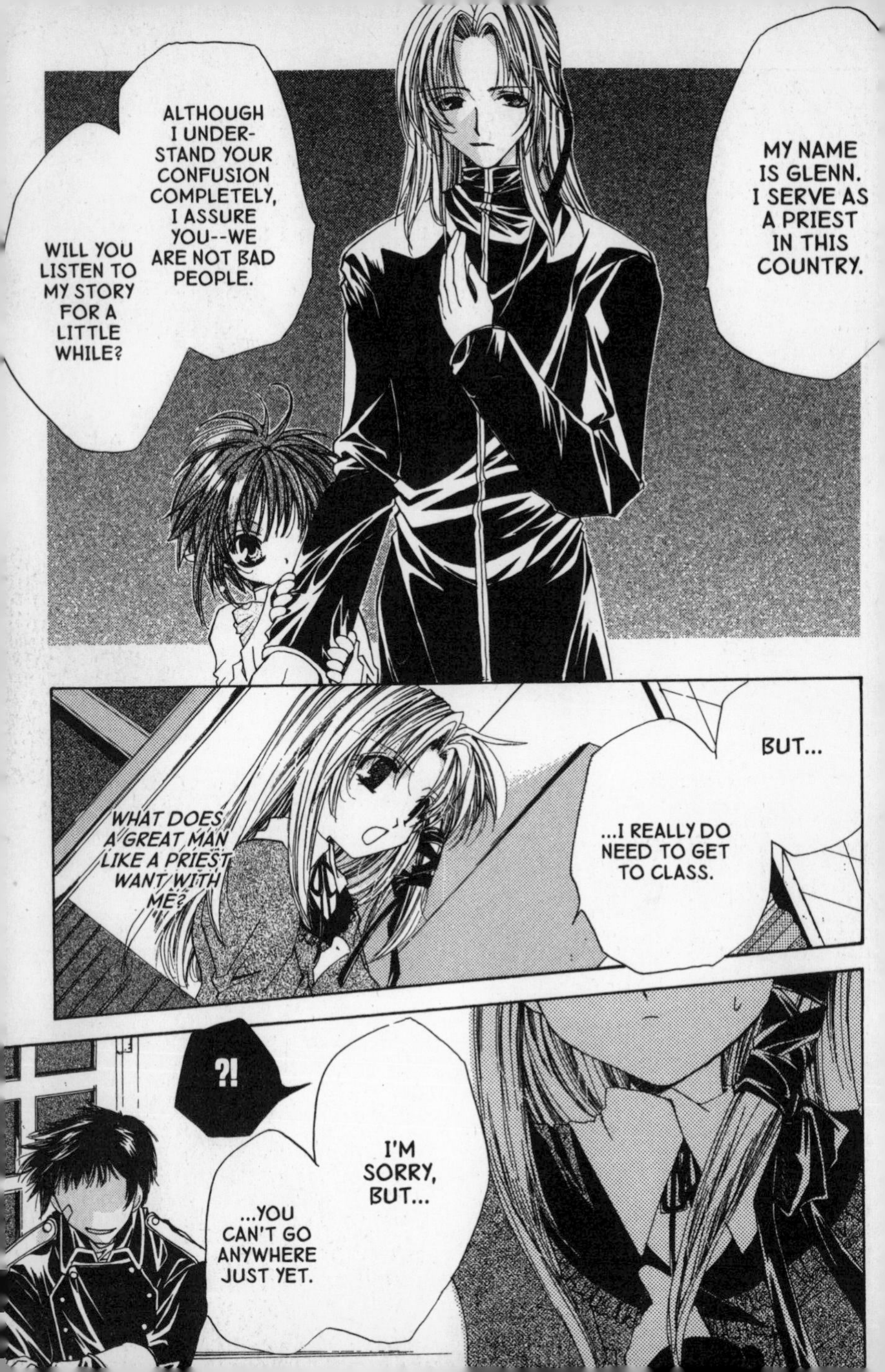
MY NAME IS GLENN. I SERVE AS A PRIEST IN THIS COUNTRY.
ALTHOUGH I UNDER-STAND YOUR CONFUSION COMPLETELY, I ASSURE YOU--WE ARE NOT BAD PEOPLE.
WILL YOU LISTEN TO MY STORY FOR A LITTLE WHILE?
BUT...
...I REALLY DO NEED TO GET TO CLASS.
WHAT DOES A GREAT MAN LIKE A PRIEST WANT WITH ME?
I'M SORRY, BUT...
...YOU CAN'T GO ANYWHERE JUST YET.
?!

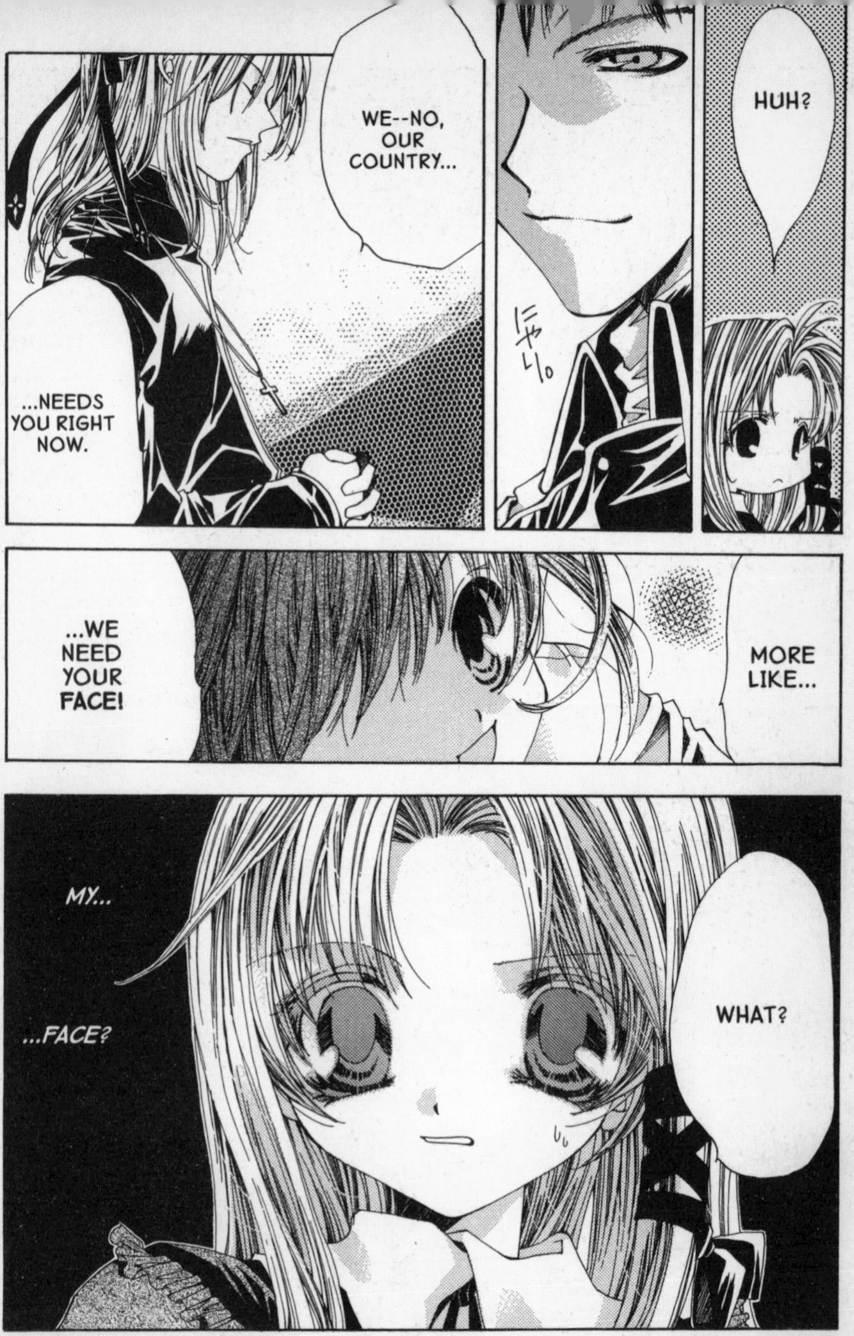
HUH?
にやり。
WE--NO, OUR COUNTRY...
...NEEDS YOU RIGHT NOW.
MORE LIKE...
...WE NEED YOUR FACE!
WHAT?
MY...
...FACE?

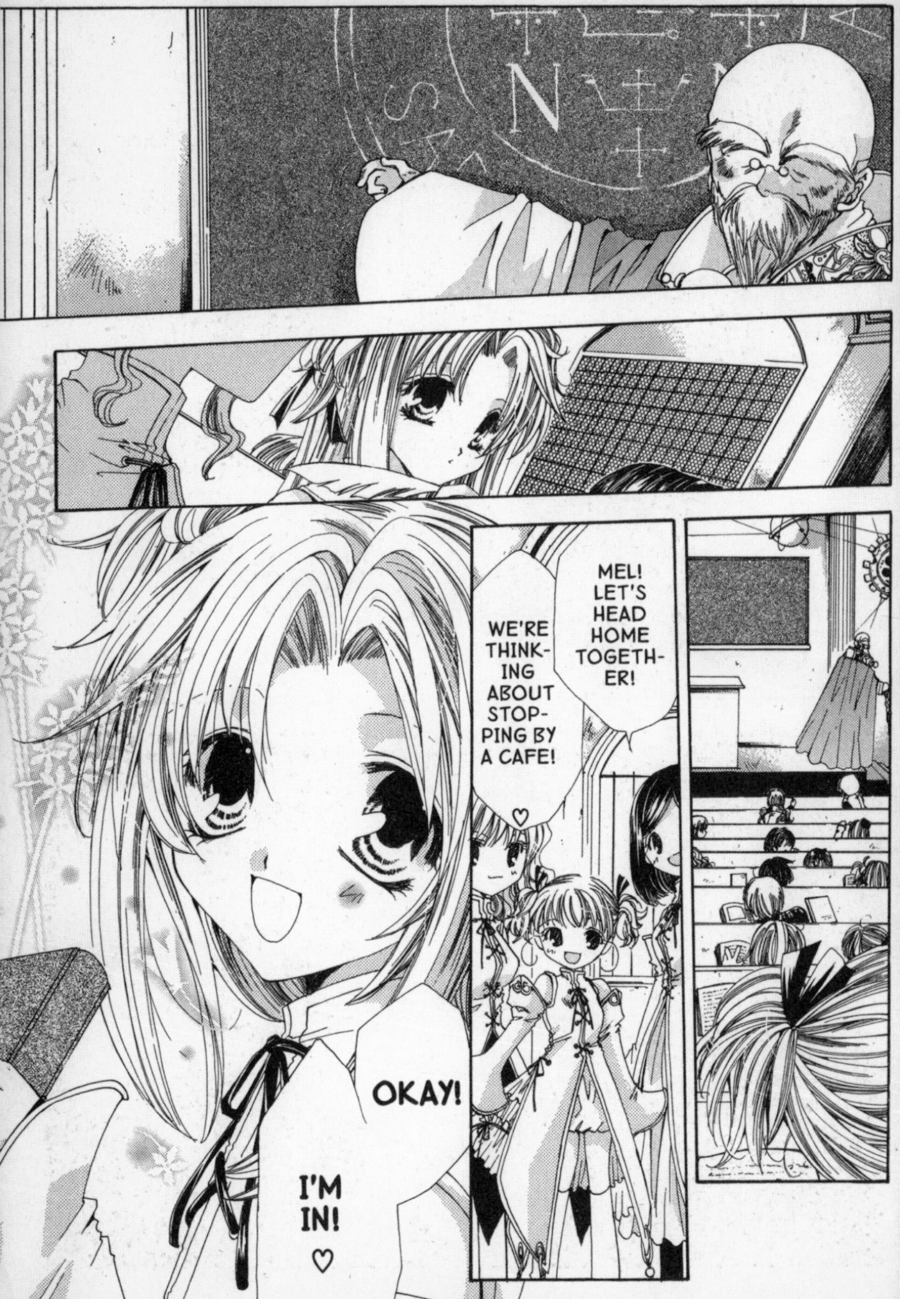
MEL! LET'S HEAD HOME TOGETHER!
WE'RE THINKING ABOUT STOPPING BY A CAFE! ♡
OKAY!
I'M IN! ♡

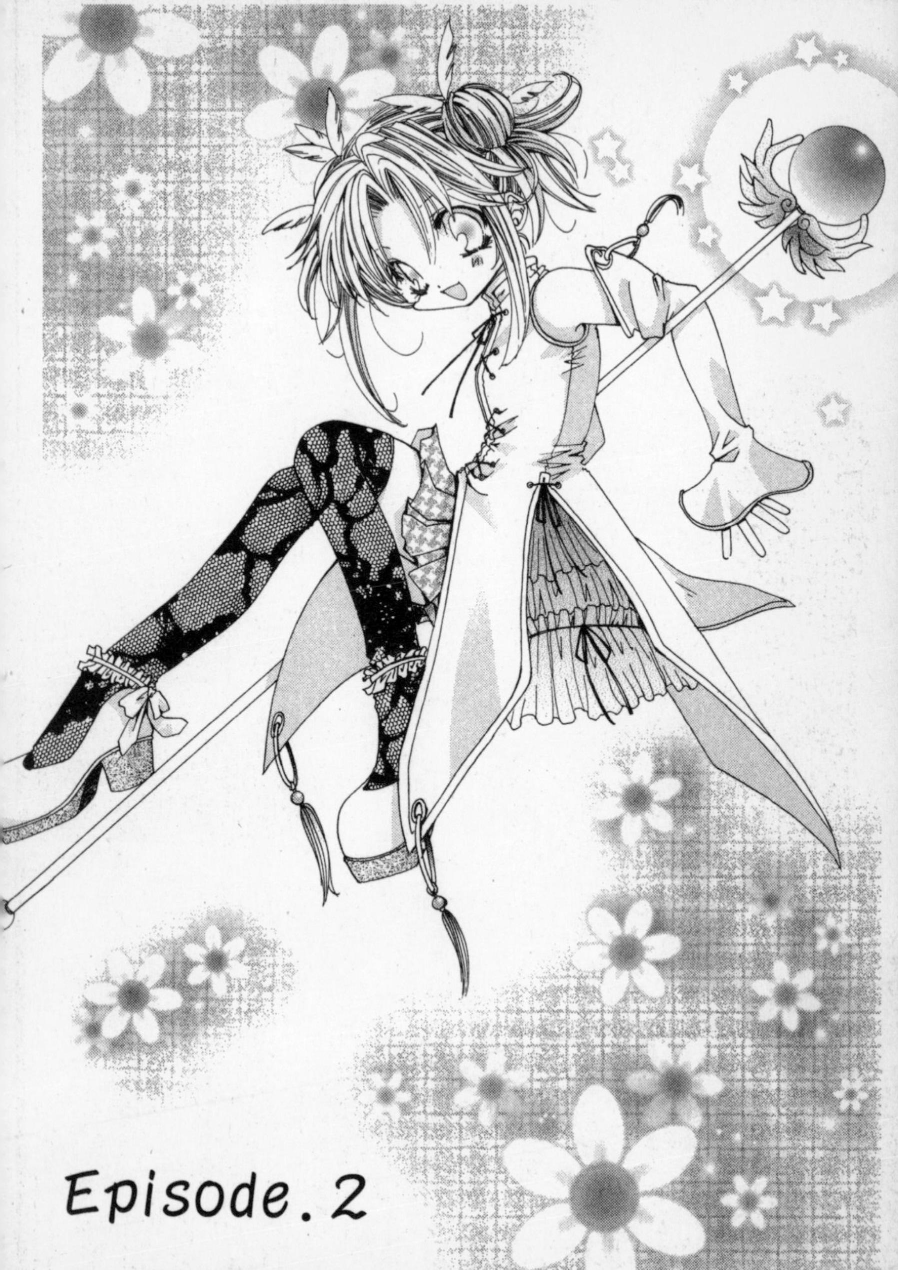

Episode. 2

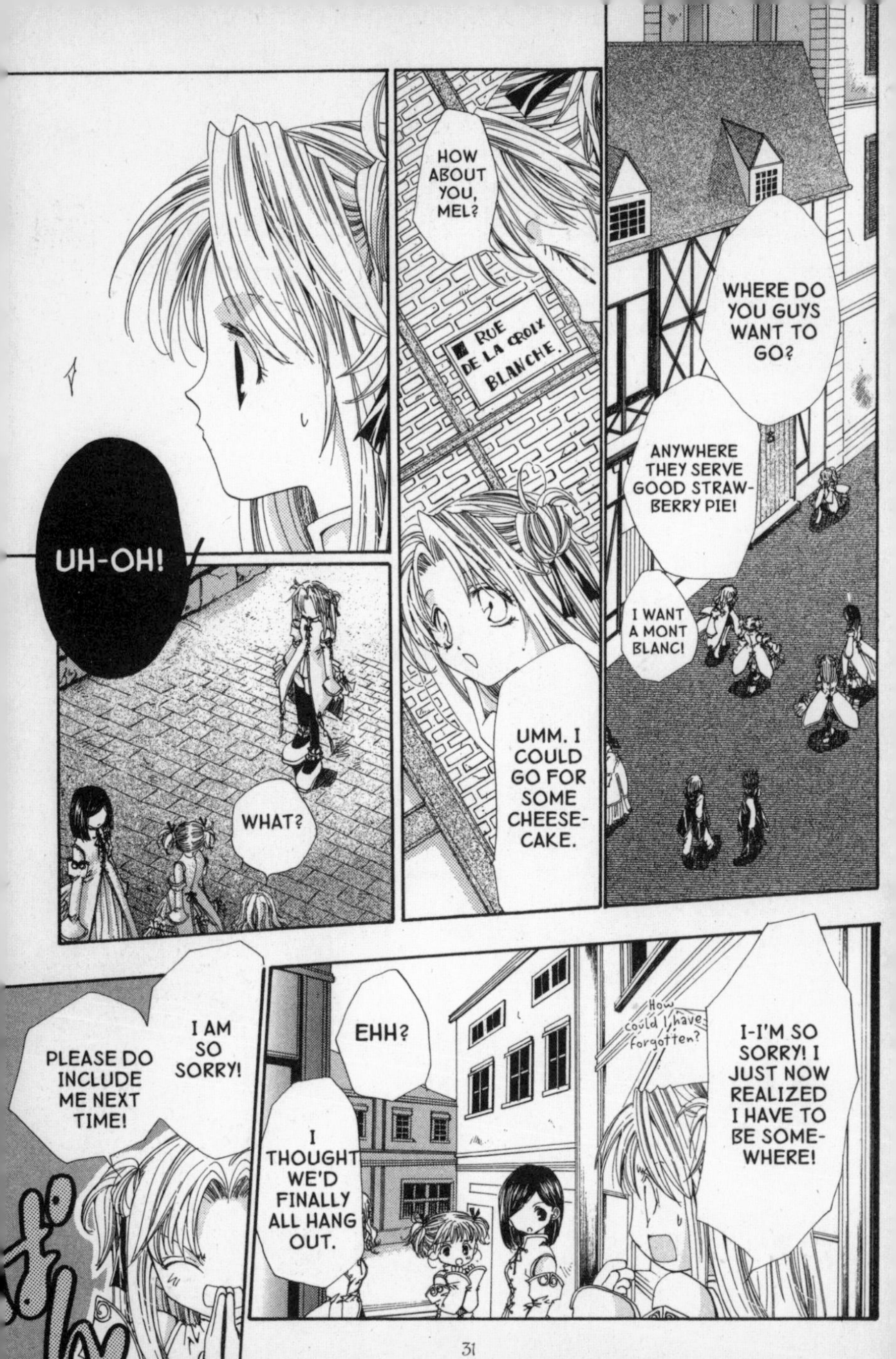
WHERE DO YOU GUYS WANT TO GO?
ANYWHERE THEY SERVE GOOD STRAW-BERRY PIE!
I WANT A MONT BLANC!
HOW ABOUT YOU, MEL?
RUE DE LA CROIX BLANCHE.
UMM. I COULD GO FOR SOME CHEESE-CAKE.
UH-OH!
WHAT?
How could I have forgotten?
I-I'M SO SORRY! I JUST NOW REALIZED I HAVE TO BE SOME-WHERE!
EHH?
I THOUGHT WE'D FINALLY ALL HANG OUT.
I AM SO SORRY!
PLEASE DO INCLUDE ME NEXT TIME!

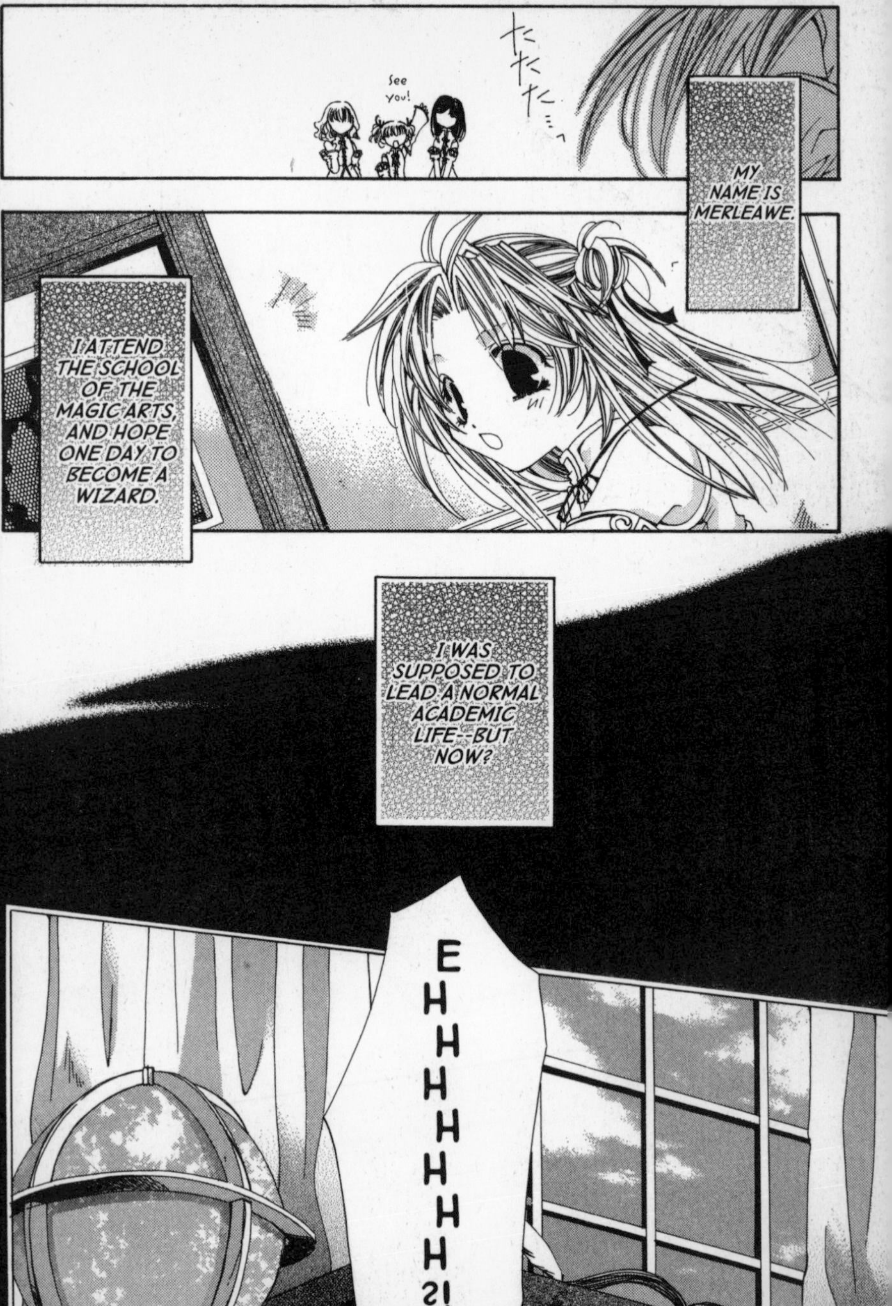
たたた…
See you!
MY NAME IS MERLEAWE.
I ATTEND THE SCHOOL OF THE MAGIC ARTS, AND HOPE ONE DAY TO BECOME A WIZARD.
I WAS SUPPOSED TO LEAD A NORMAL ACADEMIC LIFE--BUT NOW?
EHHHHHHH?!

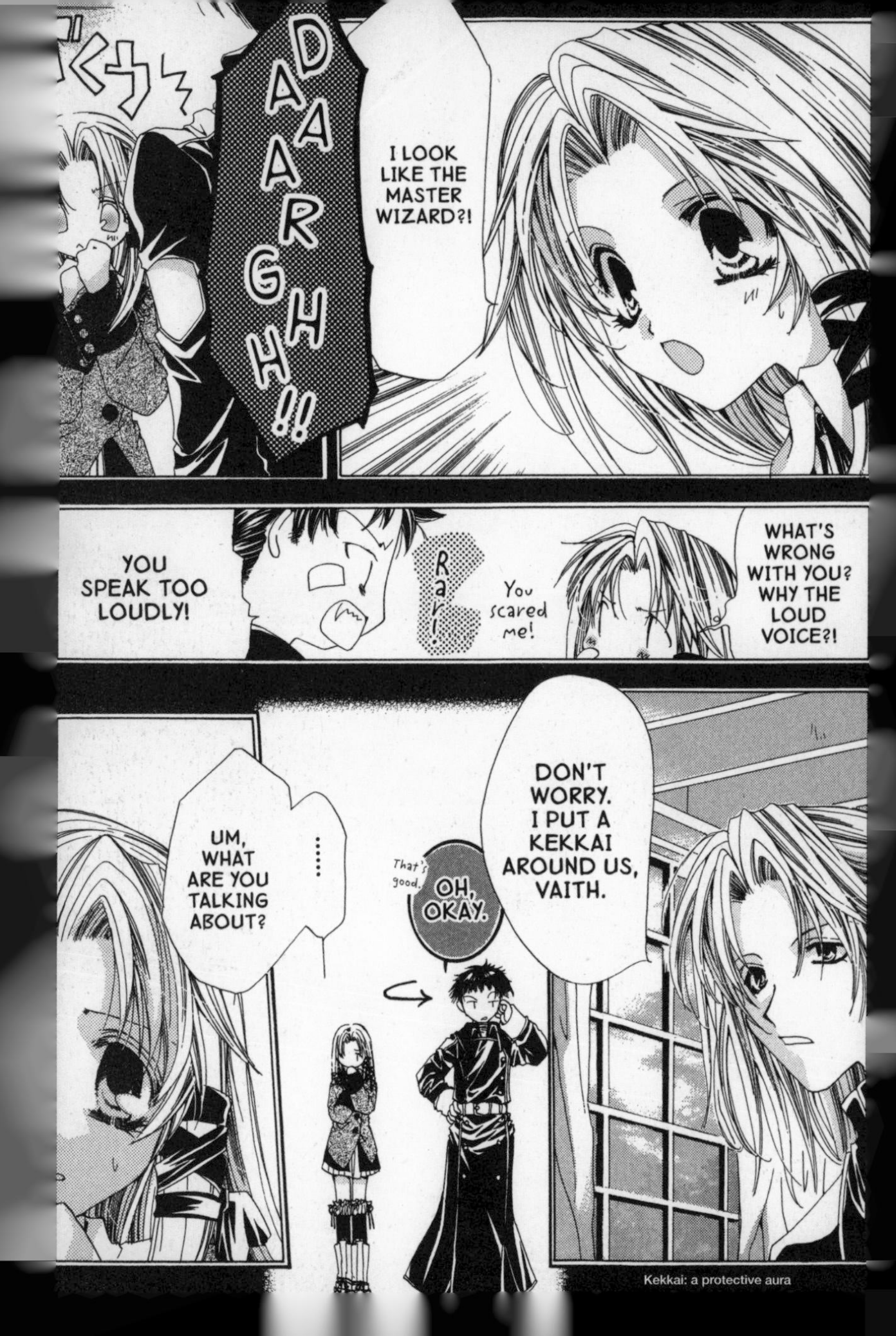
I LOOK LIKE THE MASTER WIZARD?!
DAARGHH!!
WHAT'S WRONG WITH YOU? WHY THE LOUD VOICE?!
You scared me!
Rar!
YOU SPEAK TOO LOUDLY!
DON'T WORRY. I PUT A KEKKAI AROUND US, VAITH.
OH, OKAY.
That's good.
......
UM, WHAT ARE YOU TALKING ABOUT?

Kekkai: a protective aura

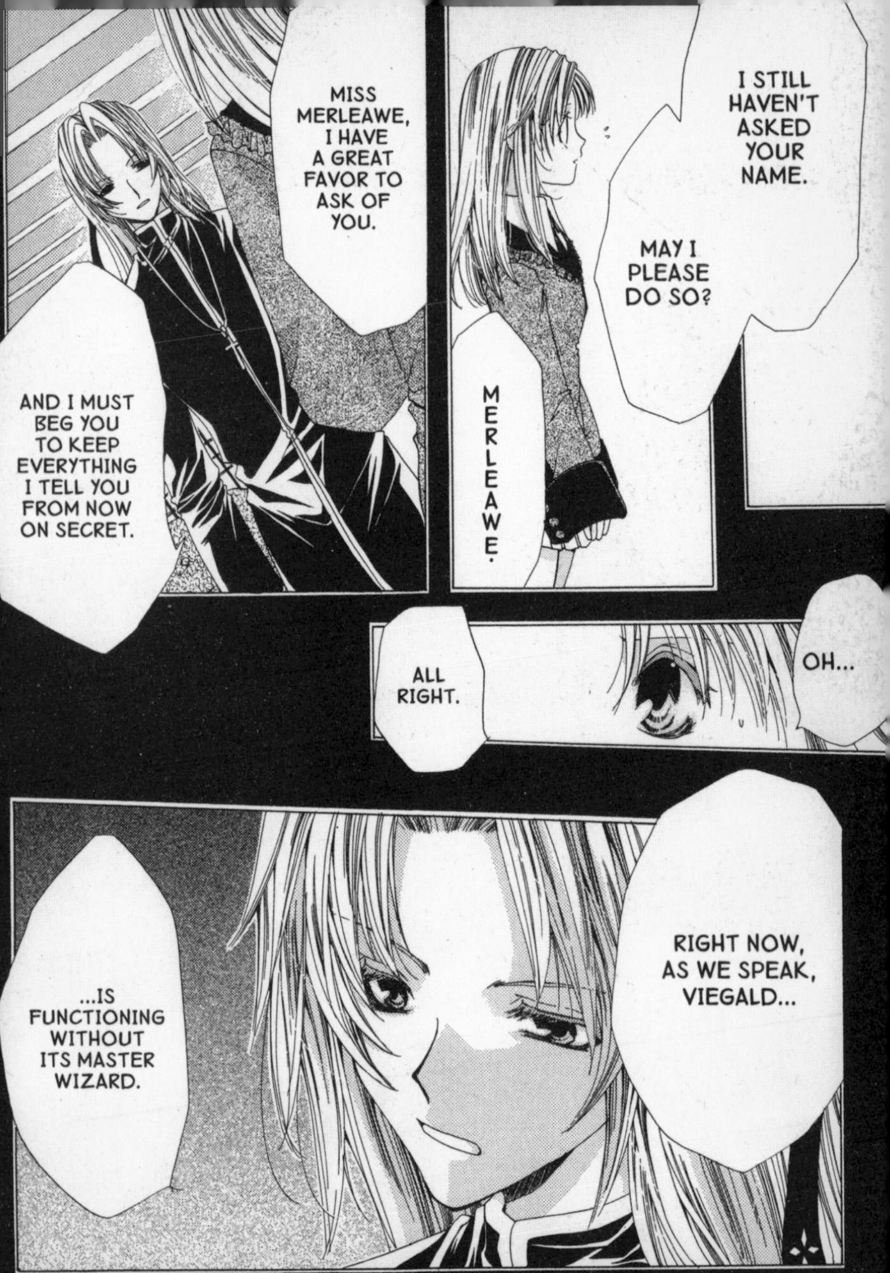

I STILL HAVEN'T ASKED YOUR NAME.
MAY I PLEASE DO SO?
MERLEAWE.
MISS MERLEAWE, I HAVE A GREAT FAVOR TO ASK OF YOU.
AND I MUST BEG YOU TO KEEP EVERYTHING I TELL YOU FROM NOW ON SECRET.
OH...
ALL RIGHT.
RIGHT NOW, AS WE SPEAK, VIEGALD...
...IS FUNCTIONING WITHOUT ITS MASTER WIZARD.

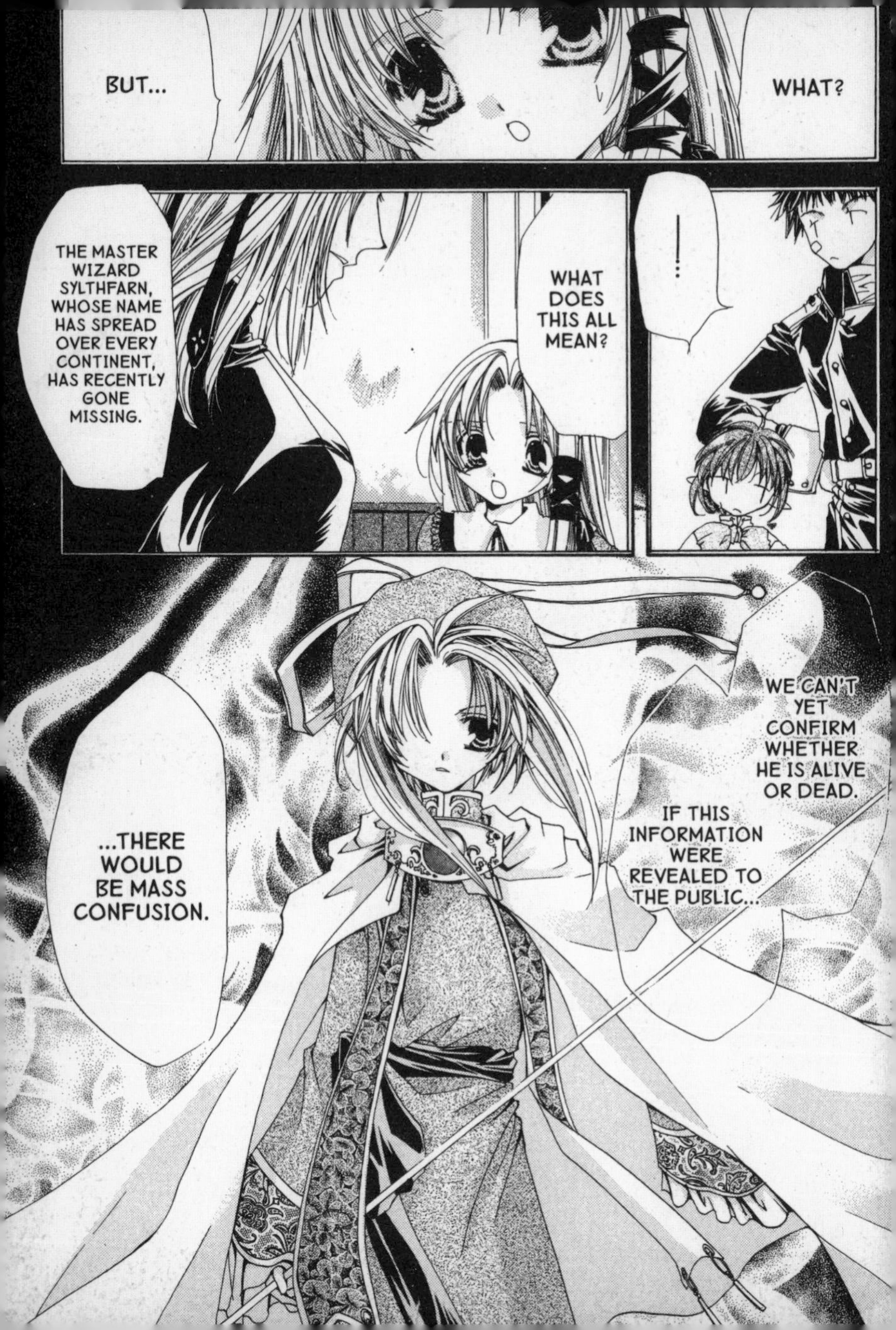
WHAT?
BUT...
!...
WHAT DOES THIS ALL MEAN?
THE MASTER WIZARD SYLTHFARN, WHOSE NAME HAS SPREAD OVER EVERY CONTINENT, HAS RECENTLY GONE MISSING.
WE CAN'T YET CONFIRM WHETHER HE IS ALIVE OR DEAD.
IF THIS INFORMATION WERE REVEALED TO THE PUBLIC...
...THERE WOULD BE MASS CONFUSION.

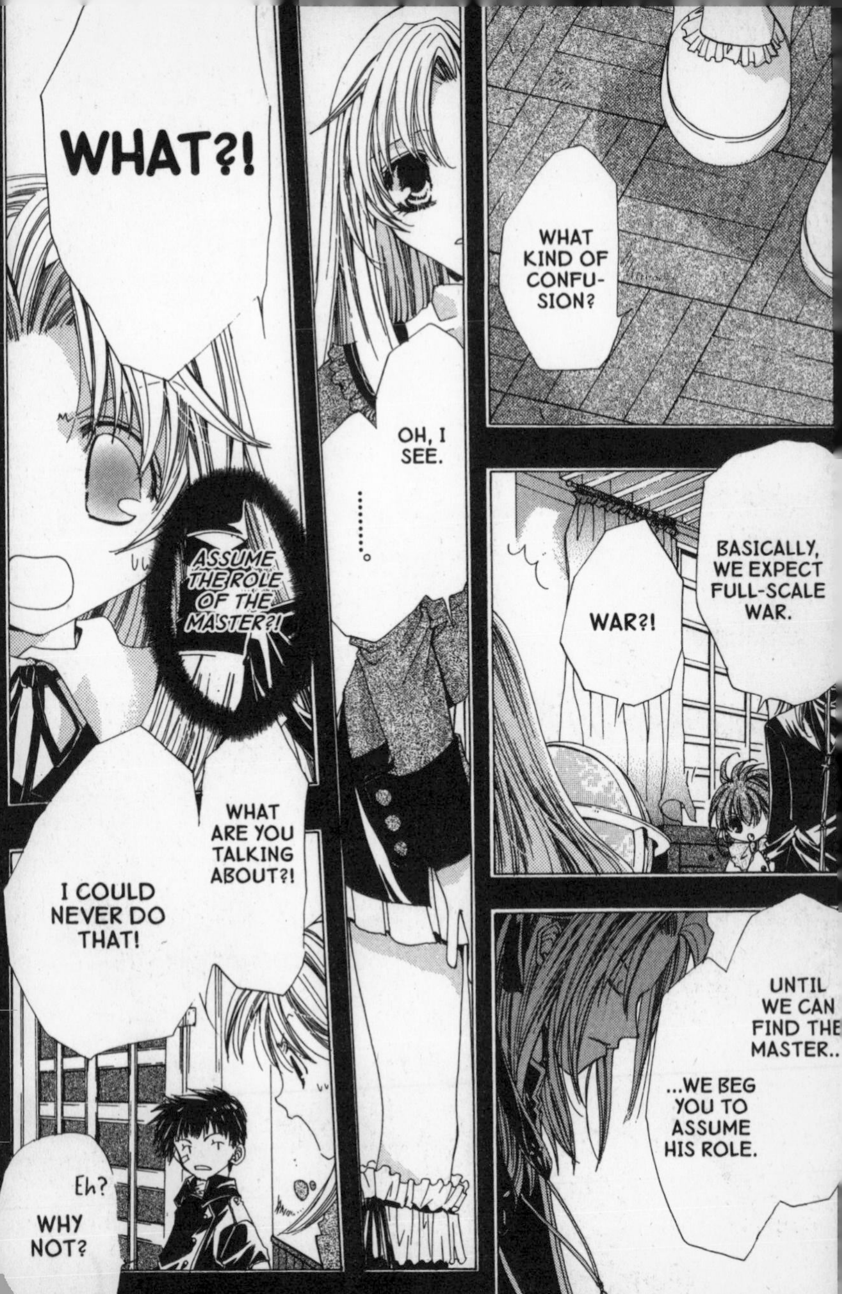
WHAT KIND OF CONFU-SION?
BASICALLY, WE EXPECT FULL-SCALE WAR.
WAR?!
UNTIL WE CAN FIND THE MASTER..
...WE BEG YOU TO ASSUME HIS ROLE.
OH, I SEE.
......
WHAT?!
ASSUME THE ROLE OF THE MASTER?!
WHAT ARE YOU TALKING ABOUT?!
I COULD NEVER DO THAT!
Eh?
WHY NOT?

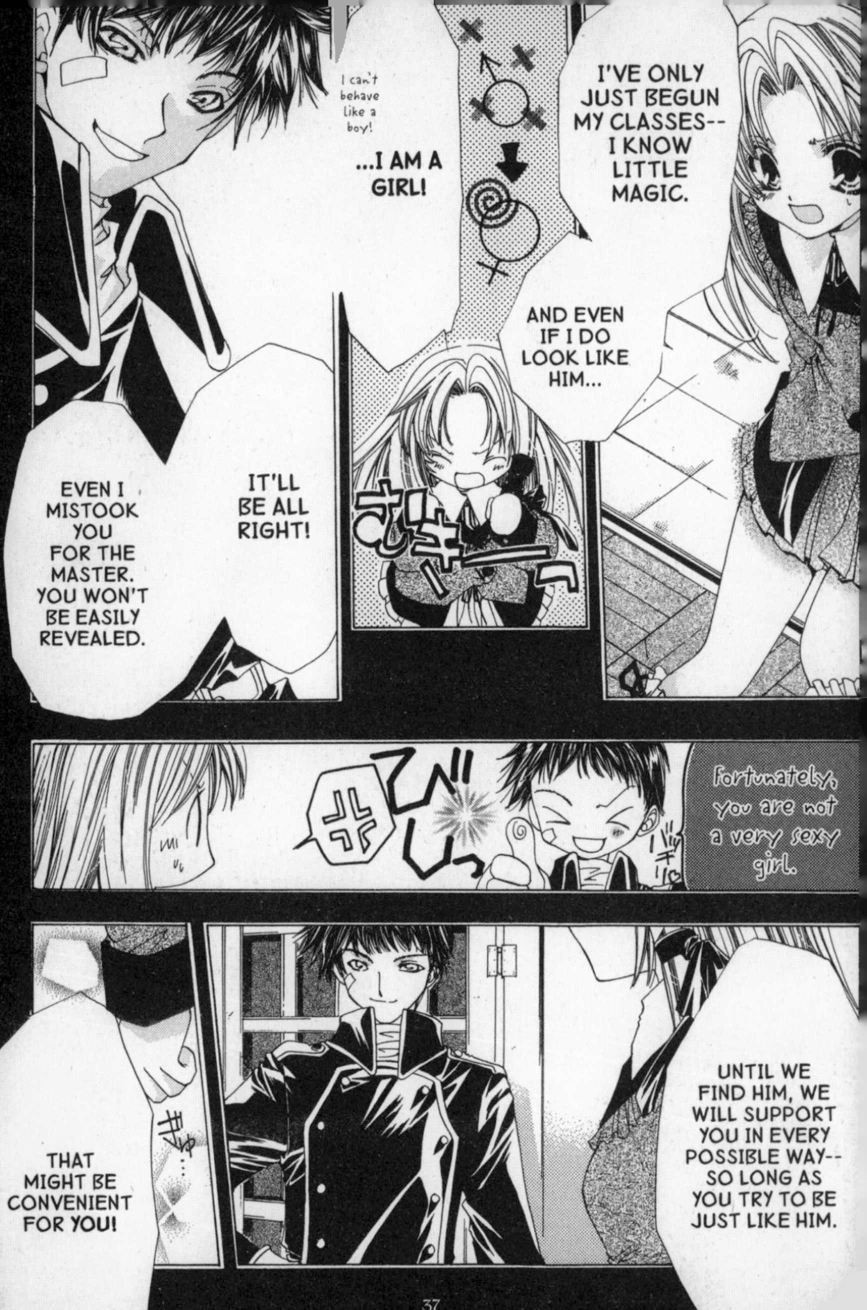
I'VE ONLY JUST BEGUN MY CLASSES-- I KNOW LITTLE MAGIC.
...I AM A GIRL!
I can't behave like a boy!
AND EVEN IF I DO LOOK LIKE HIM...
IT'LL BE ALL RIGHT!
EVEN I MISTOOK YOU FOR THE MASTER. YOU WON'T BE EASILY REVEALED.
Fortunately, you are not a very sexy girl.
UNTIL WE FIND HIM, WE WILL SUPPORT YOU IN EVERY POSSIBLE WAY-- SO LONG AS YOU TRY TO BE JUST LIKE HIM.
THAT MIGHT BE CONVENIENT FOR YOU!

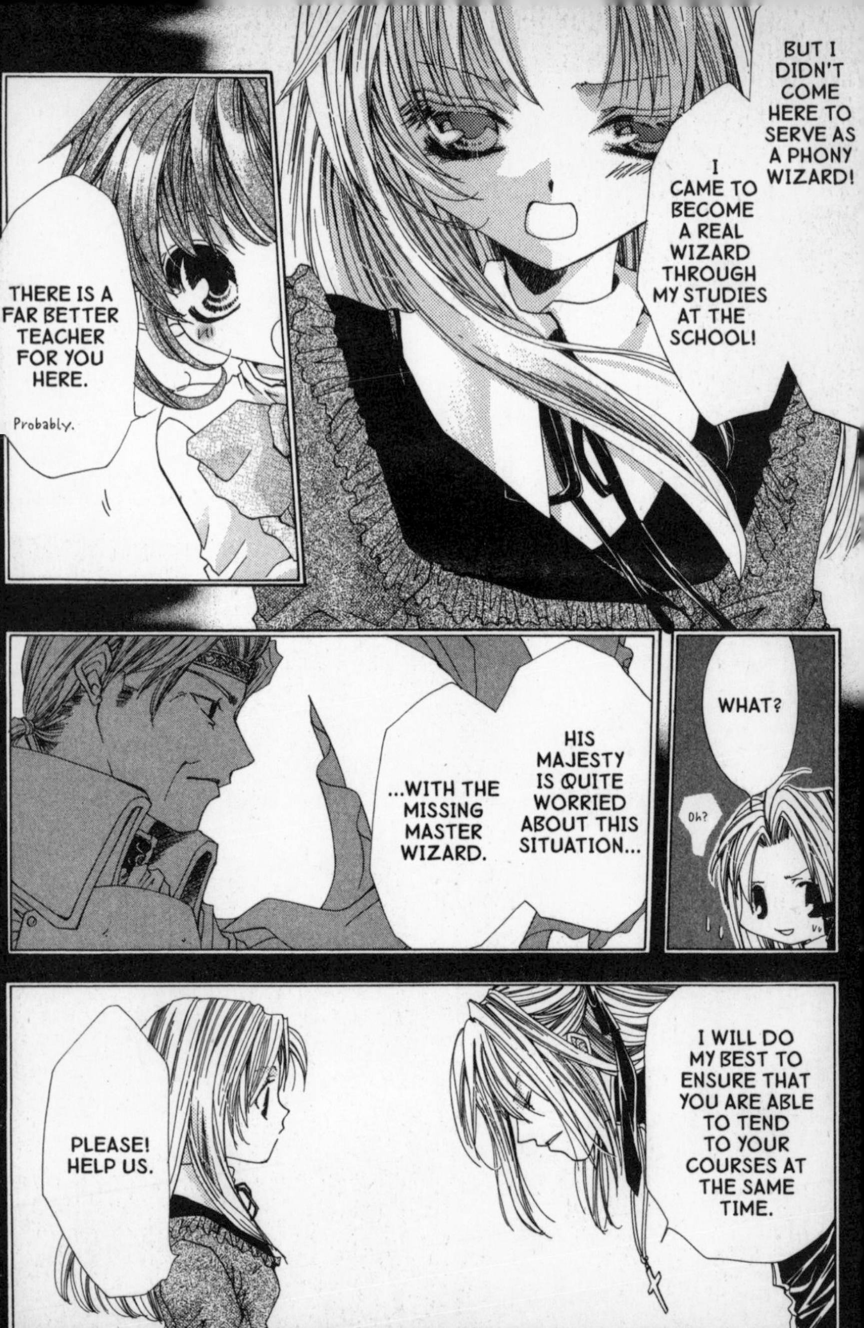
BUT I DIDN'T COME HERE TO SERVE AS A PHONY WIZARD!
I CAME TO BECOME A REAL WIZARD THROUGH MY STUDIES AT THE SCHOOL!
THERE IS A FAR BETTER TEACHER FOR YOU HERE.
Probably.
WHAT?
Oh?
HIS MAJESTY IS QUITE WORRIED ABOUT THIS SITUATION...
...WITH THE MISSING MASTER WIZARD.
I WILL DO MY BEST TO ENSURE THAT YOU ARE ABLE TO TEND TO YOUR COURSES AT THE SAME TIME.
PLEASE! HELP US.

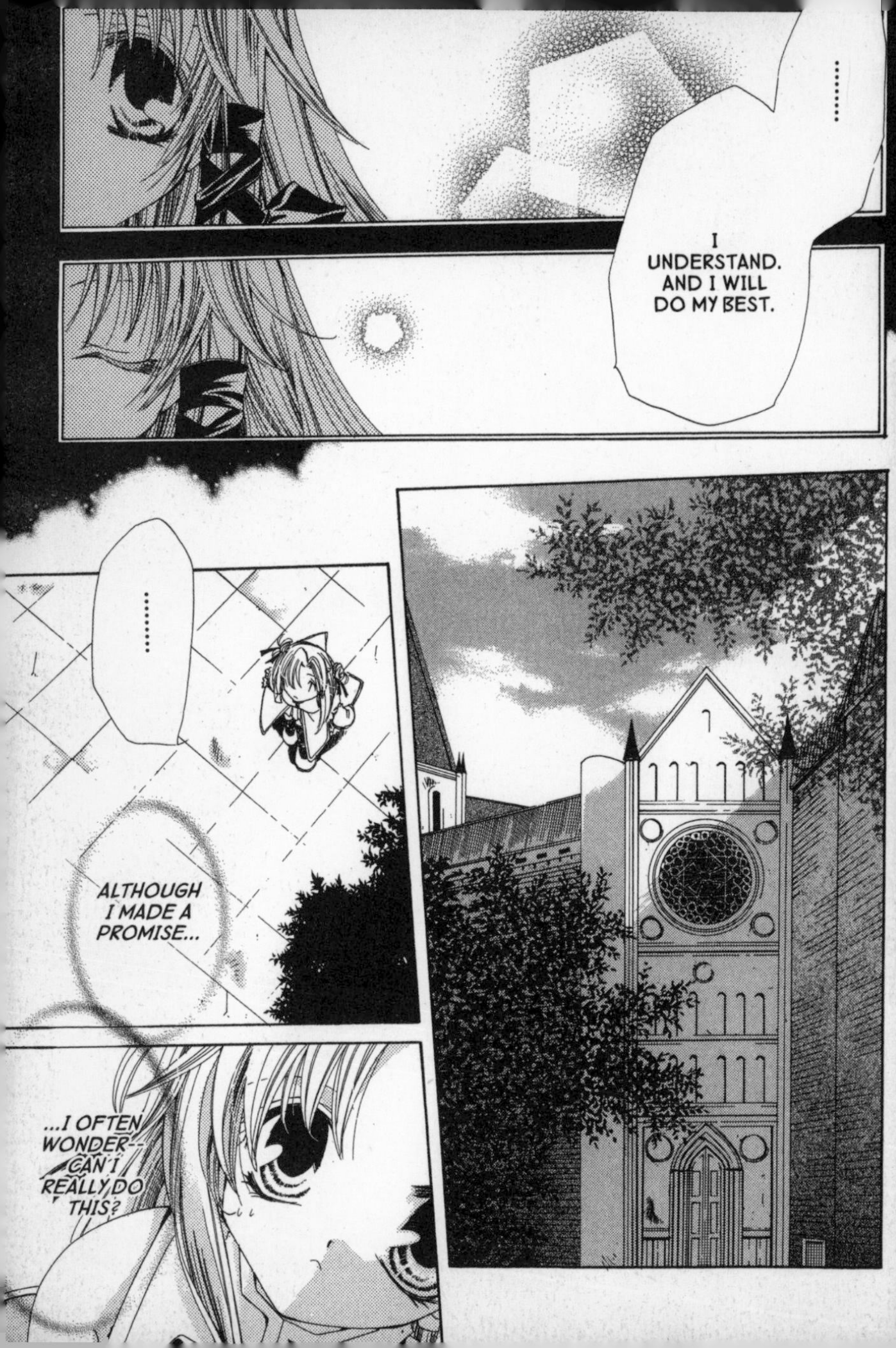
......
I UNDERSTAND. AND I WILL DO MY BEST.
......
ALTHOUGH I MADE A PROMISE...
...I OFTEN WONDER--CAN I REALLY DO THIS?

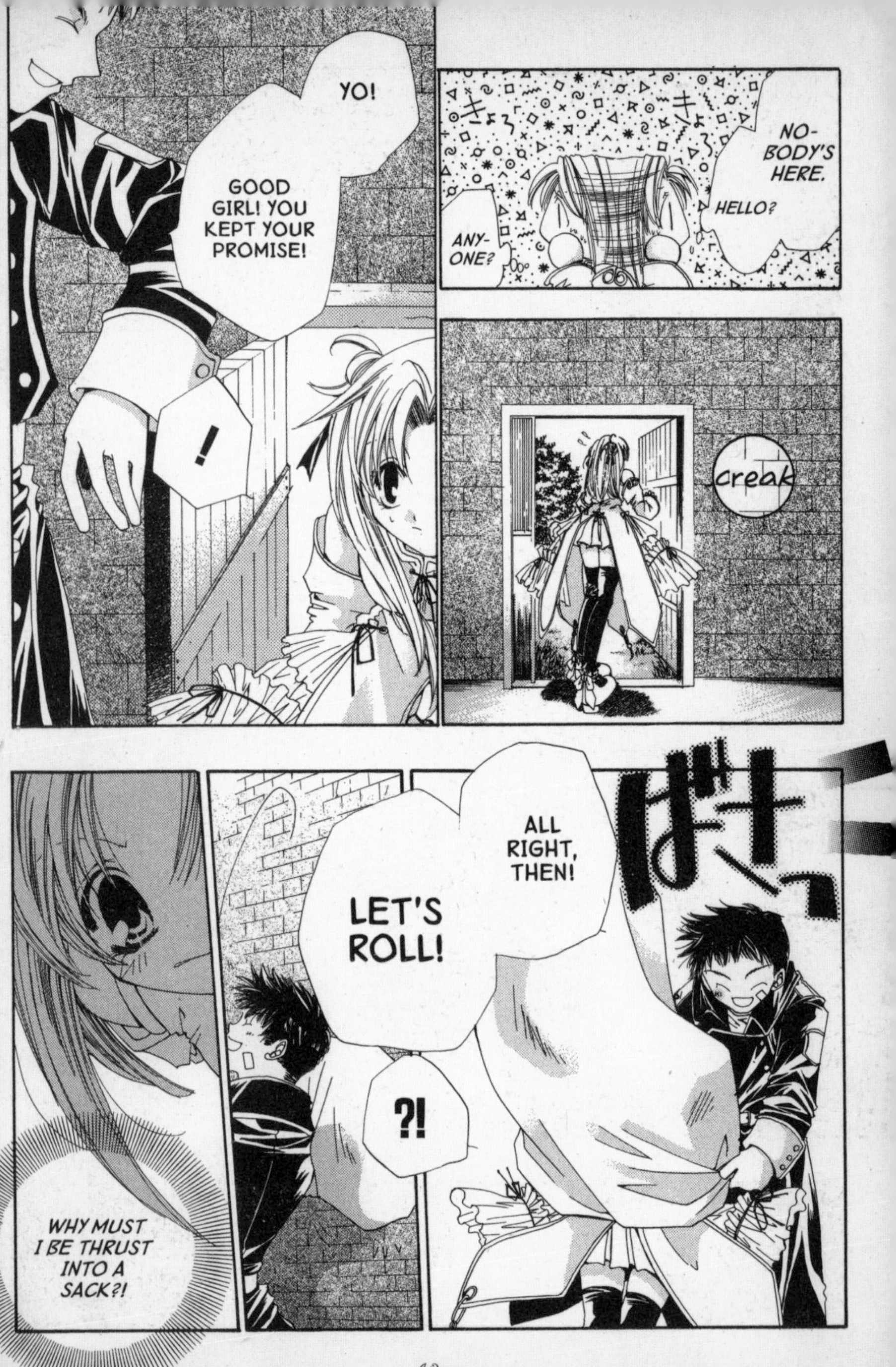
NO-BODY'S HERE.
HELLO?
ANY-ONE?
creak
YO!
GOOD GIRL! YOU KEPT YOUR PROMISE!
!
ばっ
ALL RIGHT, THEN!
LET'S ROLL!
?!
WHY MUST I BE THRUST INTO A SACK?!

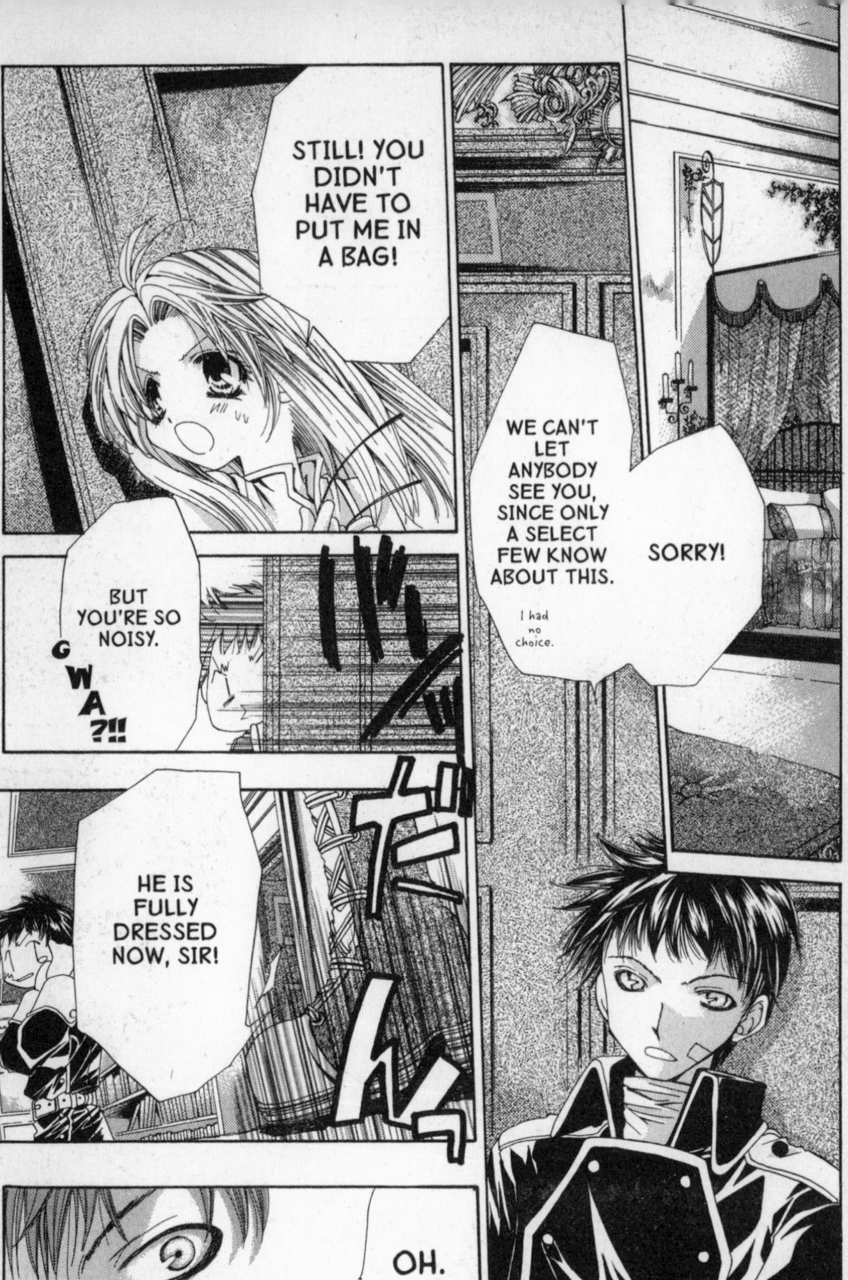
STILL! YOU DIDN'T HAVE TO PUT ME IN A BAG!
BUT YOU'RE SO NOISY.
GWA?!!
WE CAN'T LET ANYBODY SEE YOU, SINCE ONLY A SELECT FEW KNOW ABOUT THIS.
I had no choice.
SORRY!
HE IS FULLY DRESSED NOW, SIR!
OH.

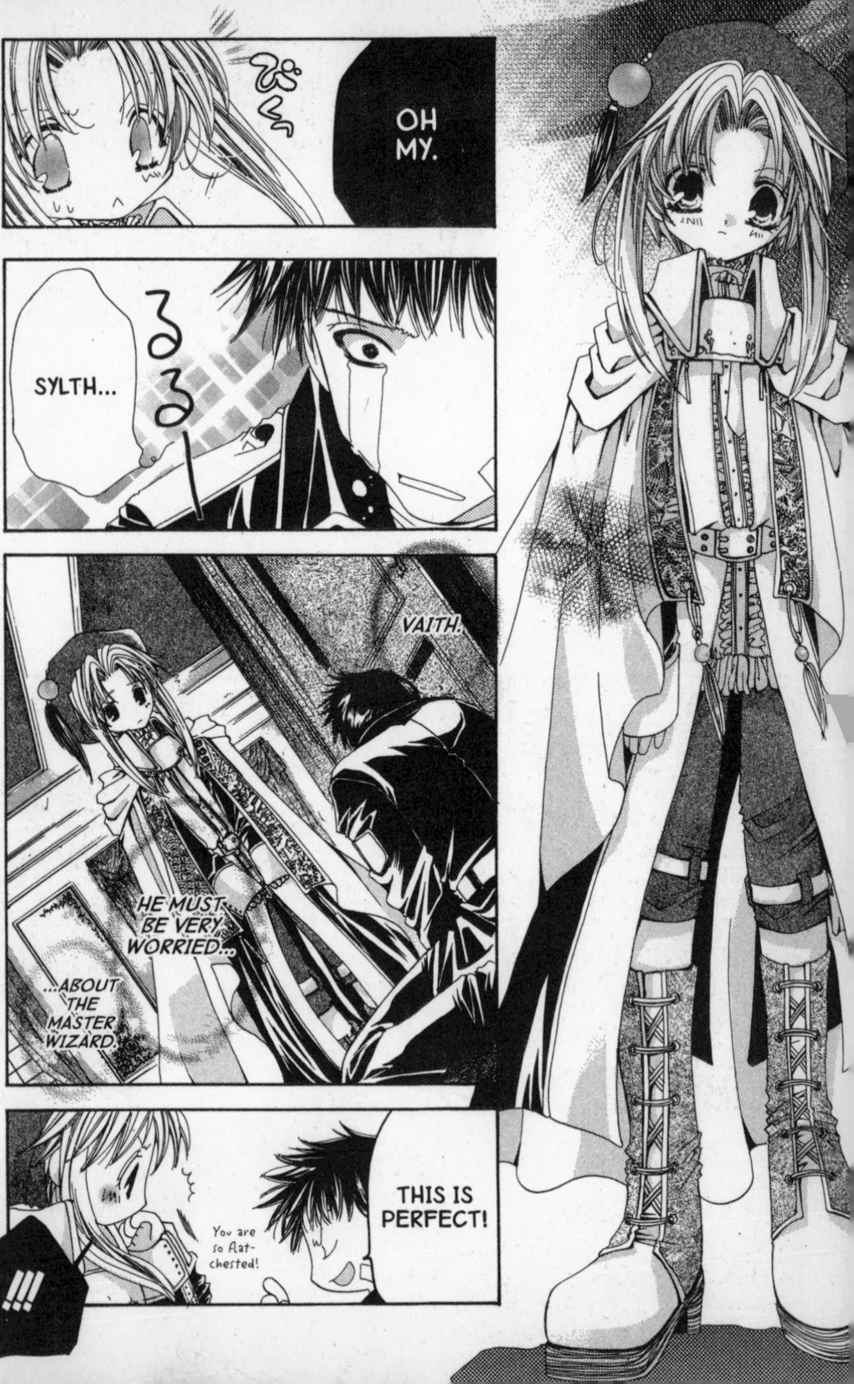
OH MY.
びく
SYLTH...
るる
VAITH.
HE MUST BE VERY WORRIED...
...ABOUT THE MASTER WIZARD.
THIS IS PERFECT!
You are so flat-chested!
!!!

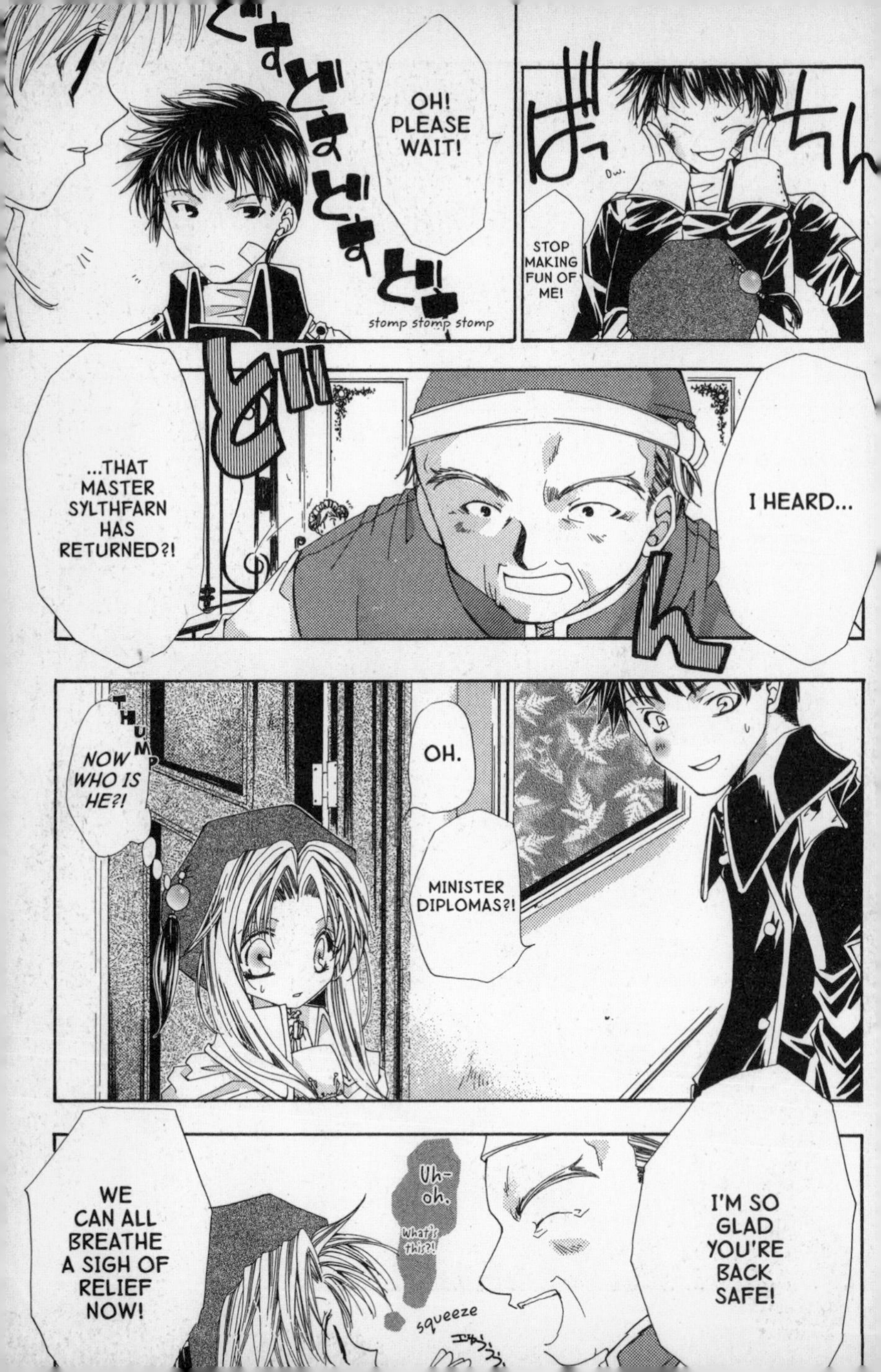
ばっちん
Ow.
STOP MAKING FUN OF ME!
OH! PLEASE WAIT!
stomp stomp stomp
I HEARD...
...THAT MASTER SYLTHFARN HAS RETURNED?!
OH.
MINISTER DIPLOMAS?!
THUMP
NOW WHO IS HE?!
I'M SO GLAD YOU'RE BACK SAFE!
Uh-oh.
What's this?!
WE CAN ALL BREATHE A SIGH OF RELIEF NOW!
squeeze

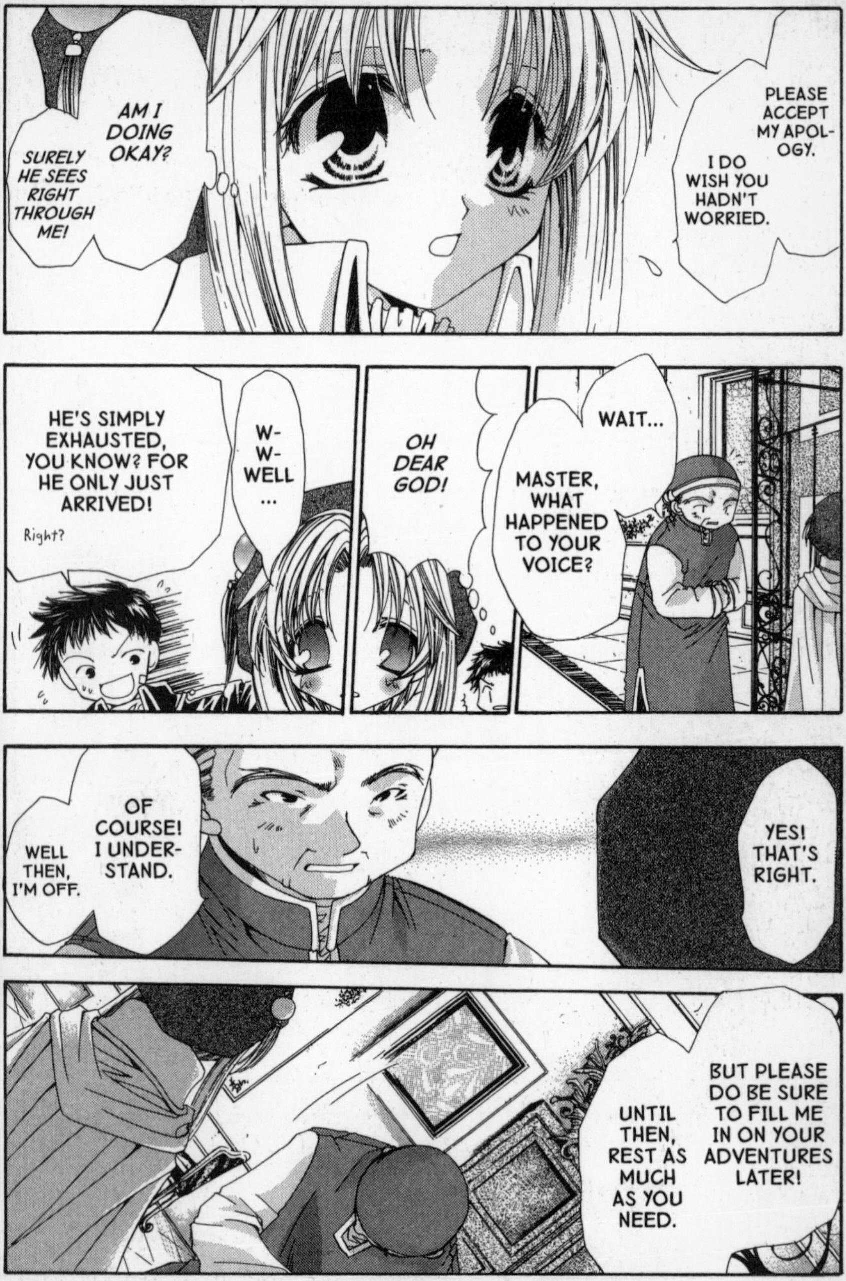
PLEASE ACCEPT MY APOLOGY.
I DO WISH YOU HADN'T WORRIED.
AM I DOING OKAY?
SURELY HE SEES RIGHT THROUGH ME!
WAIT...
MASTER, WHAT HAPPENED TO YOUR VOICE?
OH DEAR GOD!
W-W-WELL ...
HE'S SIMPLY EXHAUSTED, YOU KNOW? FOR HE ONLY JUST ARRIVED!
Right?
YES! THAT'S RIGHT.
OF COURSE! I UNDERSTAND.
WELL THEN, I'M OFF.
BUT PLEASE DO BE SURE TO FILL ME IN ON YOUR ADVENTURES LATER!
UNTIL THEN, REST AS MUCH AS YOU NEED.

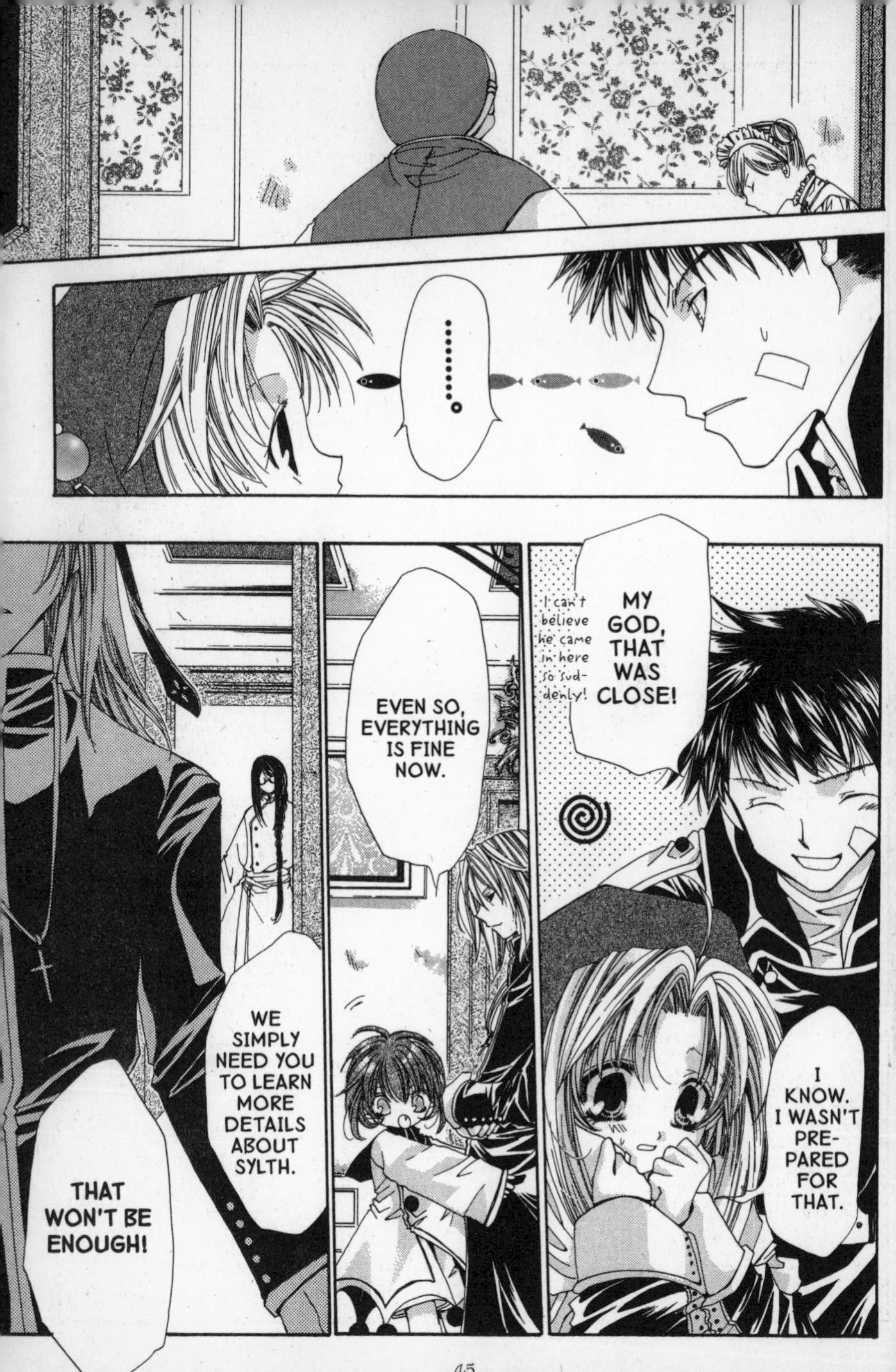
......
MY GOD, THAT WAS CLOSE!
I can't believe he came in here so suddenly!
I KNOW. I WASN'T PRE-PARED FOR THAT.
EVEN SO, EVERYTHING IS FINE NOW.
WE SIMPLY NEED YOU TO LEARN MORE DETAILS ABOUT SYLTH.
THAT WON'T BE ENOUGH!

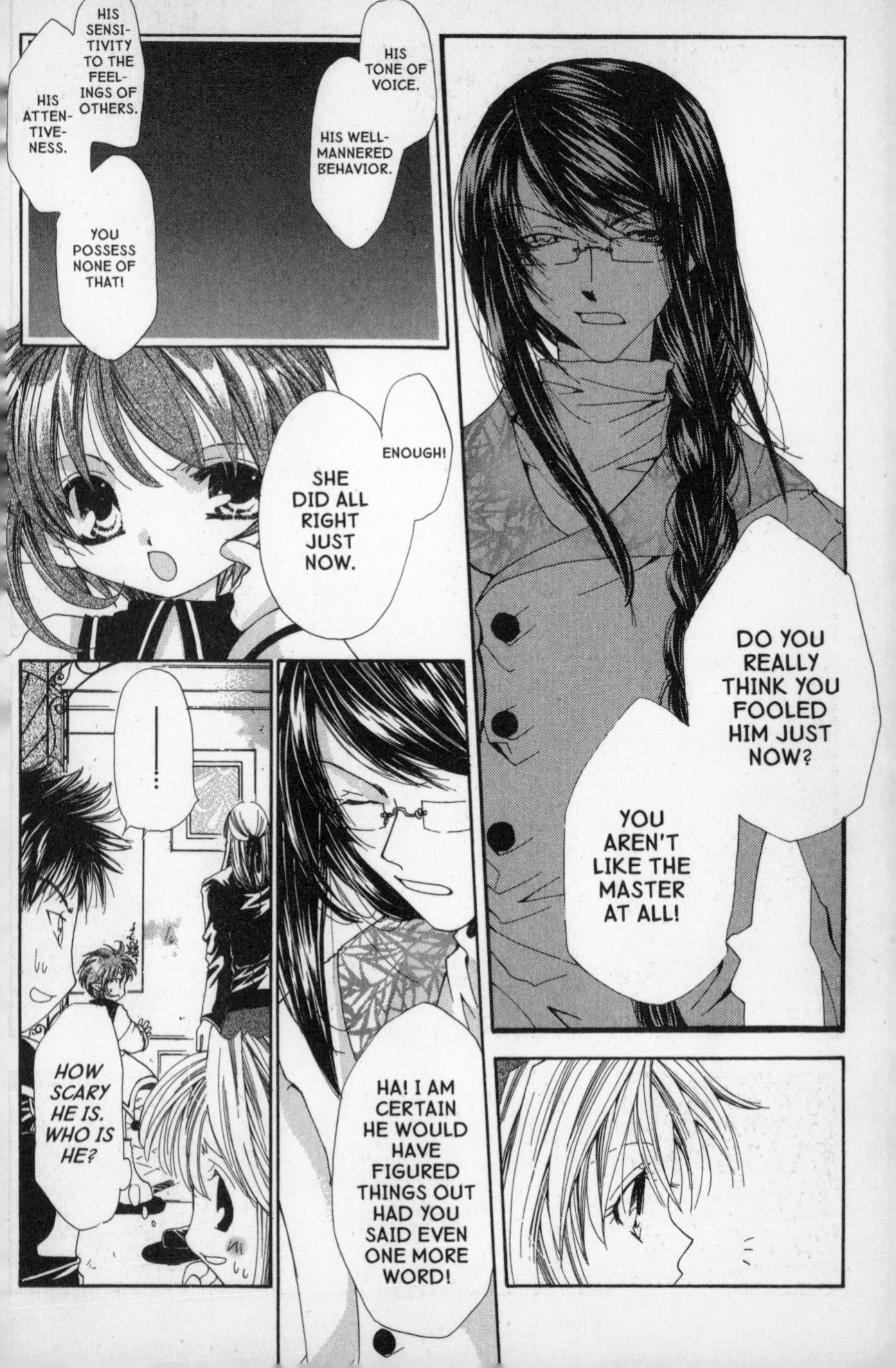
DO YOU REALLY THINK YOU FOOLED HIM JUST NOW?
YOU AREN'T LIKE THE MASTER AT ALL!
HIS TONE OF VOICE.
HIS WELL-MANNERED BEHAVIOR.
HIS SENSITIVITY TO THE FEELINGS OF OTHERS.
HIS ATTENTIVENESS.
YOU POSSESS NONE OF THAT!
ENOUGH!
SHE DID ALL RIGHT JUST NOW.
HA! I AM CERTAIN HE WOULD HAVE FIGURED THINGS OUT HAD YOU SAID EVEN ONE MORE WORD!
......!
HOW SCARY HE IS. WHO IS HE?

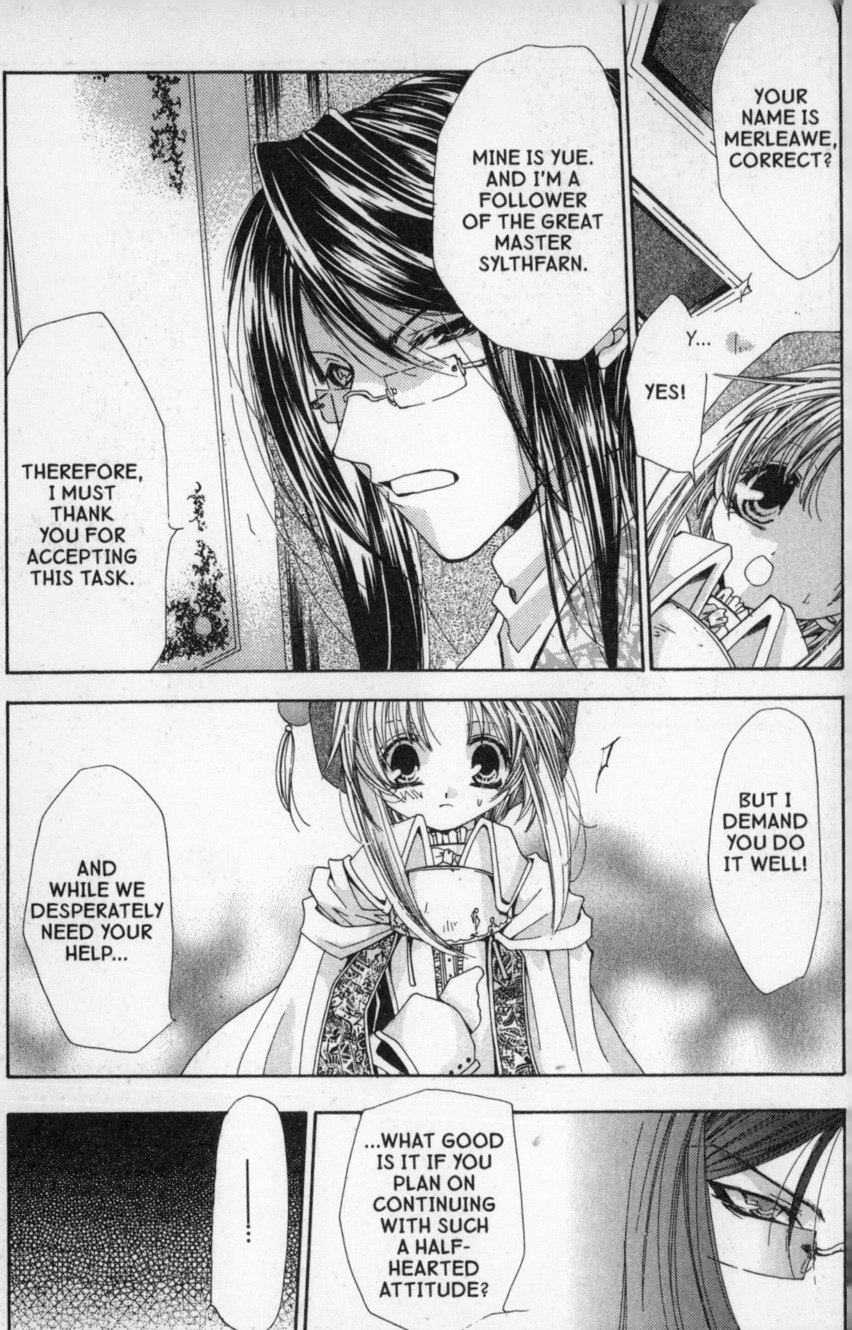

YOUR NAME IS MERLEAWE, CORRECT?
Y...
YES!
MINE IS YUE. AND I'M A FOLLOWER OF THE GREAT MASTER SYLTHFARN.
THEREFORE, I MUST THANK YOU FOR ACCEPTING THIS TASK.
BUT I DEMAND YOU DO IT WELL!
AND WHILE WE DESPERATELY NEED YOUR HELP...
...WHAT GOOD IS IT IF YOU PLAN ON CONTINUING WITH SUCH A HALF-HEARTED ATTITUDE?
......!

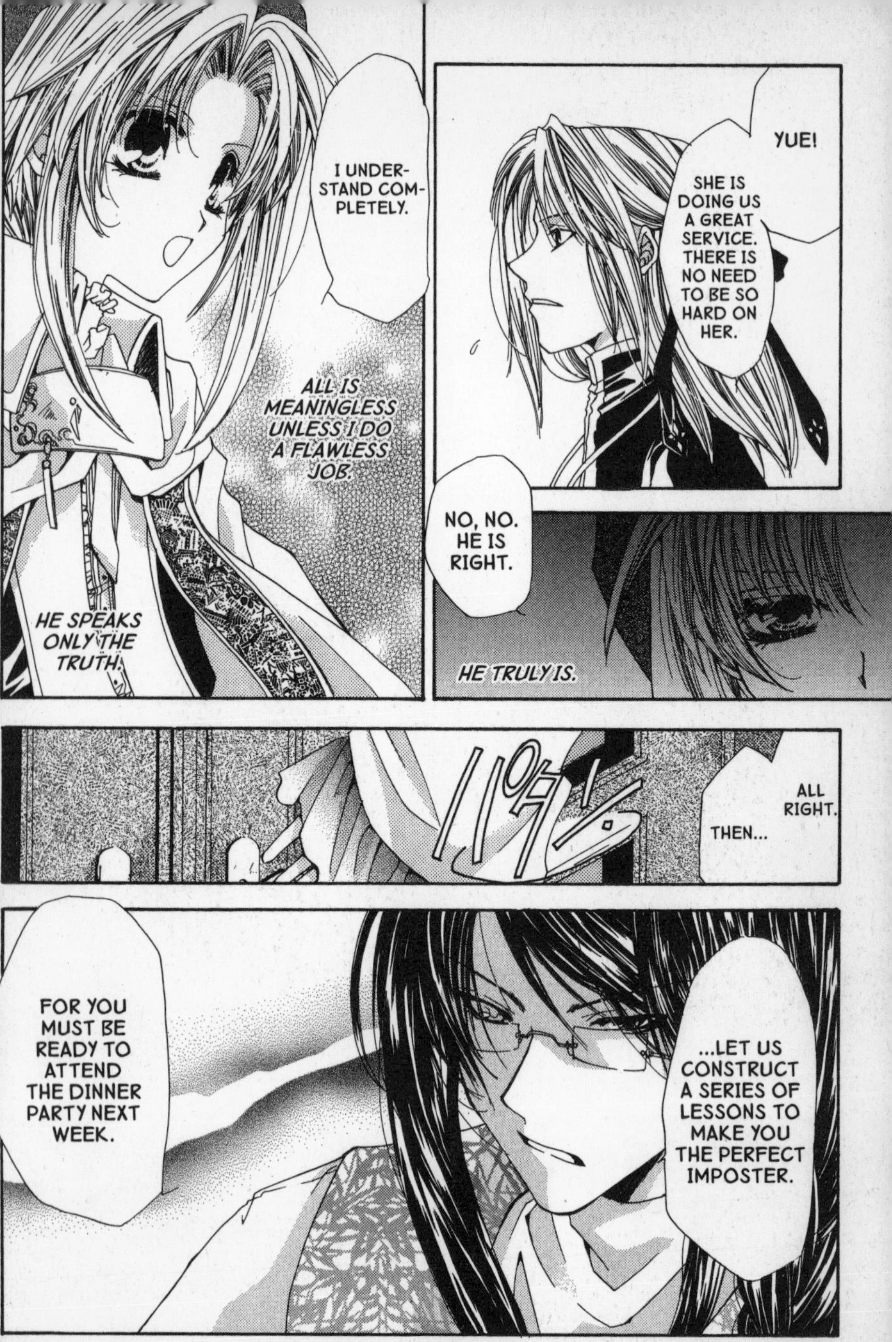
YUE!
SHE IS DOING US A GREAT SERVICE. THERE IS NO NEED TO BE SO HARD ON HER.
NO, NO. HE IS RIGHT.
HE TRULY IS.
I UNDER-STAND COM-PLETELY.
ALL IS MEANINGLESS UNLESS I DO A FLAWLESS JOB.
HE SPEAKS ONLY THE TRUTH.
ALL RIGHT.
THEN...
...LET US CONSTRUCT A SERIES OF LESSONS TO MAKE YOU THE PERFECT IMPOSTER.
FOR YOU MUST BE READY TO ATTEND THE DINNER PARTY NEXT WEEK.

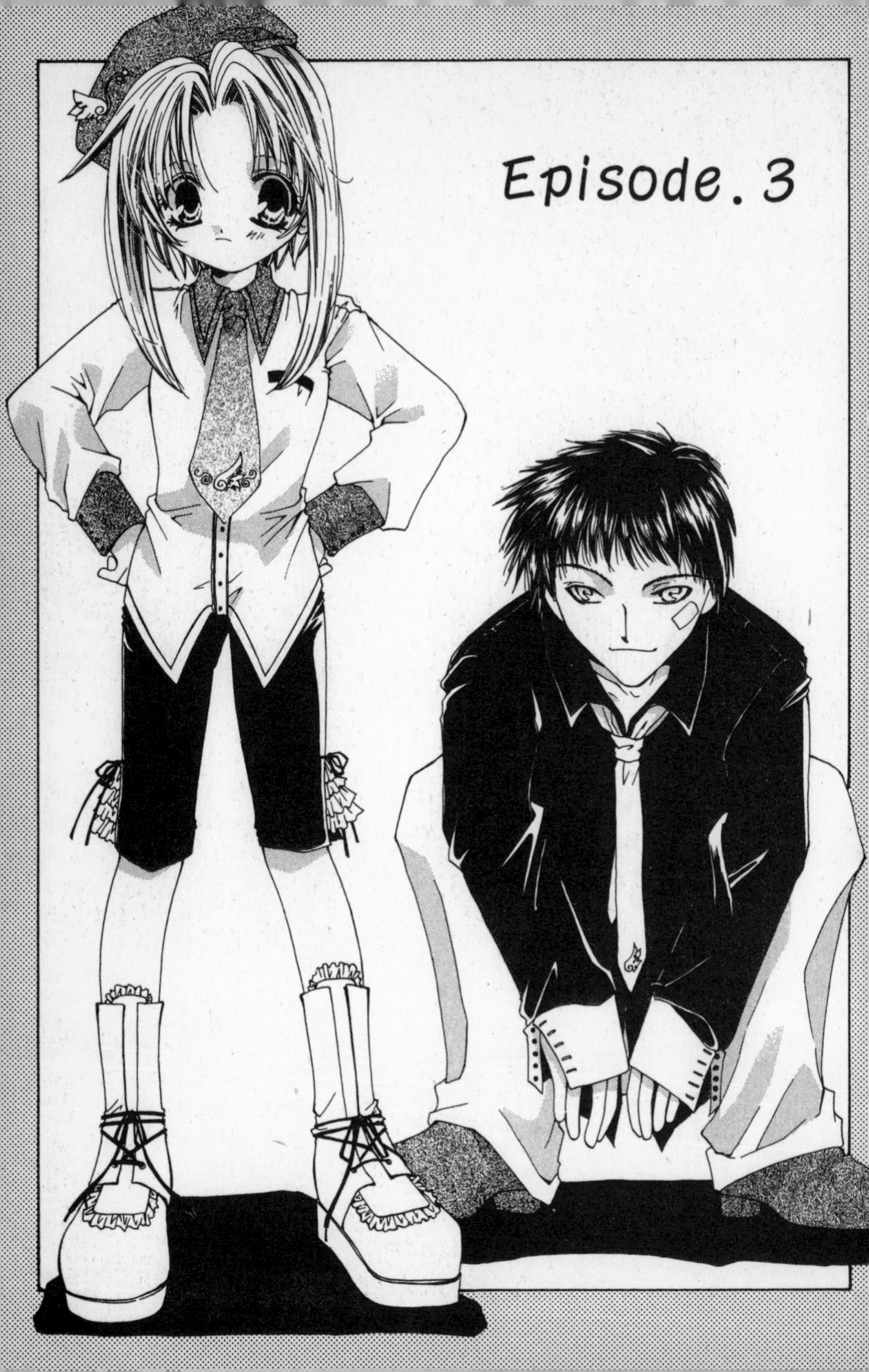
Episode. 3

EEEK!!

UM?!

50

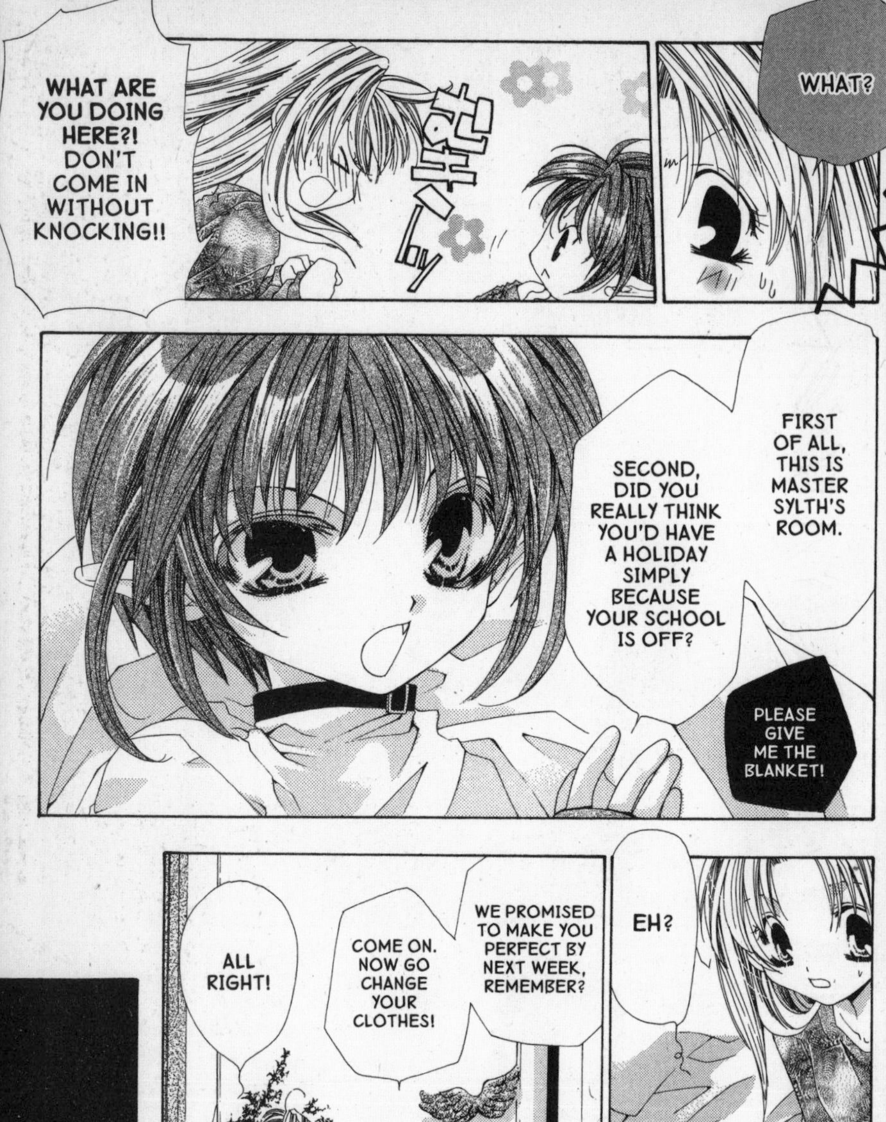
WHAT?
WHAT ARE YOU DOING HERE?! DON'T COME IN WITHOUT KNOCKING!!
FIRST OF ALL, THIS IS MASTER SYLTH'S ROOM.
SECOND, DID YOU REALLY THINK YOU'D HAVE A HOLIDAY SIMPLY BECAUSE YOUR SCHOOL IS OFF?
PLEASE GIVE ME THE BLANKET!
EH?
WE PROMISED TO MAKE YOU PERFECT BY NEXT WEEK, REMEMBER?
COME ON. NOW GO CHANGE YOUR CLOTHES!
ALL RIGHT!

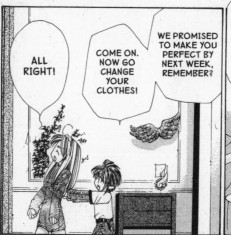

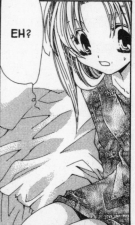

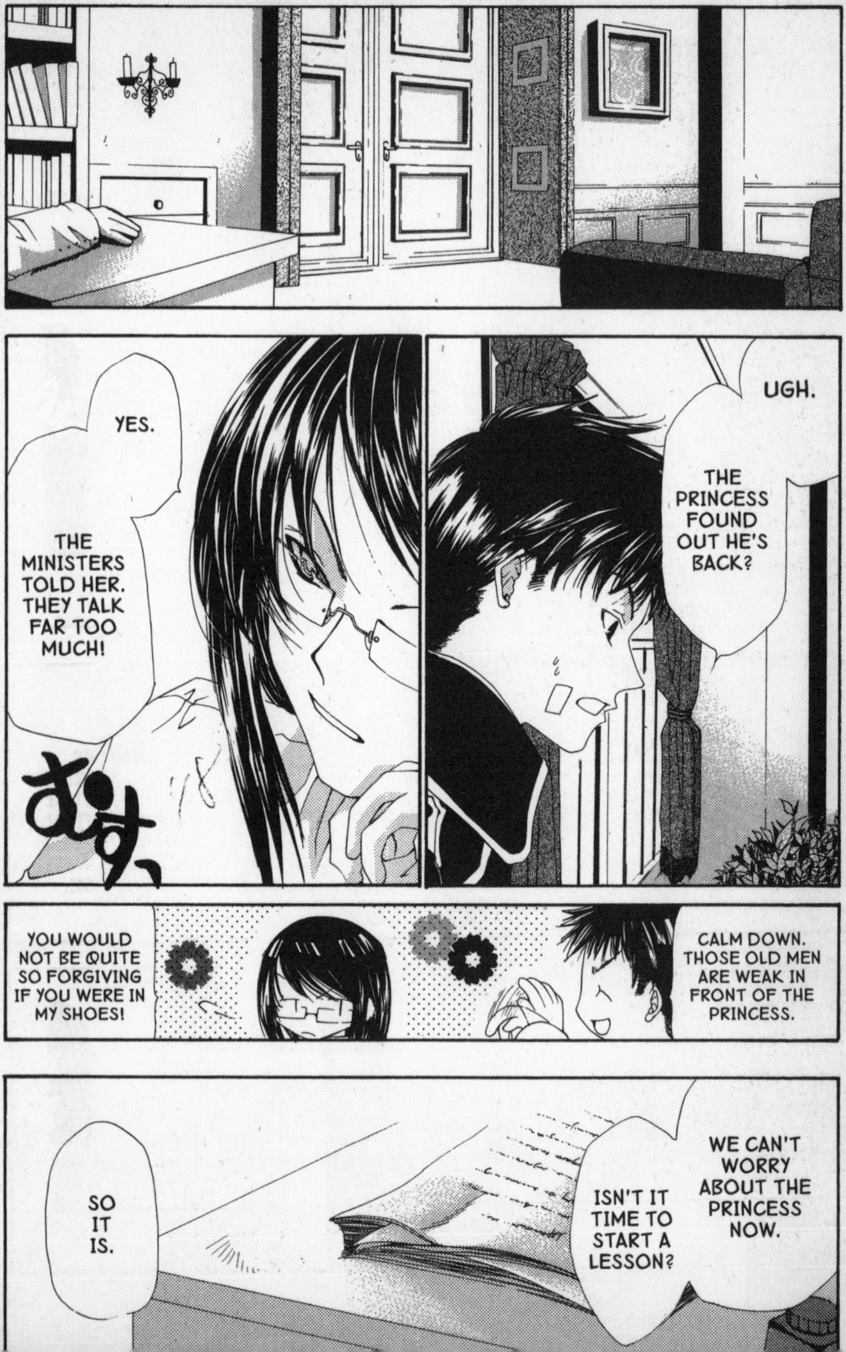
UGH.
THE PRINCESS FOUND OUT HE'S BACK?
YES.
THE MINISTERS TOLD HER. THEY TALK FAR TOO MUCH!
むす
CALM DOWN. THOSE OLD MEN ARE WEAK IN FRONT OF THE PRINCESS.
YOU WOULD NOT BE QUITE SO FORGIVING IF YOU WERE IN MY SHOES!
WE CAN'T WORRY ABOUT THE PRINCESS NOW.
ISN'T IT TIME TO START A LESSON?
SO IT IS.

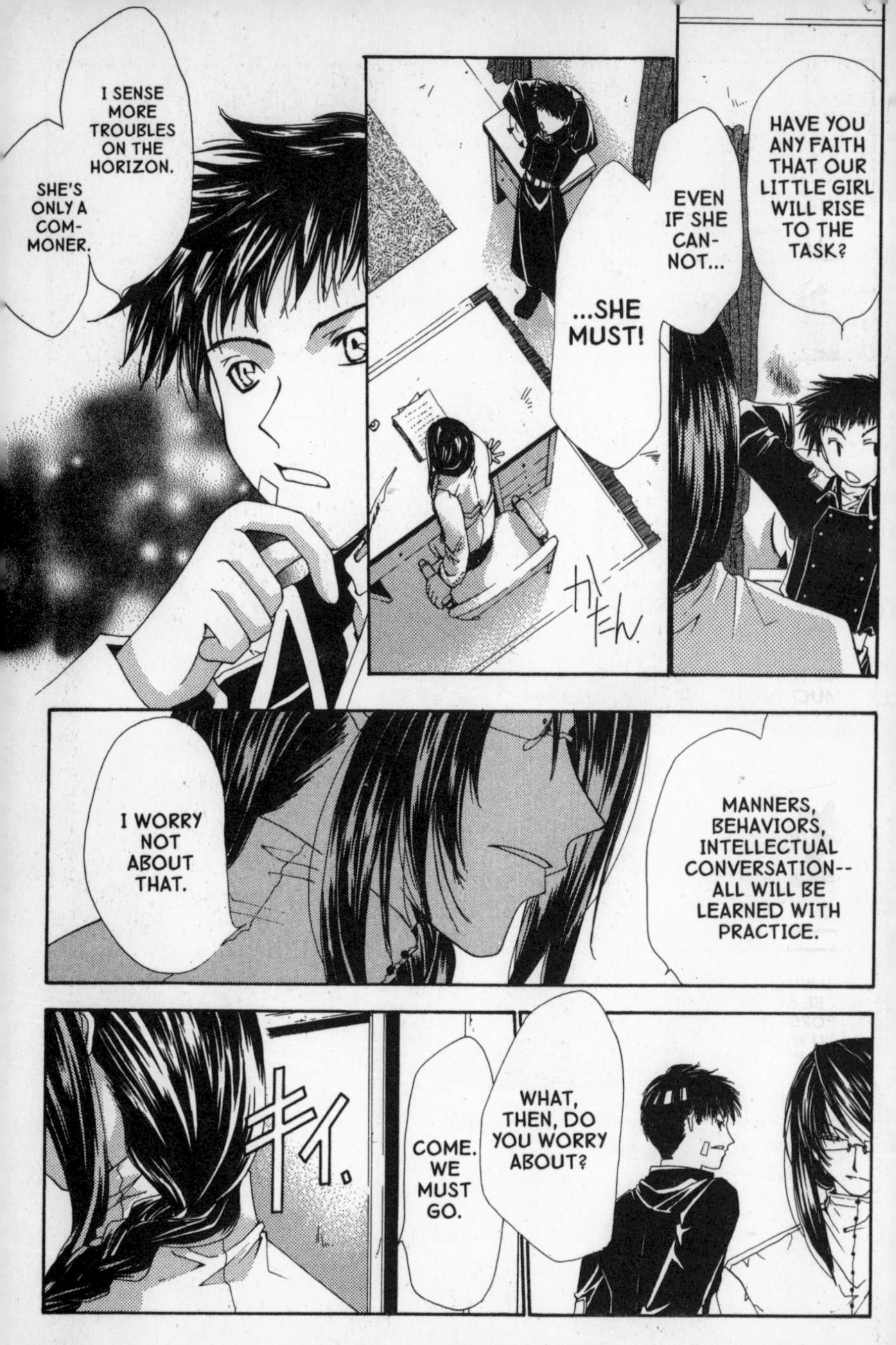
HAVE YOU ANY FAITH THAT OUR LITTLE GIRL WILL RISE TO THE TASK?
EVEN IF SHE CAN-NOT...
...SHE MUST!
ガたん
I SENSE MORE TROUBLES ON THE HORIZON.
SHE'S ONLY A COM-MONER.
MANNERS, BEHAVIORS, INTELLECTUAL CONVERSATION--ALL WILL BE LEARNED WITH PRACTICE.
I WORRY NOT ABOUT THAT.
WHAT, THEN, DO YOU WORRY ABOUT?
COME. WE MUST GO.
キイ.

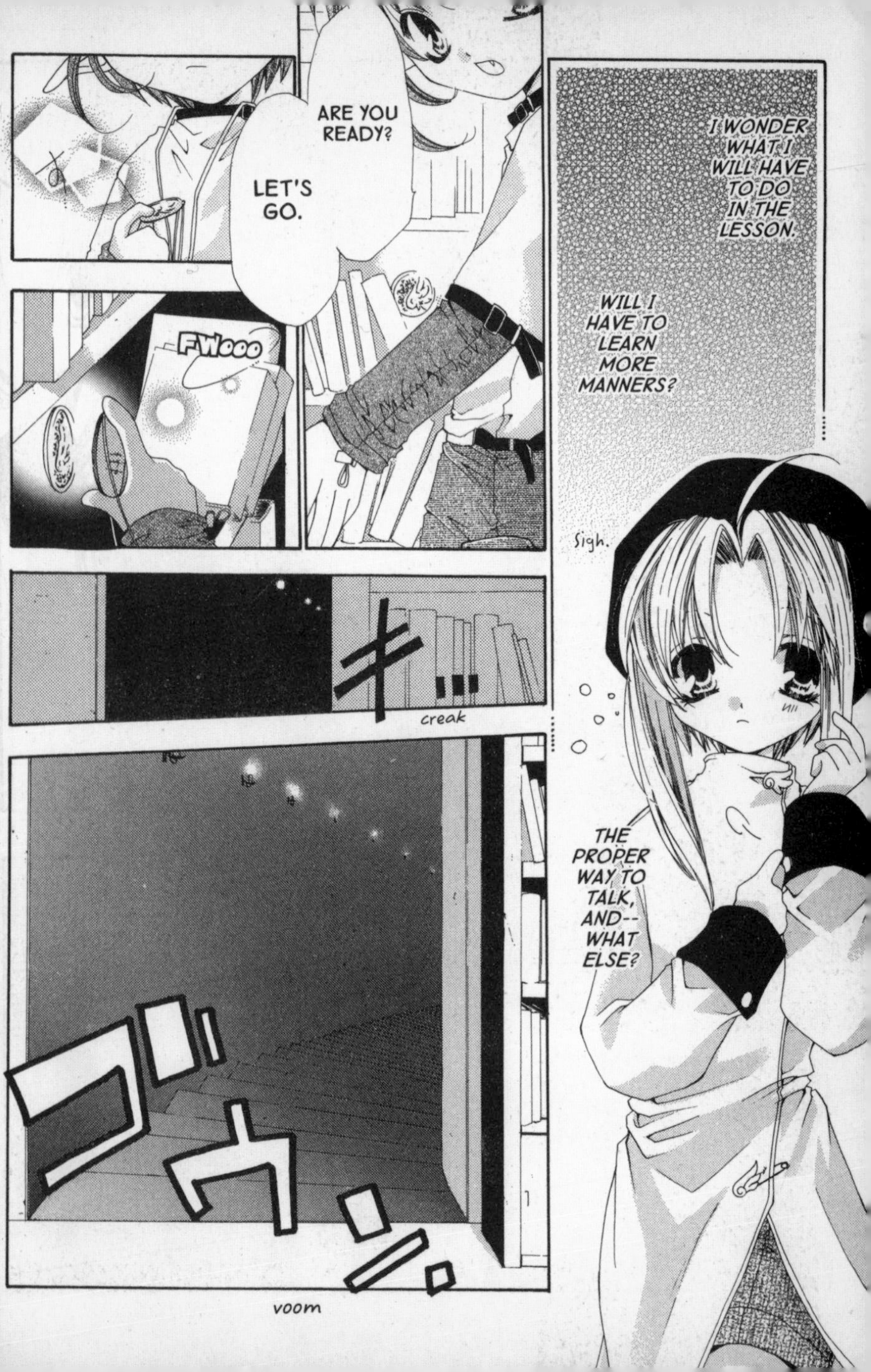
I WONDER WHAT I WILL HAVE TO DO IN THE LESSON.
WILL I HAVE TO LEARN MORE MANNERS?
Sigh.
THE PROPER WAY TO TALK, AND-- WHAT ELSE?
ARE YOU READY?
LET'S GO.
FWOOO
creak
voom

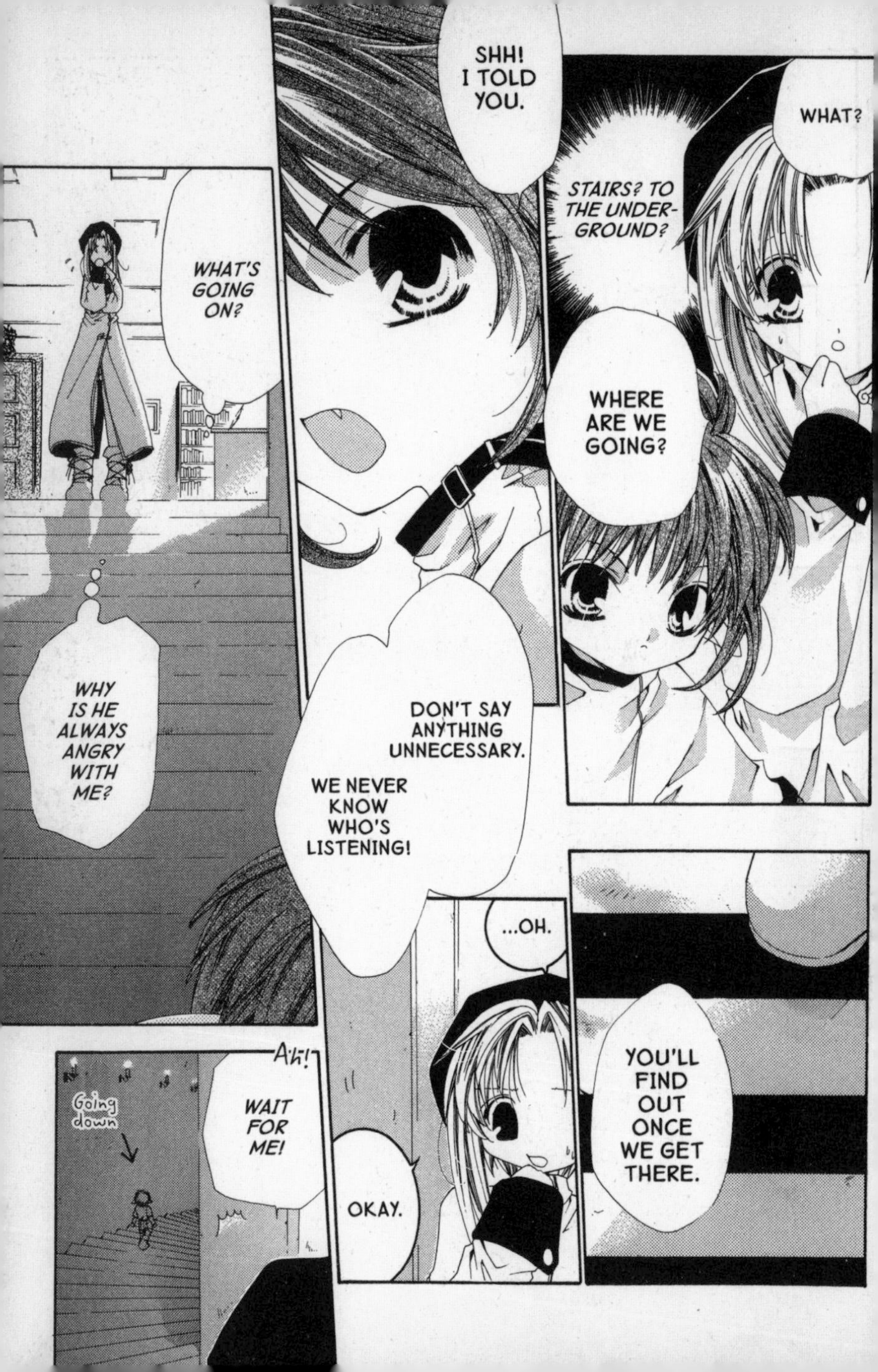
WHAT?
STAIRS? TO THE UNDERGROUND?
WHERE ARE WE GOING?
SHH! I TOLD YOU.
DON'T SAY ANYTHING UNNECESSARY.
WE NEVER KNOW WHO'S LISTENING!
WHAT'S GOING ON?
WHY IS HE ALWAYS ANGRY WITH ME?
YOU'LL FIND OUT ONCE WE GET THERE.
...OH.
OKAY.
Ah!
WAIT FOR ME!
Going down

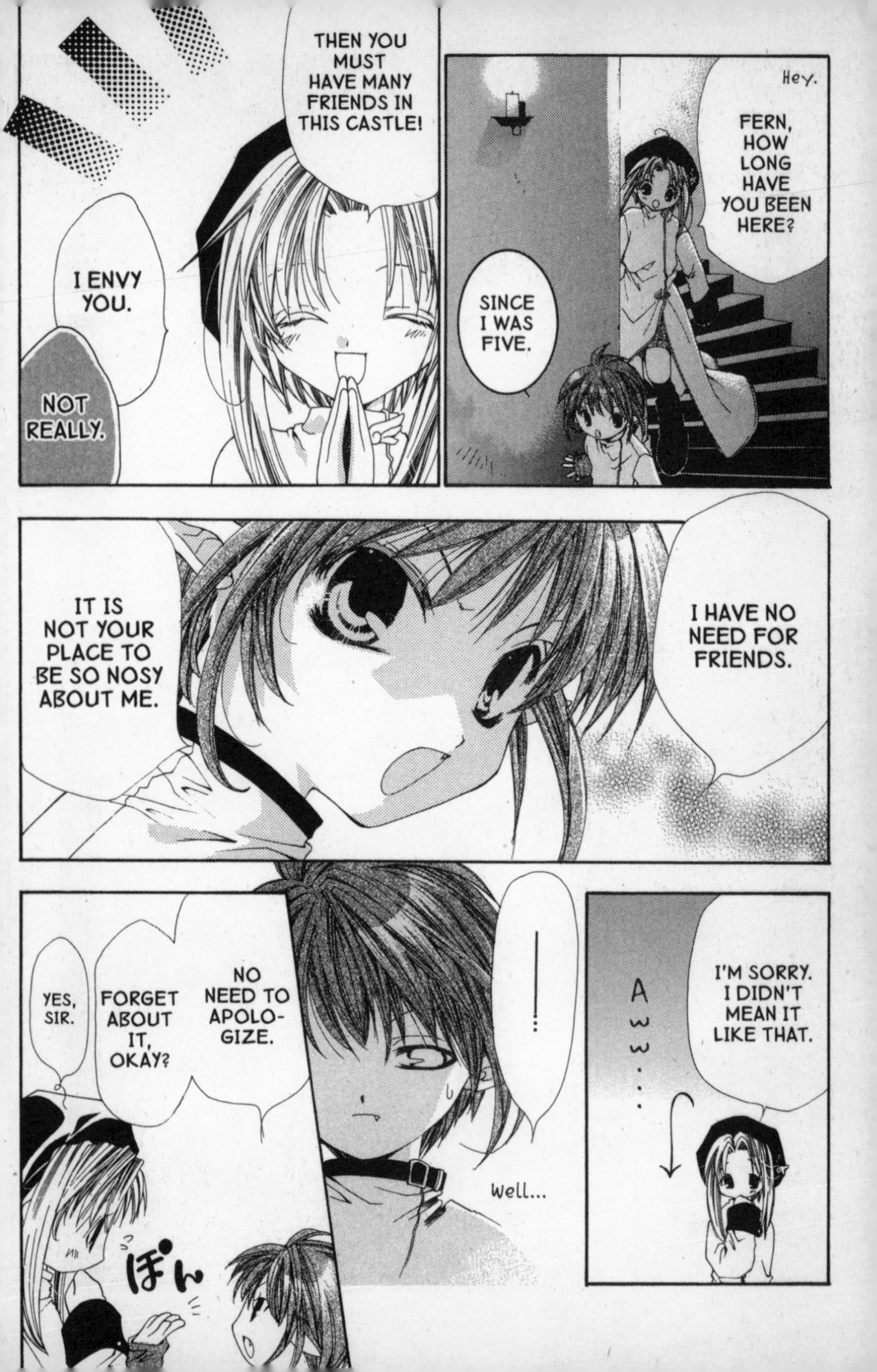
Hey.
FERN, HOW LONG HAVE YOU BEEN HERE?
SINCE I WAS FIVE.
THEN YOU MUST HAVE MANY FRIENDS IN THIS CASTLE!
I ENVY YOU.
NOT REALLY.
I HAVE NO NEED FOR FRIENDS.
IT IS NOT YOUR PLACE TO BE SO NOSY ABOUT ME.
I'M SORRY. I DIDN'T MEAN IT LIKE THAT.
Aww...
—!
Well...
NO NEED TO APOLOGIZE.
FORGET ABOUT IT, OKAY?
YES, SIR.
ぽん

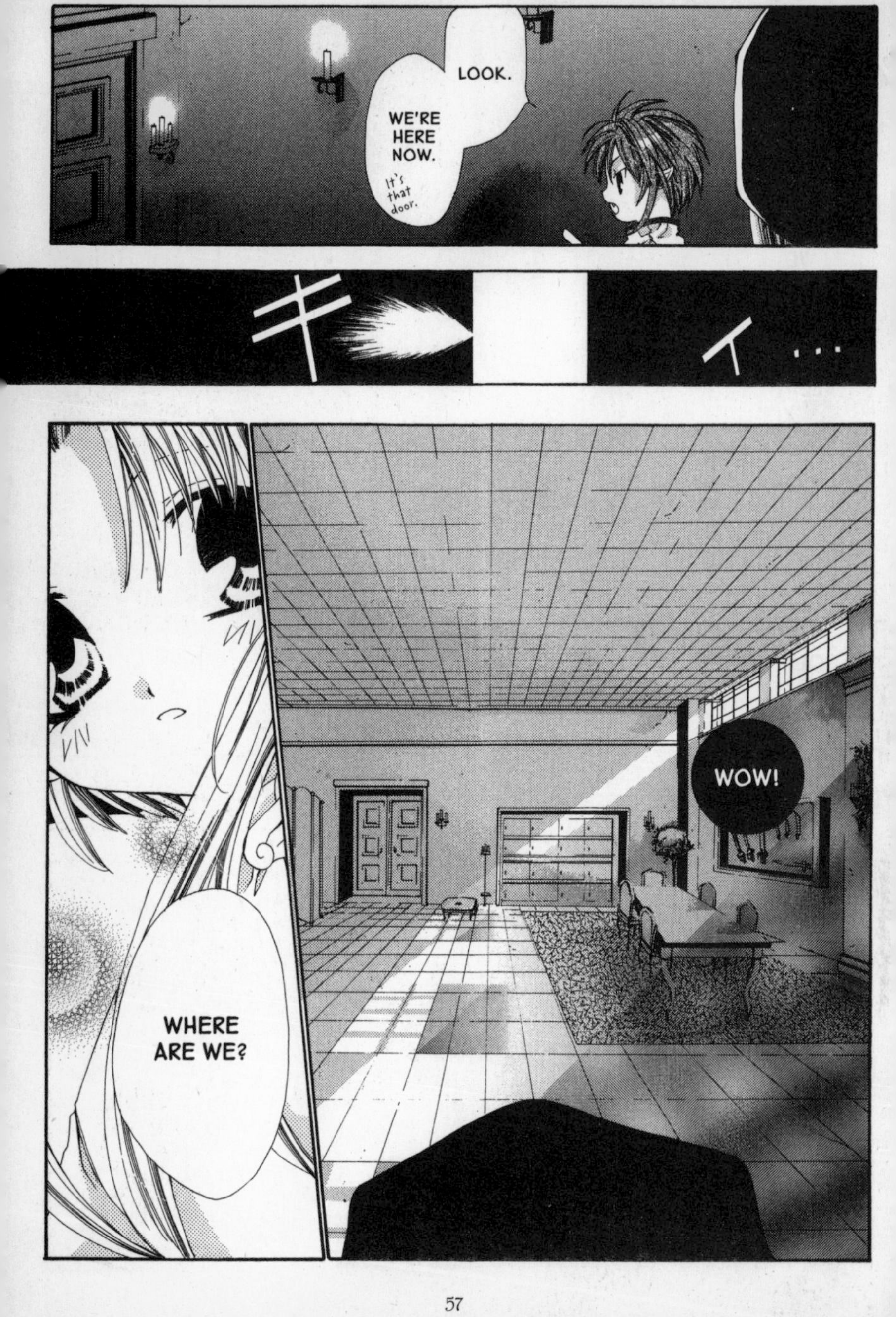
LOOK.
WE'RE HERE NOW.
It's that door.
キイ...
WOW!
WHERE ARE WE?

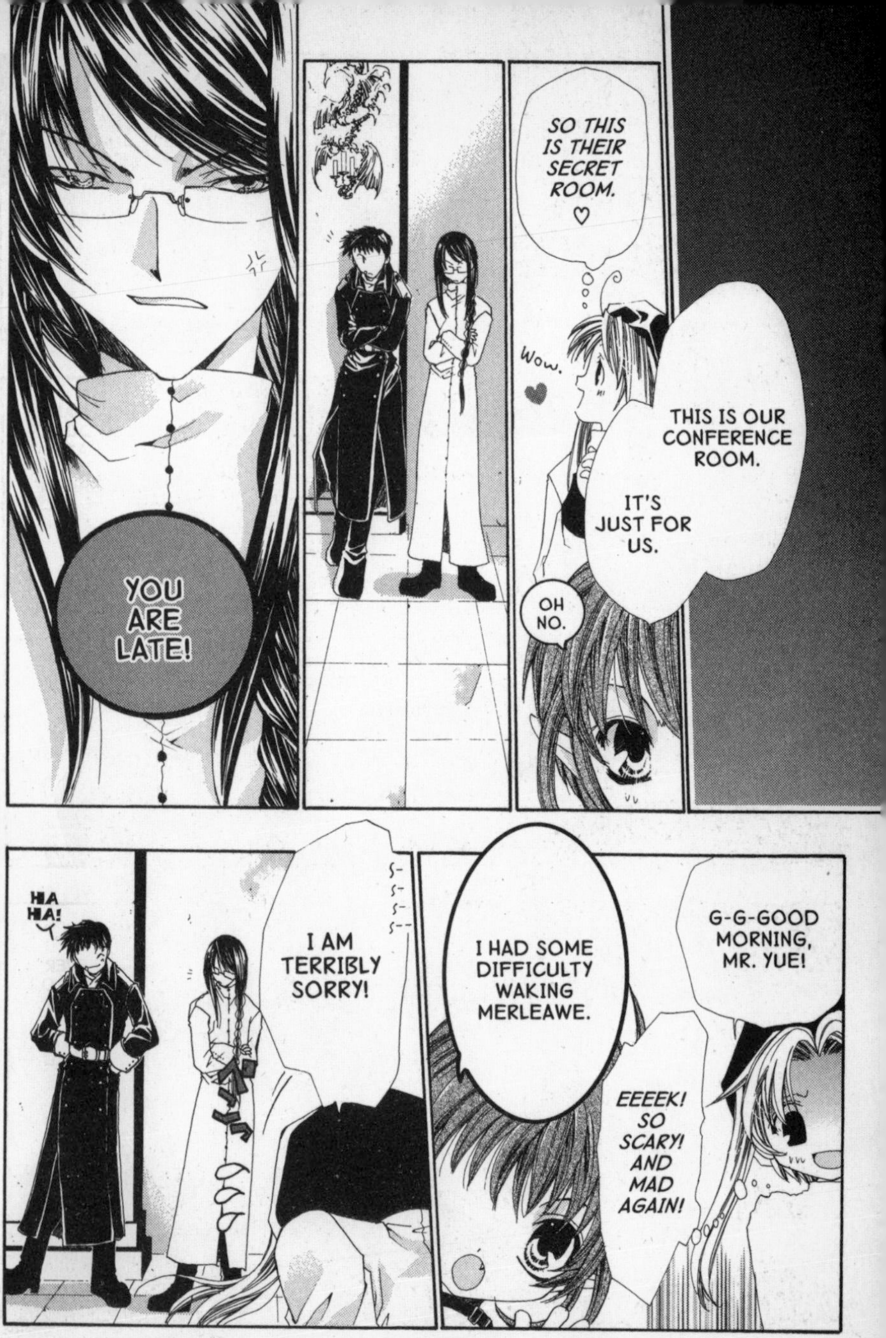
SO THIS IS THEIR SECRET ROOM. ♡
THIS IS OUR CONFERENCE ROOM.
IT'S JUST FOR US.
Wow.
OH NO.
YOU ARE LATE!
G-G-GOOD MORNING, MR. YUE!
EEEEK! SO SCARY! AND MAD AGAIN!
I HAD SOME DIFFICULTY WAKING MERLEAWE.
I AM TERRIBLY SORRY!
HA HA!

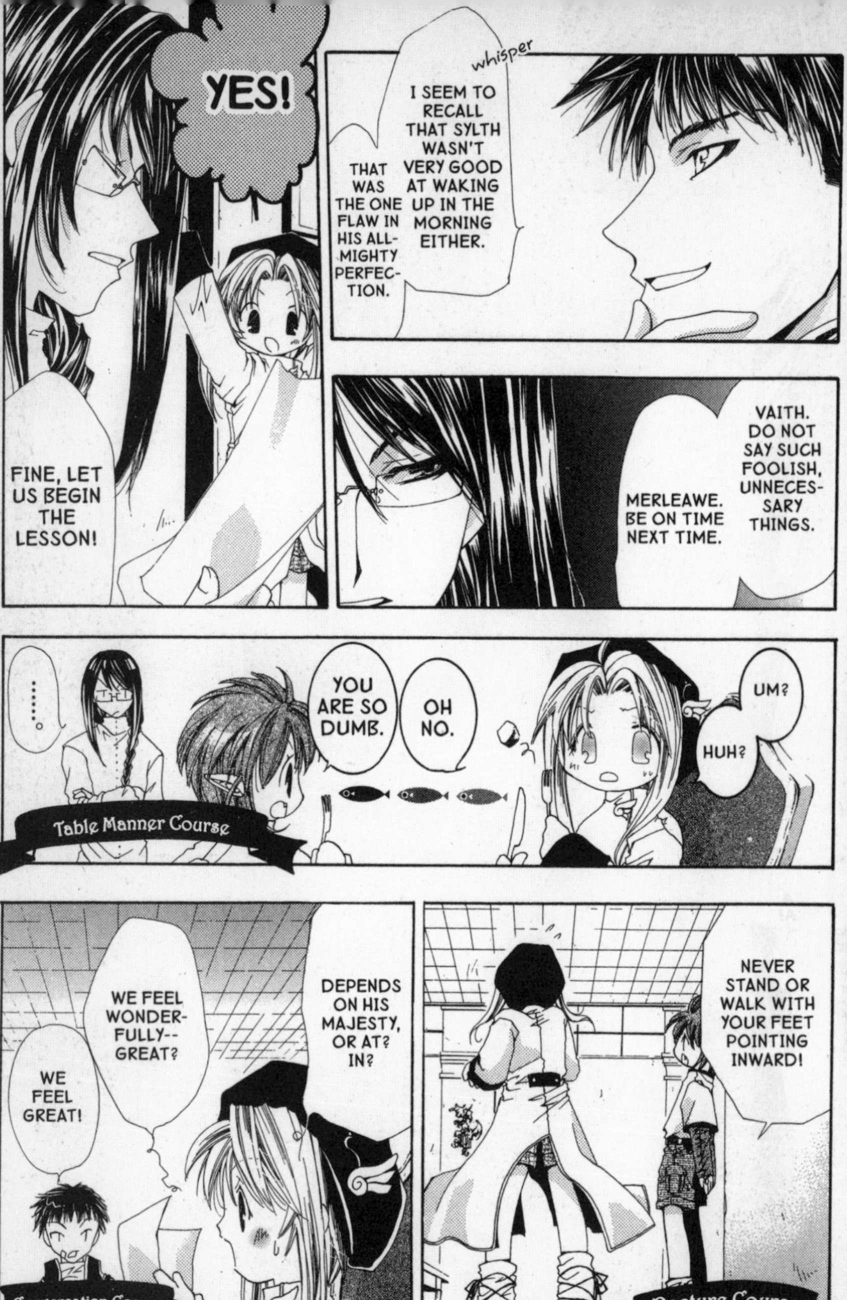

whisper
I SEEM TO RECALL THAT SYLTH WASN'T VERY GOOD AT WAKING UP IN THE MORNING EITHER.
THAT WAS THE ONE FLAW IN HIS ALL-MIGHTY PERFECTION.
VAITH. DO NOT SAY SUCH FOOLISH, UNNECESSARY THINGS.
MERLEAWE. BE ON TIME NEXT TIME.
YES!
FINE, LET US BEGIN THE LESSON!
UM?
HUH?
OH NO.
YOU ARE SO DUMB.
......
Table Manner Course
NEVER STAND OR WALK WITH YOUR FEET POINTING INWARD!
Posture Course
DEPENDS ON HIS MAJESTY, OR AT? IN?
WE FEEL WONDERFULLY--GREAT?
WE FEEL GREAT!
Conversation Course

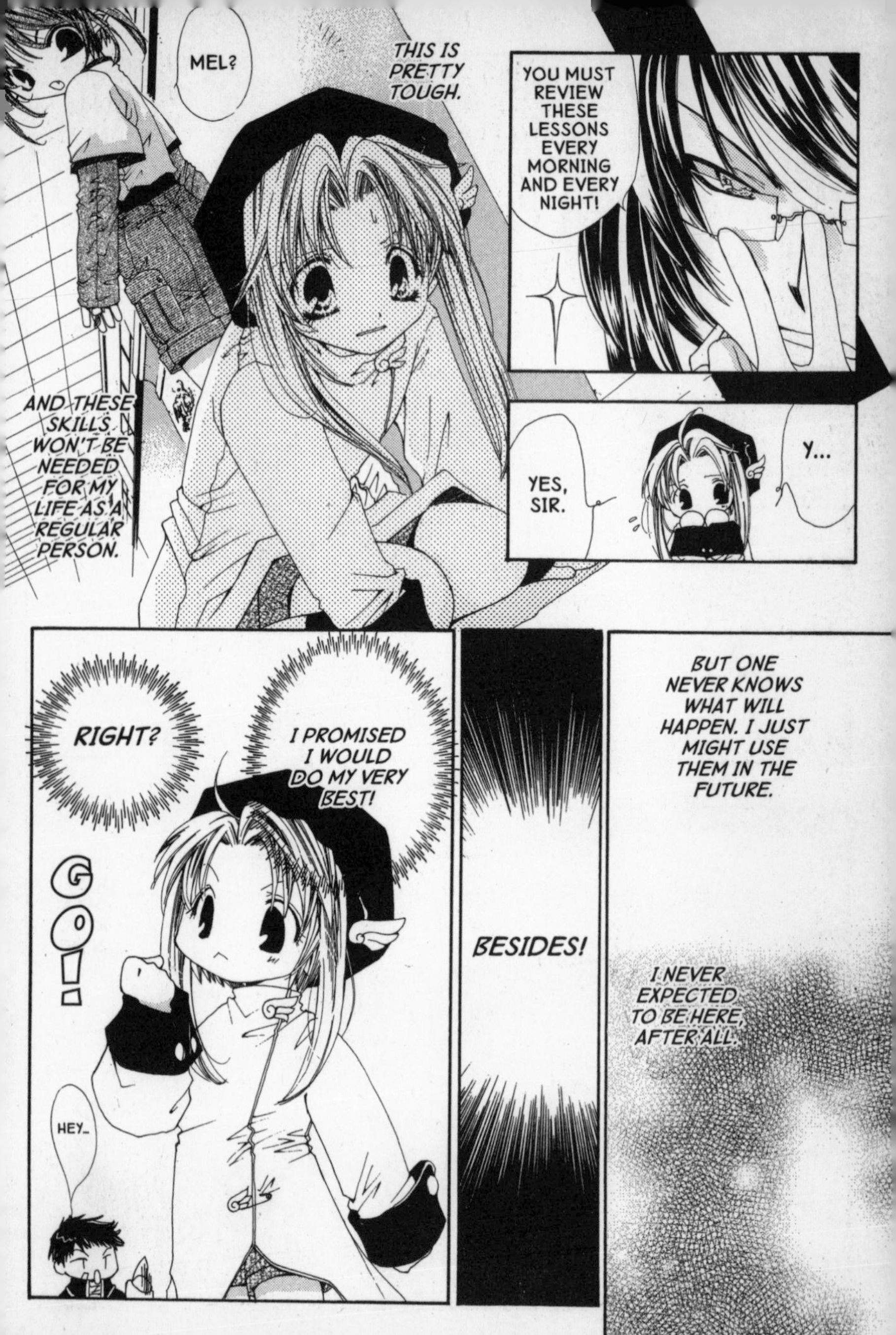
YOU MUST REVIEW THESE LESSONS EVERY MORNING AND EVERY NIGHT!
Y...
YES, SIR.
THIS IS PRETTY TOUGH.
MEL?
AND THESE SKILLS WON'T BE NEEDED FOR MY LIFE AS A REGULAR PERSON.
BUT ONE NEVER KNOWS WHAT WILL HAPPEN. I JUST MIGHT USE THEM IN THE FUTURE.
I NEVER EXPECTED TO BE HERE, AFTER ALL.
BESIDES!
I PROMISED I WOULD DO MY VERY BEST!
RIGHT?
GO!
HEY...

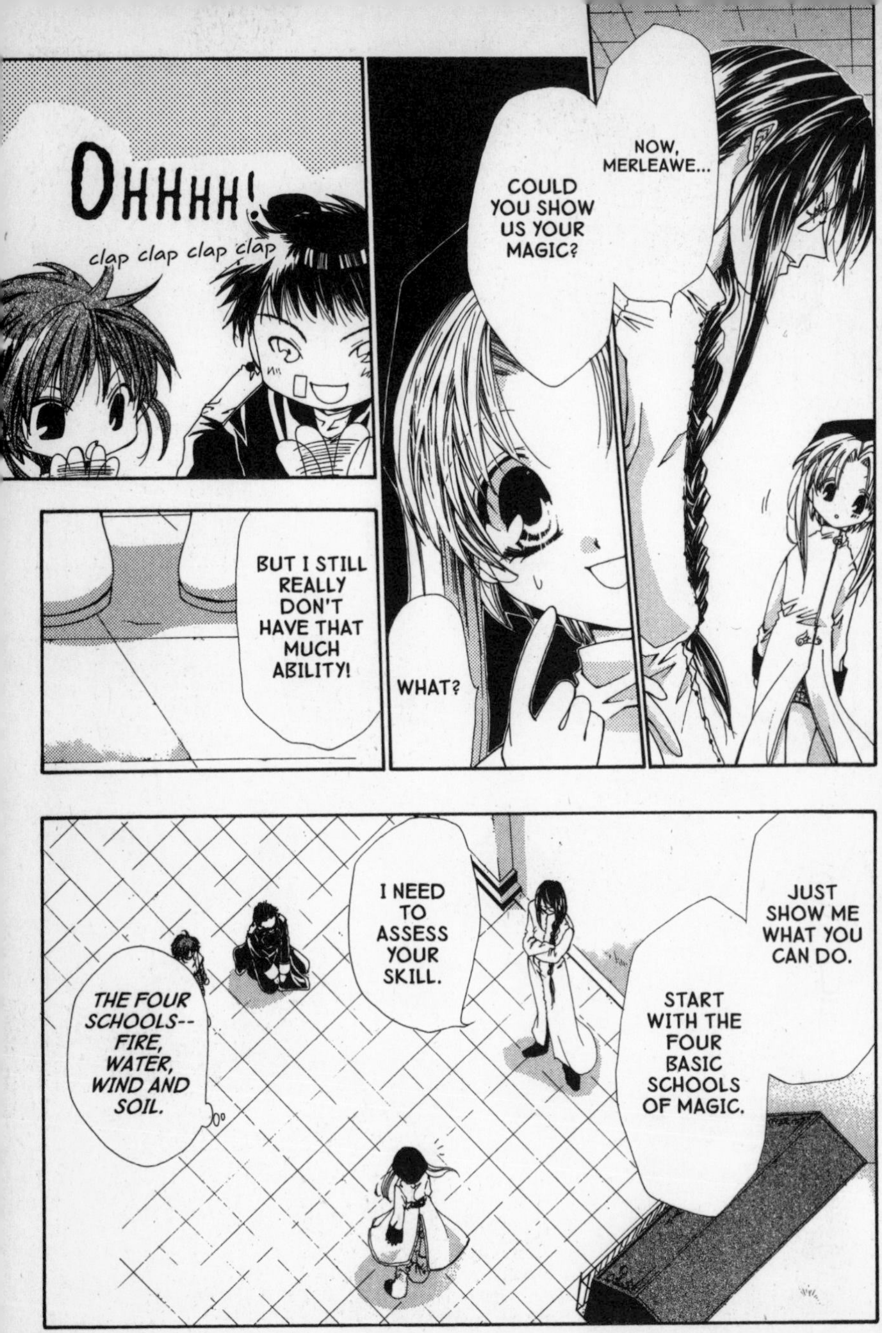
NOW, MERLEAWE... COULD YOU SHOW US YOUR MAGIC?
WHAT?
OHHHH!
clap clap clap clap
BUT I STILL REALLY DON'T HAVE THAT MUCH ABILITY!
JUST SHOW ME WHAT YOU CAN DO.
START WITH THE FOUR BASIC SCHOOLS OF MAGIC.
I NEED TO ASSESS YOUR SKILL.
THE FOUR SCHOOLS--FIRE, WATER, WIND AND SOIL.

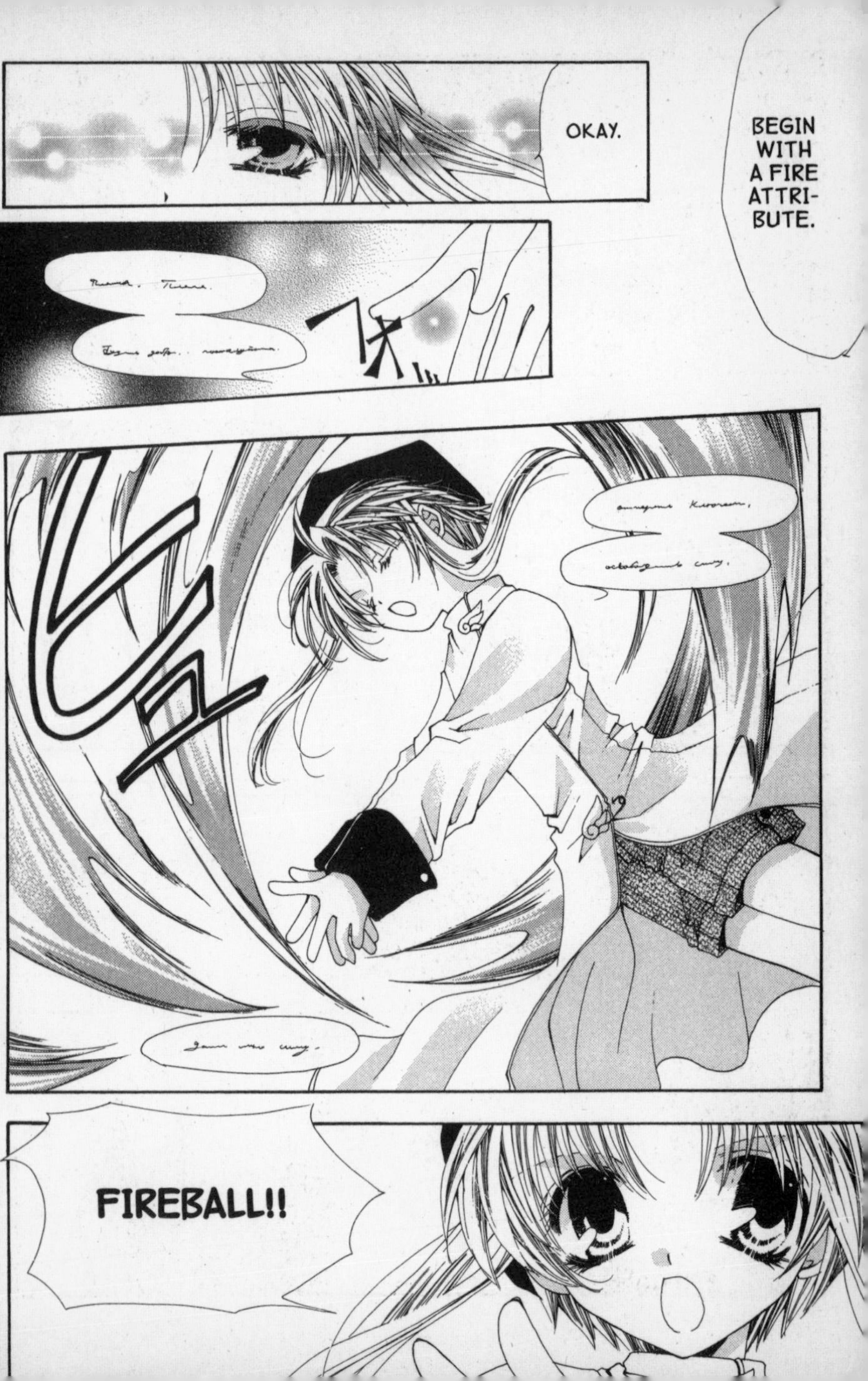
BEGIN WITH A FIRE ATTRI-BUTE.
OKAY.
FIREBALL!!

URGH.

......。

OH...

NO.

!!

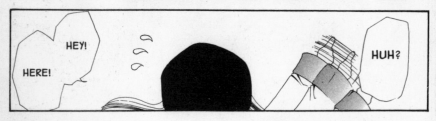

HEY!

HERE!

HUH?

YES!

WIND.

NEXT.

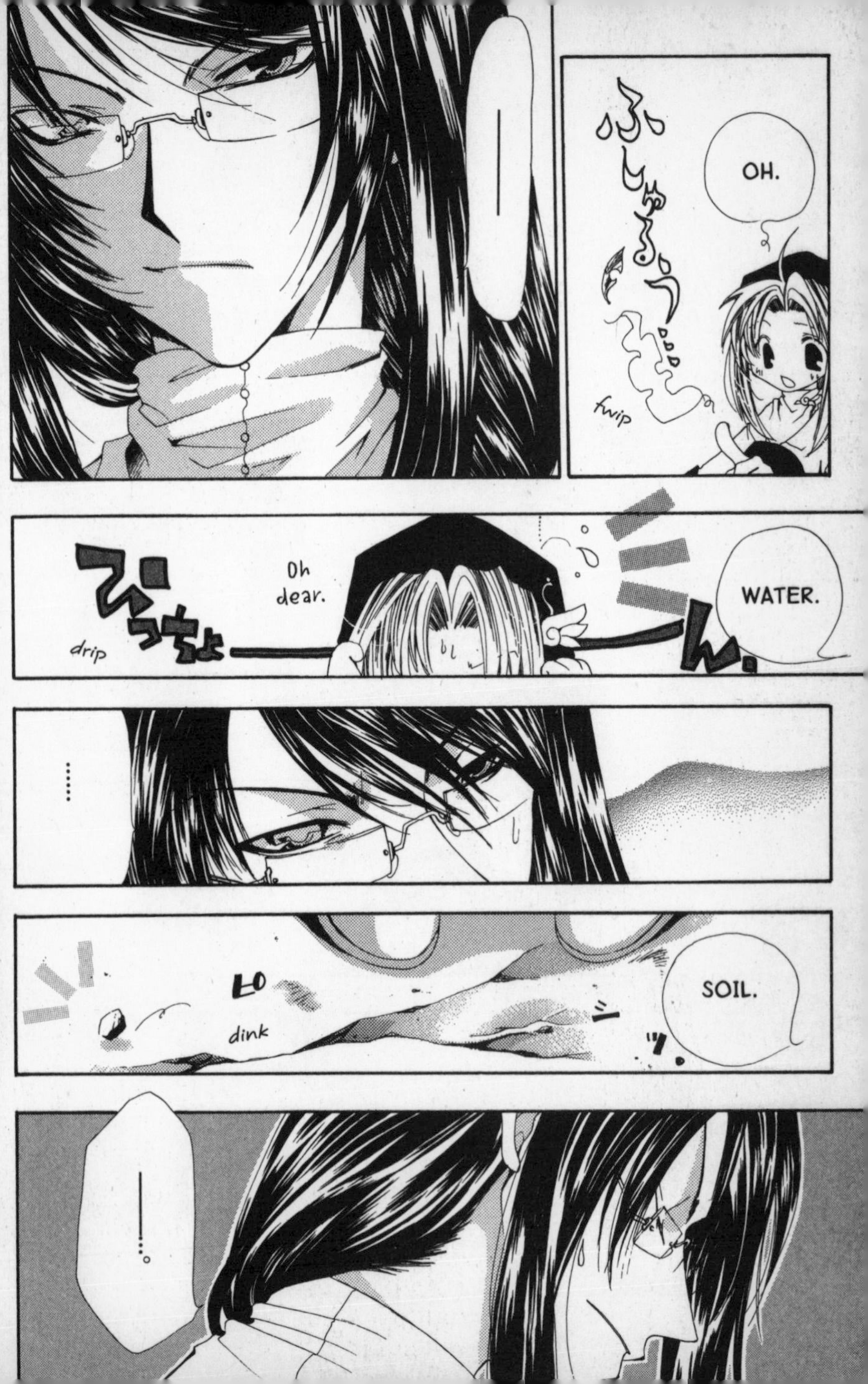
OH.
fwip
—
WATER.
Oh dear.
drip
……
SOIL.
dink
—…

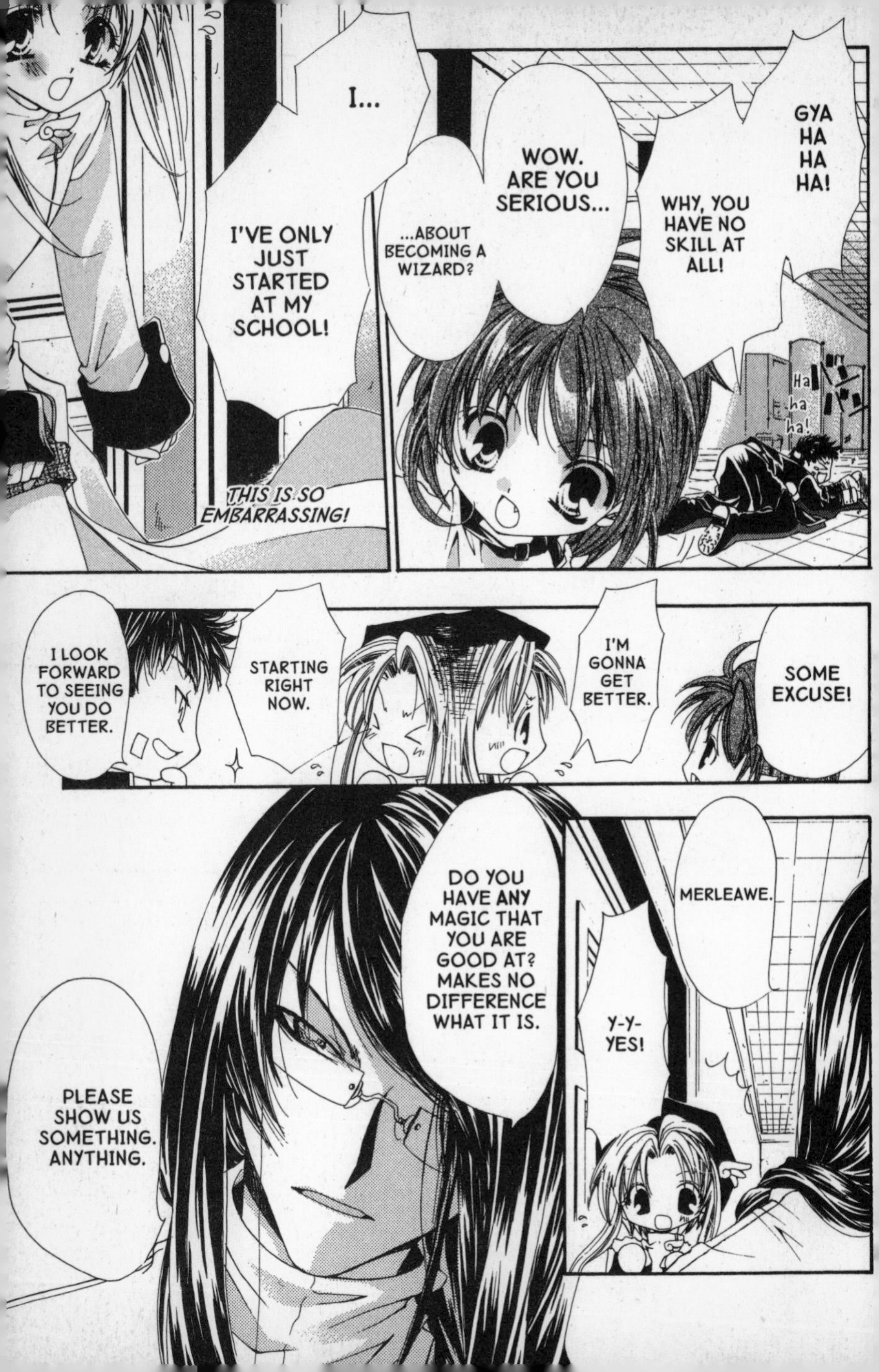
GYA HA HA HA!
WHY, YOU HAVE NO SKILL AT ALL!
WOW. ARE YOU SERIOUS...
...ABOUT BECOMING A WIZARD?
Ha ha ha!
I...
I'VE ONLY JUST STARTED AT MY SCHOOL!
THIS IS SO EMBARRASSING!
SOME EXCUSE!
I'M GONNA GET BETTER.
STARTING RIGHT NOW.
I LOOK FORWARD TO SEEING YOU DO BETTER.
MERLEAWE.
Y-Y-YES!
DO YOU HAVE ANY MAGIC THAT YOU ARE GOOD AT? MAKES NO DIFFERENCE WHAT IT IS.
PLEASE SHOW US SOMETHING. ANYTHING.

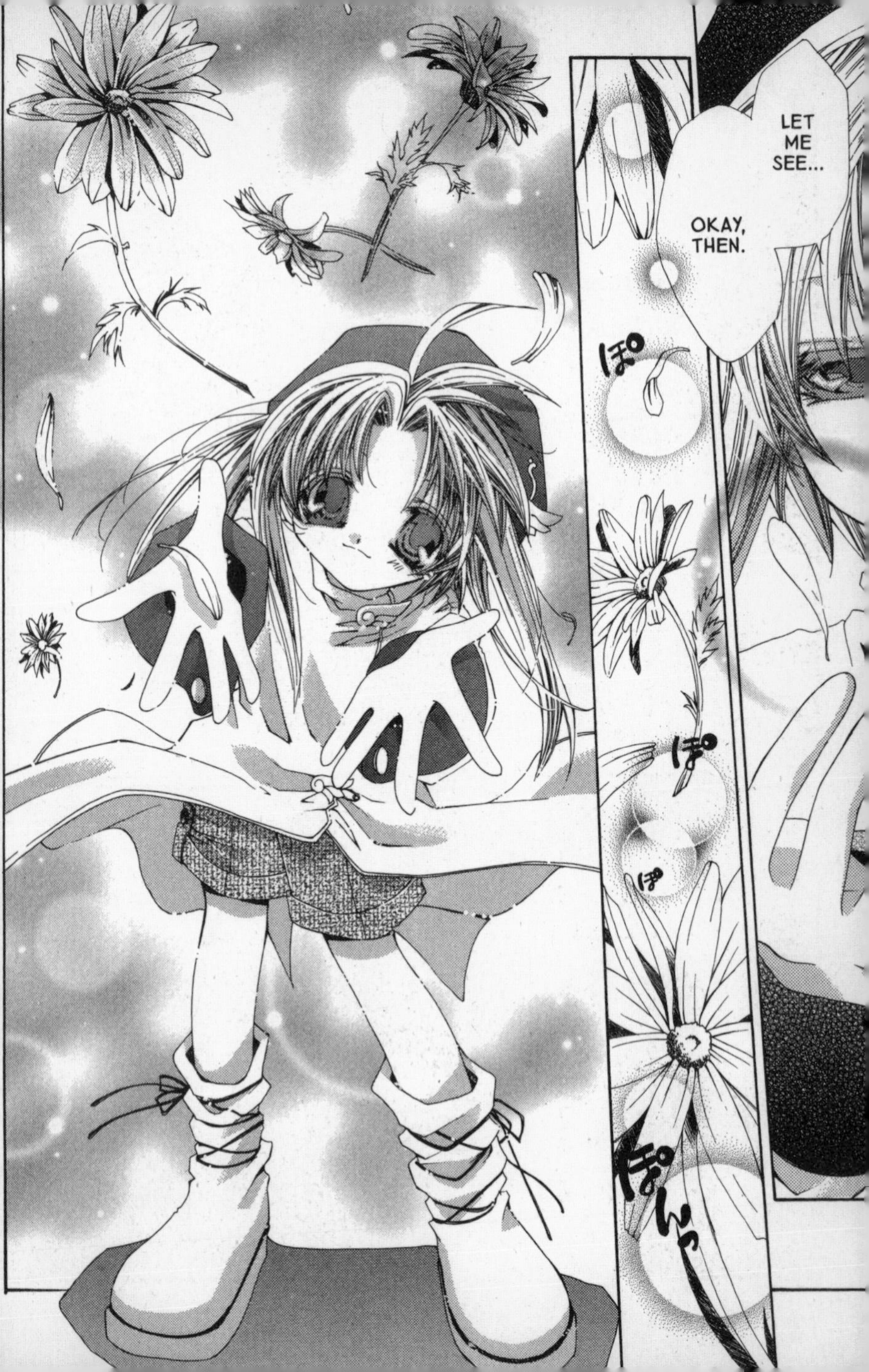
LET ME SEE...
OKAY, THEN.
ぽ
ぽ
ぽ
ぽんっ

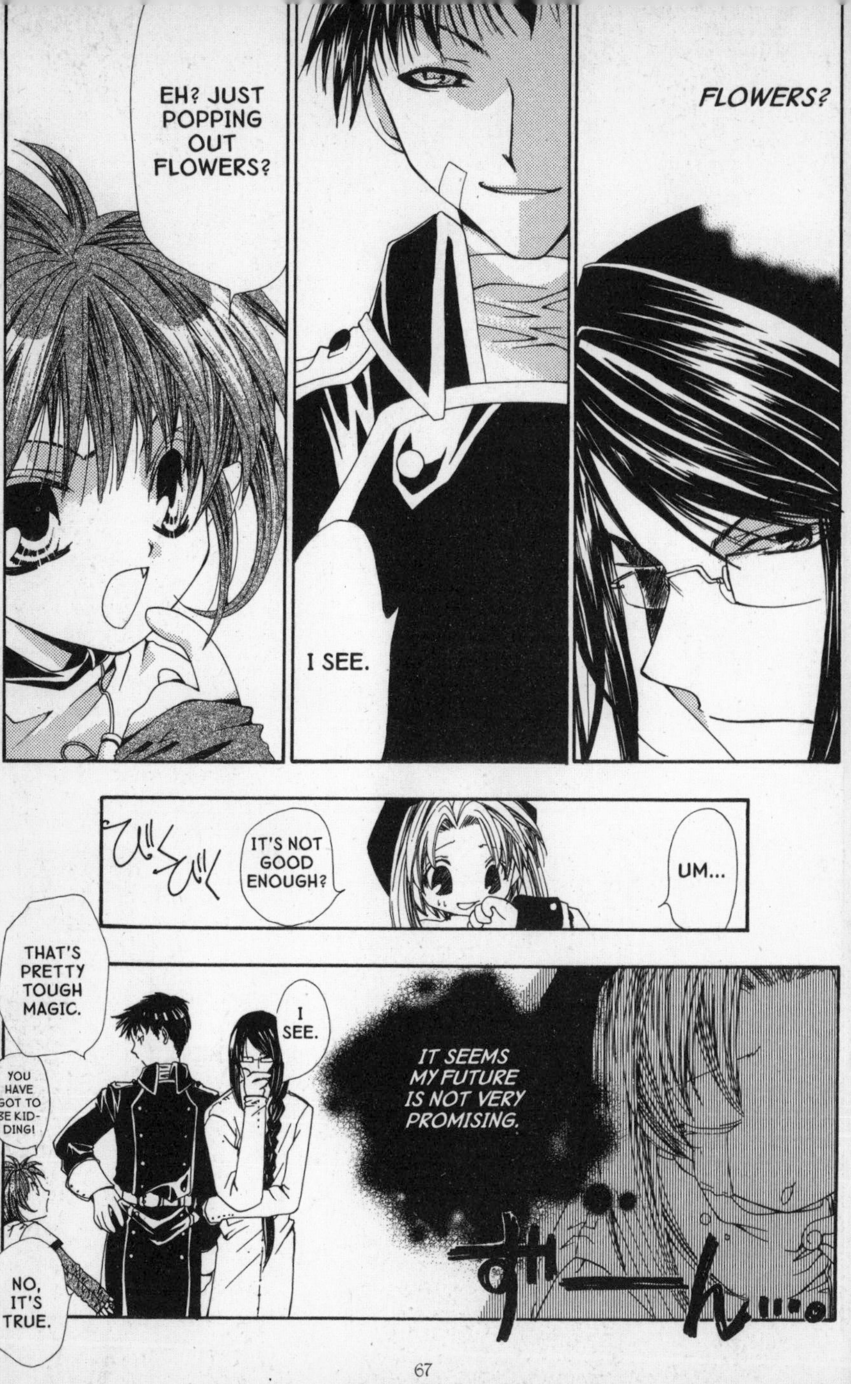
FLOWERS?
I SEE.
EH? JUST POPPING OUT FLOWERS?
UM...
IT'S NOT GOOD ENOUGH?
IT SEEMS MY FUTURE IS NOT VERY PROMISING.
I SEE.
THAT'S PRETTY TOUGH MAGIC.
YOU HAVE GOT TO BE KID-DING!
NO, IT'S TRUE.

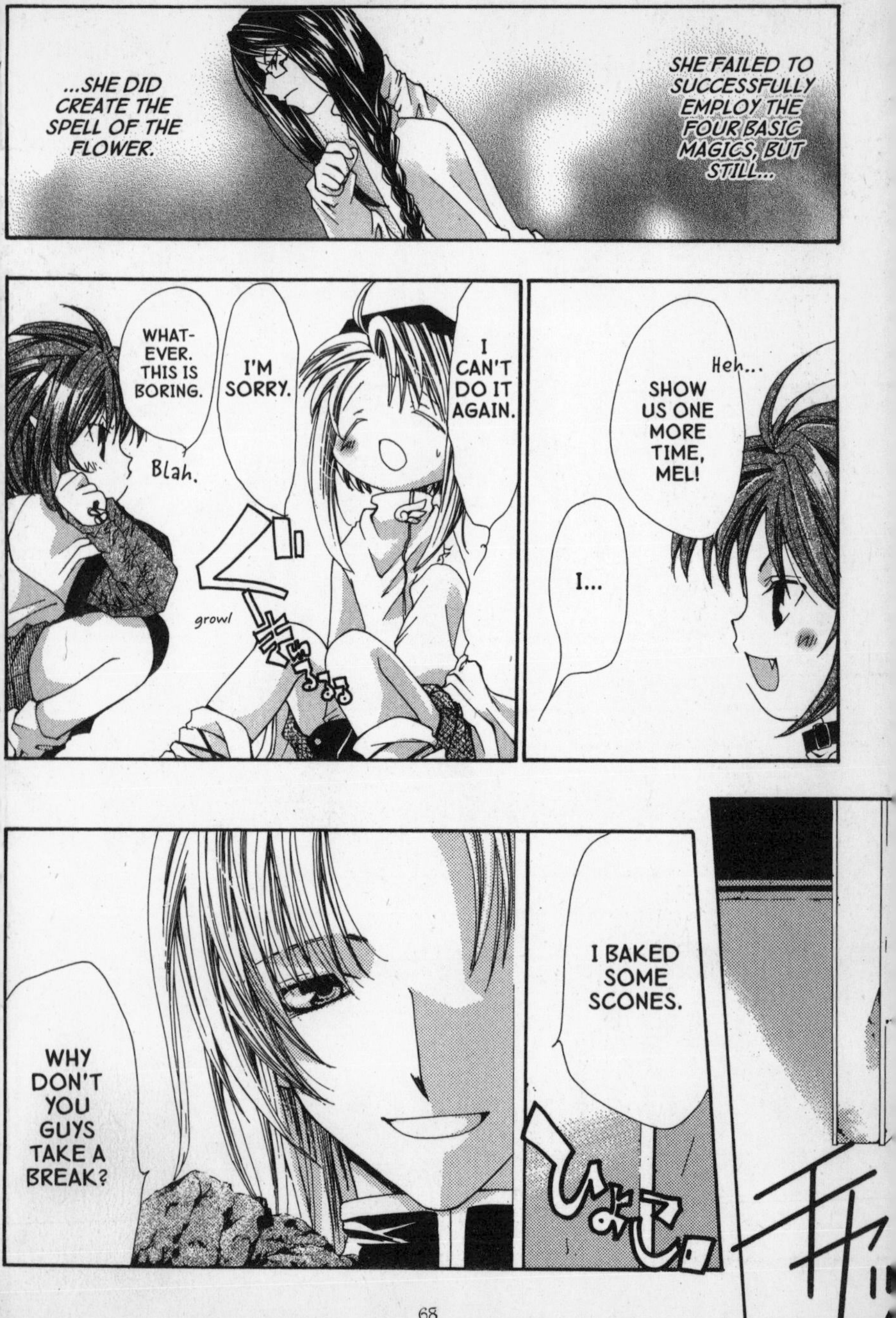
SHE FAILED TO SUCCESSFULLY EMPLOY THE FOUR BASIC MAGICS, BUT STILL...
...SHE DID CREATE THE SPELL OF THE FLOWER.
Heh...
SHOW US ONE MORE TIME, MEL!
I...
I CAN'T DO IT AGAIN.
I'M SORRY.
WHAT-EVER. THIS IS BORING.
Blah.
growl
I BAKED SOME SCONES.
WHY DON'T YOU GUYS TAKE A BREAK?

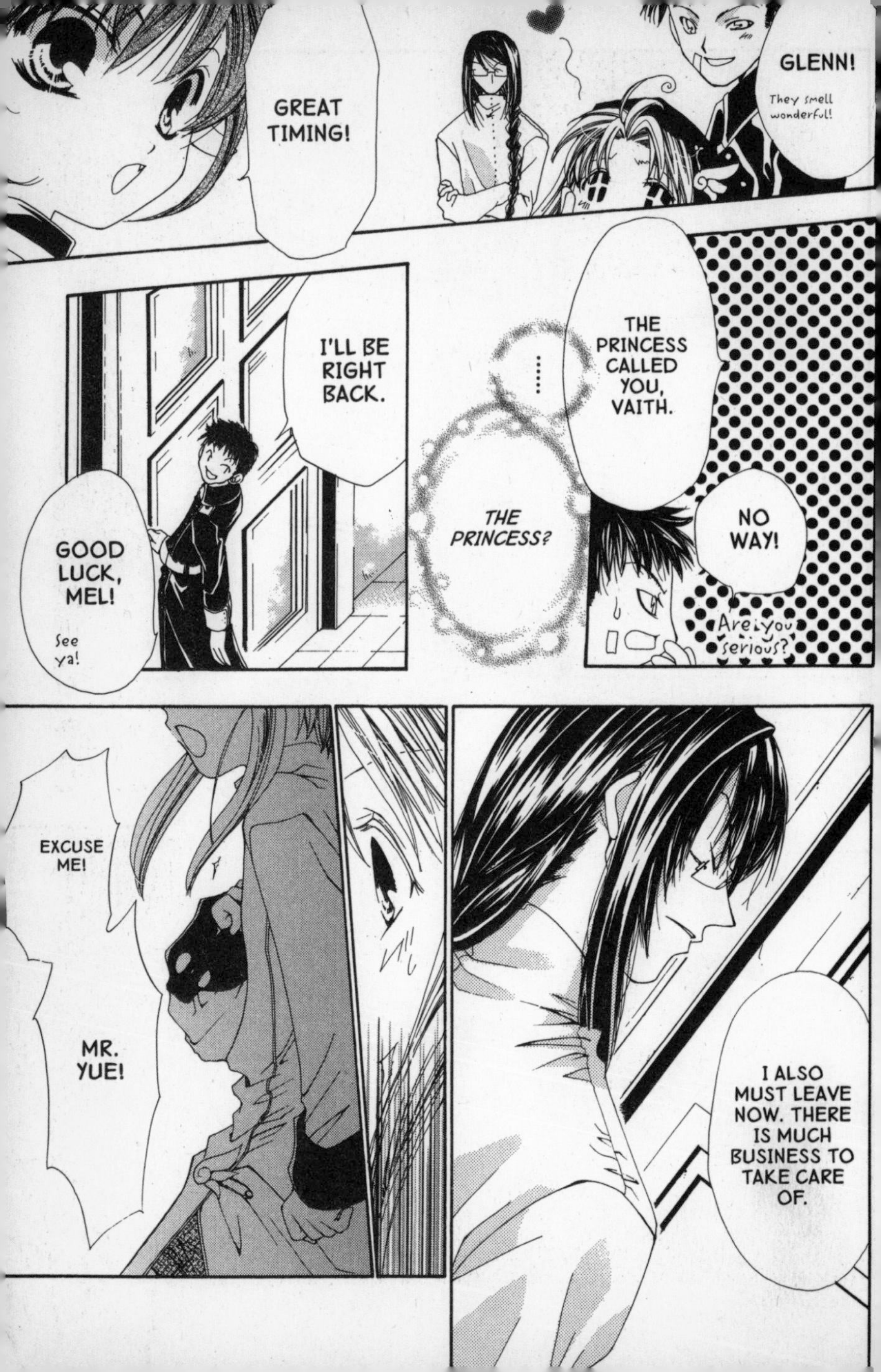
GLENN!
They smell wonderful!
GREAT TIMING!
THE PRINCESS CALLED YOU, VAITH.
......
THE PRINCESS?
NO WAY!
Are you serious?
I'LL BE RIGHT BACK.
GOOD LUCK, MEL!
See ya!
I ALSO MUST LEAVE NOW. THERE IS MUCH BUSINESS TO TAKE CARE OF.
EXCUSE ME!
MR. YUE!

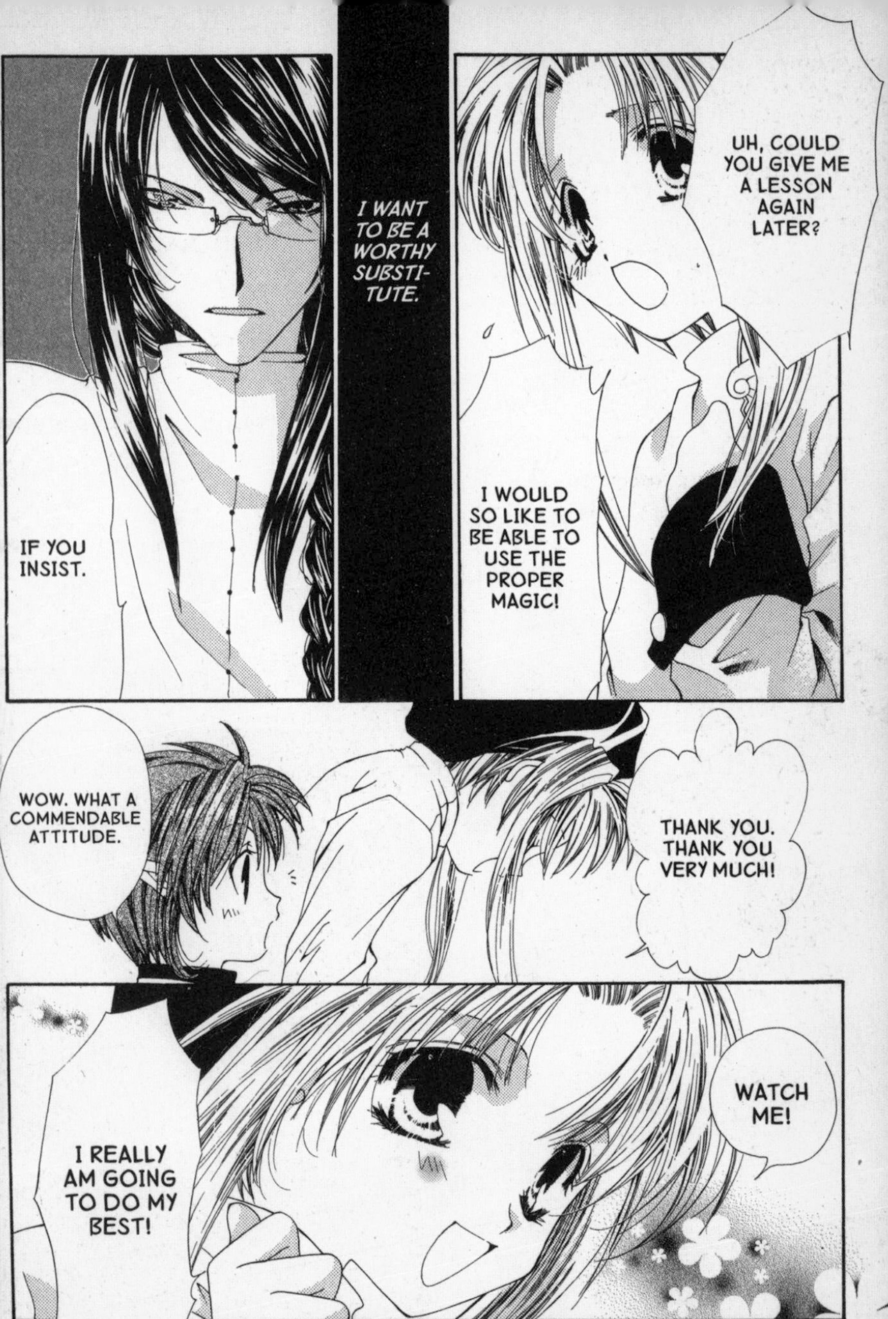
UH, COULD YOU GIVE ME A LESSON AGAIN LATER?
I WOULD SO LIKE TO BE ABLE TO USE THE PROPER MAGIC!
I WANT TO BE A WORTHY SUBSTITUTE.
IF YOU INSIST.
THANK YOU. THANK YOU VERY MUCH!
WOW. WHAT A COMMENDABLE ATTITUDE.
WATCH ME!
I REALLY AM GOING TO DO MY BEST!

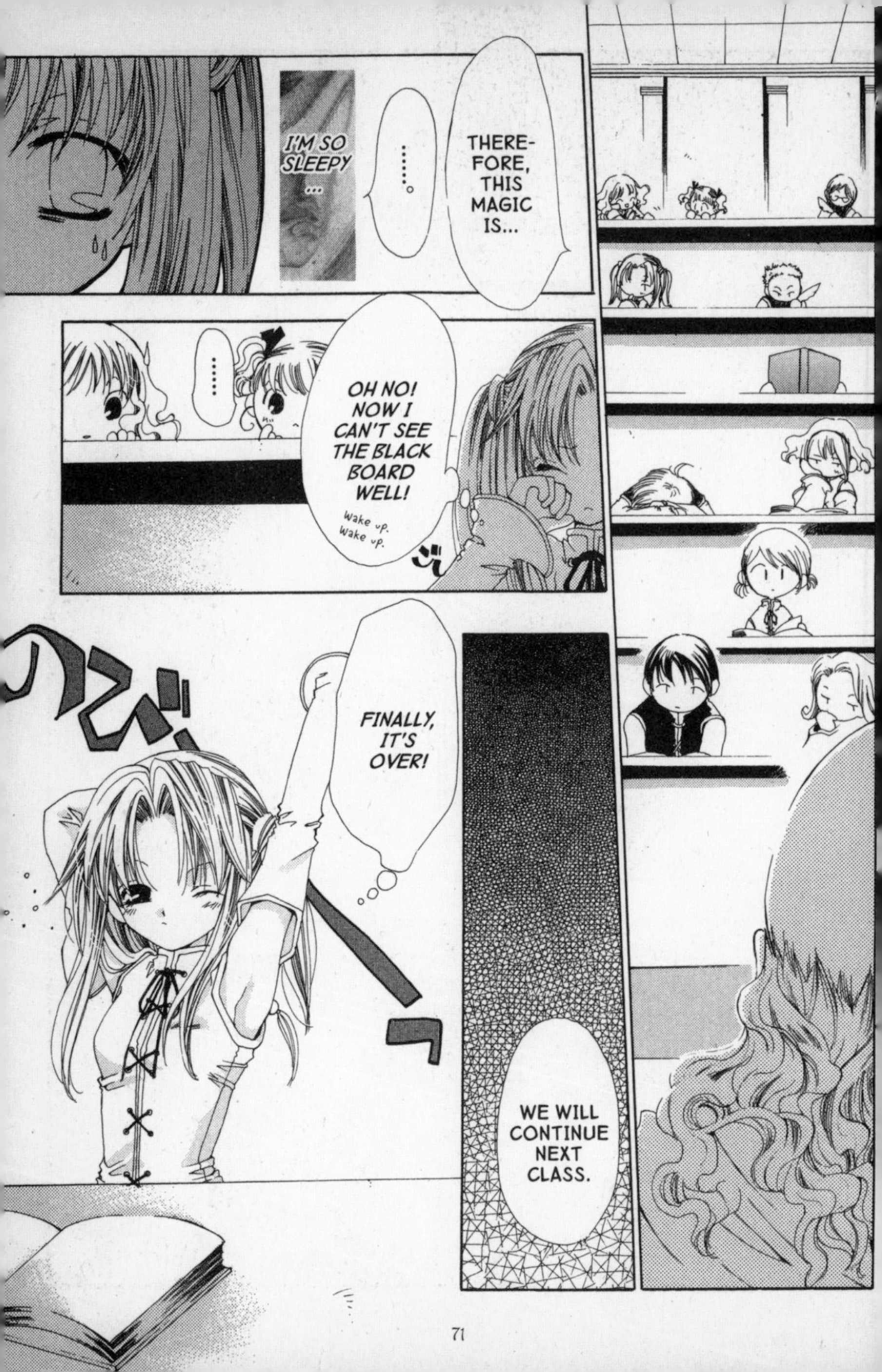
THEREFORE, THIS MAGIC IS...
......
I'M SO SLEEPY...
OH NO! NOW I CAN'T SEE THE BLACK BOARD WELL!
Wake up. Wake up.
......
WE WILL CONTINUE NEXT CLASS.
FINALLY, IT'S OVER!
のび

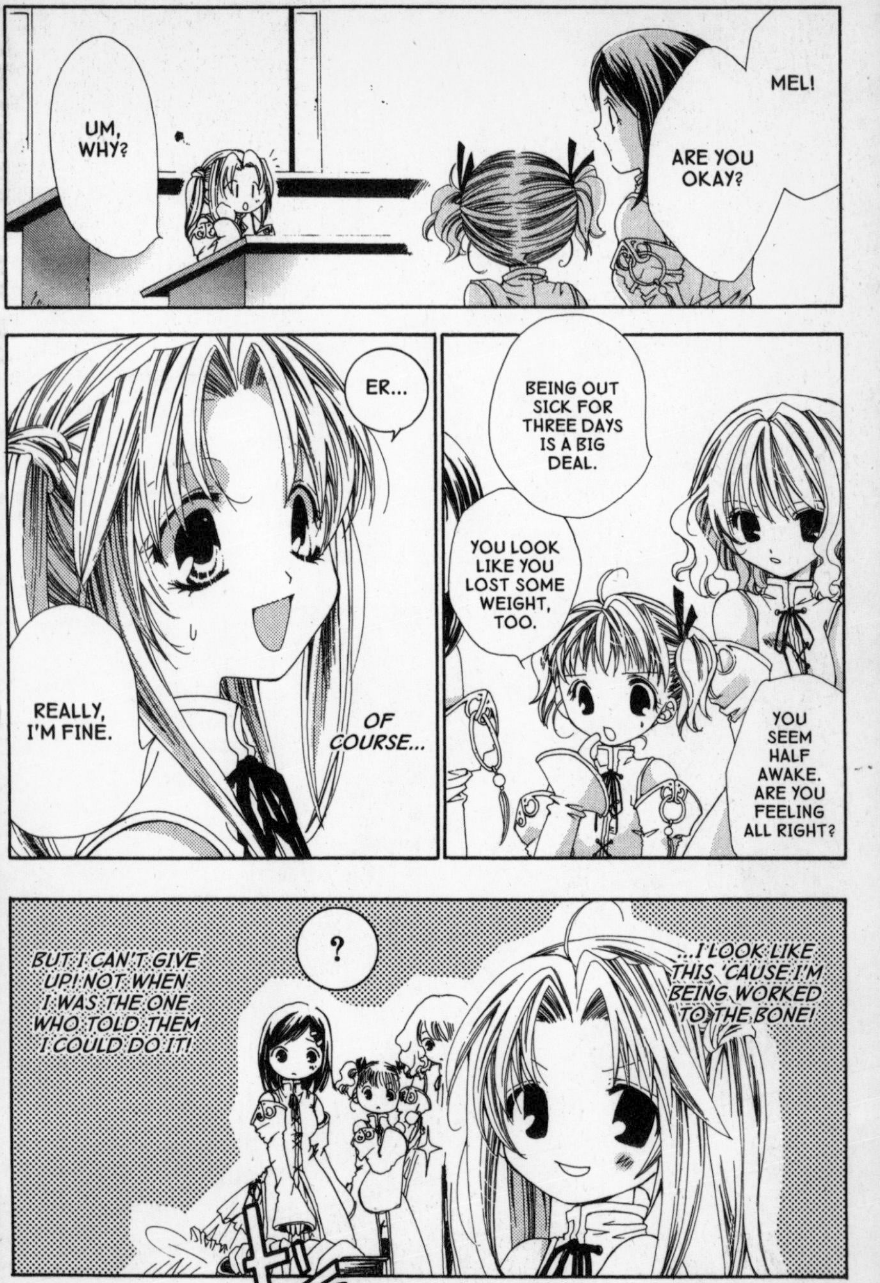
MEL!
ARE YOU OKAY?
UM, WHY?
BEING OUT SICK FOR THREE DAYS IS A BIG DEAL.
YOU LOOK LIKE YOU LOST SOME WEIGHT, TOO.
YOU SEEM HALF AWAKE. ARE YOU FEELING ALL RIGHT?
ER...
REALLY, I'M FINE.
OF COURSE...
...I LOOK LIKE THIS 'CAUSE I'M BEING WORKED TO THE BONE!
?
BUT I CAN'T GIVE UP! NOT WHEN I WAS THE ONE WHO TOLD THEM I COULD DO IT!

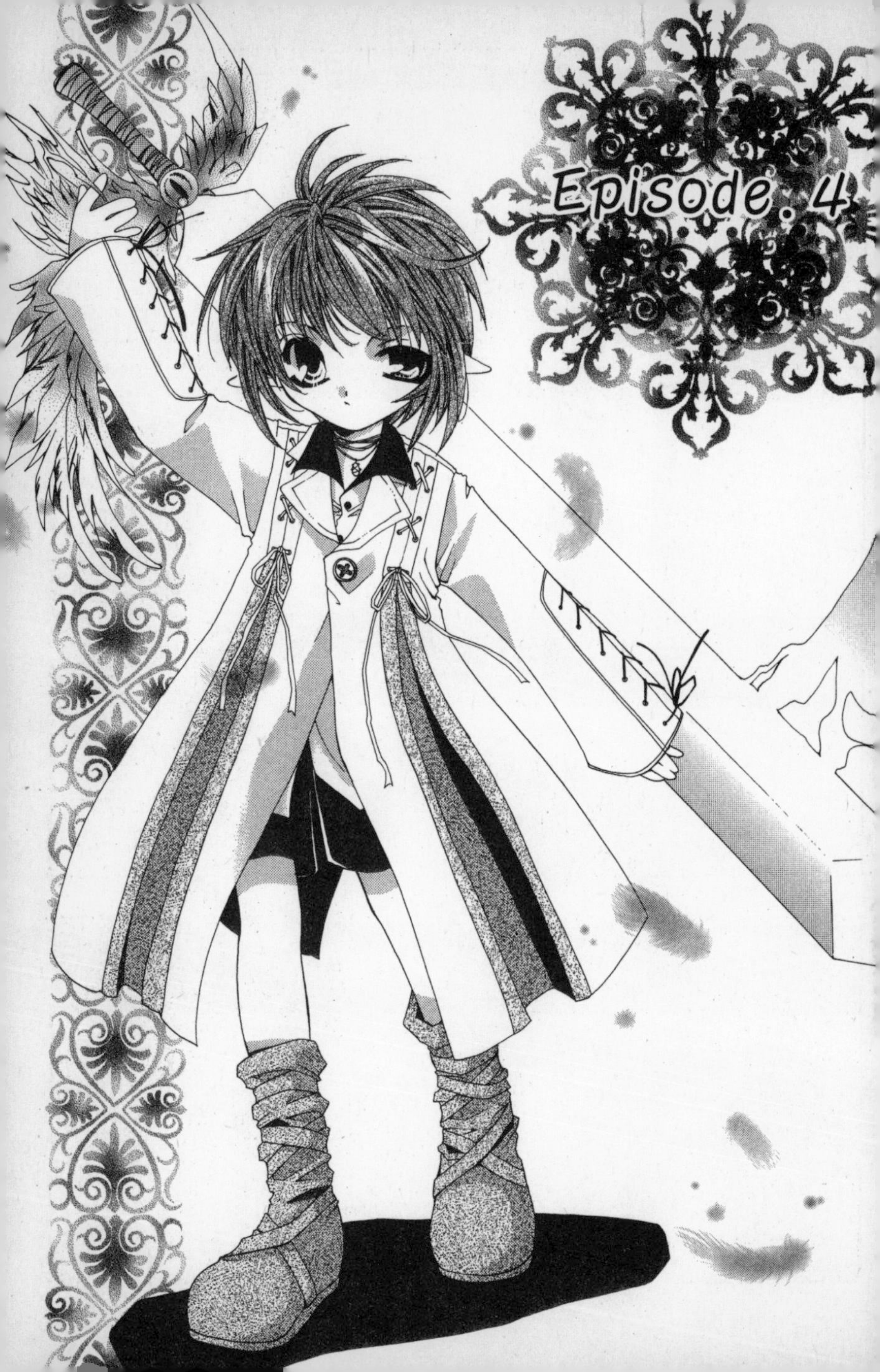
Episode. 4

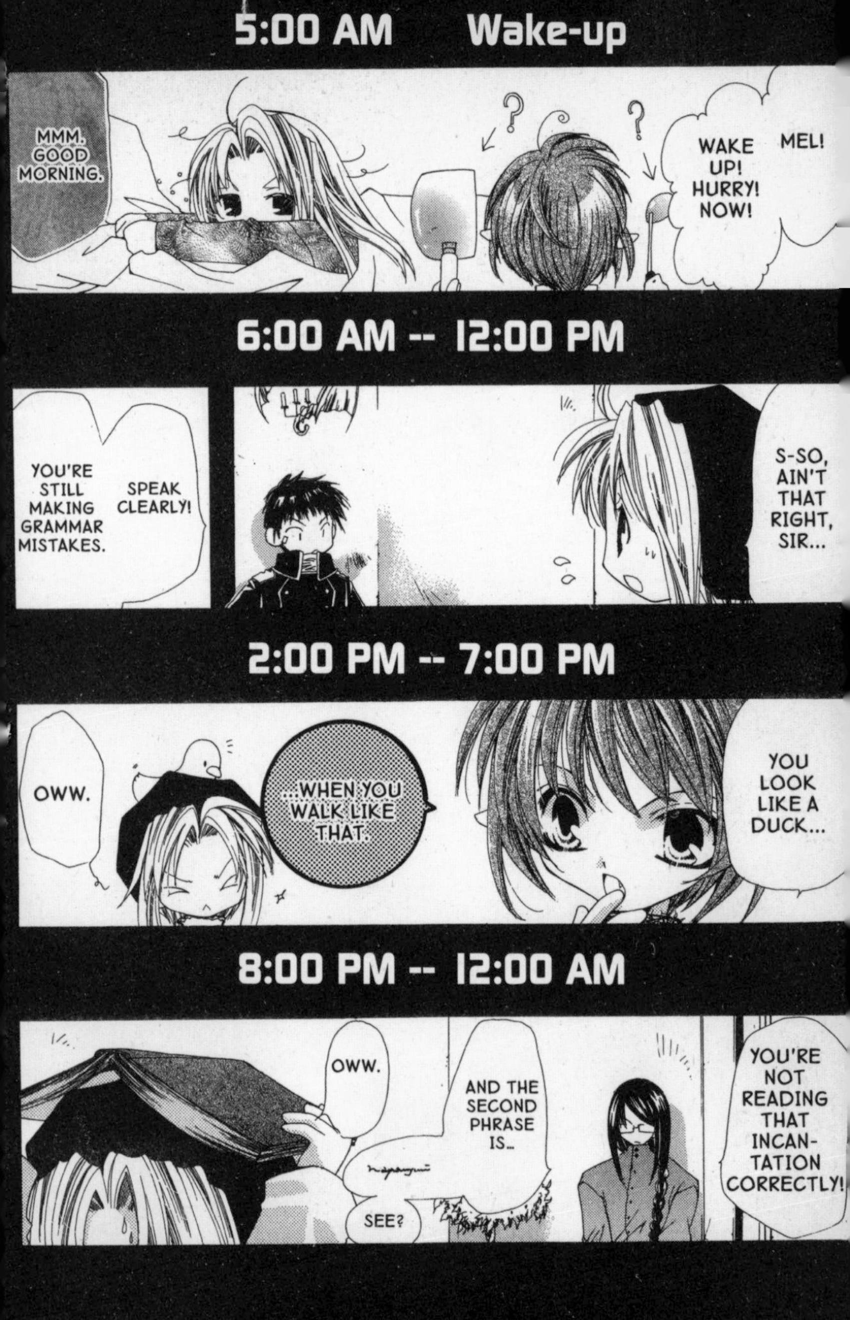
5:00 AM Wake-up
MEL!
WAKE UP! HURRY! NOW!
MMM. GOOD MORNING.
6:00 AM -- 12:00 PM
S-SO, AIN'T THAT RIGHT, SIR...
SPEAK CLEARLY!
YOU'RE STILL MAKING GRAMMAR MISTAKES.
2:00 PM -- 7:00 PM
YOU LOOK LIKE A DUCK...
...WHEN YOU WALK LIKE THAT.
OWW.
8:00 PM -- 12:00 AM
YOU'RE NOT READING THAT INCANTATION CORRECTLY!
AND THE SECOND PHRASE IS...
OWW.
SEE?

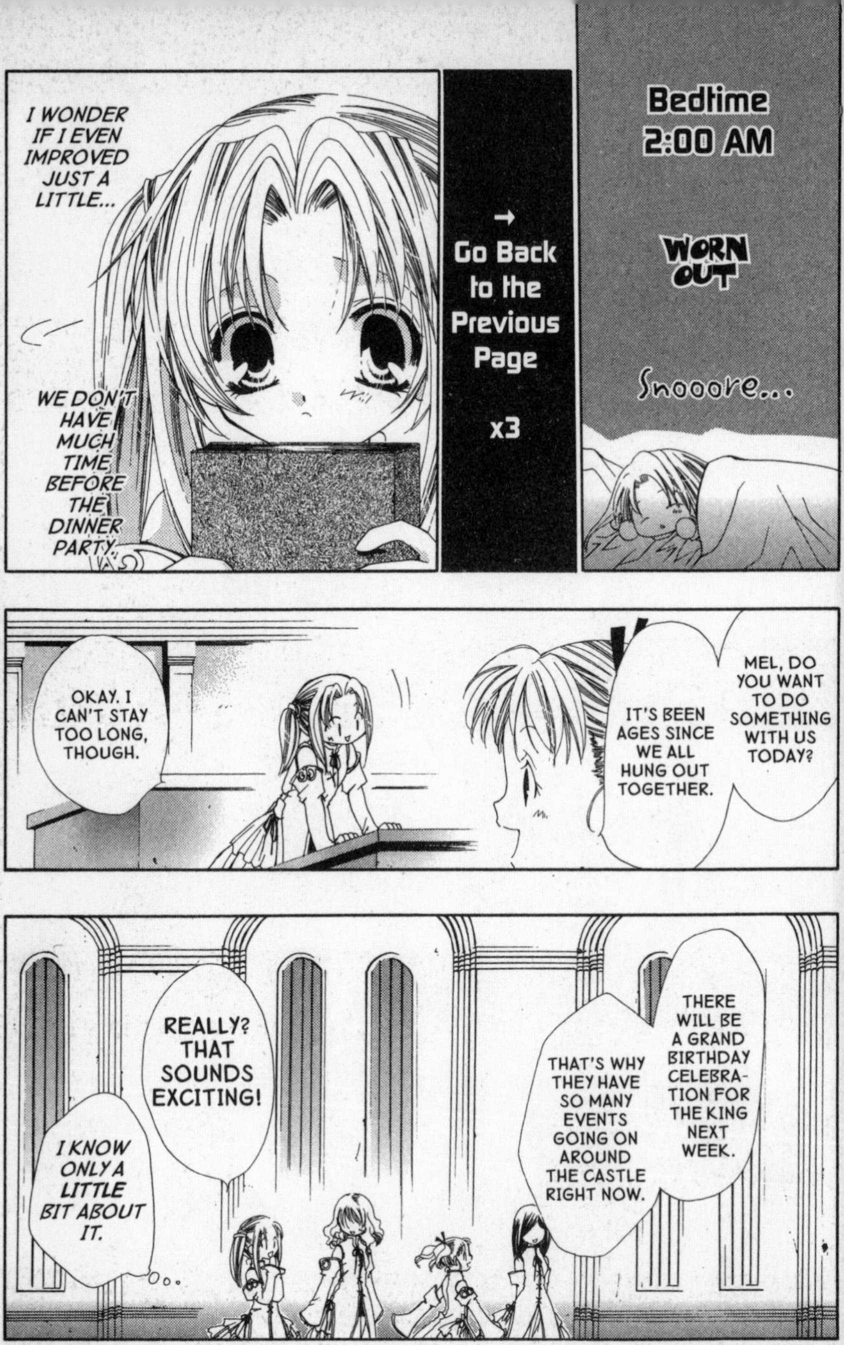
Bedtime 2:00 AM
WORN OUT
Snooore...
→ Go Back to the Previous Page x3
I WONDER IF I EVEN IMPROVED JUST A LITTLE...
WE DON'T HAVE MUCH TIME BEFORE THE DINNER PARTY.
MEL, DO YOU WANT TO DO SOMETHING WITH US TODAY?
IT'S BEEN AGES SINCE WE ALL HUNG OUT TOGETHER.
OKAY. I CAN'T STAY TOO LONG, THOUGH.
THERE WILL BE A GRAND BIRTHDAY CELEBRATION FOR THE KING NEXT WEEK.
THAT'S WHY THEY HAVE SO MANY EVENTS GOING ON AROUND THE CASTLE RIGHT NOW.
REALLY? THAT SOUNDS EXCITING!
I KNOW ONLY A LITTLE BIT ABOUT IT.

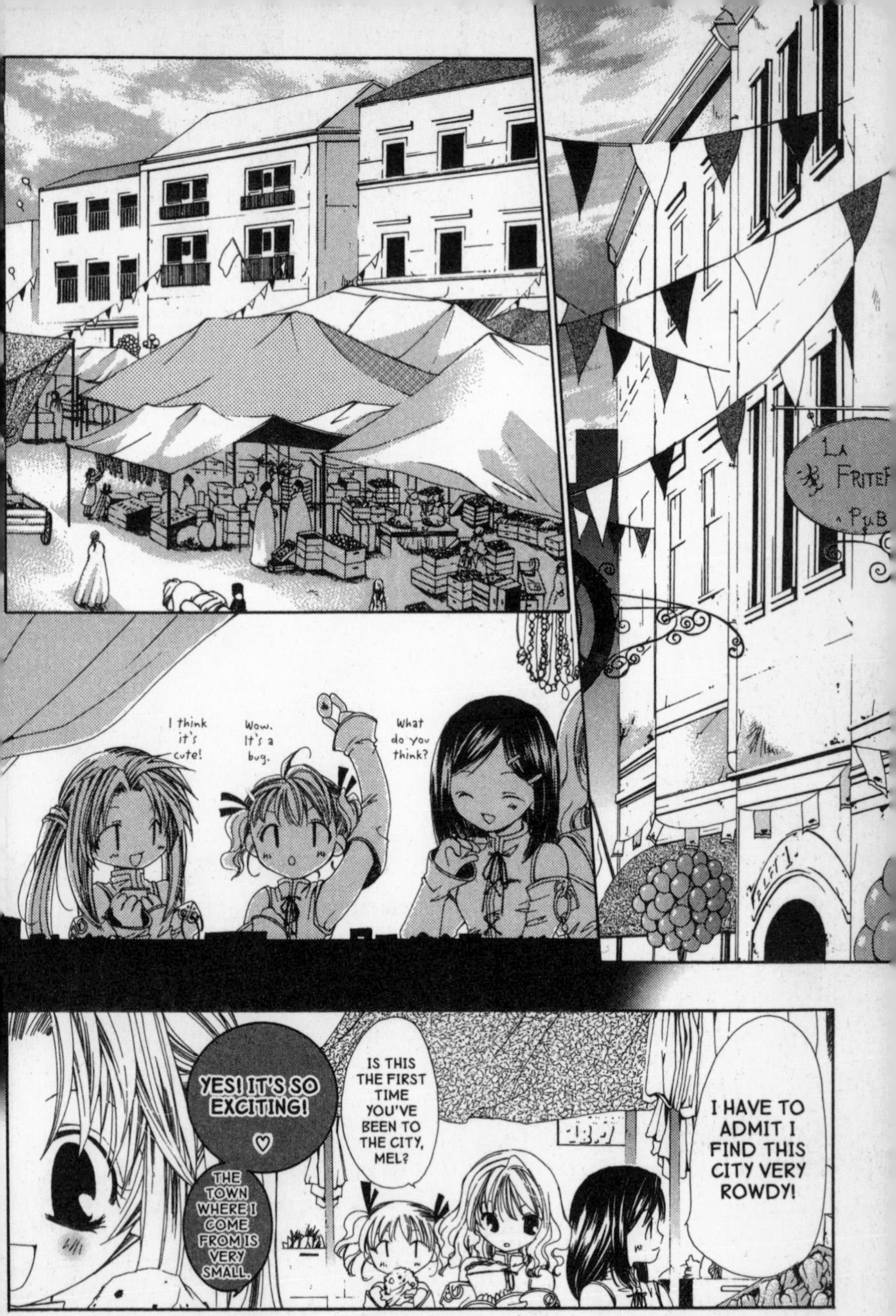
What do you think?
Wow. It's a bug.
I think it's cute!
I HAVE TO ADMIT I FIND THIS CITY VERY ROWDY!
IS THIS THE FIRST TIME YOU'VE BEEN TO THE CITY, MEL?
YES! IT'S SO EXCITING! ♡
THE TOWN WHERE I COME FROM IS VERY SMALL.

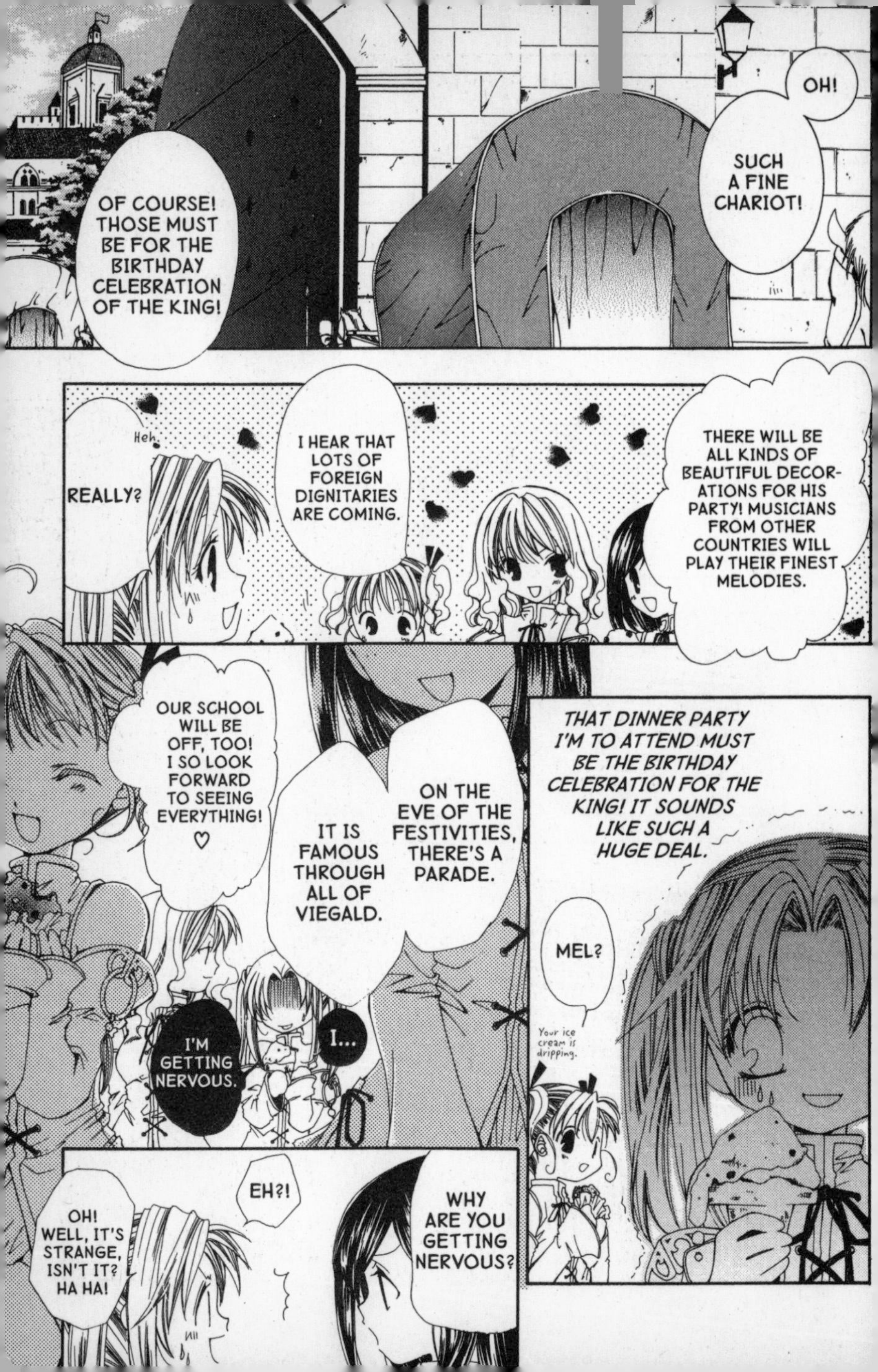

OH!
SUCH A FINE CHARIOT!
OF COURSE! THOSE MUST BE FOR THE BIRTHDAY CELEBRATION OF THE KING!
THERE WILL BE ALL KINDS OF BEAUTIFUL DECORATIONS FOR HIS PARTY! MUSICIANS FROM OTHER COUNTRIES WILL PLAY THEIR FINEST MELODIES.
I HEAR THAT LOTS OF FOREIGN DIGNITARIES ARE COMING.
Heh.
REALLY?
ON THE EVE OF THE FESTIVITIES, THERE'S A PARADE.
IT IS FAMOUS THROUGH ALL OF VIEGALD.
OUR SCHOOL WILL BE OFF, TOO! I SO LOOK FORWARD TO SEEING EVERYTHING! ♡
I...
I'M GETTING NERVOUS.
THAT DINNER PARTY I'M TO ATTEND MUST BE THE BIRTHDAY CELEBRATION FOR THE KING! IT SOUNDS LIKE SUCH A HUGE DEAL.
MEL?
Your ice cream is dripping.
WHY ARE YOU GETTING NERVOUS?
EH?!
OH! WELL, IT'S STRANGE, ISN'T IT? HA HA!

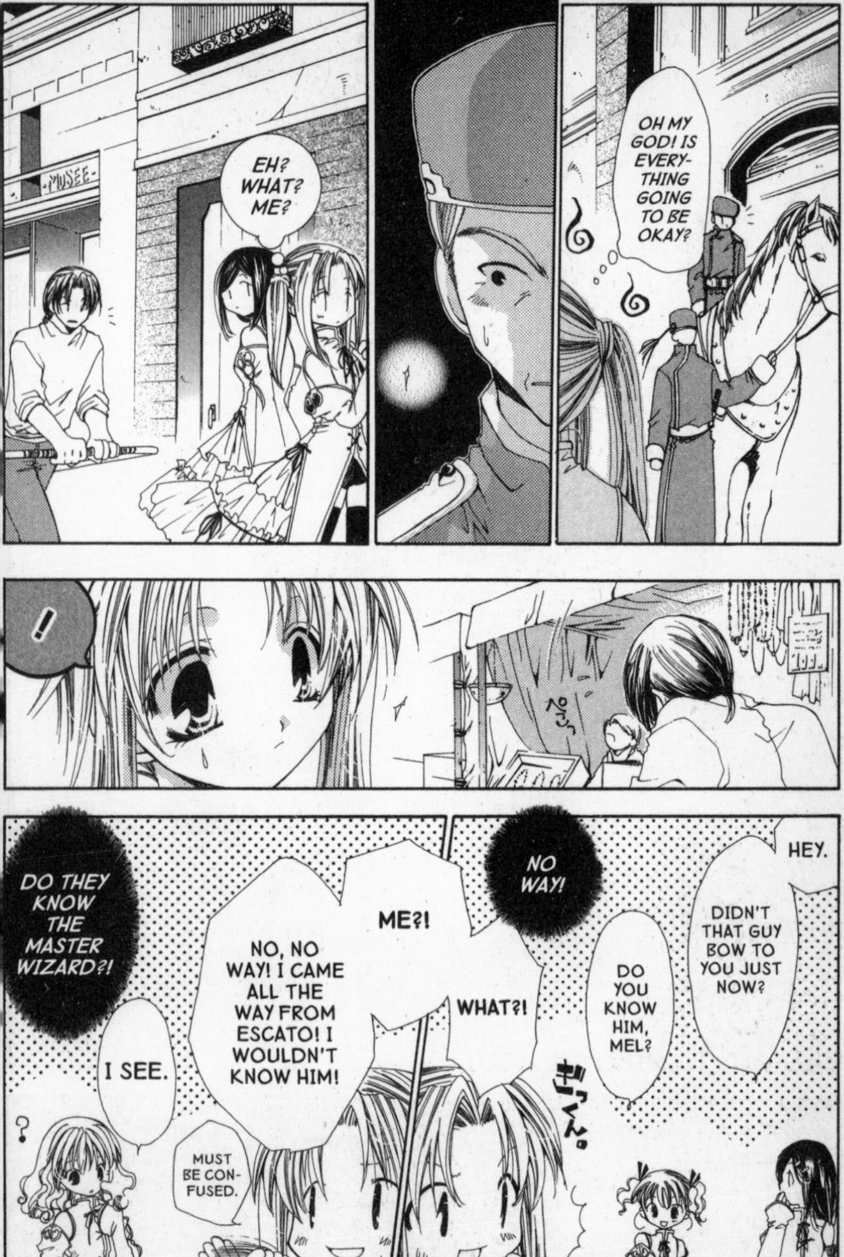
OH MY GOD! IS EVERYTHING GOING TO BE OKAY?
MUSEE
EH? WHAT? ME?
!
HEY.
DIDN'T THAT GUY BOW TO YOU JUST NOW?
DO YOU KNOW HIM, MEL?
NO WAY!
WHAT?!
ME?!
NO, NO WAY! I CAME ALL THE WAY FROM ESCATO! I WOULDN'T KNOW HIM!
DO THEY KNOW THE MASTER WIZARD?!
I SEE.
?
MUST BE CONFUSED.

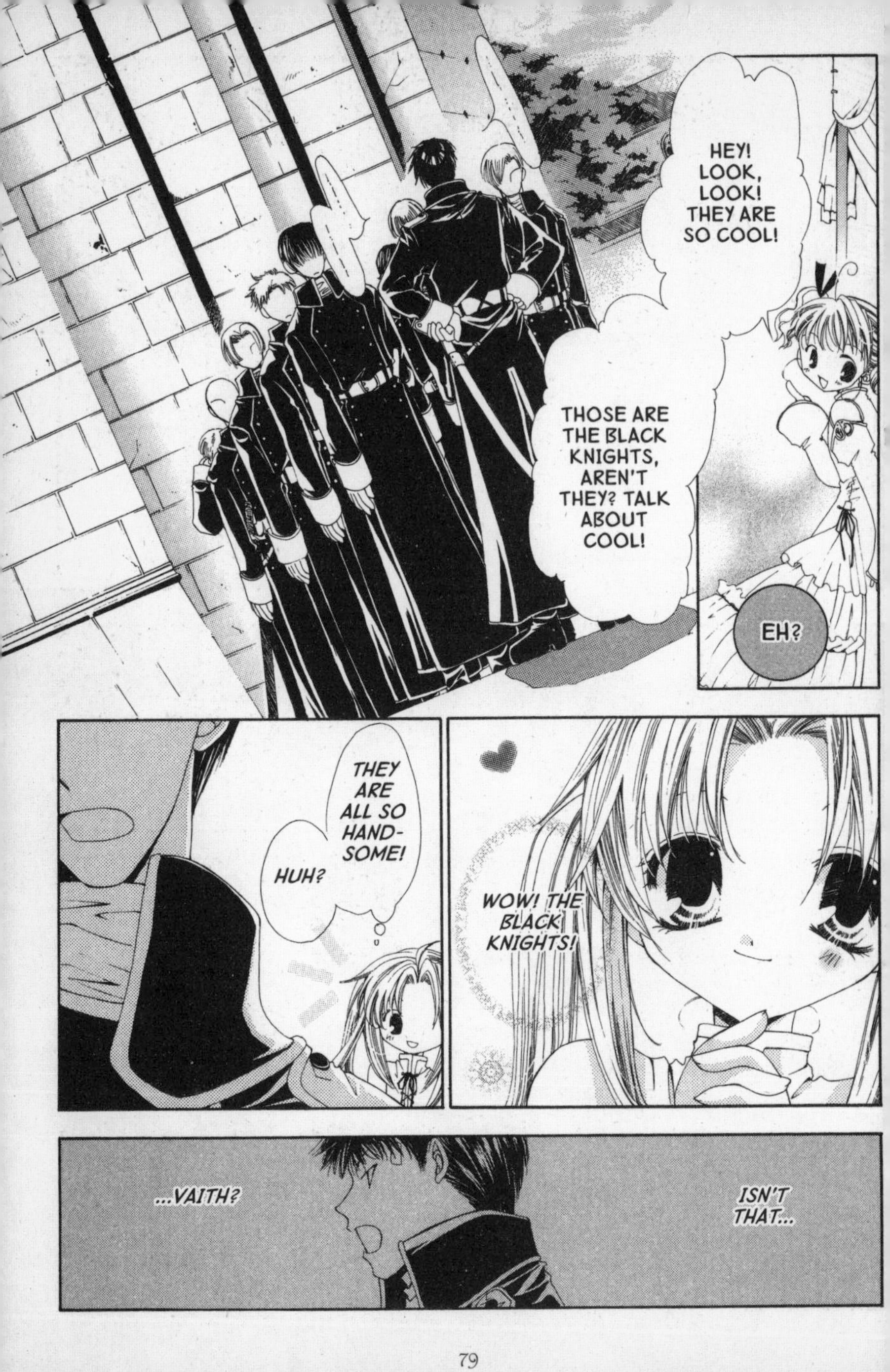

HEY! LOOK, LOOK! THEY ARE SO COOL!
THOSE ARE THE BLACK KNIGHTS, AREN'T THEY? TALK ABOUT COOL!
EH?
WOW! THE BLACK KNIGHTS!
THEY ARE ALL SO HAND-SOME!
HUH?
ISN'T THAT...
...VAITH?

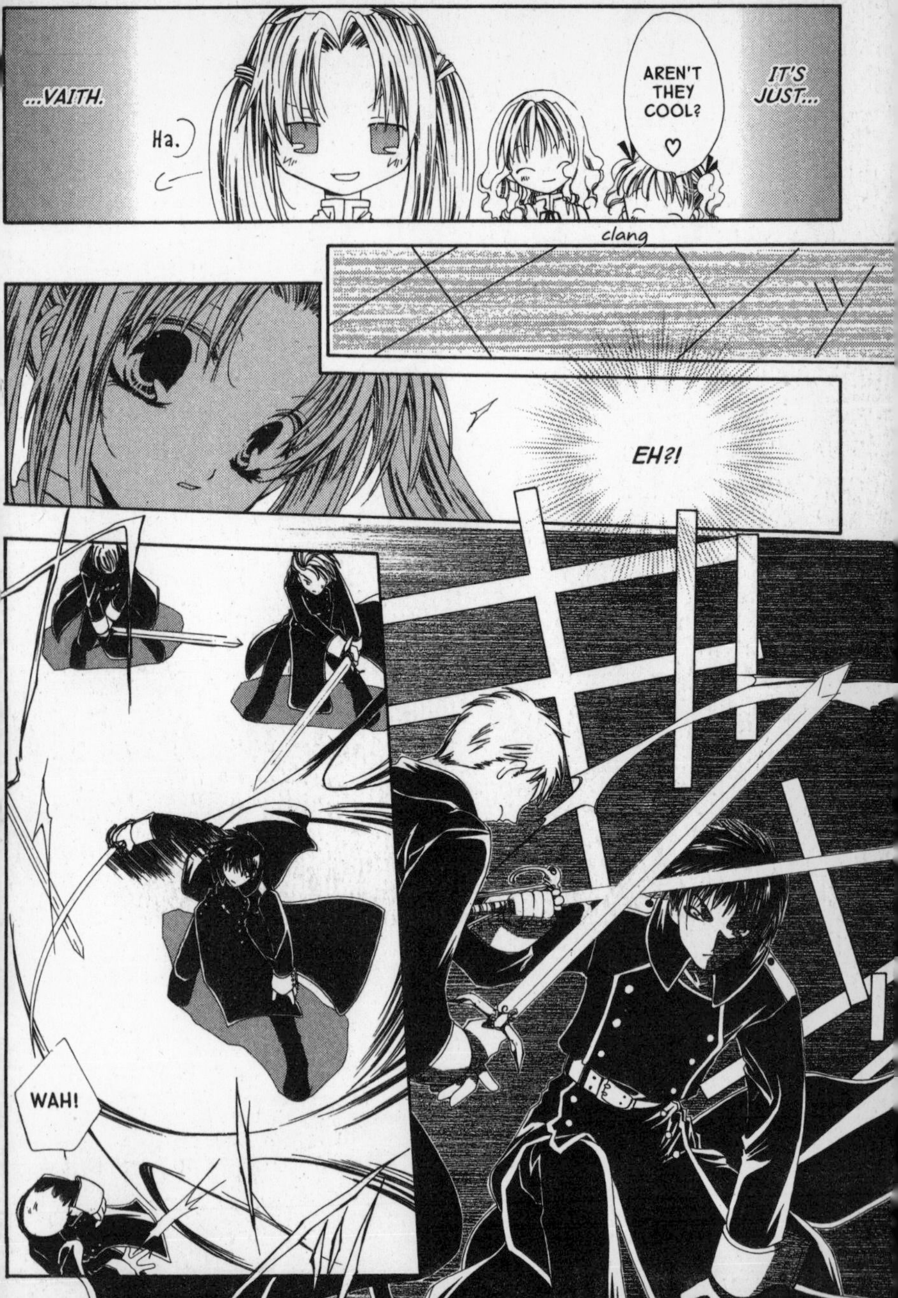
IT'S JUST...
AREN'T THEY COOL? ♡
Ha.
...VAITH.
clang
EH?!
WAH!

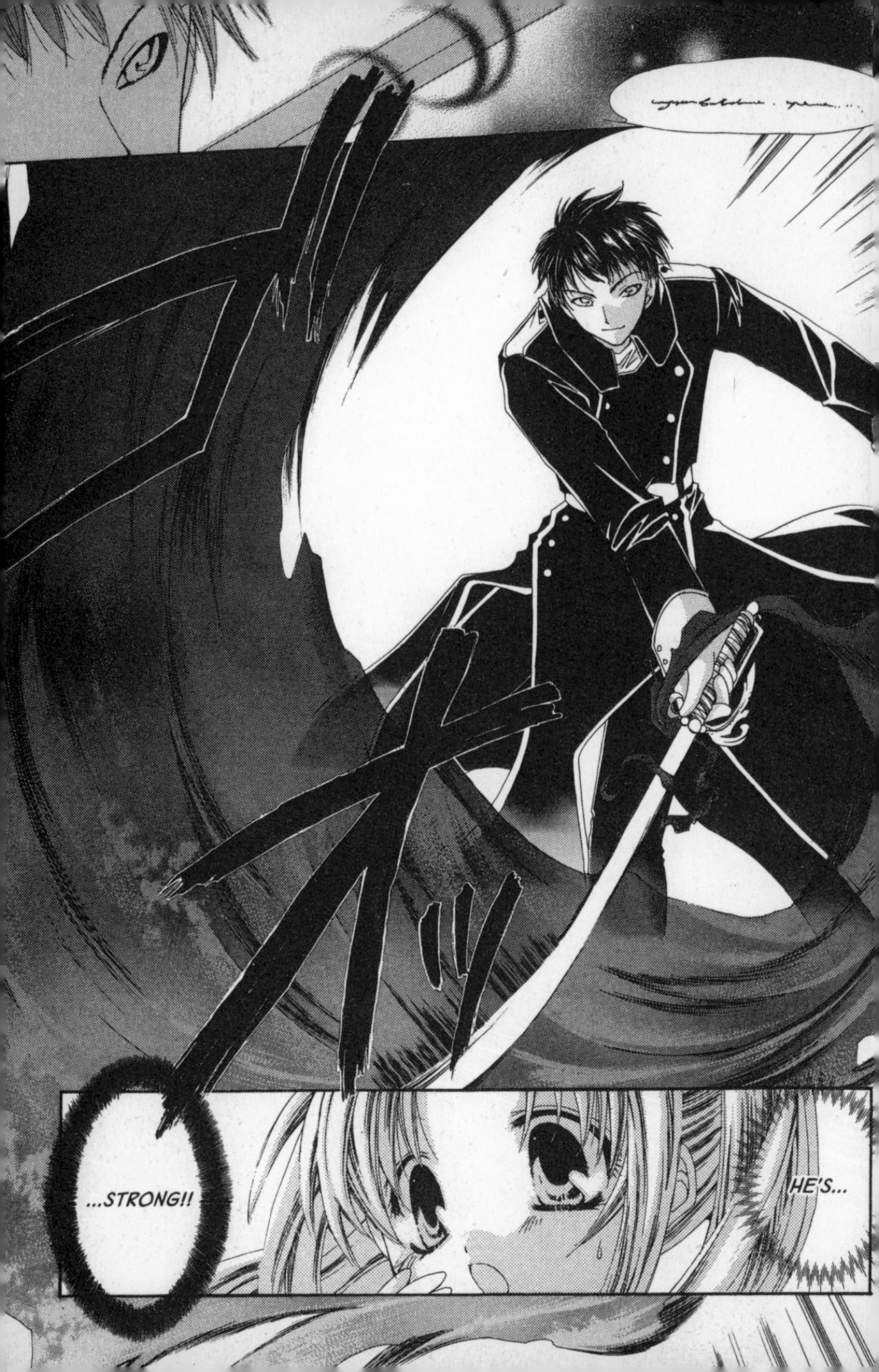
HE'S...
...STRONG!!

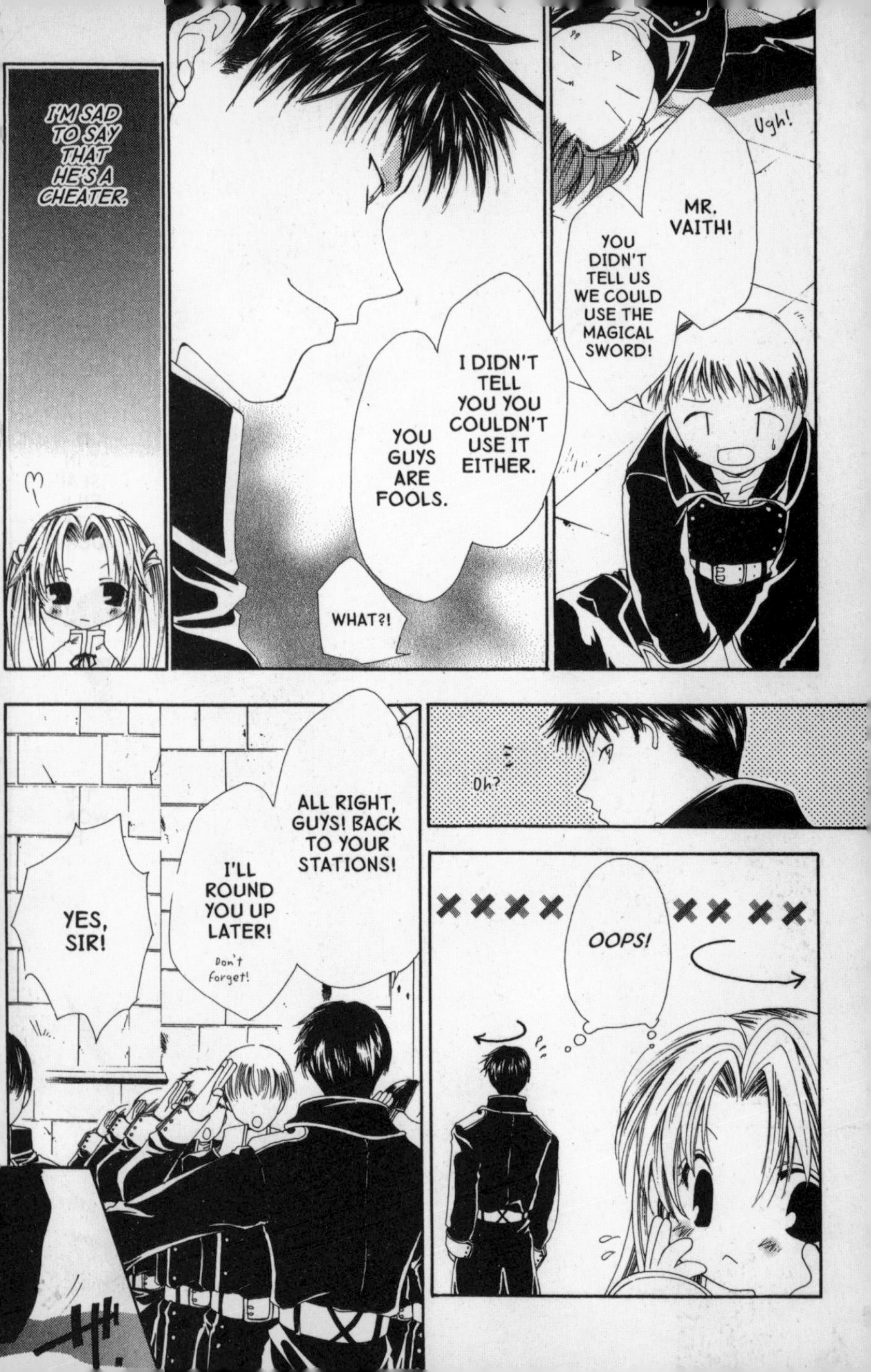
Ugh!
MR. VAITH!
YOU DIDN'T TELL US WE COULD USE THE MAGICAL SWORD!
I DIDN'T TELL YOU YOU COULDN'T USE IT EITHER.
YOU GUYS ARE FOOLS.
WHAT?!
I'M SAD TO SAY THAT HE'S A CHEATER.
Oh?
OOPS!
ALL RIGHT, GUYS! BACK TO YOUR STATIONS!
I'LL ROUND YOU UP LATER!
Don't forget!
YES, SIR!

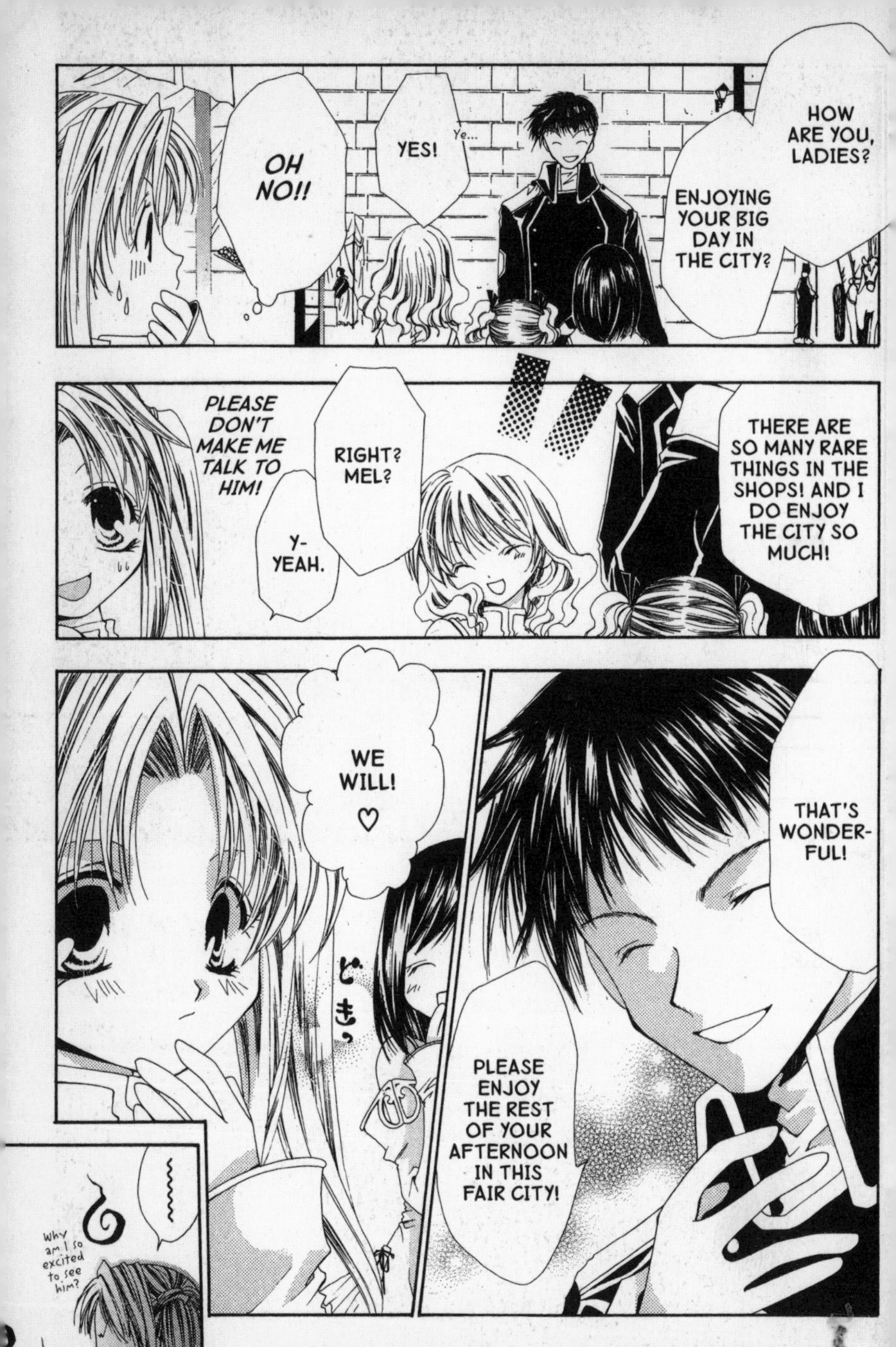
HOW ARE YOU, LADIES?
ENJOYING YOUR BIG DAY IN THE CITY?
Ye...
YES!
OH NO!!
THERE ARE SO MANY RARE THINGS IN THE SHOPS! AND I DO ENJOY THE CITY SO MUCH!
RIGHT? MEL?
Y-YEAH.
PLEASE DON'T MAKE ME TALK TO HIM!
THAT'S WONDER-FUL!
PLEASE ENJOY THE REST OF YOUR AFTERNOON IN THIS FAIR CITY!
WE WILL! ♡
どき、
Why am I so excited to see him?

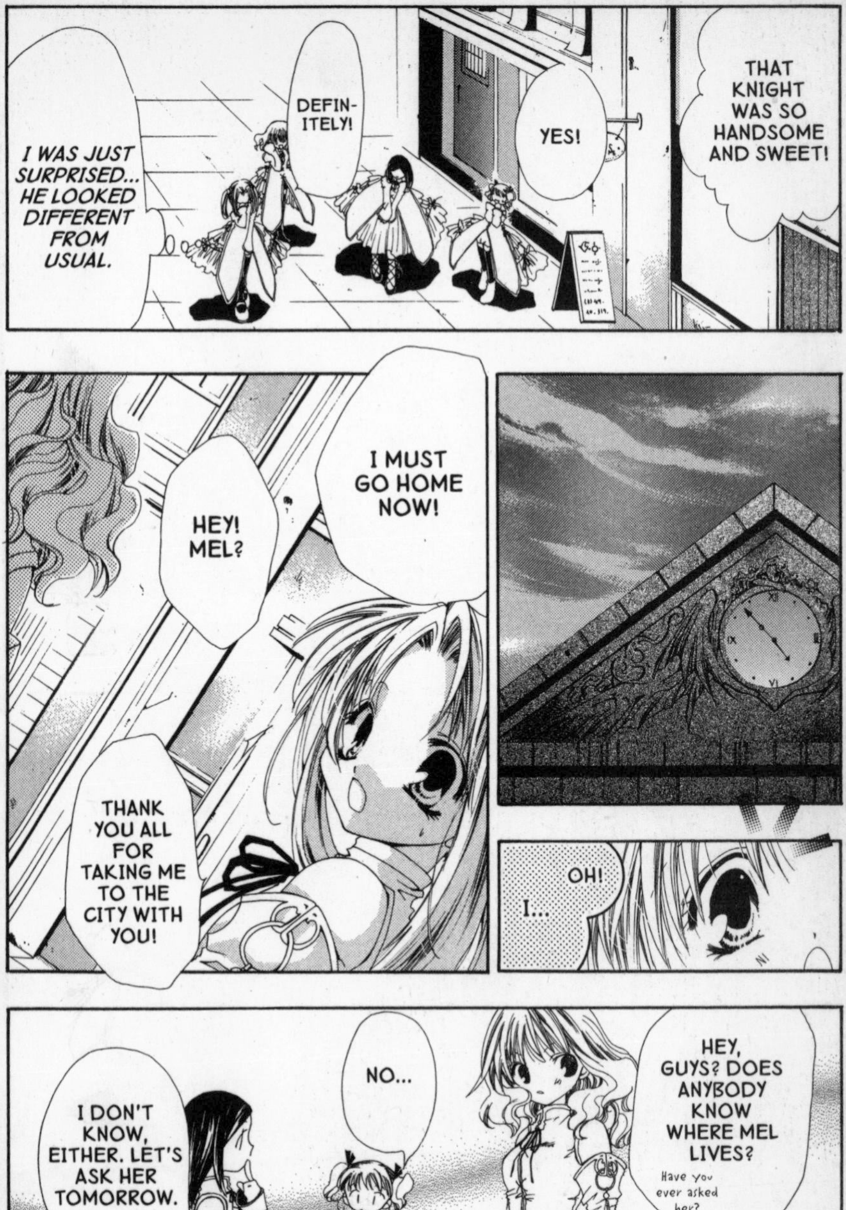
THAT KNIGHT WAS SO HANDSOME AND SWEET!
YES!
DEFIN-ITELY!
I WAS JUST SURPRISED... HE LOOKED DIFFERENT FROM USUAL.
OH!
I...
I MUST GO HOME NOW!
HEY! MEL?
THANK YOU ALL FOR TAKING ME TO THE CITY WITH YOU!
HEY, GUYS? DOES ANYBODY KNOW WHERE MEL LIVES?
Have you ever asked her?
NO...
I DON'T KNOW, EITHER. LET'S ASK HER TOMORROW.

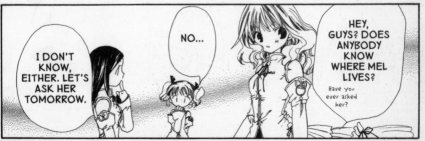

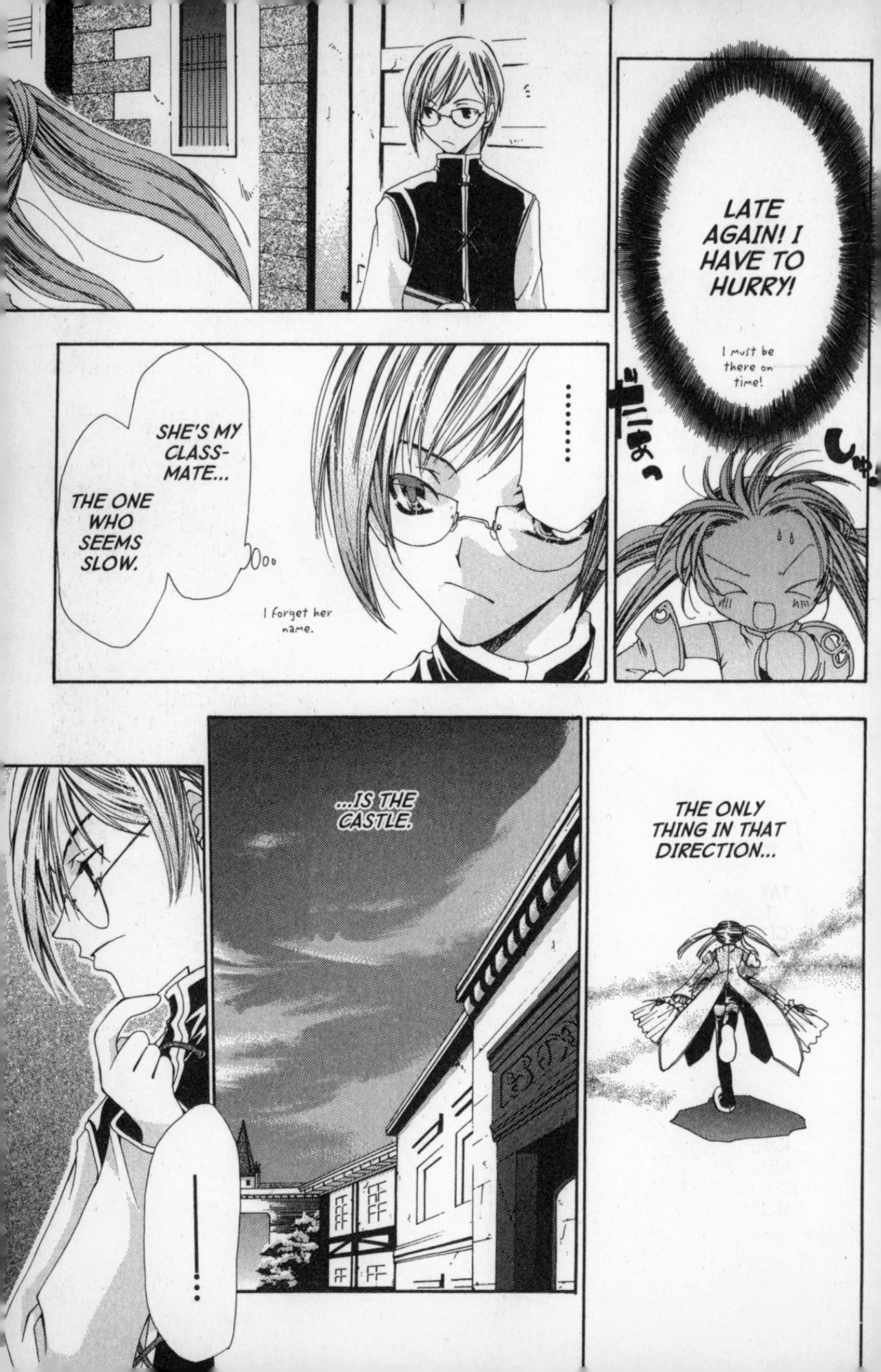

LATE AGAIN! I HAVE TO HURRY!
I must be there on time!
......
SHE'S MY CLASS-MATE... THE ONE WHO SEEMS SLOW.
I forget her name.
THE ONLY THING IN THAT DIRECTION...
...IS THE CASTLE.
......

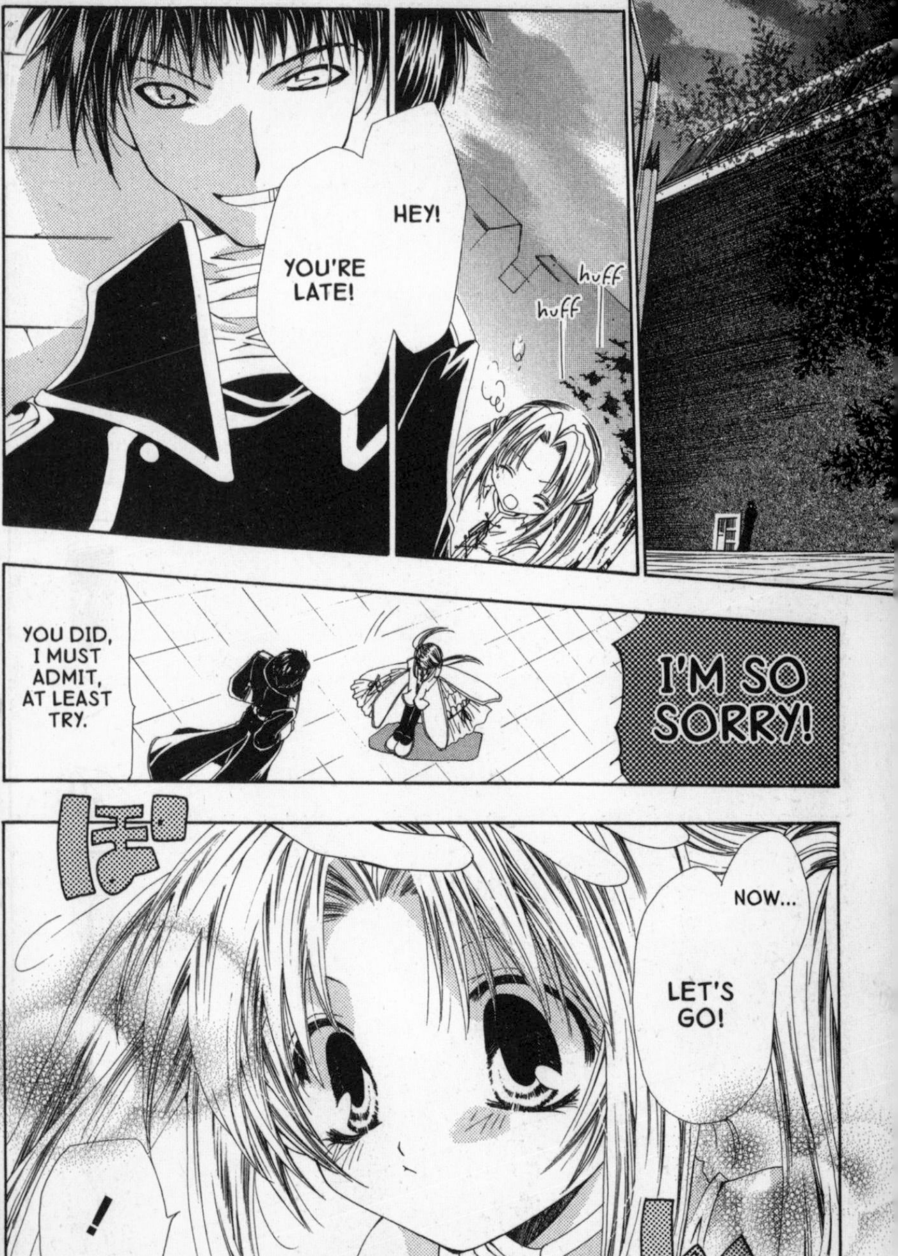
huff
huff
HEY! YOU'RE LATE!
I'M SO SORRY!
YOU DID, I MUST ADMIT, AT LEAST TRY.
ぽ
ん
NOW... LET'S GO!
!

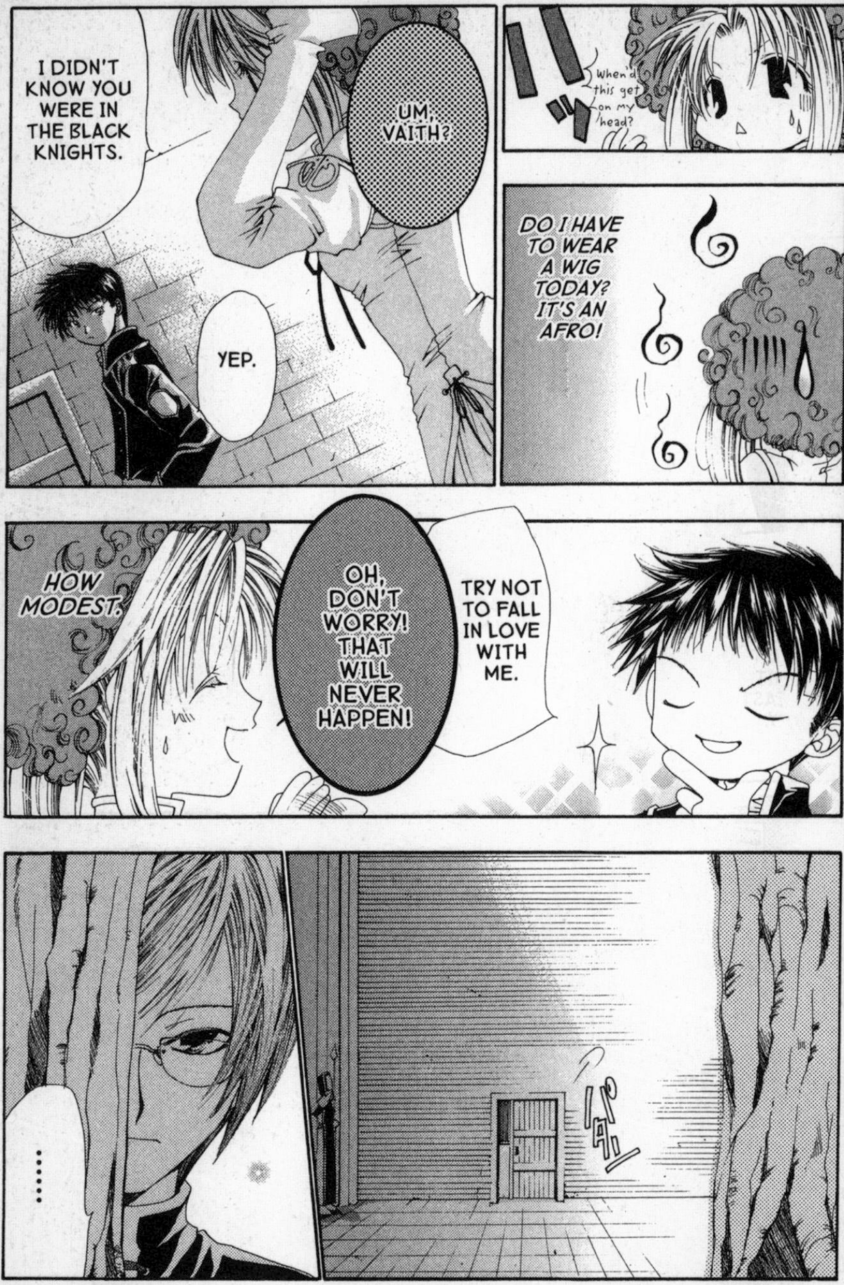

When'd this get on my head?
DO I HAVE TO WEAR A WIG TODAY? IT'S AN AFRO!
UM, VAITH?
I DIDN'T KNOW YOU WERE IN THE BLACK KNIGHTS.
YEP.
TRY NOT TO FALL IN LOVE WITH ME.
OH, DON'T WORRY! THAT WILL NEVER HAPPEN!
HOW MODEST.
......

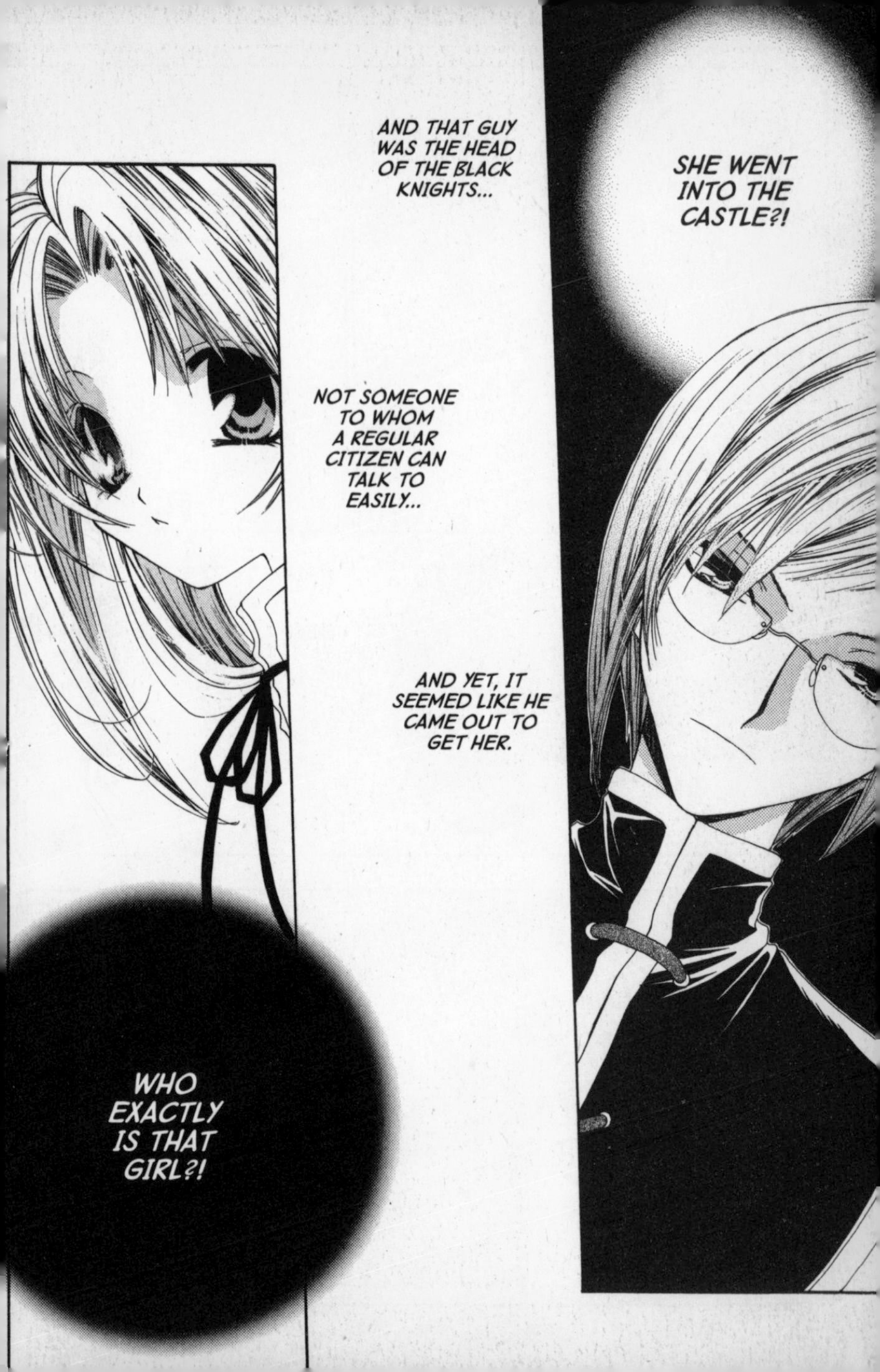
SHE WENT INTO THE CASTLE?!
AND THAT GUY WAS THE HEAD OF THE BLACK KNIGHTS...
NOT SOMEONE TO WHOM A REGULAR CITIZEN CAN TALK TO EASILY...
AND YET, IT SEEMED LIKE HE CAME OUT TO GET HER.
WHO EXACTLY IS THAT GIRL?!

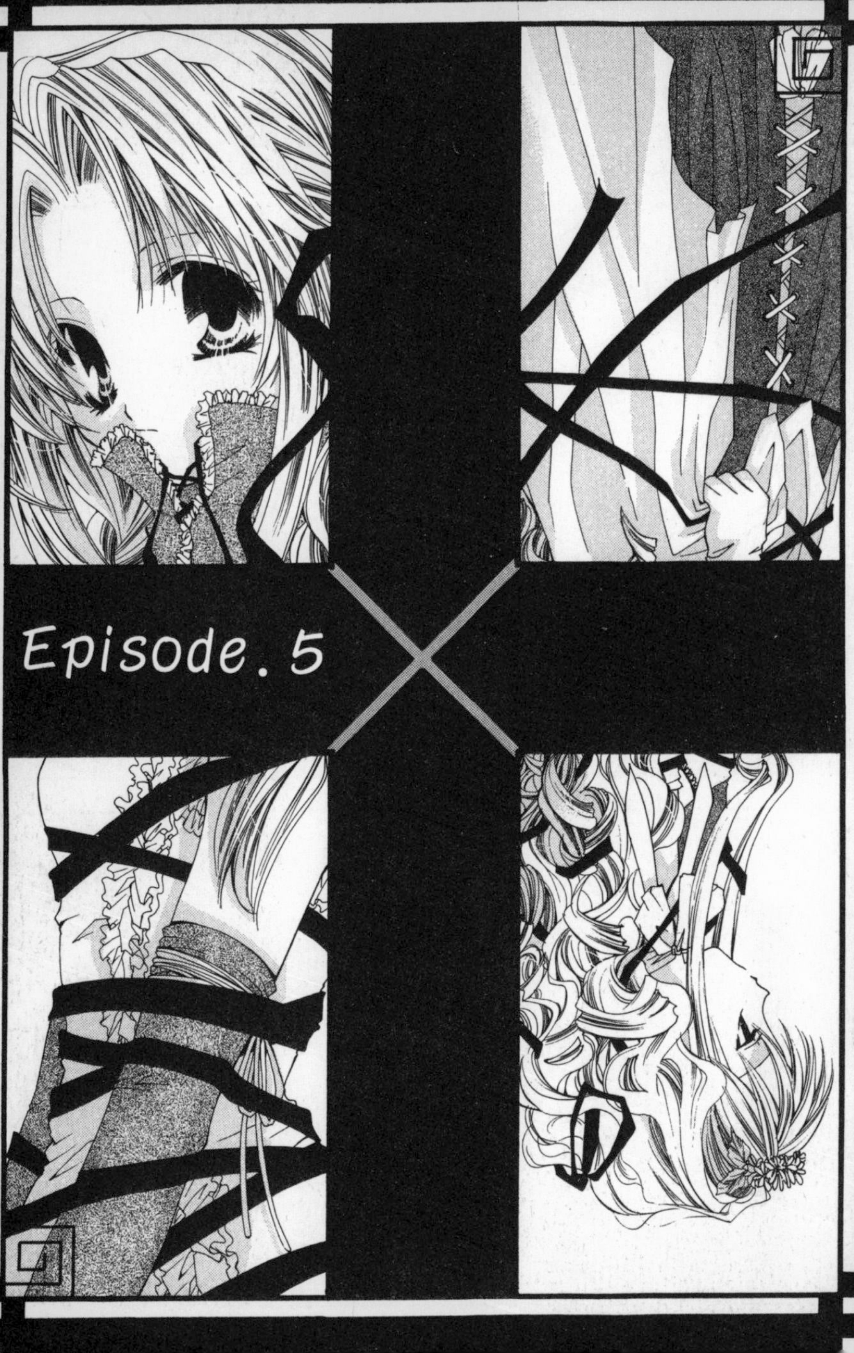
Episode. 5

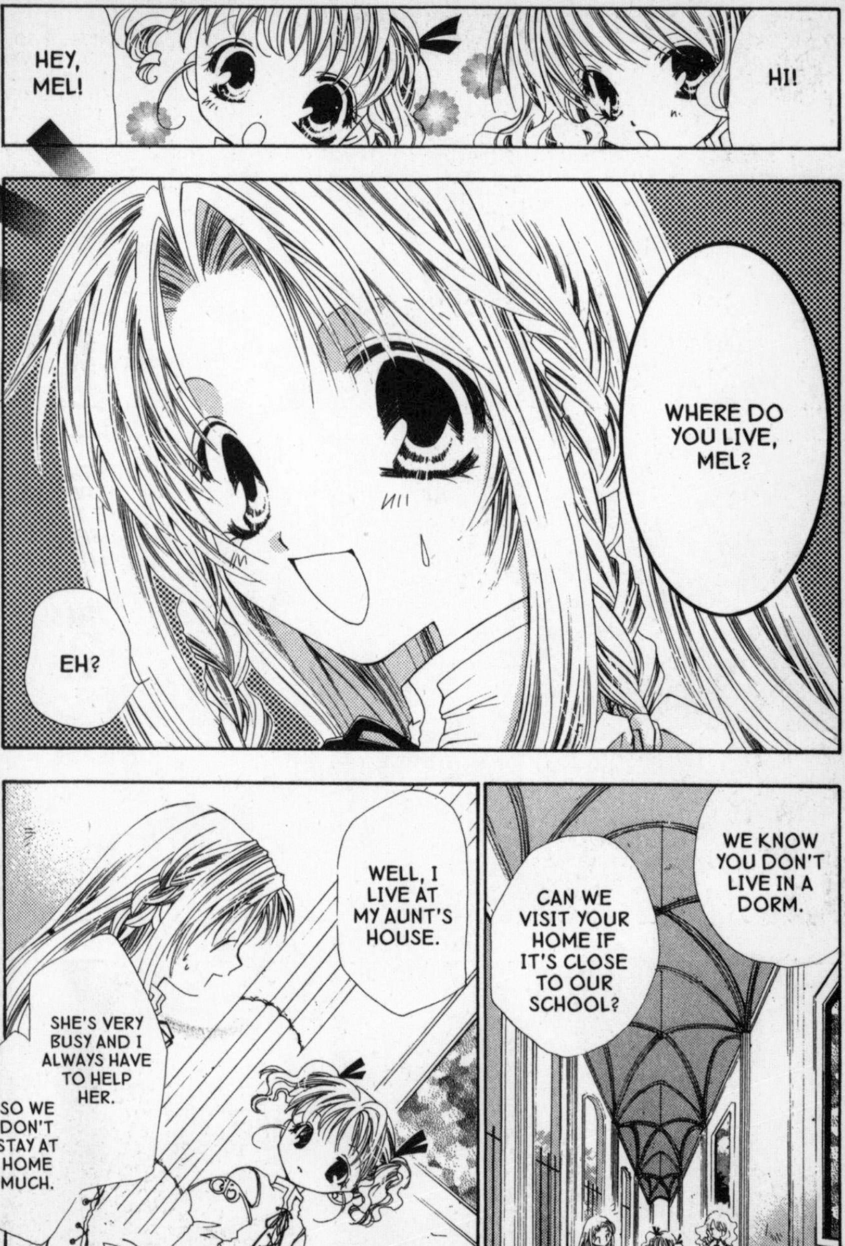
HI!
HEY, MEL!
WHERE DO YOU LIVE, MEL?
EH?
WE KNOW YOU DON'T LIVE IN A DORM.
CAN WE VISIT YOUR HOME IF IT'S CLOSE TO OUR SCHOOL?
WELL, I LIVE AT MY AUNT'S HOUSE.
SHE'S VERY BUSY AND I ALWAYS HAVE TO HELP HER.
SO WE DON'T STAY AT HOME MUCH.

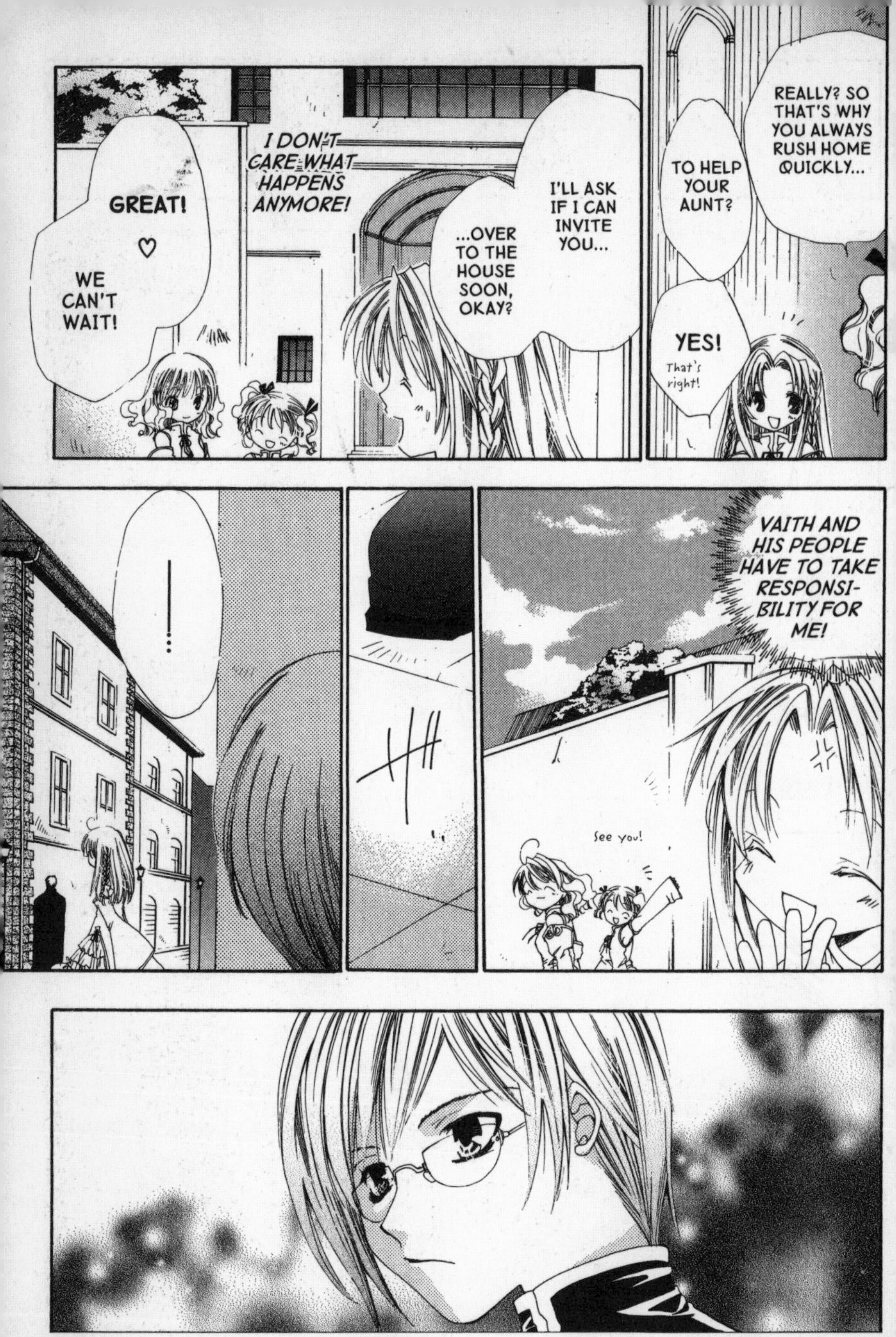
REALLY? SO THAT'S WHY YOU ALWAYS RUSH HOME QUICKLY...
TO HELP YOUR AUNT?
YES!
That's right!
I'LL ASK IF I CAN INVITE YOU...
...OVER TO THE HOUSE SOON, OKAY?
I DON'T CARE WHAT HAPPENS ANYMORE!
GREAT! ♡ WE CAN'T WAIT!
VAITH AND HIS PEOPLE HAVE TO TAKE RESPONSI-BILITY FOR ME!
See you!
—...

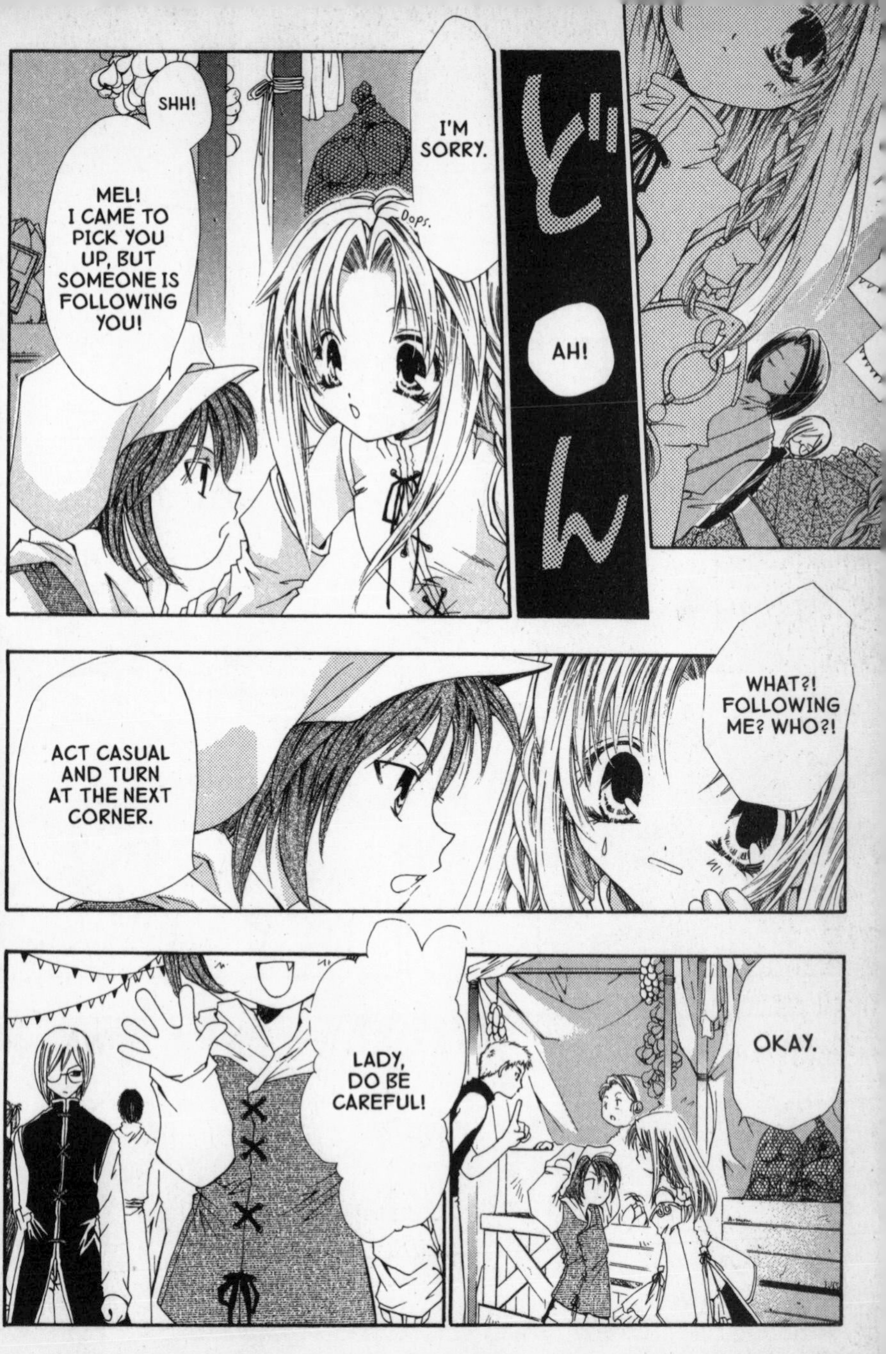
どしん
AH!
I'M SORRY.
Oops.
SHH!
MEL! I CAME TO PICK YOU UP, BUT SOMEONE IS FOLLOWING YOU!
WHAT?! FOLLOWING ME? WHO?!
ACT CASUAL AND TURN AT THE NEXT CORNER.
OKAY.
LADY, DO BE CAREFUL!

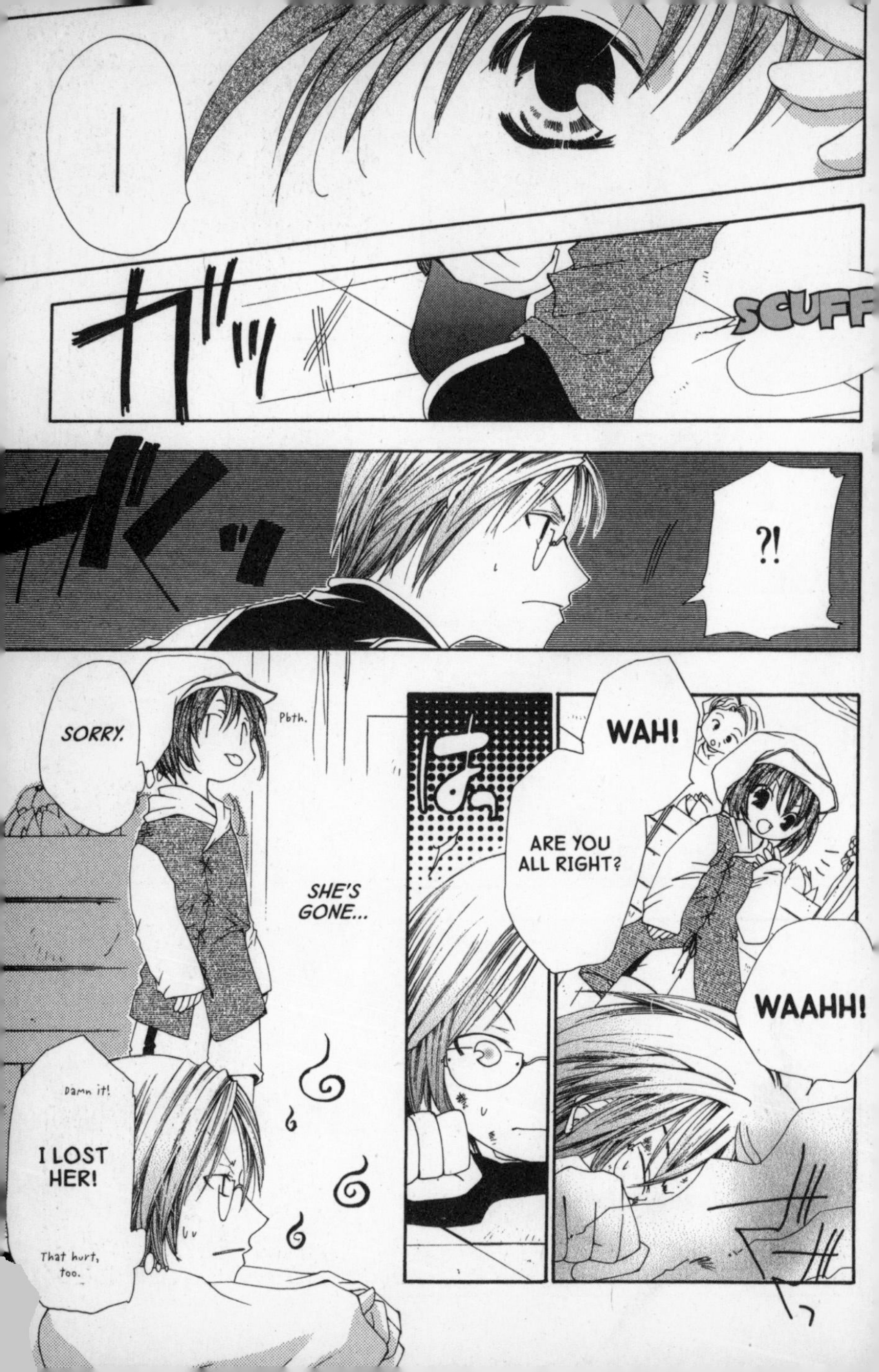
SCUFF
?!
WAH!
WAAHH!
ARE YOU ALL RIGHT?
SORRY.
Pbth.
SHE'S GONE...
Damn it!
I LOST HER!
That hurt, too.

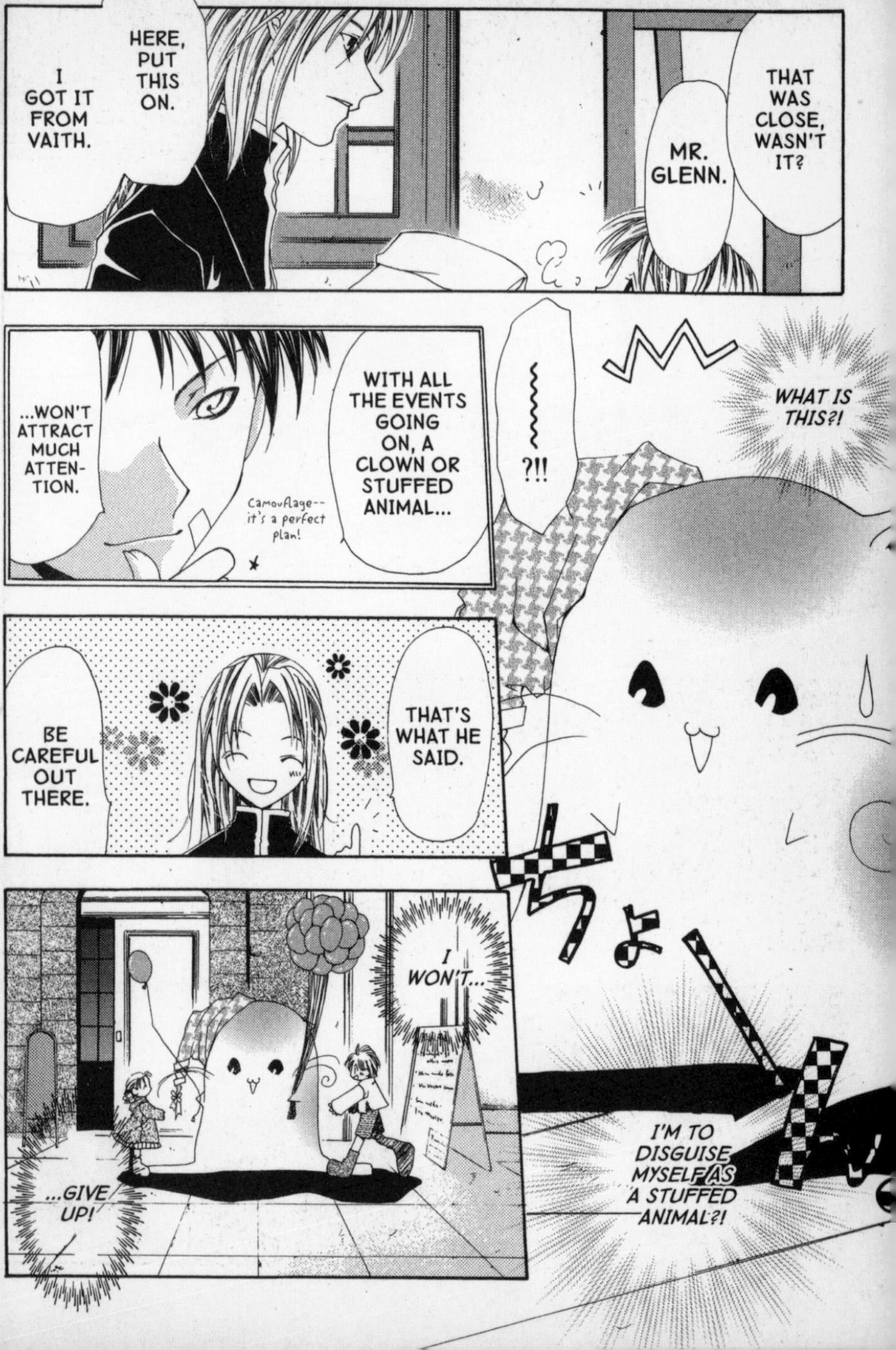
THAT WAS CLOSE, WASN'T IT?
MR. GLENN.
HERE, PUT THIS ON.
I GOT IT FROM VAITH.
WITH ALL THE EVENTS GOING ON, A CLOWN OR STUFFED ANIMAL...
...WON'T ATTRACT MUCH ATTENTION.
Camouflage--it's a perfect plan!
THAT'S WHAT HE SAID.
BE CAREFUL OUT THERE.
~~~ ?!!
WHAT IS THIS?!
ちょ
I'M TO DISGUISE MYSELF AS A STUFFED ANIMAL?!
I WON'T...
...GIVE UP!
~~~

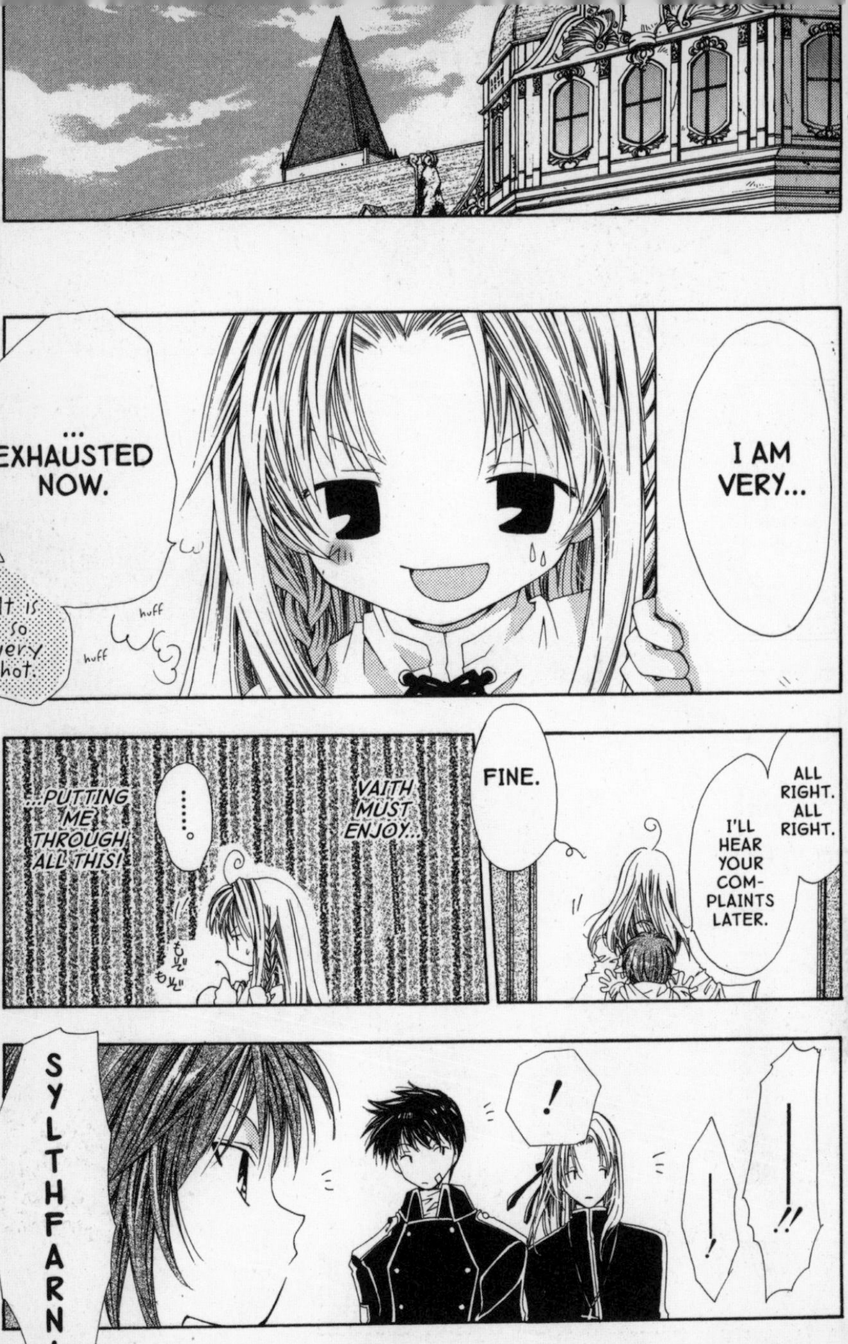
I AM VERY...
...EXHAUSTED NOW.
It is so very hot.
huff huff
ALL RIGHT. ALL RIGHT.
I'LL HEAR YOUR COMPLAINTS LATER.
FINE.
VAITH MUST ENJOY...
......。
...PUTTING ME THROUGH ALL THIS!
もぞもぞ
—!!
—!
!
SYLTHFARN!

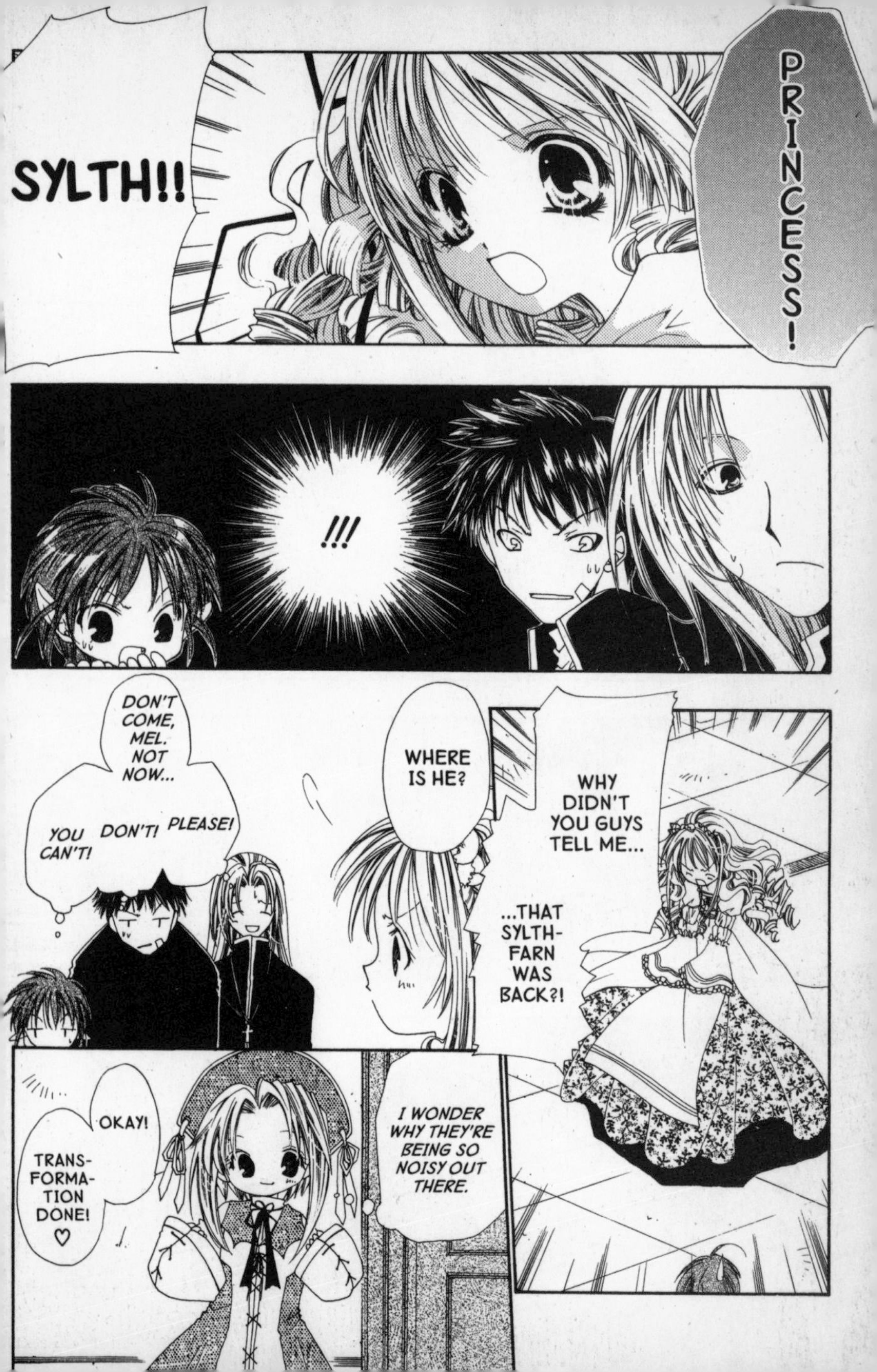
PRINCESS!
SYLTH!!
!!!
WHY DIDN'T YOU GUYS TELL ME...
...THAT SYLTH-FARN WAS BACK?!
WHERE IS HE?
DON'T COME, MEL. NOT NOW...
PLEASE!
DON'T!
YOU CAN'T!
I WONDER WHY THEY'RE BEING SO NOISY OUT THERE.
OKAY!
TRANS-FORMA-TION DONE! ♡

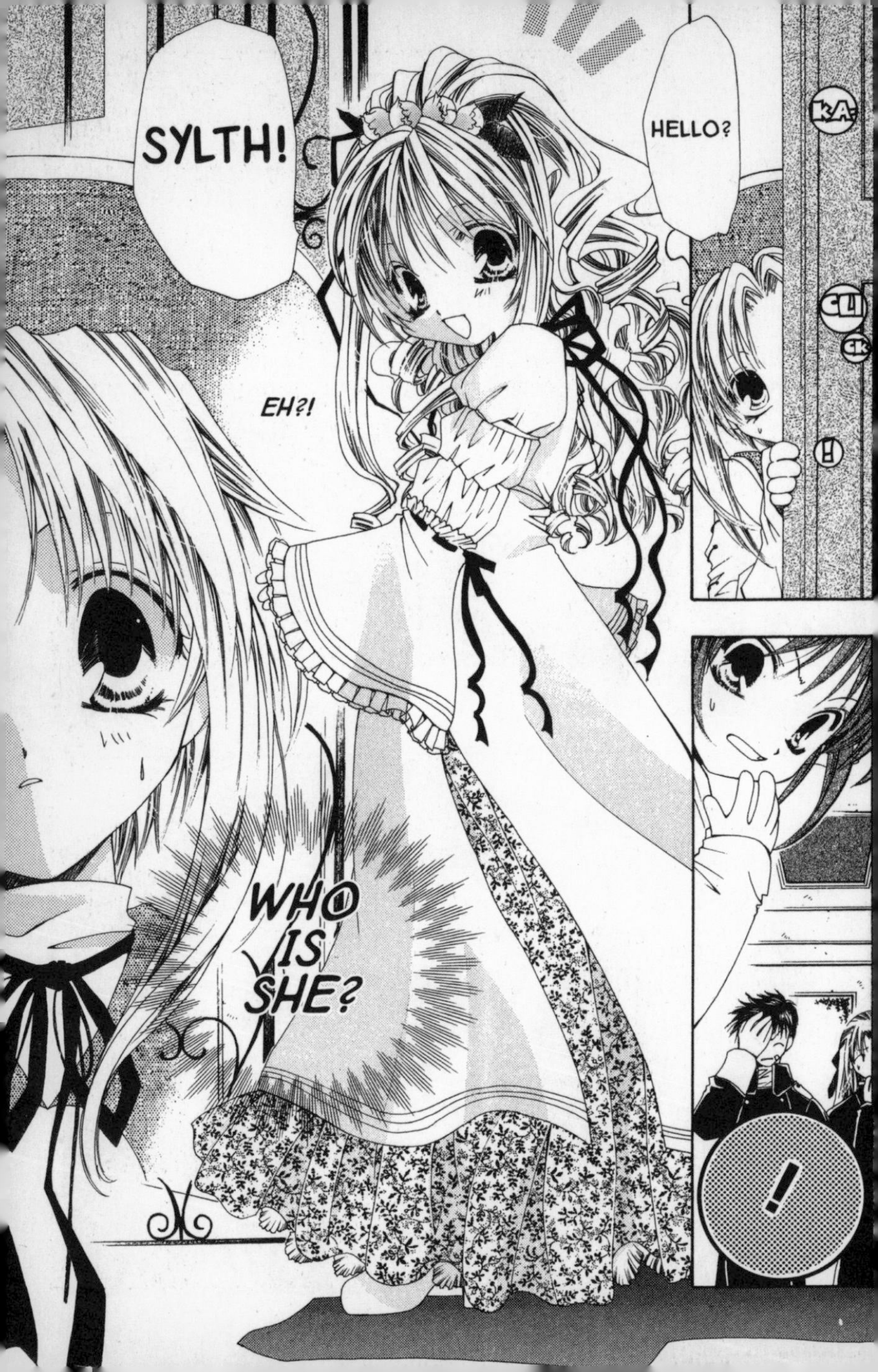
KA-
CLI
CK
!
HELLO?
SYLTH!
EH?!
WHO IS SHE?

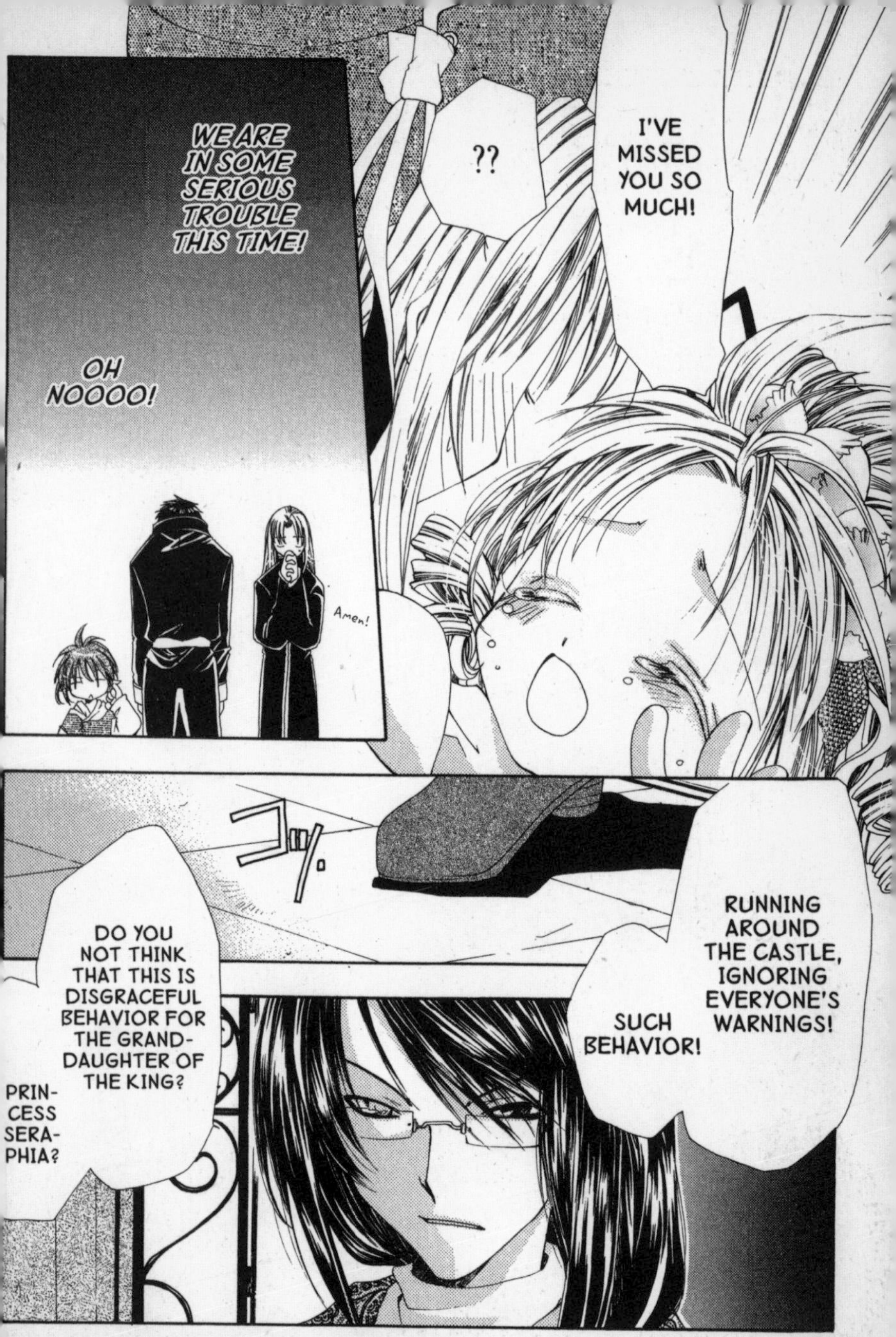
I'VE MISSED YOU SO MUCH!
??
WE ARE IN SOME SERIOUS TROUBLE THIS TIME!
OH NOOOO!
Amen!
RUNNING AROUND THE CASTLE, IGNORING EVERYONE'S WARNINGS!
SUCH BEHAVIOR!
DO YOU NOT THINK THAT THIS IS DISGRACEFUL BEHAVIOR FOR THE GRAND-DAUGHTER OF THE KING?
PRIN-CESS SERA-PHIA?

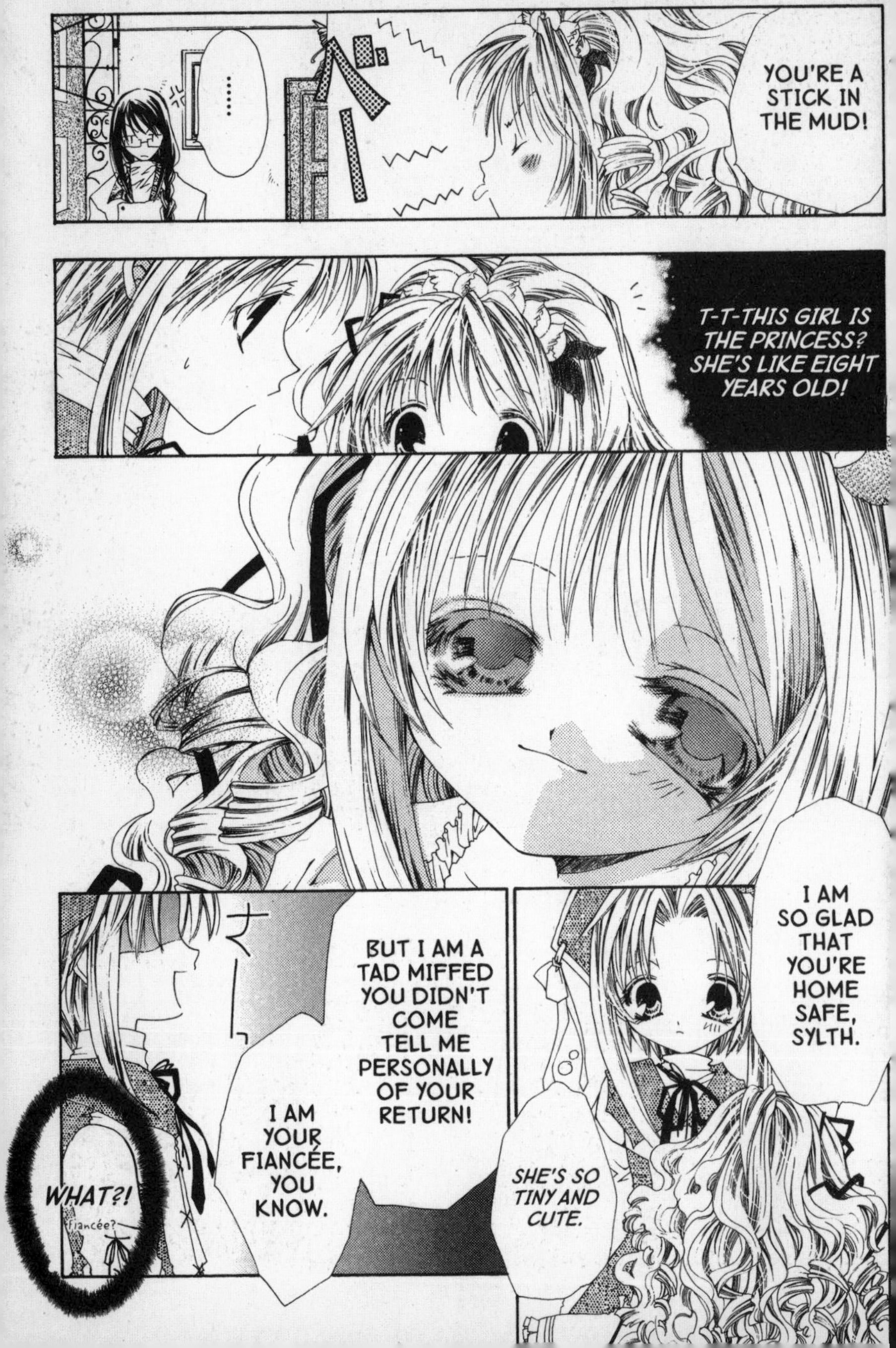
YOU'RE A STICK IN THE MUD!
......
T-T-THIS GIRL IS THE PRINCESS? SHE'S LIKE EIGHT YEARS OLD!
I AM SO GLAD THAT YOU'RE HOME SAFE, SYLTH.
SHE'S SO TINY AND CUTE.
BUT I AM A TAD MIFFED YOU DIDN'T COME TELL ME PERSONALLY OF YOUR RETURN!
I AM YOUR FIANCÉE, YOU KNOW.
WHAT?!
fiancée?

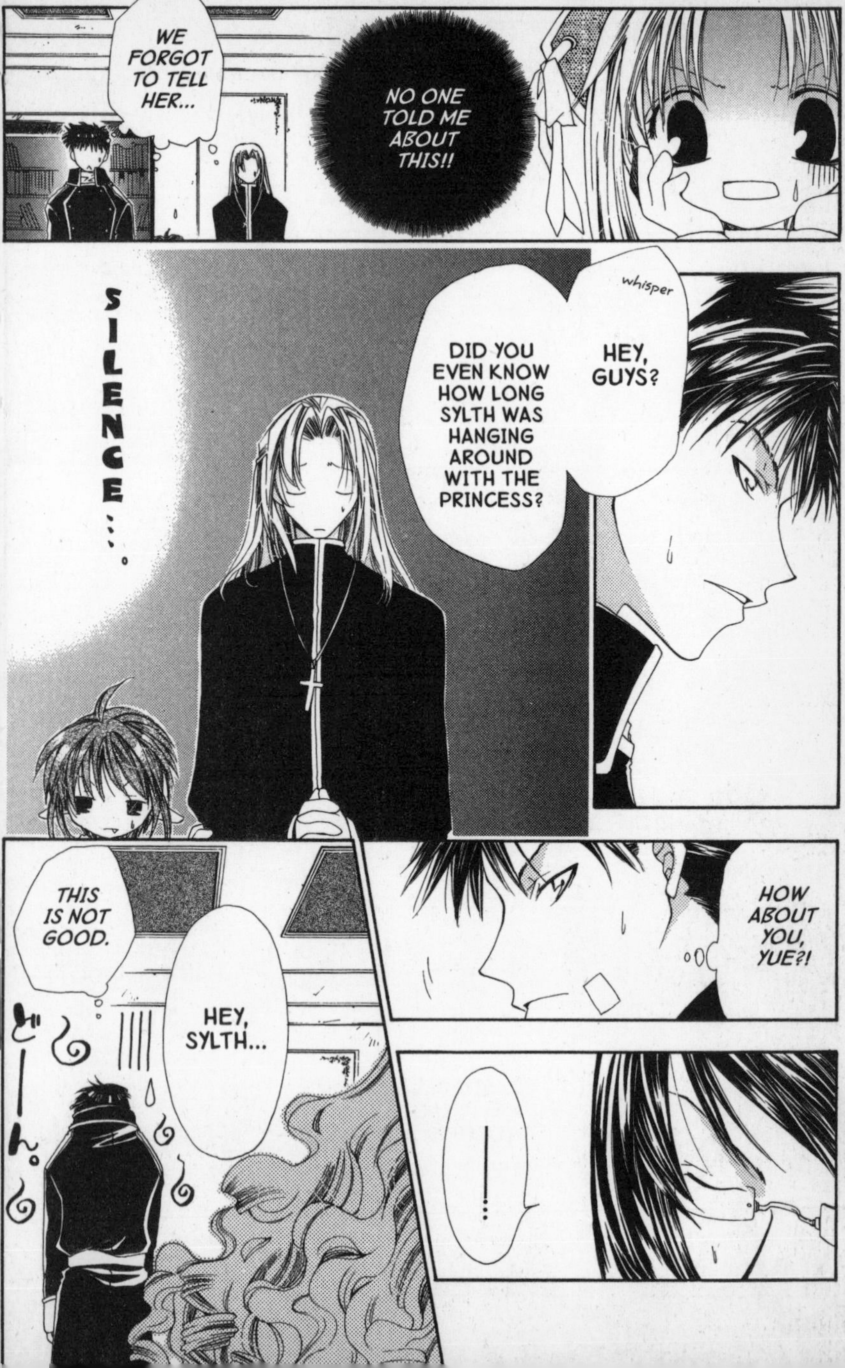
NO ONE TOLD ME ABOUT THIS!!
WE FORGOT TO TELL HER...
whisper
HEY, GUYS?
DID YOU EVEN KNOW HOW LONG SYLTH WAS HANGING AROUND WITH THE PRINCESS?
SILENCE...
HOW ABOUT YOU, YUE?!
HEY, SYLTH...
THIS IS NOT GOOD.
どーん。

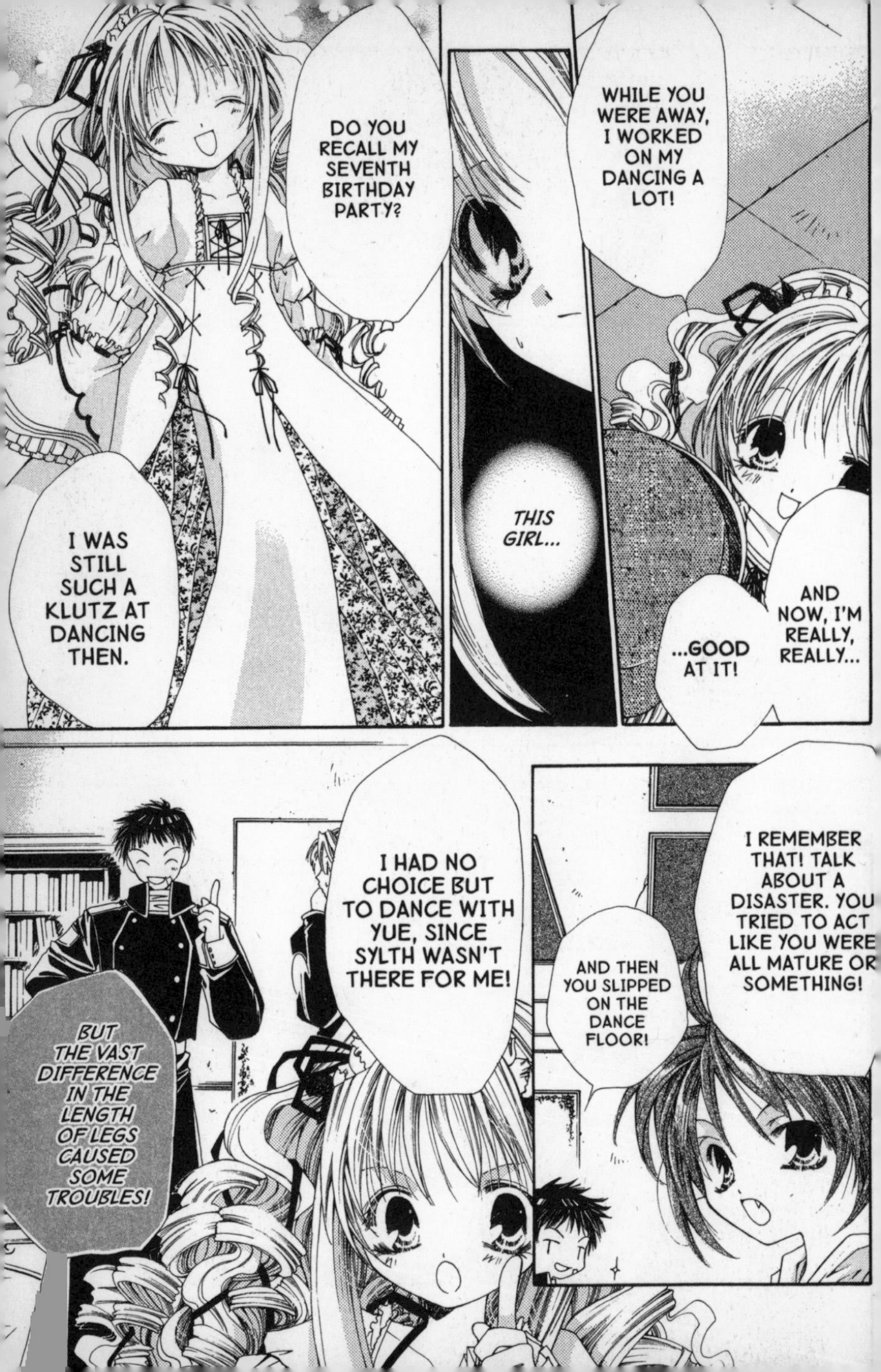
WHILE YOU WERE AWAY, I WORKED ON MY DANCING A LOT!
AND NOW, I'M REALLY, REALLY...
...GOOD AT IT!
THIS GIRL...
DO YOU RECALL MY SEVENTH BIRTHDAY PARTY?
I WAS STILL SUCH A KLUTZ AT DANCING THEN.
I REMEMBER THAT! TALK ABOUT A DISASTER. YOU TRIED TO ACT LIKE YOU WERE ALL MATURE OR SOMETHING!
AND THEN YOU SLIPPED ON THE DANCE FLOOR!
I HAD NO CHOICE BUT TO DANCE WITH YUE, SINCE SYLTH WASN'T THERE FOR ME!
BUT THE VAST DIFFERENCE IN THE LENGTH OF LEGS CAUSED SOME TROUBLES!

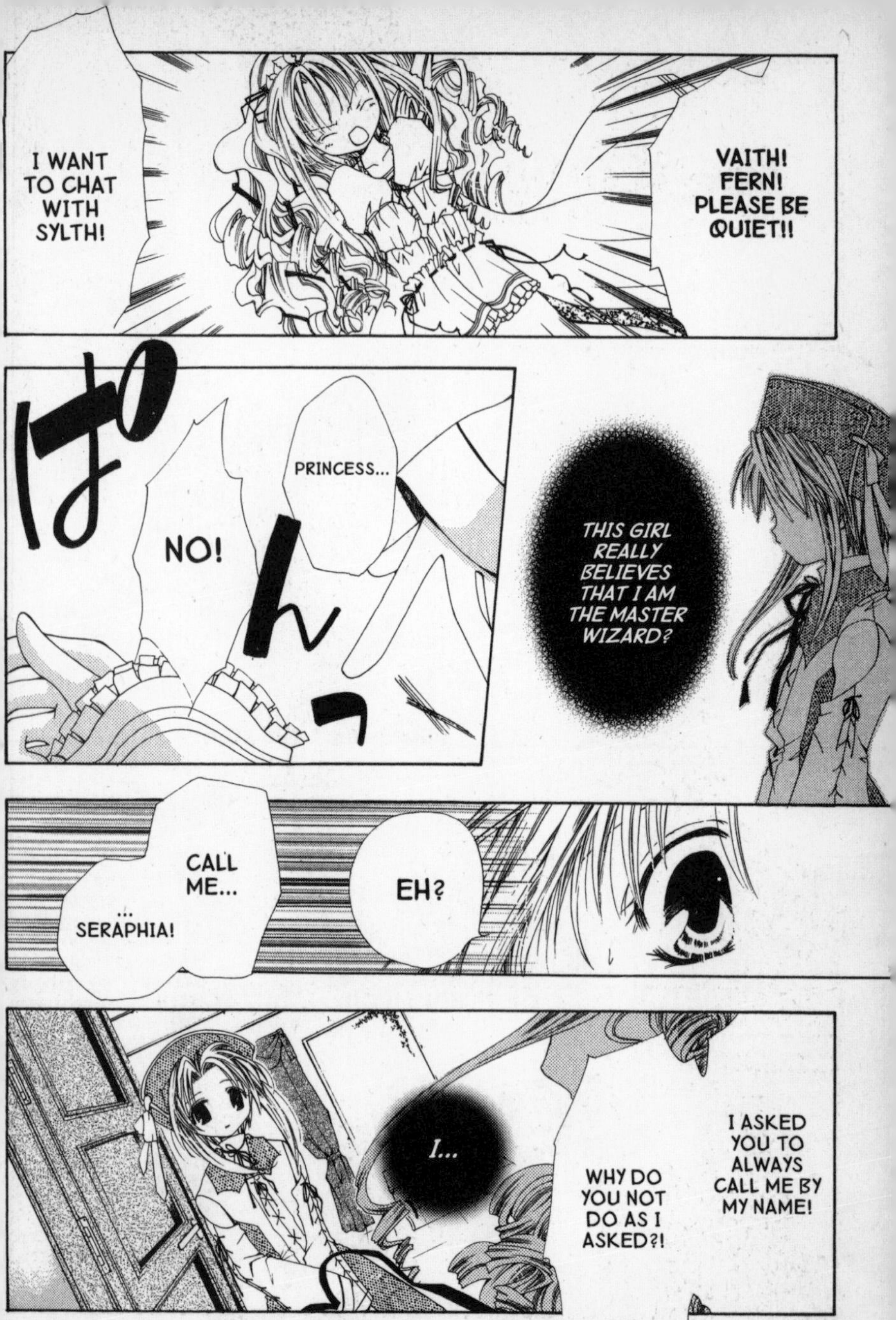
VAITH! FERN! PLEASE BE QUIET!!
I WANT TO CHAT WITH SYLTH!
THIS GIRL REALLY BELIEVES THAT I AM THE MASTER WIZARD?
PRINCESS...
NO!
ぱんっ
EH?
CALL ME...
...SERAPHIA!
I ASKED YOU TO ALWAYS CALL ME BY MY NAME!
WHY DO YOU NOT DO AS I ASKED?!
I...

I'M OFF TO MY ROOM NOW.

I'M SORRY.

I AM BEING SO DISHONEST WITH HER.

SYLTH?

PLEASE GIVE ME A KISS.

UM, WELL...

WHAT?

EH?!

Give her a kiss?!

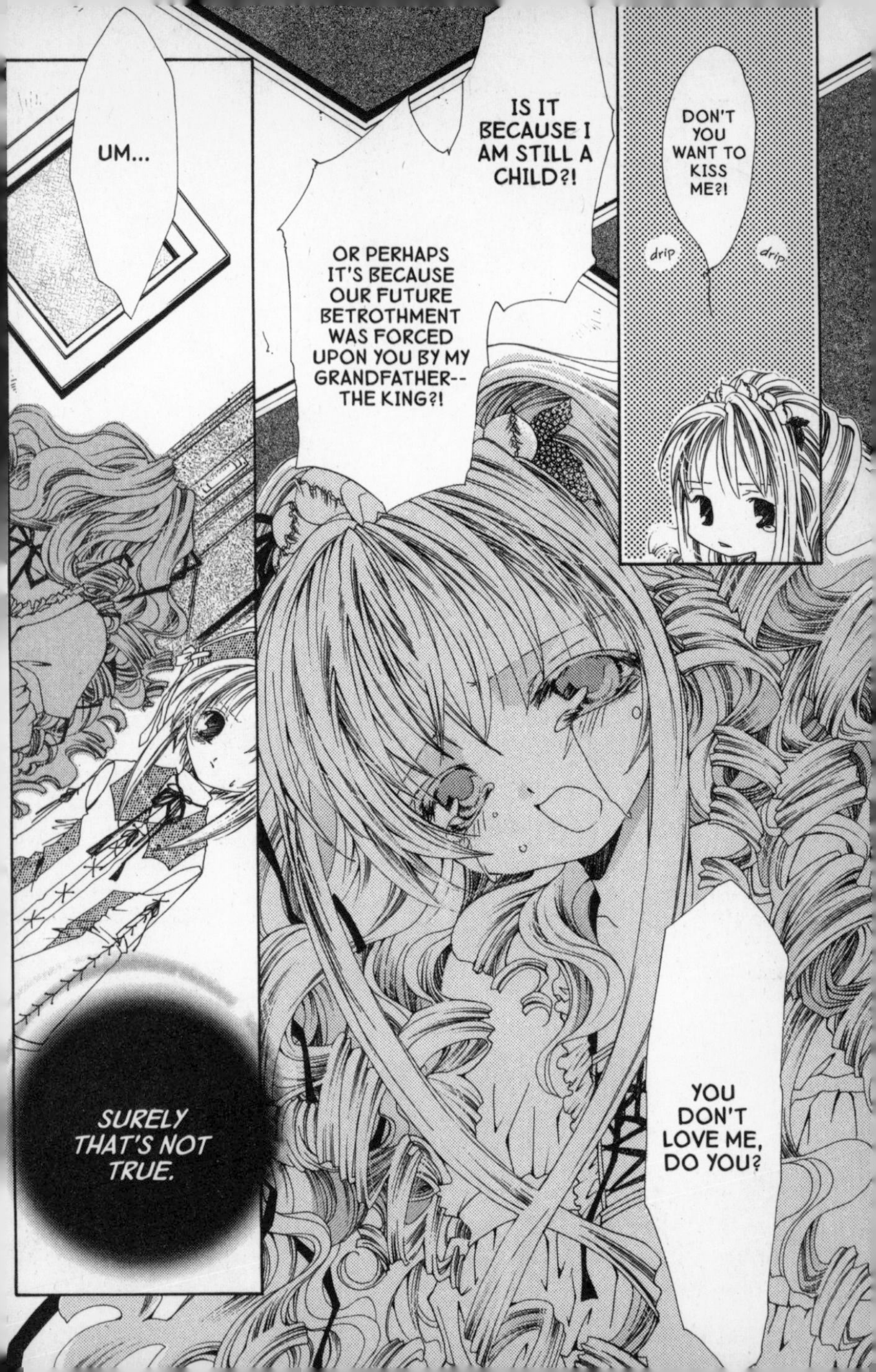
DON'T YOU WANT TO KISS ME?!
drip
drip
IS IT BECAUSE I AM STILL A CHILD?!
OR PERHAPS IT'S BECAUSE OUR FUTURE BETROTHMENT WAS FORCED UPON YOU BY MY GRANDFATHER-- THE KING?!
YOU DON'T LOVE ME, DO YOU?
UM...
SURELY THAT'S NOT TRUE.

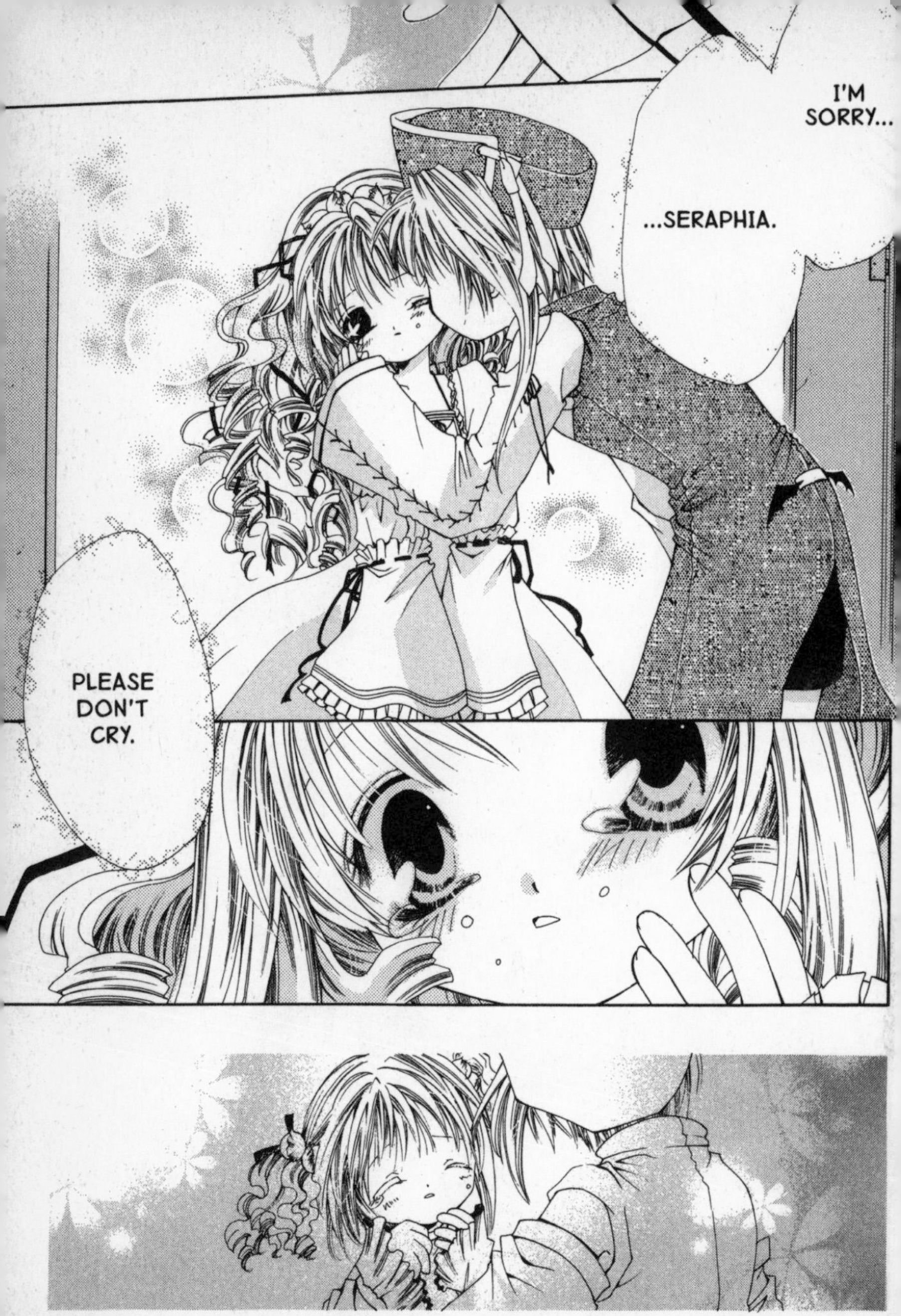
I'M SORRY...
...SERAPHIA.
PLEASE DON'T CRY.

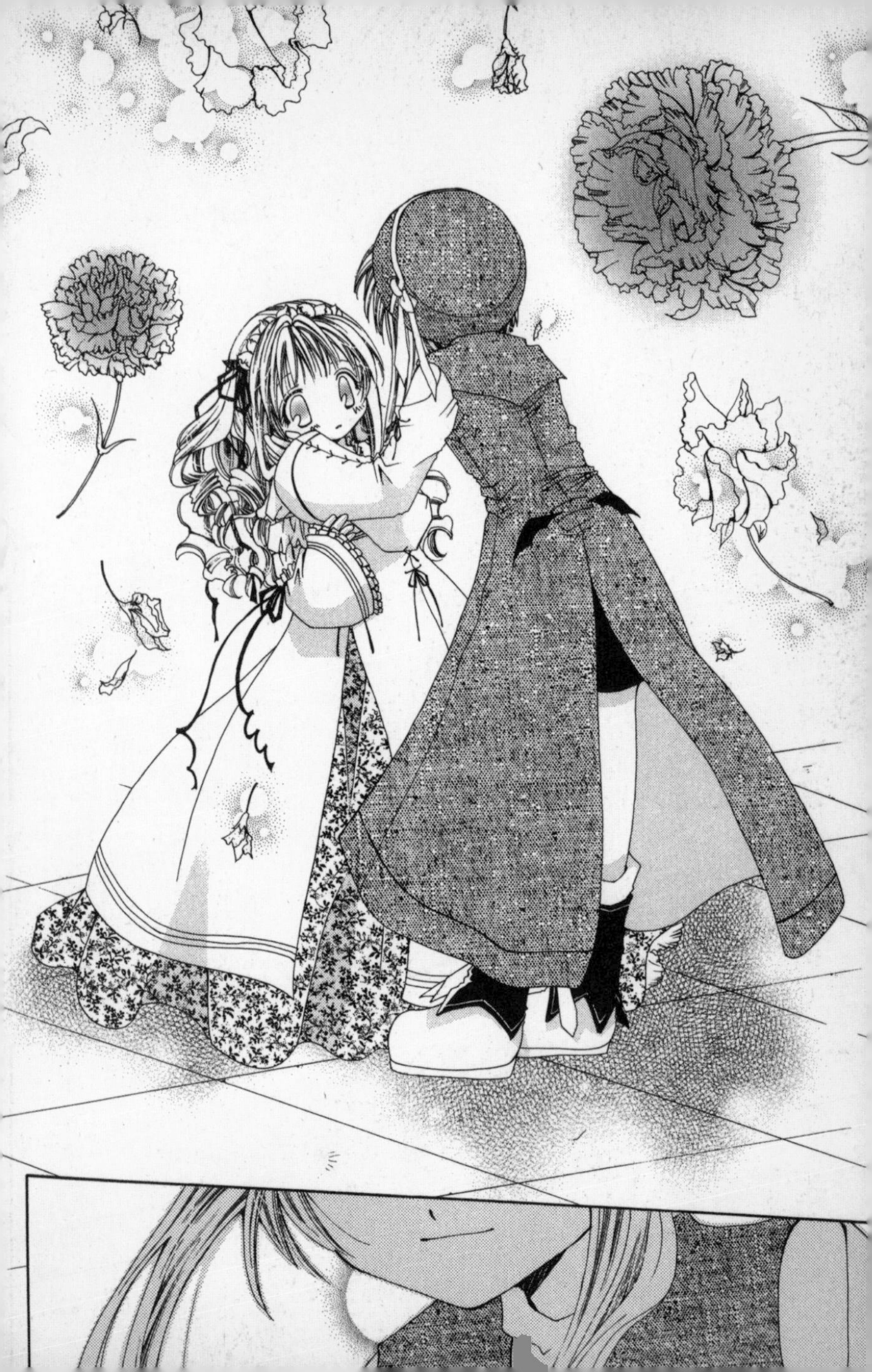

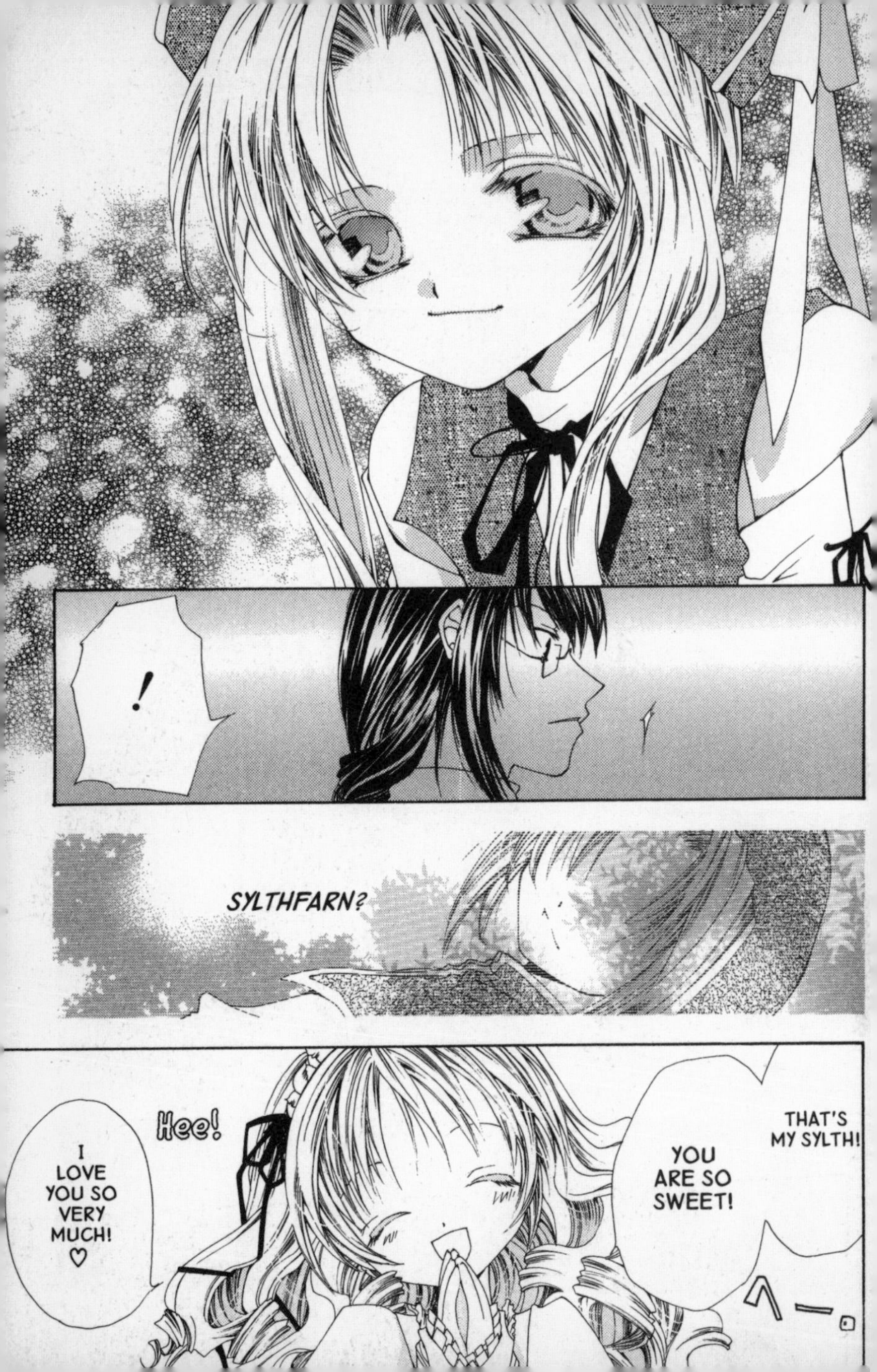
!
SYLTHFARN?
THAT'S MY SYLTH!
YOU ARE SO SWEET!
Hee!
I LOVE YOU SO VERY MUCH! ♡

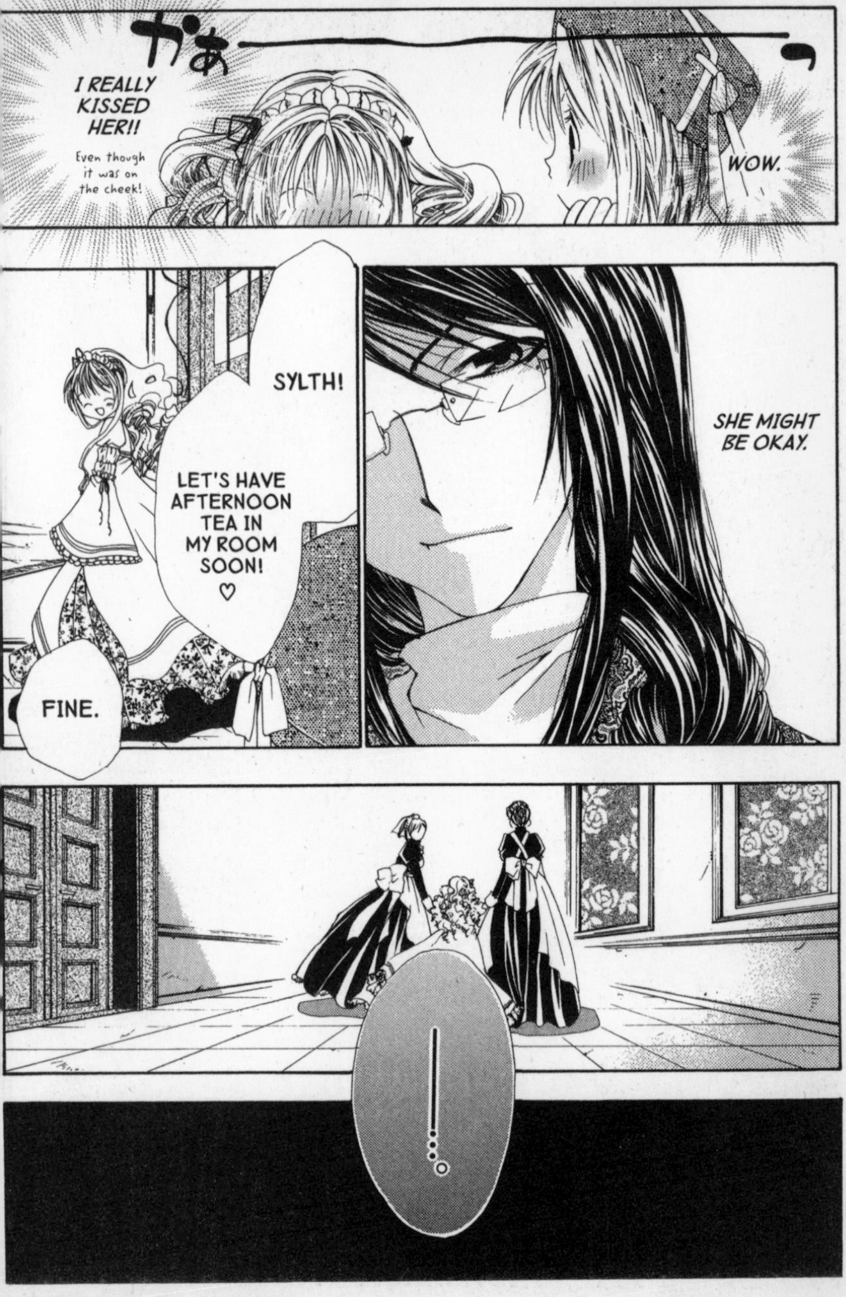
がぁーーーっ
WOW.
I REALLY KISSED HER!!
Even though it was on the cheek!
SHE MIGHT BE OKAY.
SYLTH!
LET'S HAVE AFTERNOON TEA IN MY ROOM SOON! ♡
FINE.
!...

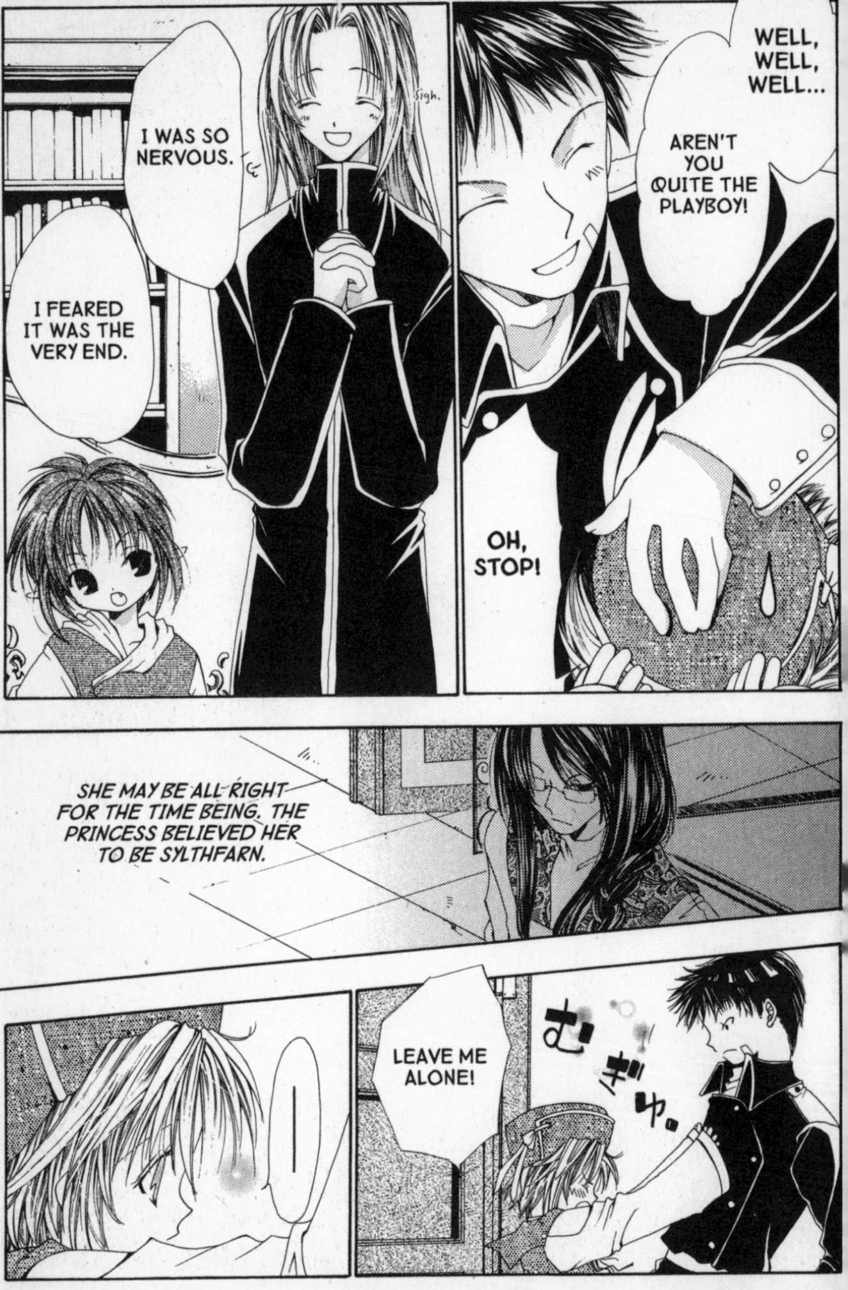
WELL, WELL, WELL...
AREN'T YOU QUITE THE PLAYBOY!
OH, STOP!
Sigh.
I WAS SO NERVOUS.
I FEARED IT WAS THE VERY END.
SHE MAY BE ALL RIGHT FOR THE TIME BEING. THE PRINCESS BELIEVED HER TO BE SYLTHFARN.
むぎゅ。
LEAVE ME ALONE!

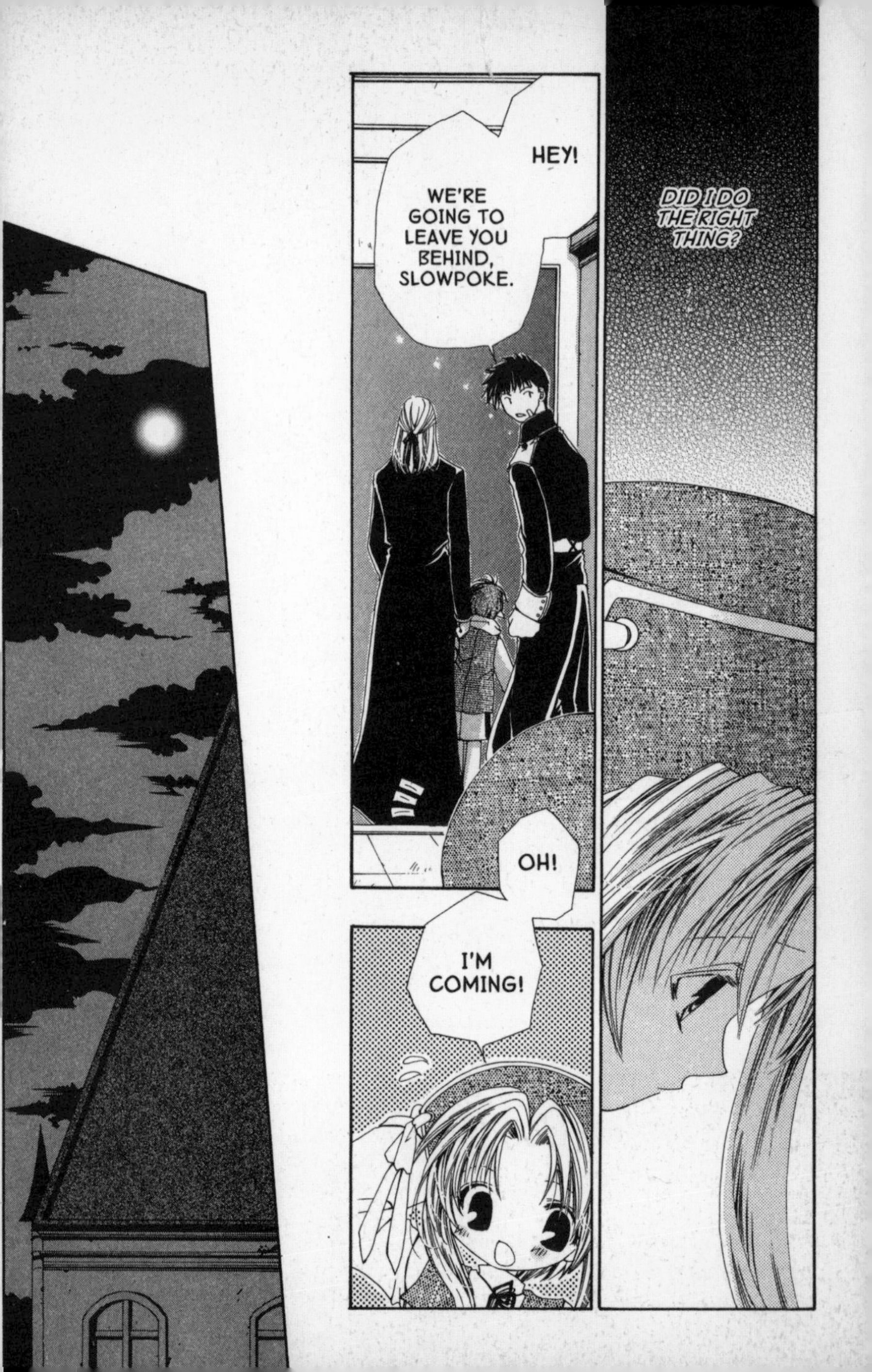
DID I DO THE RIGHT THING?
HEY!
WE'RE GOING TO LEAVE YOU BEHIND, SLOWPOKE.
OH!
I'M COMING!

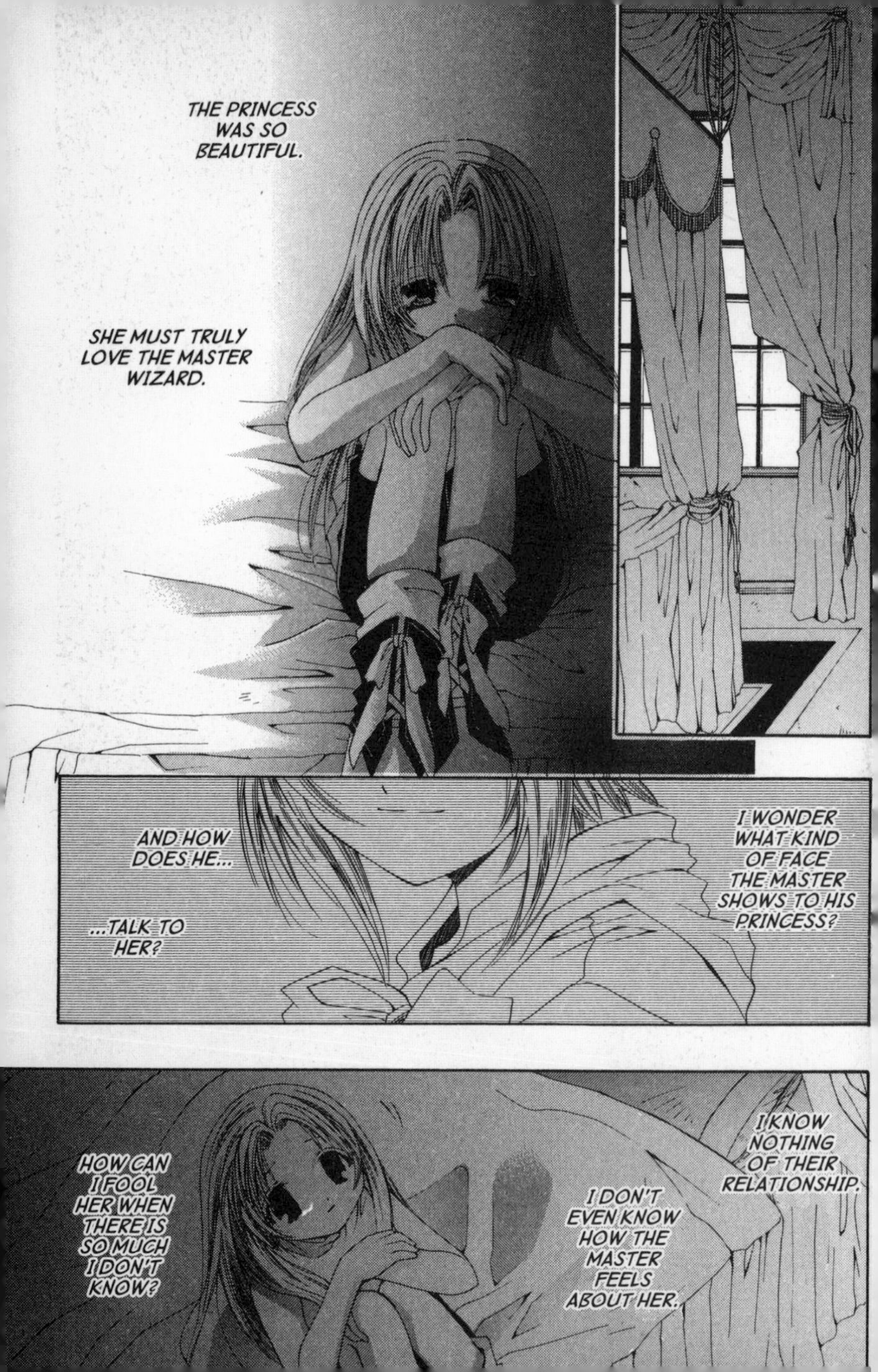
THE PRINCESS WAS SO BEAUTIFUL.
SHE MUST TRULY LOVE THE MASTER WIZARD.
I WONDER WHAT KIND OF FACE THE MASTER SHOWS TO HIS PRINCESS?
AND HOW DOES HE...
...TALK TO HER?
I KNOW NOTHING OF THEIR RELATIONSHIP.
I DON'T EVEN KNOW HOW THE MASTER FEELS ABOUT HER.
HOW CAN I FOOL HER WHEN THERE IS SO MUCH I DON'T KNOW?

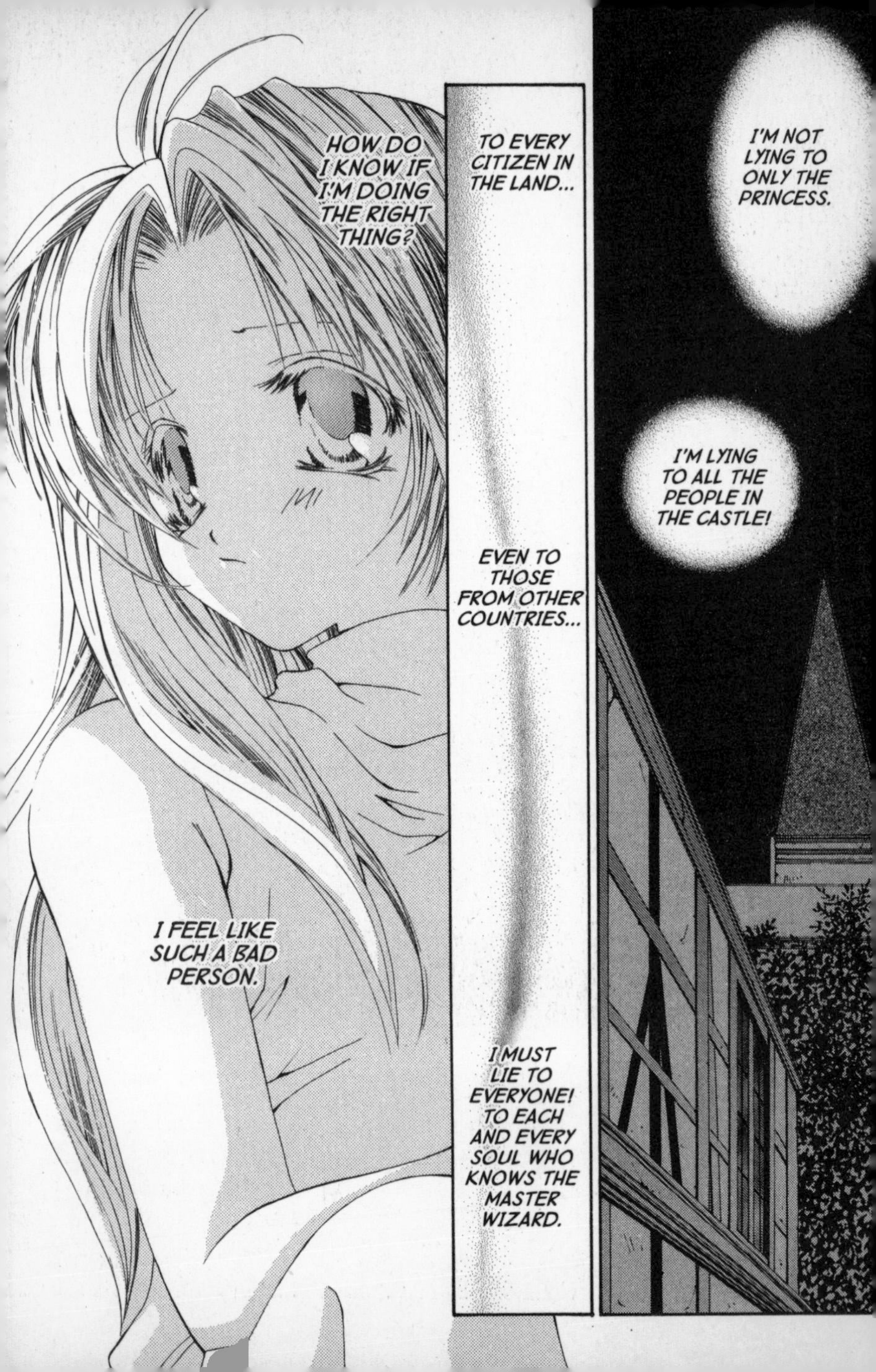
I'M NOT LYING TO ONLY THE PRINCESS.
I'M LYING TO ALL THE PEOPLE IN THE CASTLE!
TO EVERY CITIZEN IN THE LAND...
EVEN TO THOSE FROM OTHER COUNTRIES...
I MUST LIE TO EVERYONE! TO EACH AND EVERY SOUL WHO KNOWS THE MASTER WIZARD.
HOW DO I KNOW IF I'M DOING THE RIGHT THING?
I FEEL LIKE SUCH A BAD PERSON.

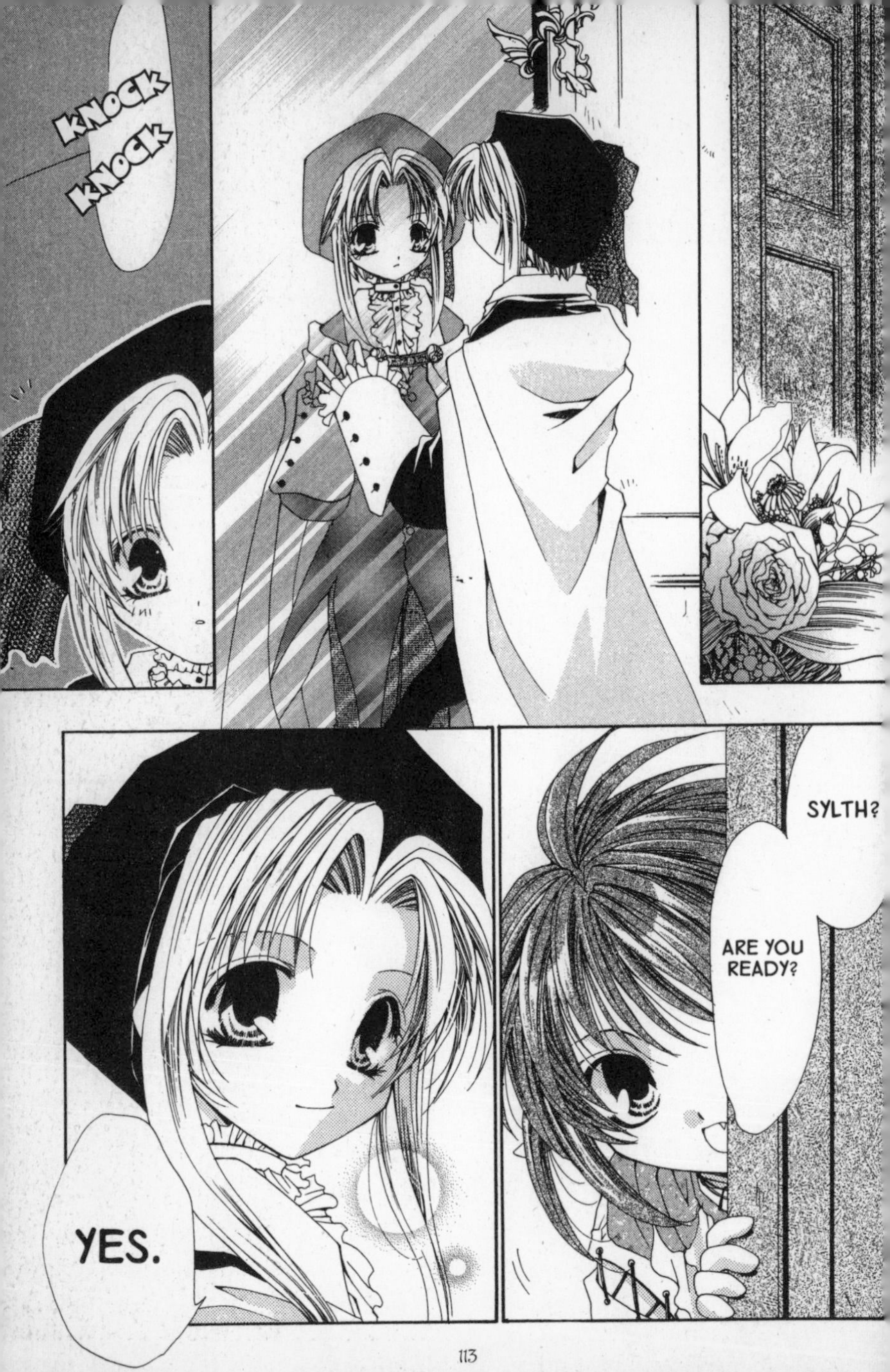
KNOCK KNOCK
SYLTH?
ARE YOU READY?
YES.

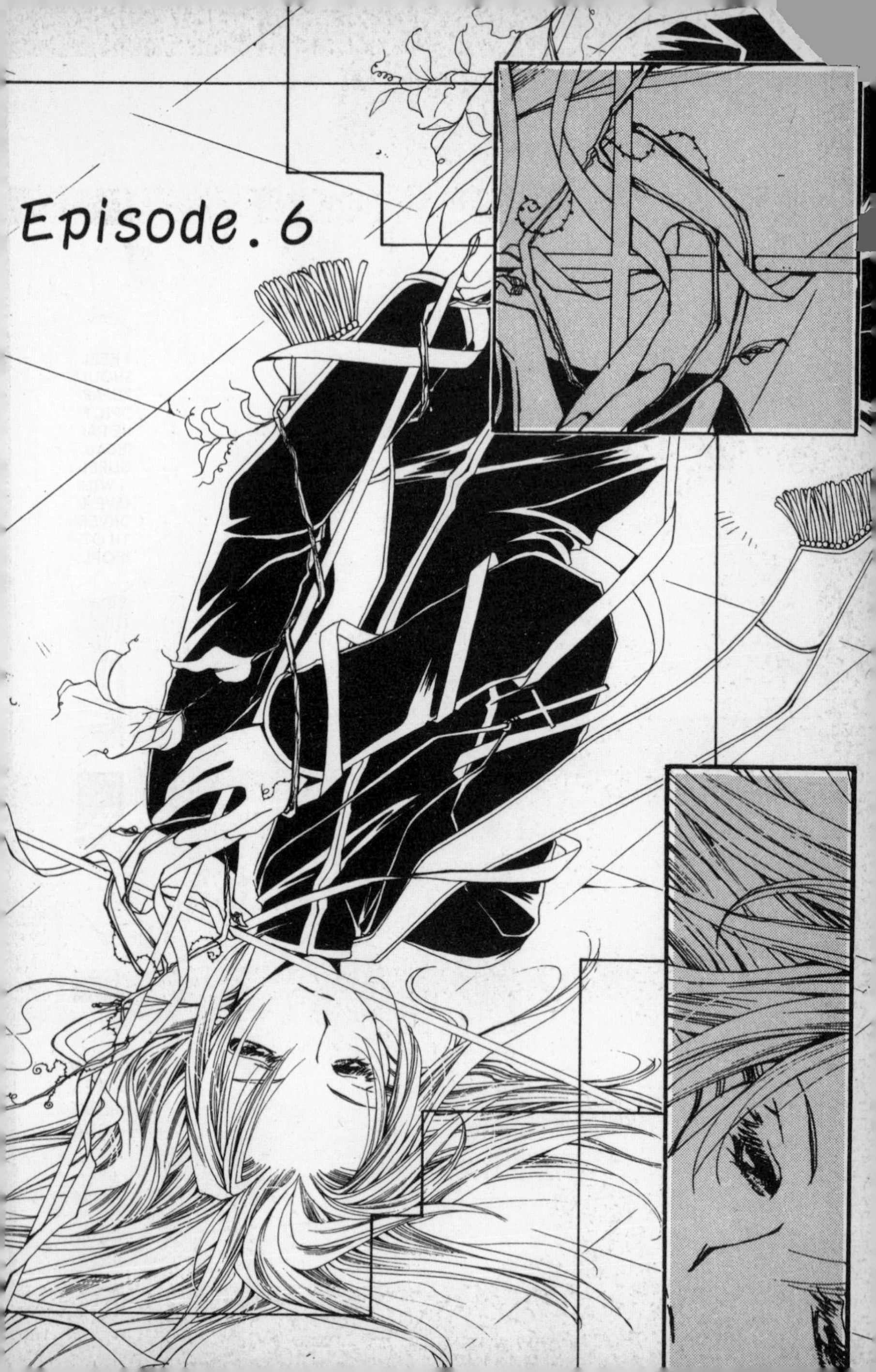
Episode. 6

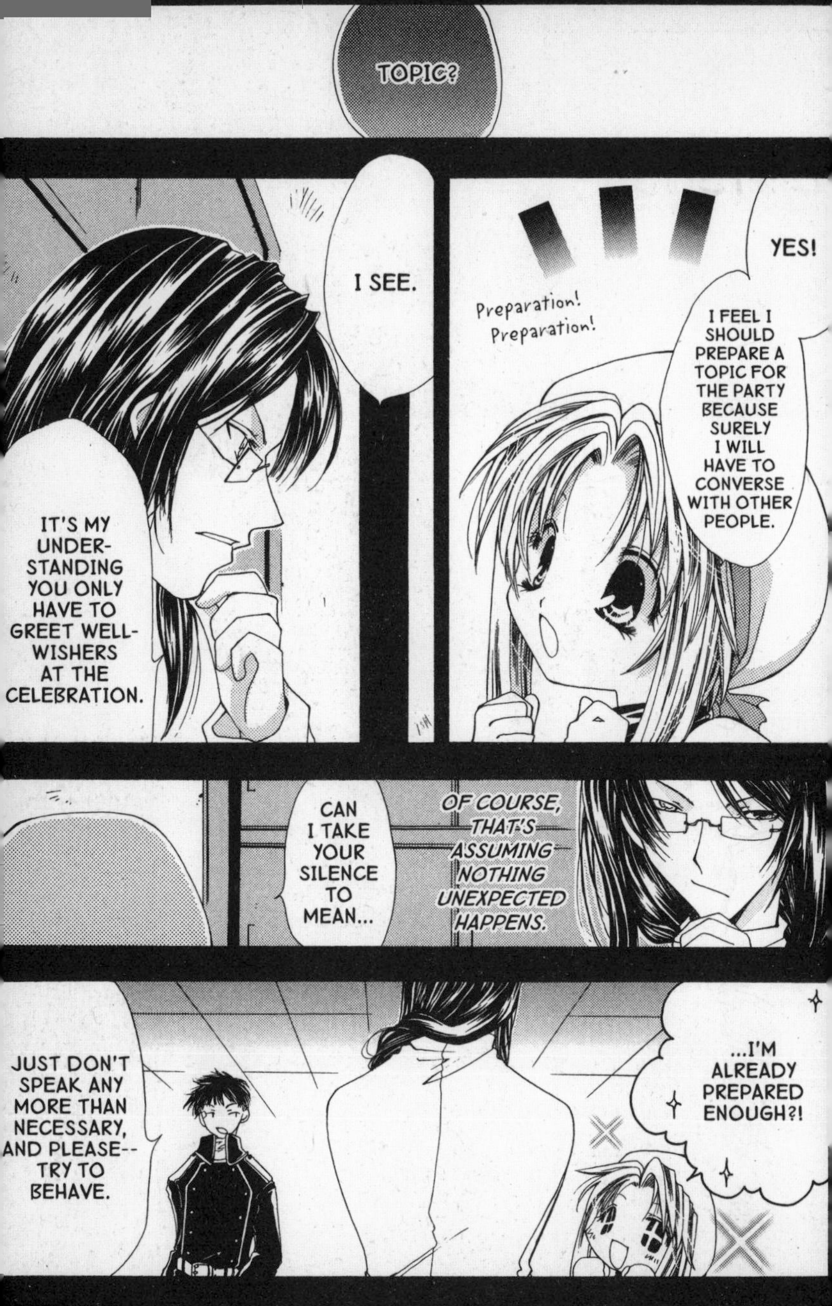
TOPIC?
YES!
I FEEL I SHOULD PREPARE A TOPIC FOR THE PARTY BECAUSE SURELY I WILL HAVE TO CONVERSE WITH OTHER PEOPLE.
Preparation! Preparation!
I SEE.
IT'S MY UNDER-STANDING YOU ONLY HAVE TO GREET WELL-WISHERS AT THE CELEBRATION.
OF COURSE, THAT'S ASSUMING NOTHING UNEXPECTED HAPPENS.
CAN I TAKE YOUR SILENCE TO MEAN...
...I'M ALREADY PREPARED ENOUGH?!
JUST DON'T SPEAK ANY MORE THAN NECESSARY, AND PLEASE--TRY TO BEHAVE.

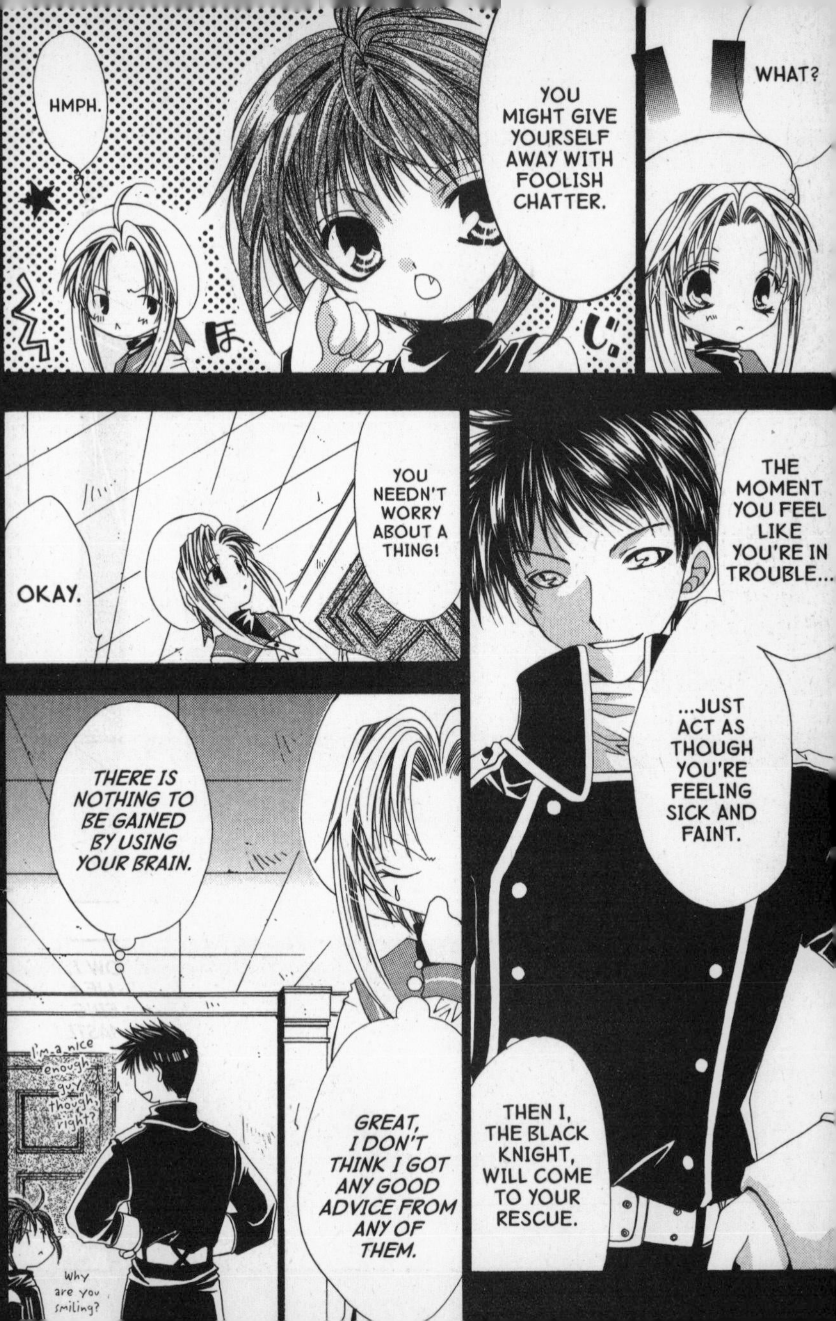
WHAT?
YOU MIGHT GIVE YOURSELF AWAY WITH FOOLISH CHATTER.
じ
ほ
HMPH.
THE MOMENT YOU FEEL LIKE YOU'RE IN TROUBLE...
...JUST ACT AS THOUGH YOU'RE FEELING SICK AND FAINT.
THEN I, THE BLACK KNIGHT, WILL COME TO YOUR RESCUE.
YOU NEEDN'T WORRY ABOUT A THING!
OKAY.
THERE IS NOTHING TO BE GAINED BY USING YOUR BRAIN.
GREAT, I DON'T THINK I GOT ANY GOOD ADVICE FROM ANY OF THEM.
I'm a nice enough guy, though, right?
Why are you smiling?

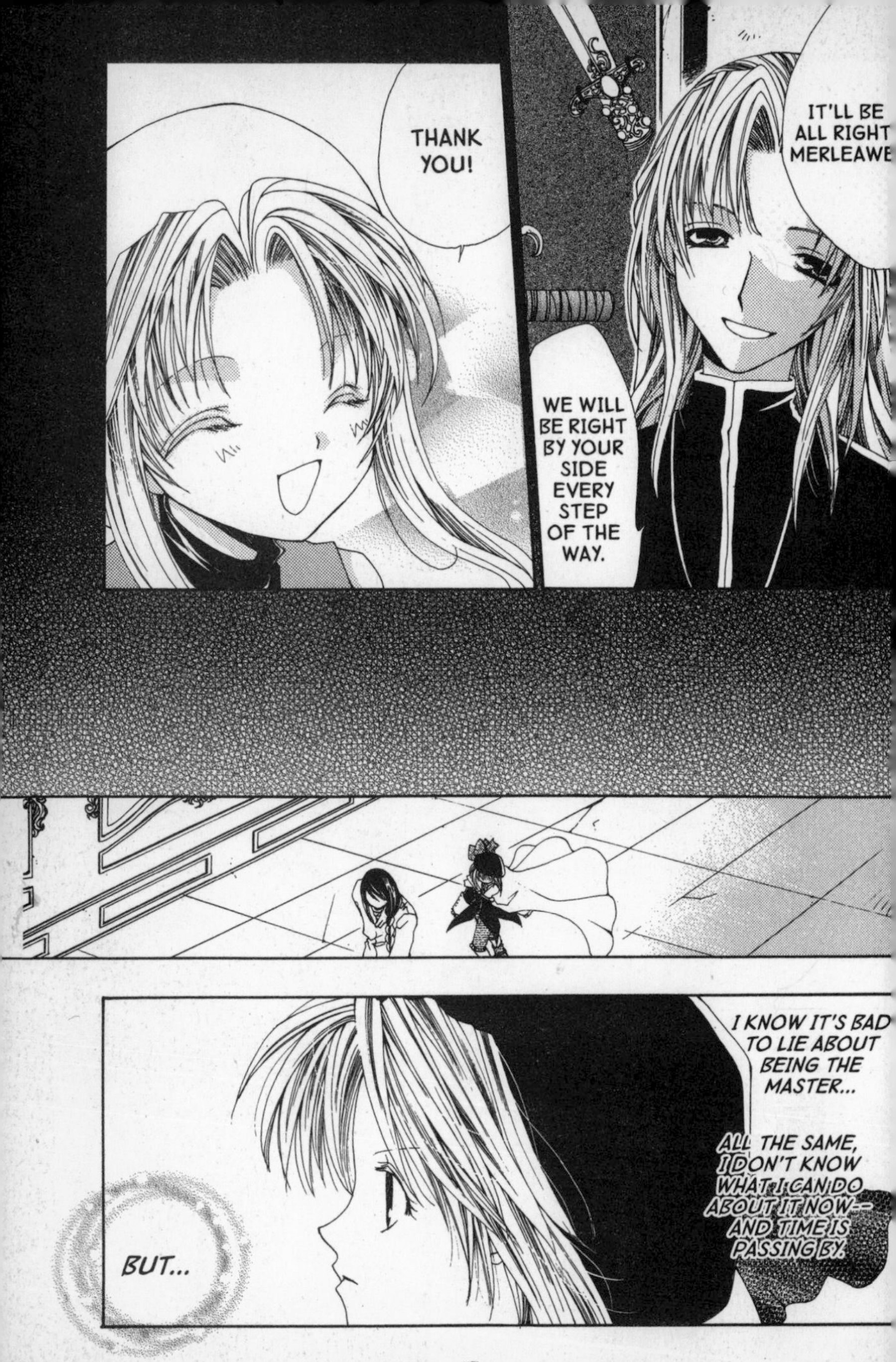
IT'LL BE ALL RIGHT MERLEAWE
WE WILL BE RIGHT BY YOUR SIDE EVERY STEP OF THE WAY.
THANK YOU!
I KNOW IT'S BAD TO LIE ABOUT BEING THE MASTER...
ALL THE SAME, I DON'T KNOW WHAT I CAN DO ABOUT IT NOW— AND TIME IS PASSING BY.
BUT...

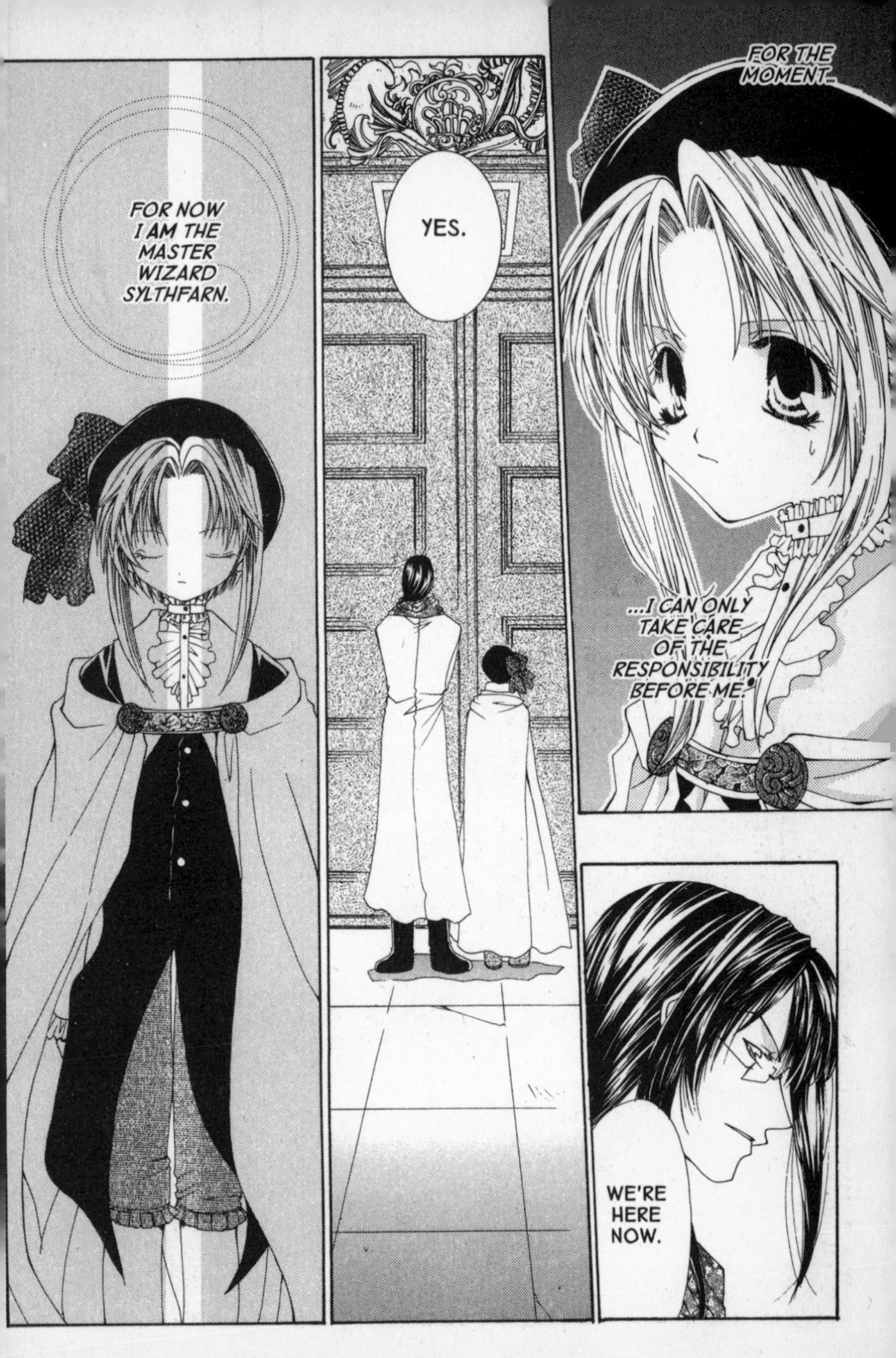
FOR THE MOMENT...
...I CAN ONLY TAKE CARE OF THE RESPONSIBILITY BEFORE ME.
WE'RE HERE NOW.
YES.
FOR NOW I AM THE MASTER WIZARD SYLTHFARN.

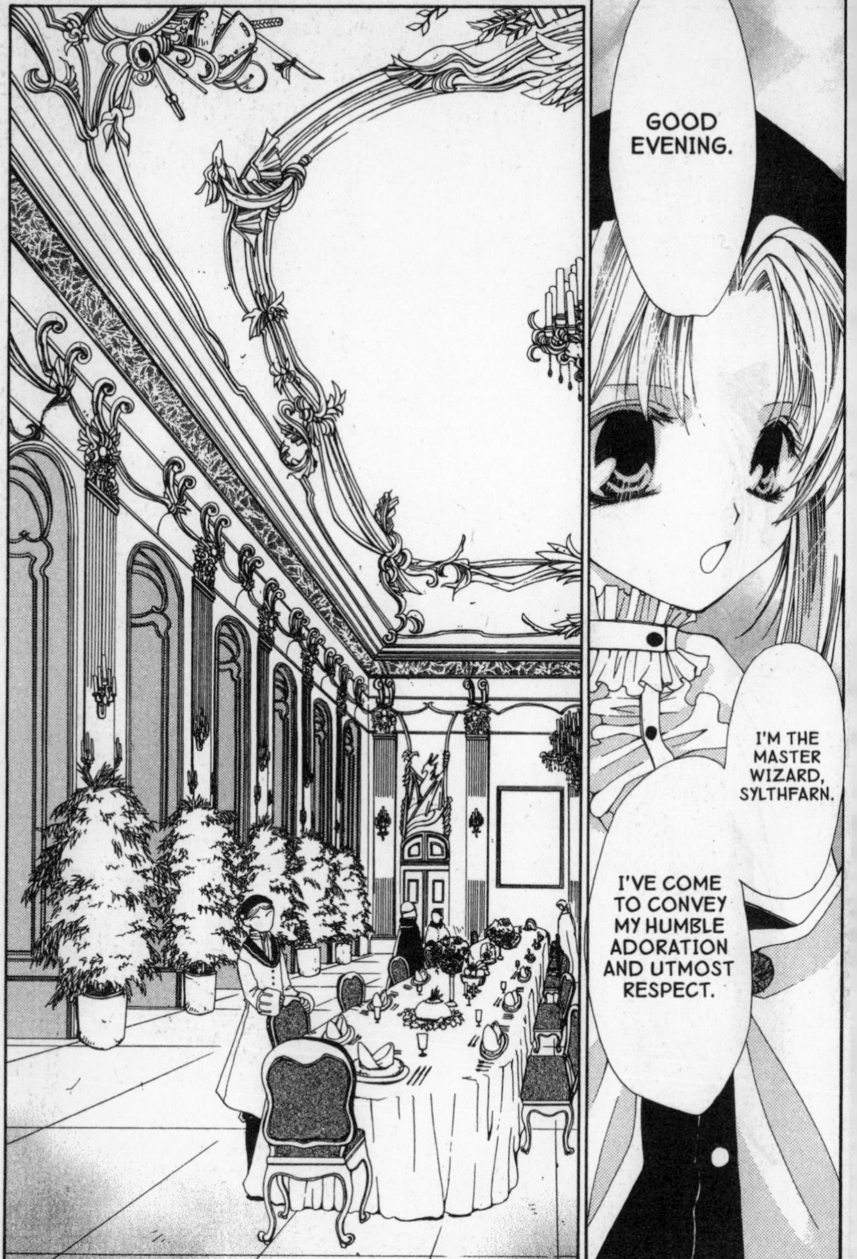
GOOD EVENING.
I'M THE MASTER WIZARD, SYLTHFARN.
I'VE COME TO CONVEY MY HUMBLE ADORATION AND UTMOST RESPECT.

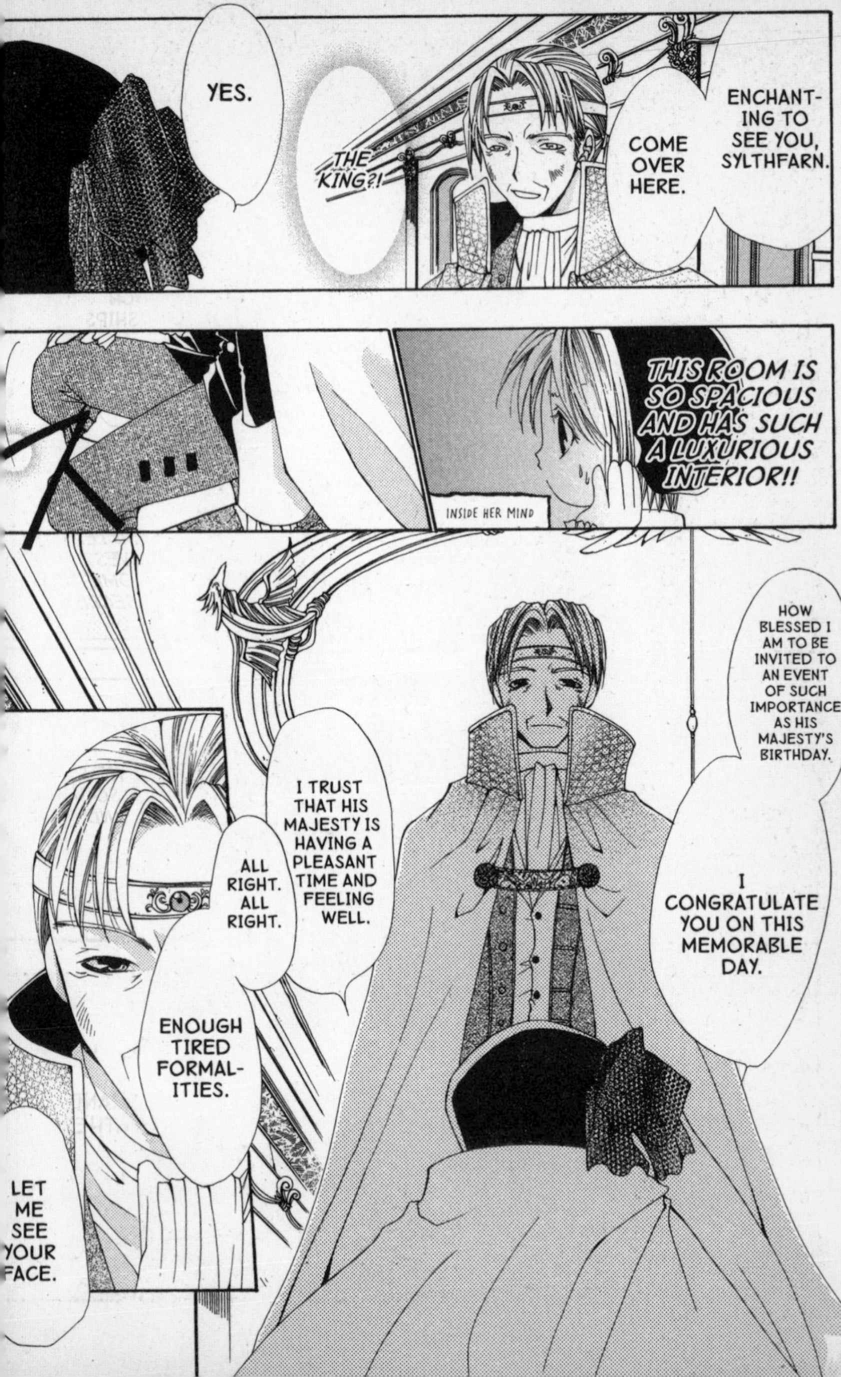
ENCHANT-ING TO SEE YOU, SYLTHFARN.
COME OVER HERE.
THE KING?!
YES.
THIS ROOM IS SO SPACIOUS AND HAS SUCH A LUXURIOUS INTERIOR!!
INSIDE HER MIND
...
HOW BLESSED I AM TO BE INVITED TO AN EVENT OF SUCH IMPORTANCE AS HIS MAJESTY'S BIRTHDAY.
I CONGRATULATE YOU ON THIS MEMORABLE DAY.
I TRUST THAT HIS MAJESTY IS HAVING A PLEASANT TIME AND FEELING WELL.
ALL RIGHT. ALL RIGHT.
ENOUGH TIRED FORMAL-ITIES.
LET ME SEE YOUR FACE.

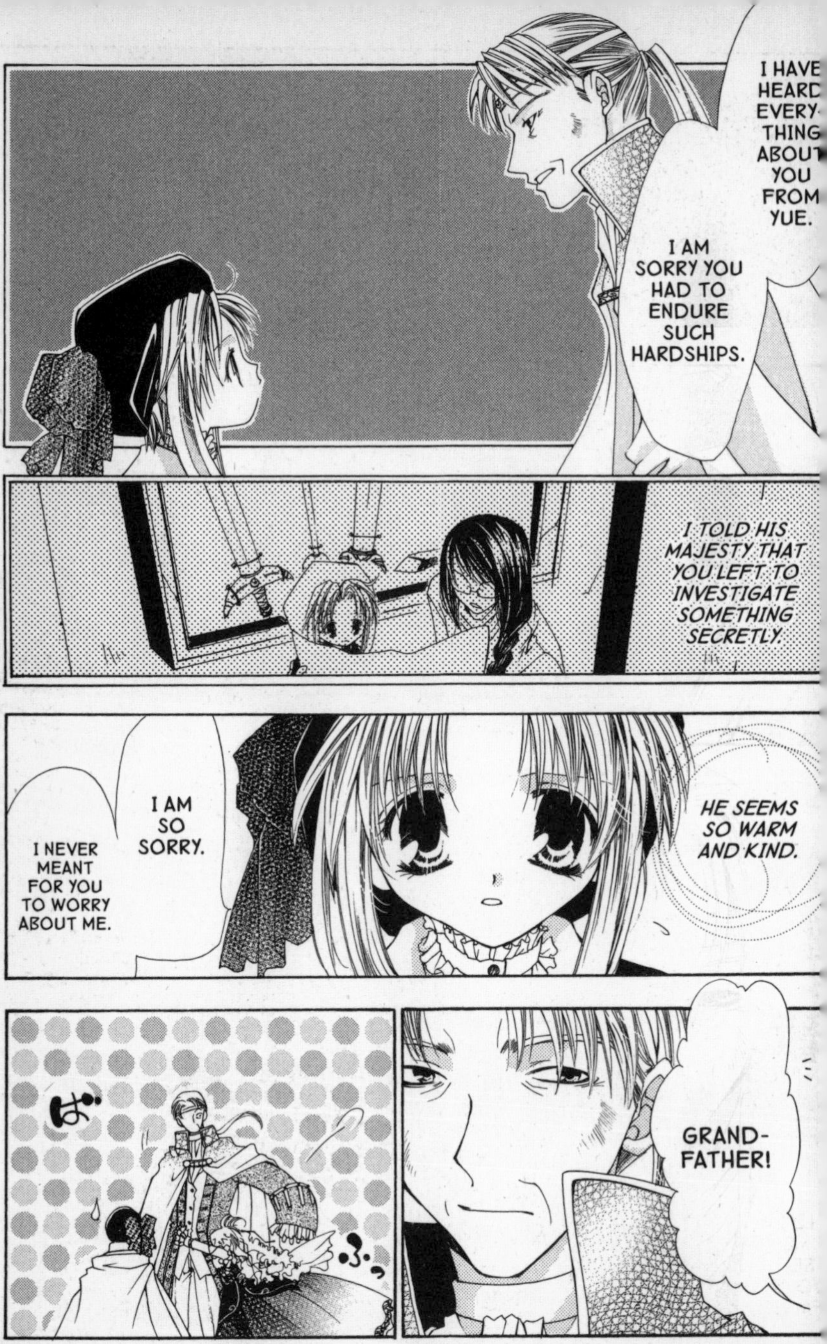
I HAVE HEARD EVERYTHING ABOUT YOU FROM YUE.
I AM SORRY YOU HAD TO ENDURE SUCH HARDSHIPS.
I TOLD HIS MAJESTY THAT YOU LEFT TO INVESTIGATE SOMETHING SECRETLY.
HE SEEMS SO WARM AND KIND.
I AM SO SORRY.
I NEVER MEANT FOR YOU TO WORRY ABOUT ME.
GRAND-FATHER!
ぱ
ふっ

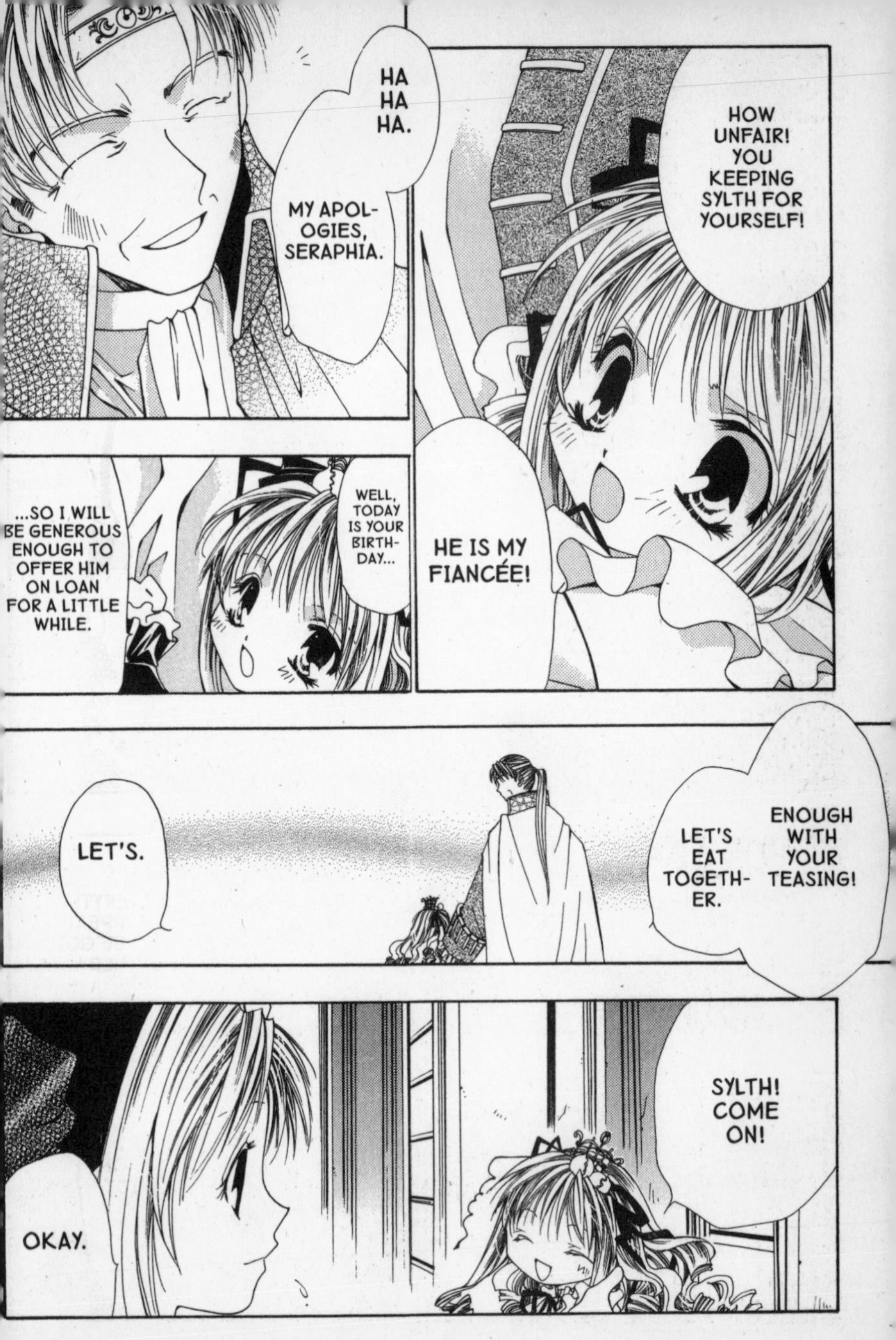
HOW UNFAIR! YOU KEEPING SYLTH FOR YOURSELF!
HA HA HA.
MY APOL-OGIES, SERAPHIA.
HE IS MY FIANCÉE!
WELL, TODAY IS YOUR BIRTH-DAY...
...SO I WILL BE GENEROUS ENOUGH TO OFFER HIM ON LOAN FOR A LITTLE WHILE.
ENOUGH WITH YOUR TEASING!
LET'S EAT TOGETH-ER.
LET'S.
SYLTH! COME ON!
OKAY.

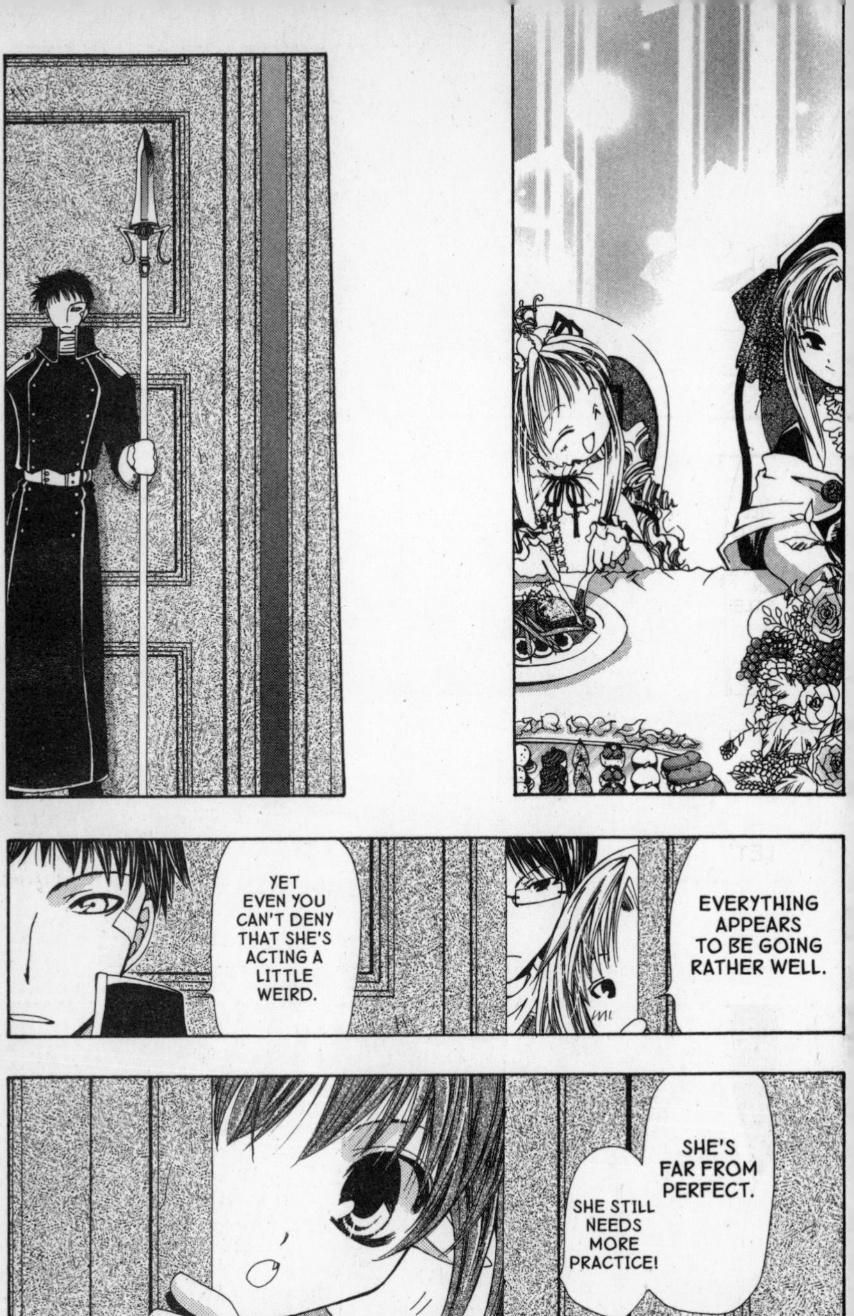
EVERYTHING APPEARS TO BE GOING RATHER WELL.
YET EVEN YOU CAN'T DENY THAT SHE'S ACTING A LITTLE WEIRD.
SHE'S FAR FROM PERFECT.
SHE STILL NEEDS MORE PRACTICE!

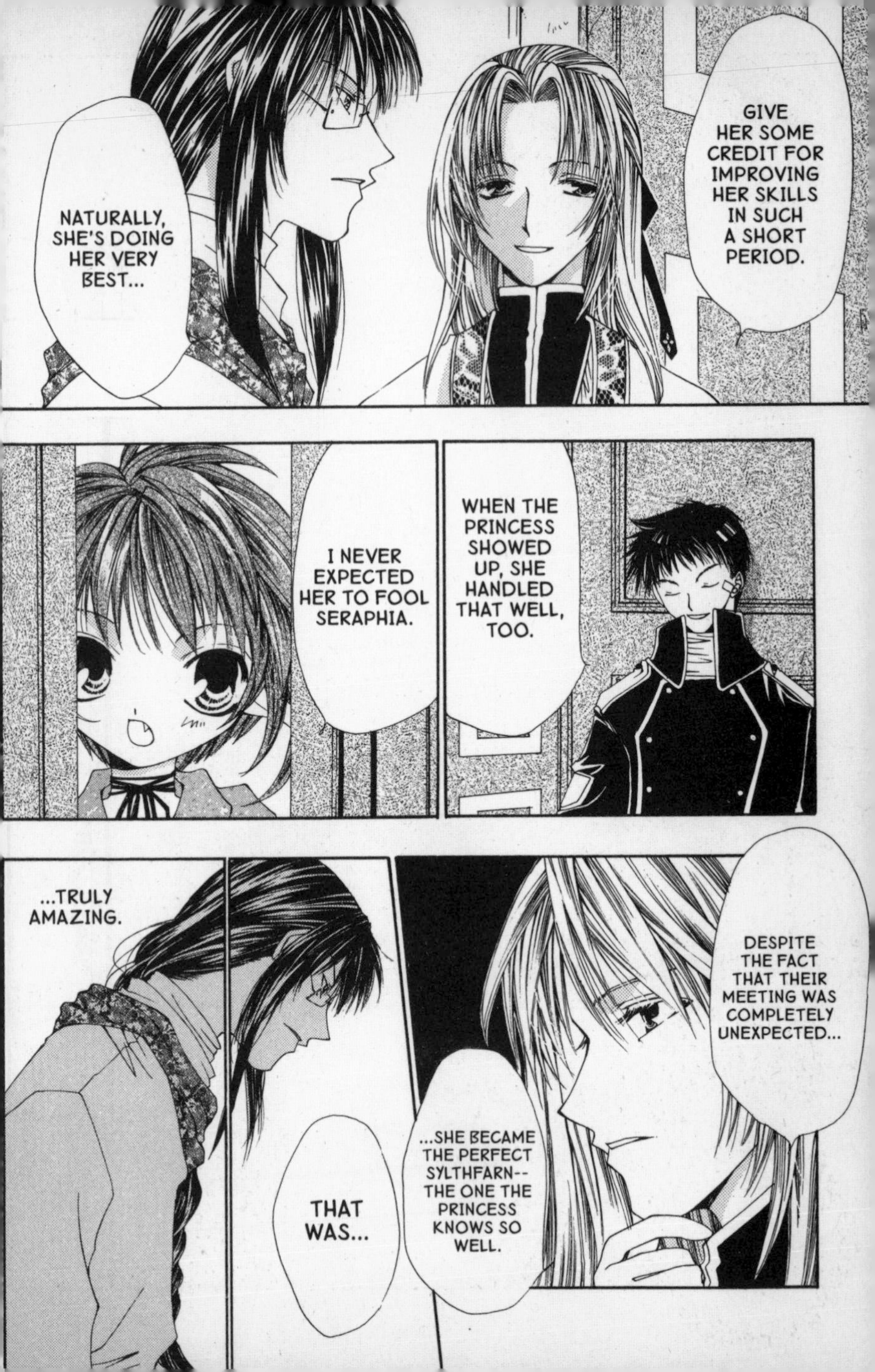
GIVE HER SOME CREDIT FOR IMPROVING HER SKILLS IN SUCH A SHORT PERIOD.
NATURALLY, SHE'S DOING HER VERY BEST...
WHEN THE PRINCESS SHOWED UP, SHE HANDLED THAT WELL, TOO.
I NEVER EXPECTED HER TO FOOL SERAPHIA.
DESPITE THE FACT THAT THEIR MEETING WAS COMPLETELY UNEXPECTED...
...SHE BECAME THE PERFECT SYLTHFARN--THE ONE THE PRINCESS KNOWS SO WELL.
THAT WAS...
...TRULY AMAZING.

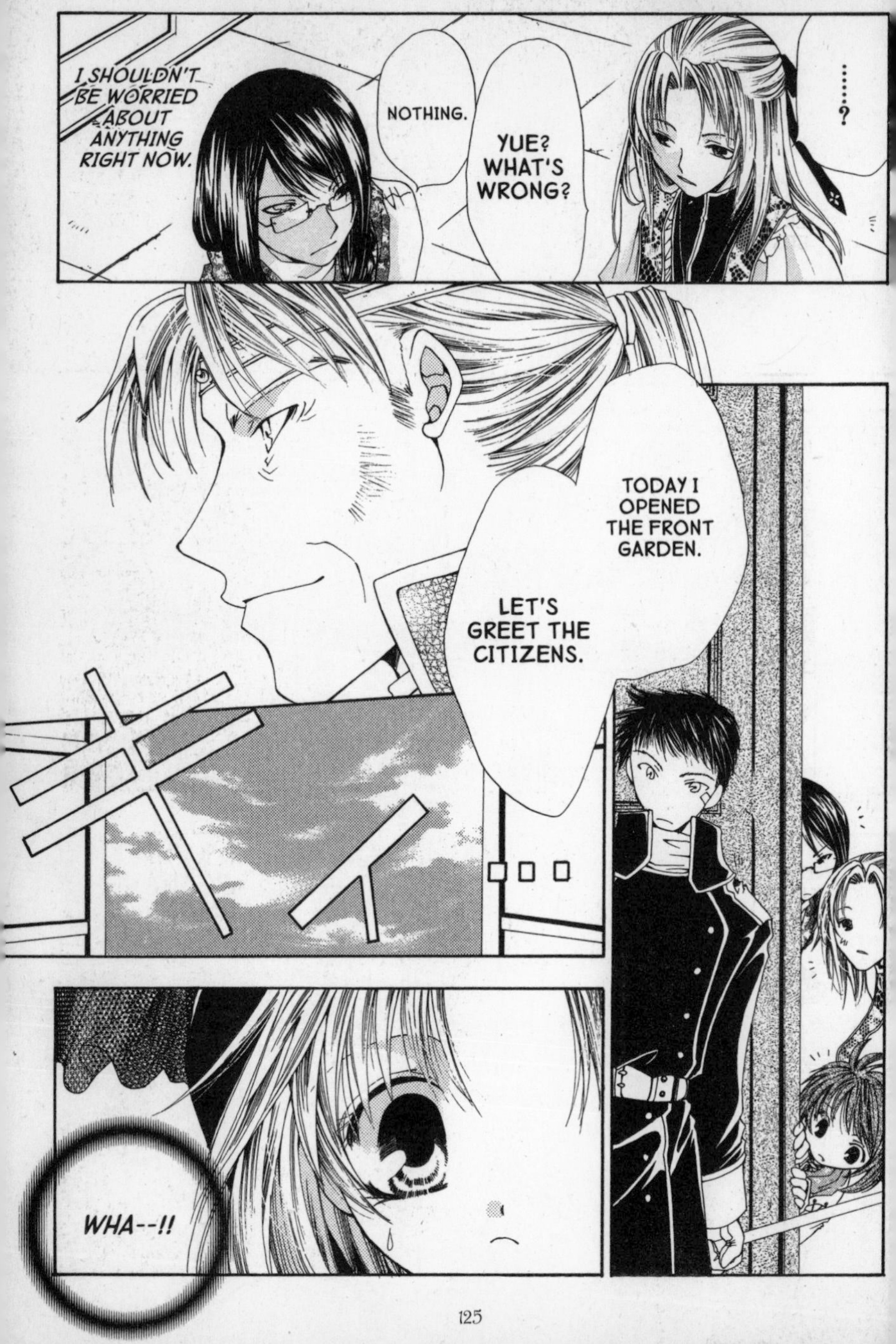
……?
YUE? WHAT'S WRONG?
NOTHING.
I SHOULDN'T BE WORRIED ABOUT ANYTHING RIGHT NOW.
TODAY I OPENED THE FRONT GARDEN.
LET'S GREET THE CITIZENS.
WHA--!!

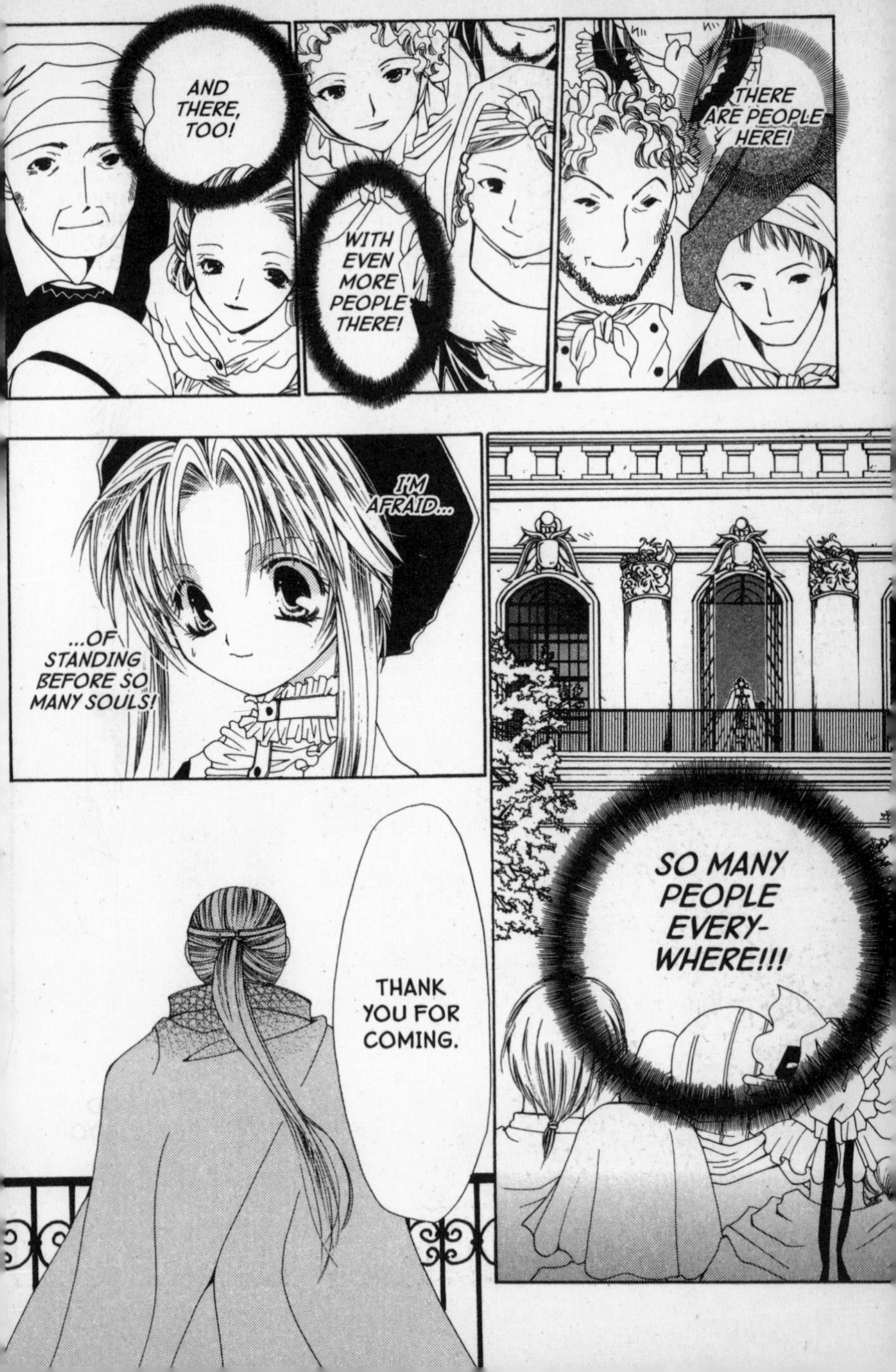
THERE ARE PEOPLE HERE!
WITH EVEN MORE PEOPLE THERE!
AND THERE, TOO!
SO MANY PEOPLE EVERY-WHERE!!!
I'M AFRAID...
...OF STANDING BEFORE SO MANY SOULS!
THANK YOU FOR COMING.

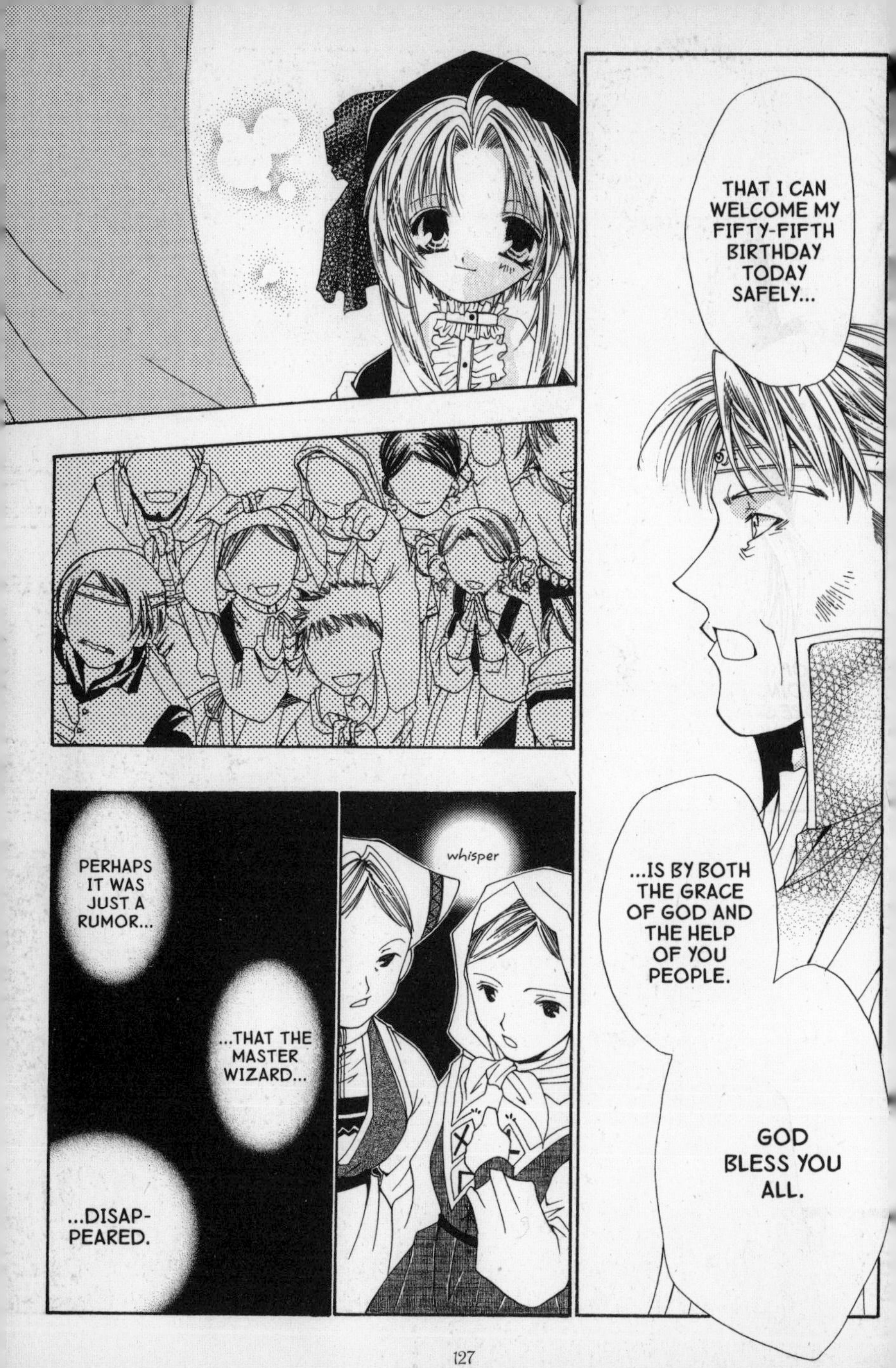
THAT I CAN WELCOME MY FIFTY-FIFTH BIRTHDAY TODAY SAFELY...
...IS BY BOTH THE GRACE OF GOD AND THE HELP OF YOU PEOPLE.
GOD BLESS YOU ALL.
whisper
PERHAPS IT WAS JUST A RUMOR...
...THAT THE MASTER WIZARD...
...DISAP-PEARED.

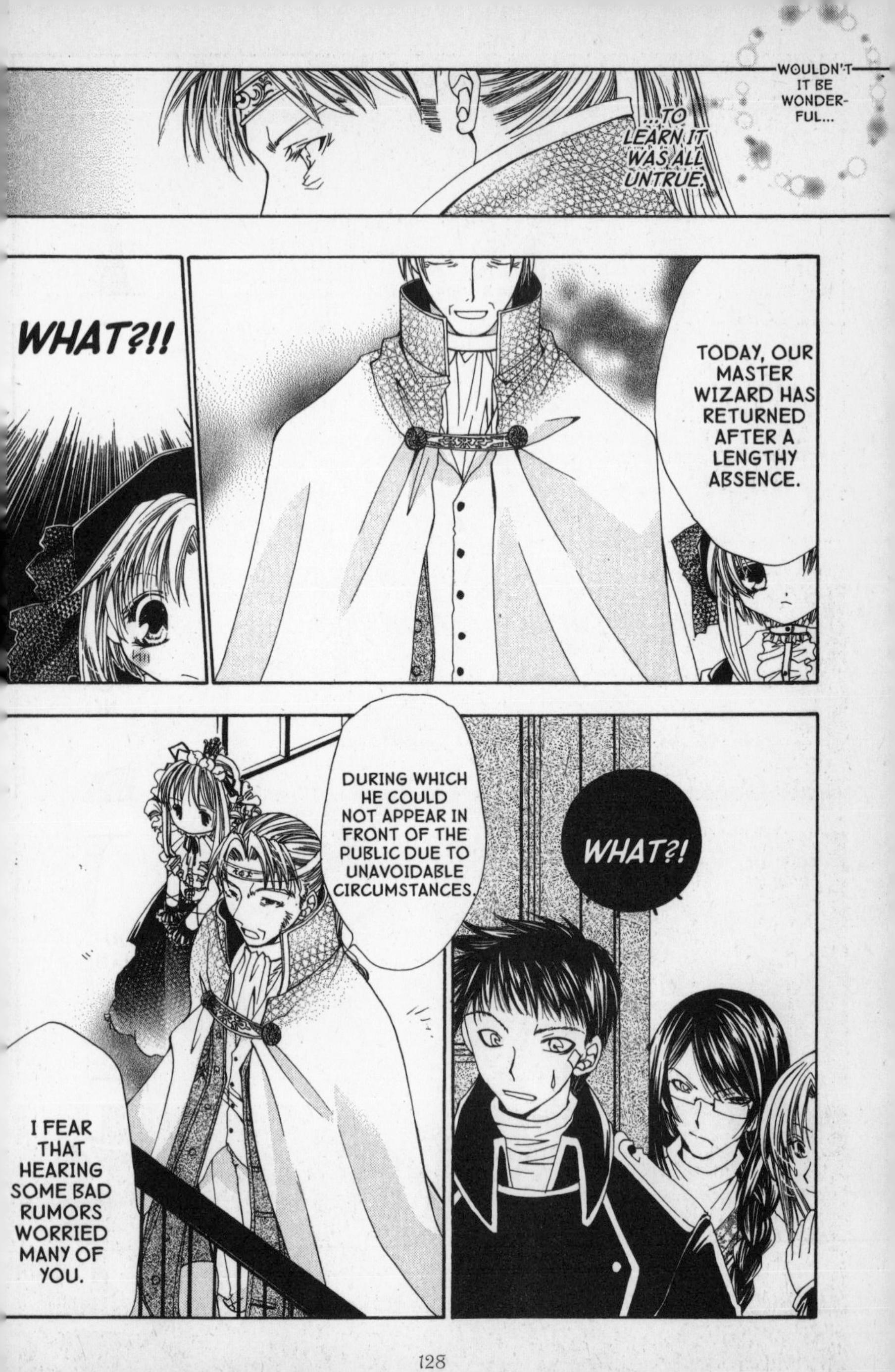
WOULDN'T IT BE WONDERFUL...
...TO LEARN IT WAS ALL UNTRUE.
TODAY, OUR MASTER WIZARD HAS RETURNED AFTER A LENGTHY ABSENCE.
WHAT?!!
WHAT?!
DURING WHICH HE COULD NOT APPEAR IN FRONT OF THE PUBLIC DUE TO UNAVOIDABLE CIRCUMSTANCES.
I FEAR THAT HEARING SOME BAD RUMORS WORRIED MANY OF YOU.

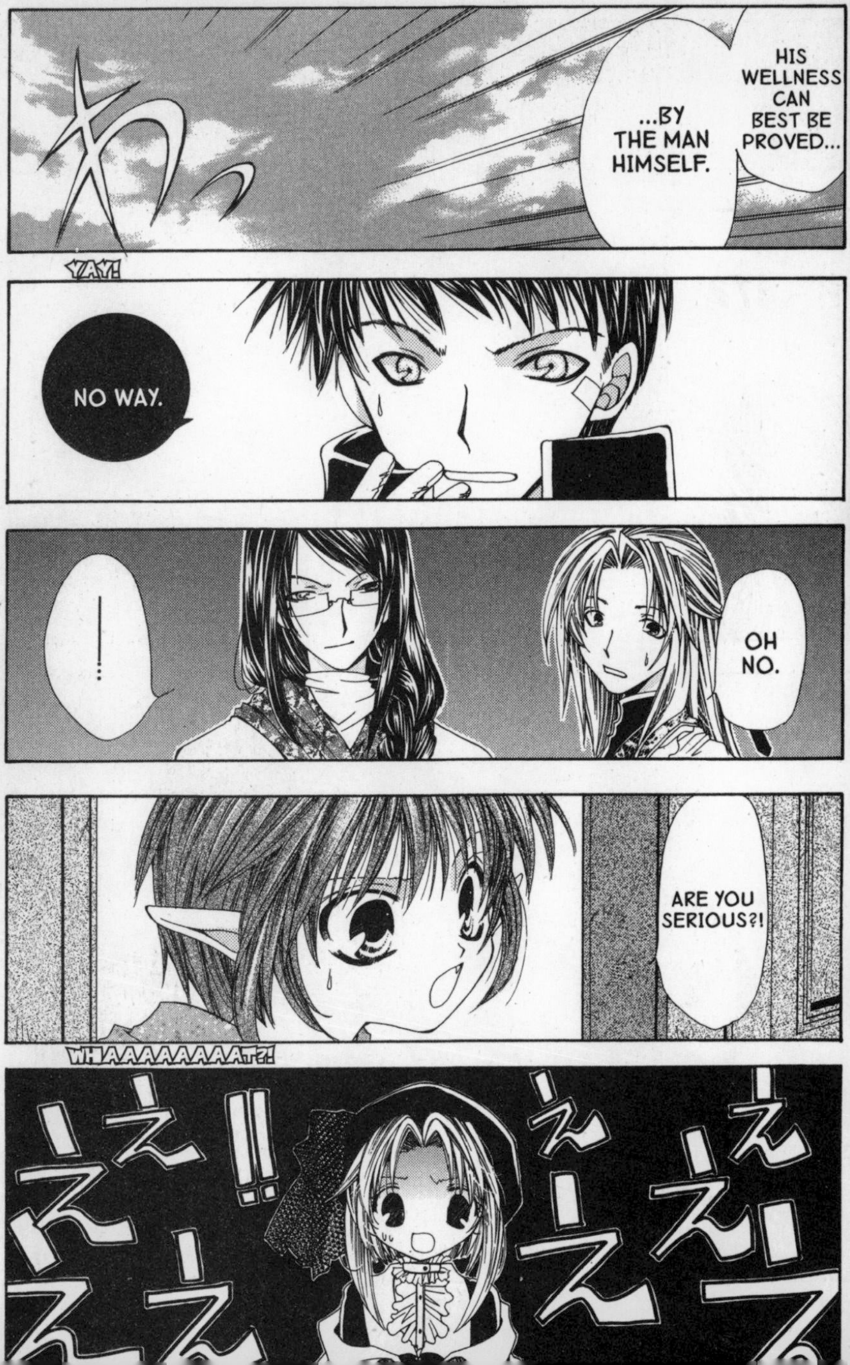
HIS WELLNESS CAN BEST BE PROVED...
...BY THE MAN HIMSELF.
YAY!
NO WAY.
OH NO.
!...
ARE YOU SERIOUS?!
WHAAAAAAAAAT?!

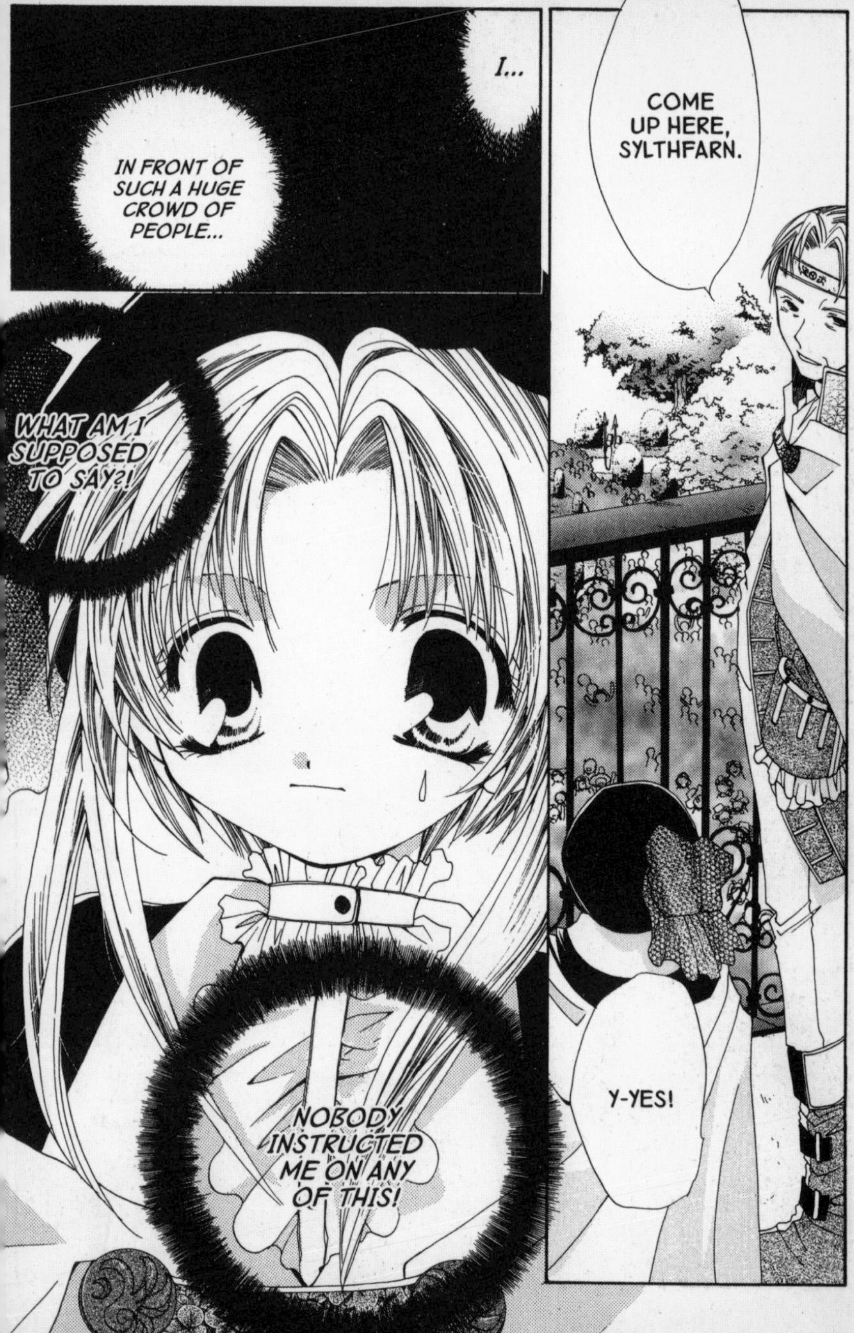
COME UP HERE, SYLTHFARN.
Y-YES!
I...
IN FRONT OF SUCH A HUGE CROWD OF PEOPLE...
WHAT AM I SUPPOSED TO SAY?!
NOBODY INSTRUCTED ME ON ANY OF THIS!

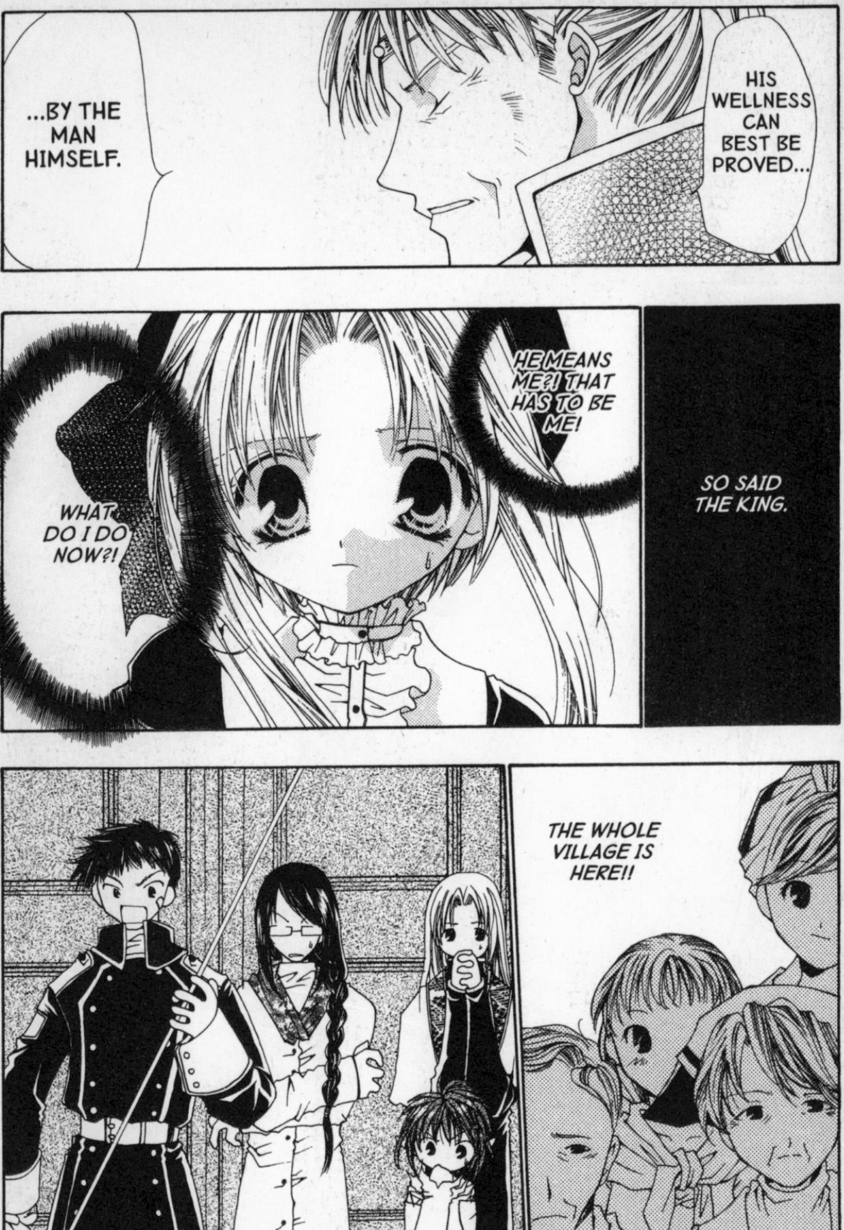
HIS WELLNESS CAN BEST BE PROVED...
...BY THE MAN HIMSELF.
SO SAID THE KING.
HE MEANS ME?! THAT HAS TO BE ME!
WHAT DO I DO NOW?!
THE WHOLE VILLAGE IS HERE!!

Episode. 7

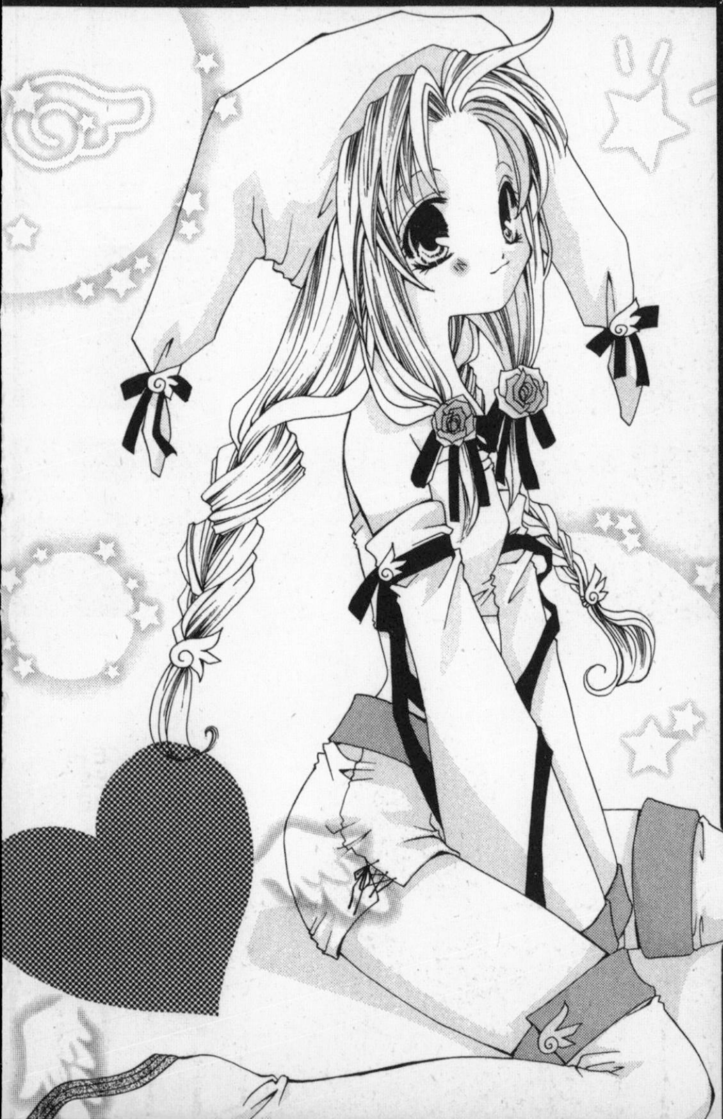

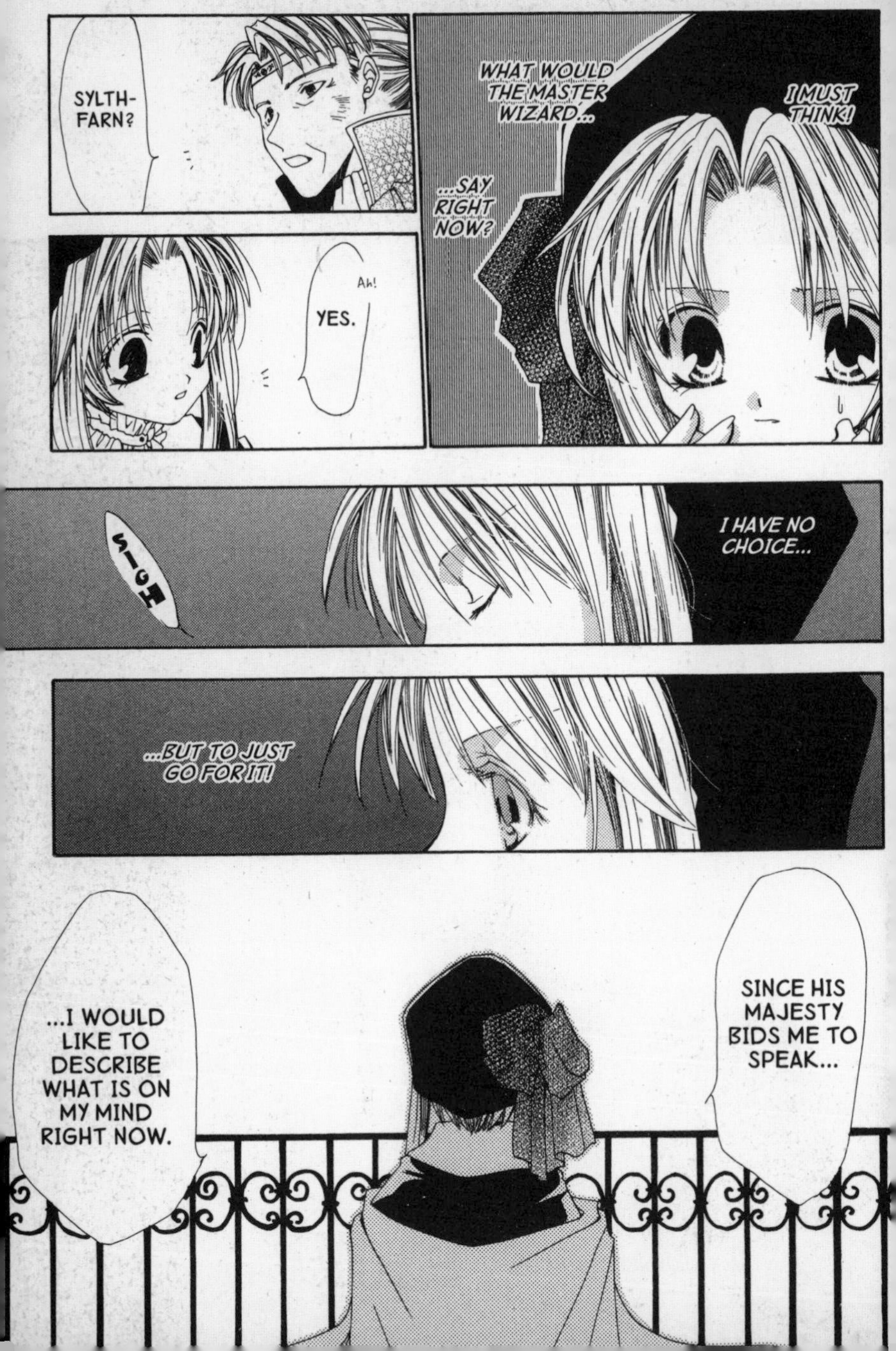
I MUST THINK!
WHAT WOULD THE MASTER WIZARD...
...SAY RIGHT NOW?
SYLTH-FARN?
Ah!
YES.
I HAVE NO CHOICE...
SIGH
...BUT TO JUST GO FOR IT!
SINCE HIS MAJESTY BIDS ME TO SPEAK...
...I WOULD LIKE TO DESCRIBE WHAT IS ON MY MIND RIGHT NOW.

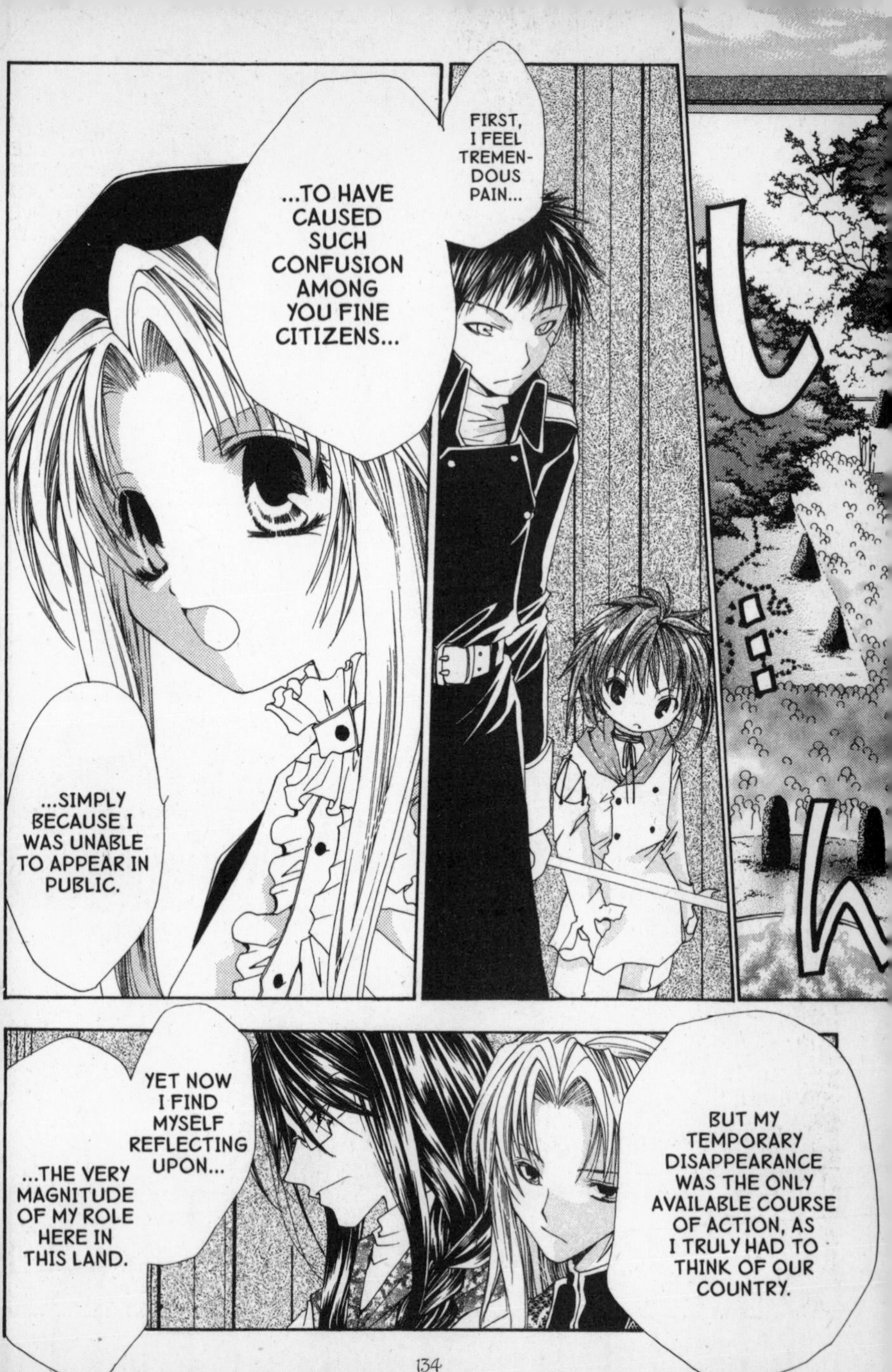
しん
FIRST, I FEEL TREMENDOUS PAIN...
...TO HAVE CAUSED SUCH CONFUSION AMONG YOU FINE CITIZENS...
...SIMPLY BECAUSE I WAS UNABLE TO APPEAR IN PUBLIC.
BUT MY TEMPORARY DISAPPEARANCE WAS THE ONLY AVAILABLE COURSE OF ACTION, AS I TRULY HAD TO THINK OF OUR COUNTRY.
YET NOW I FIND MYSELF REFLECTING UPON...
...THE VERY MAGNITUDE OF MY ROLE HERE IN THIS LAND.

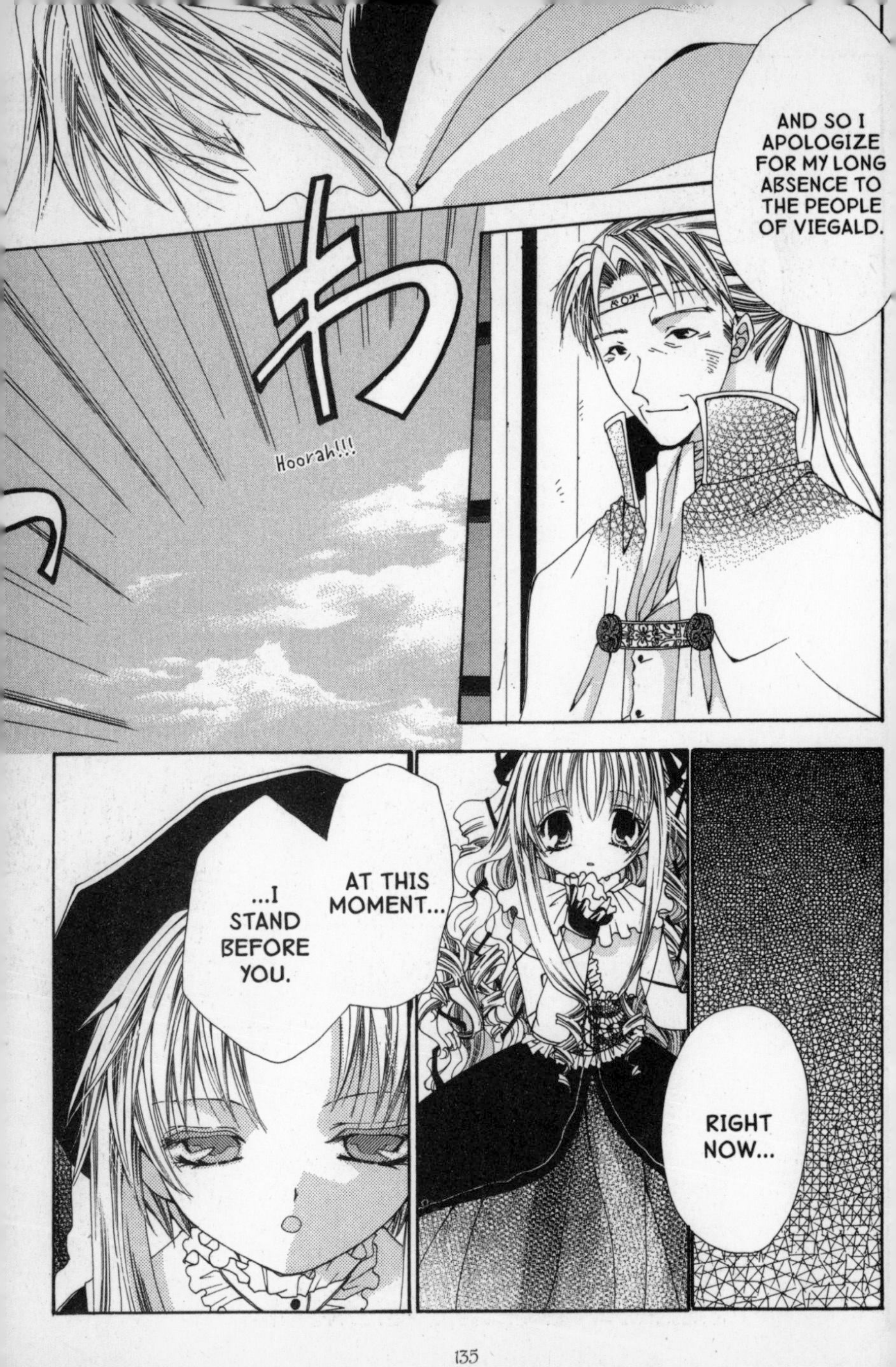
AND SO I APOLOGIZE FOR MY LONG ABSENCE TO THE PEOPLE OF VIEGALD.
わっ
Hoorah!!!
RIGHT NOW...
AT THIS MOMENT...
...I STAND BEFORE YOU.

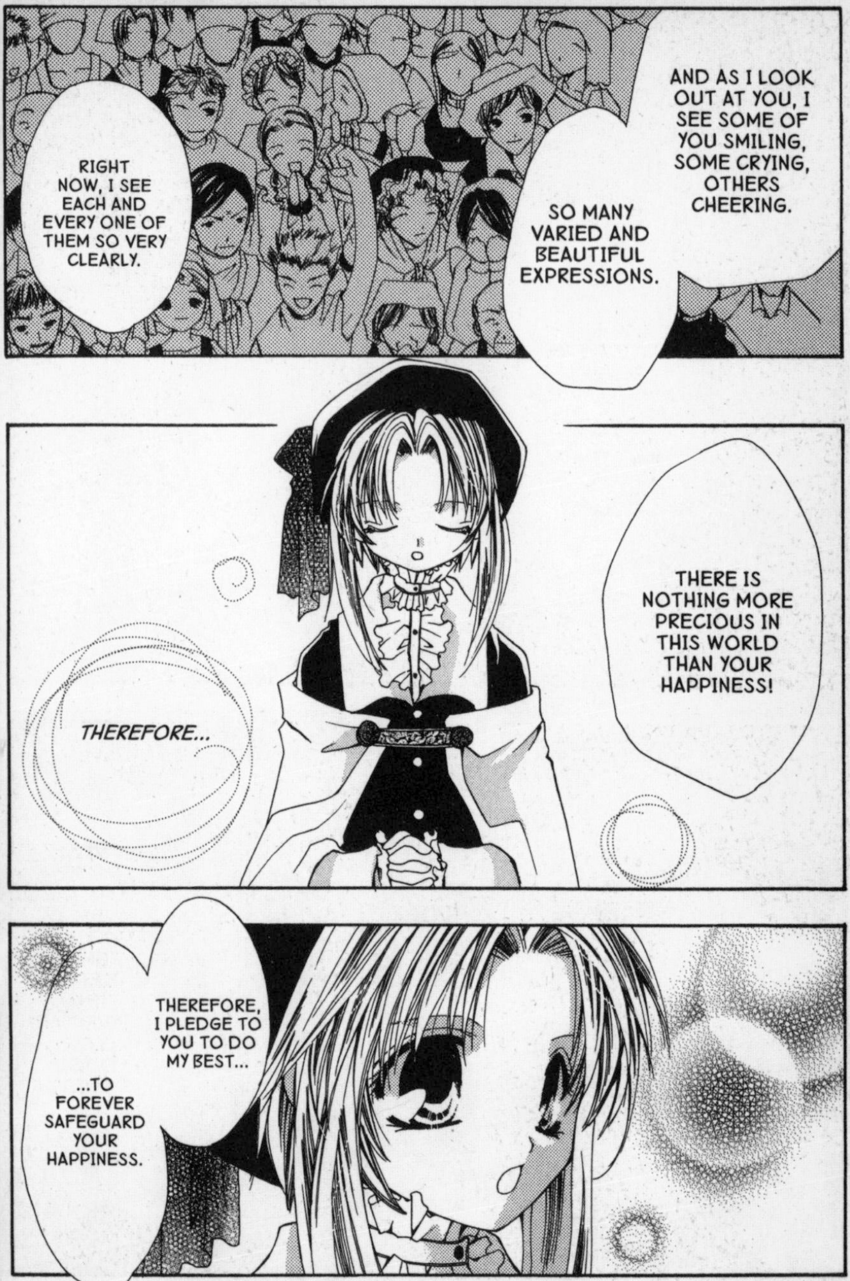
AND AS I LOOK OUT AT YOU, I SEE SOME OF YOU SMILING, SOME CRYING, OTHERS CHEERING.
SO MANY VARIED AND BEAUTIFUL EXPRESSIONS.
RIGHT NOW, I SEE EACH AND EVERY ONE OF THEM SO VERY CLEARLY.
THERE IS NOTHING MORE PRECIOUS IN THIS WORLD THAN YOUR HAPPINESS!
THEREFORE...
THEREFORE, I PLEDGE TO YOU TO DO MY BEST...
...TO FOREVER SAFEGUARD YOUR HAPPINESS.

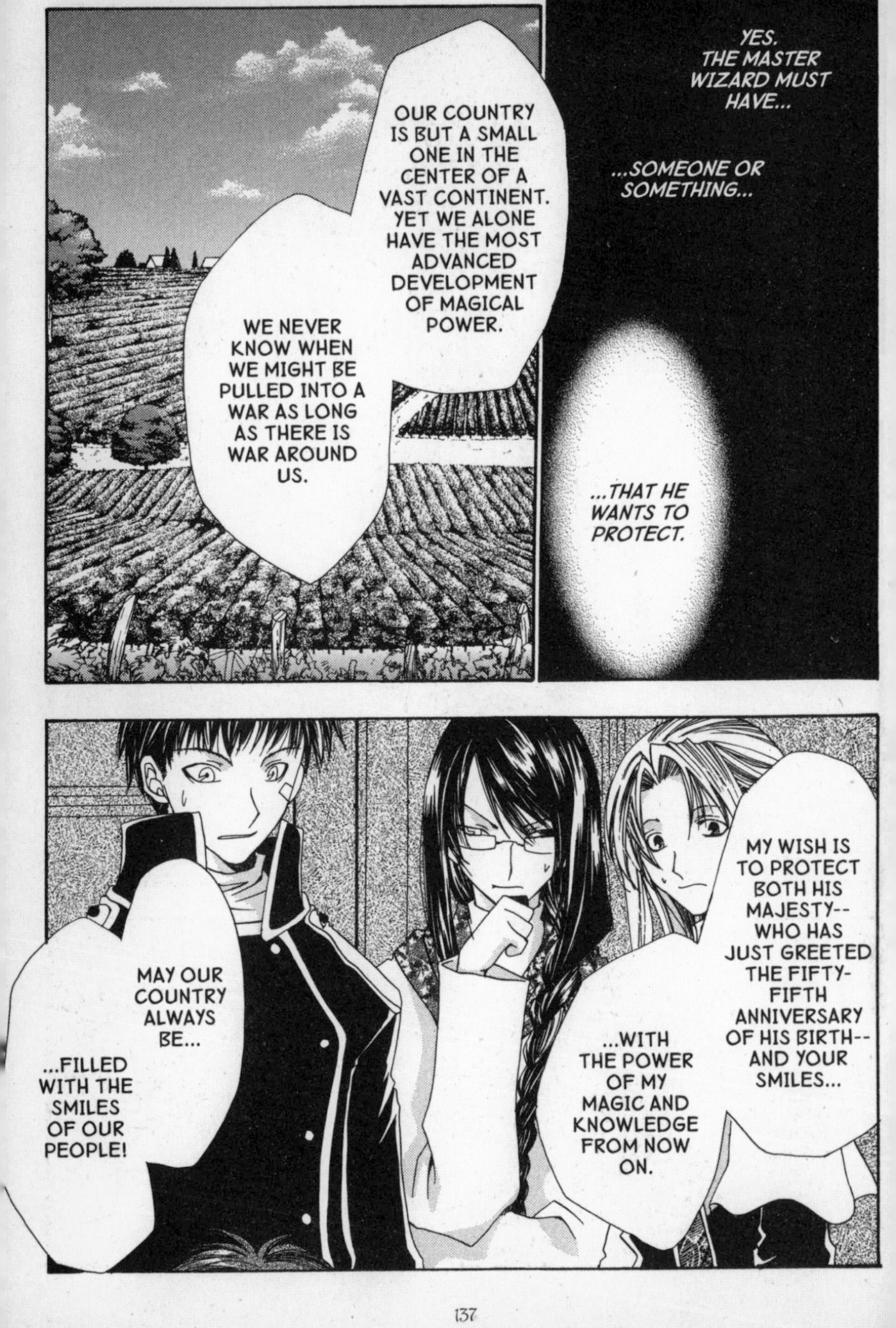
YES. THE MASTER WIZARD MUST HAVE...
...SOMEONE OR SOMETHING...
...THAT HE WANTS TO PROTECT.
OUR COUNTRY IS BUT A SMALL ONE IN THE CENTER OF A VAST CONTINENT. YET WE ALONE HAVE THE MOST ADVANCED DEVELOPMENT OF MAGICAL POWER.
WE NEVER KNOW WHEN WE MIGHT BE PULLED INTO A WAR AS LONG AS THERE IS WAR AROUND US.
MY WISH IS TO PROTECT BOTH HIS MAJESTY-- WHO HAS JUST GREETED THE FIFTY-FIFTH ANNIVERSARY OF HIS BIRTH-- AND YOUR SMILES...
...WITH THE POWER OF MY MAGIC AND KNOWLEDGE FROM NOW ON.
MAY OUR COUNTRY ALWAYS BE...
...FILLED WITH THE SMILES OF OUR PEOPLE!

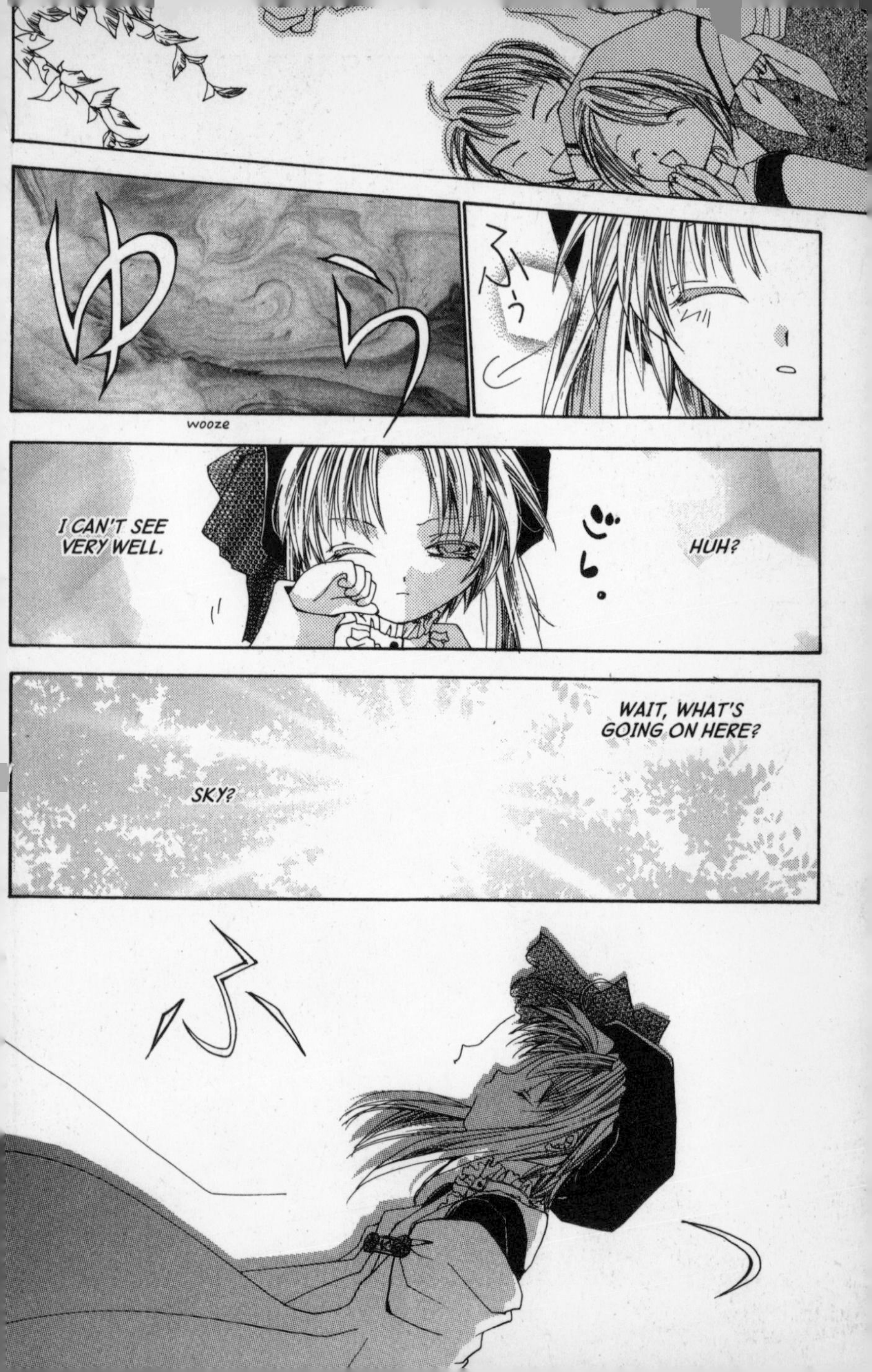
wooze
HUH?
I CAN'T SEE VERY WELL.
WAIT, WHAT'S GOING ON HERE?
SKY?

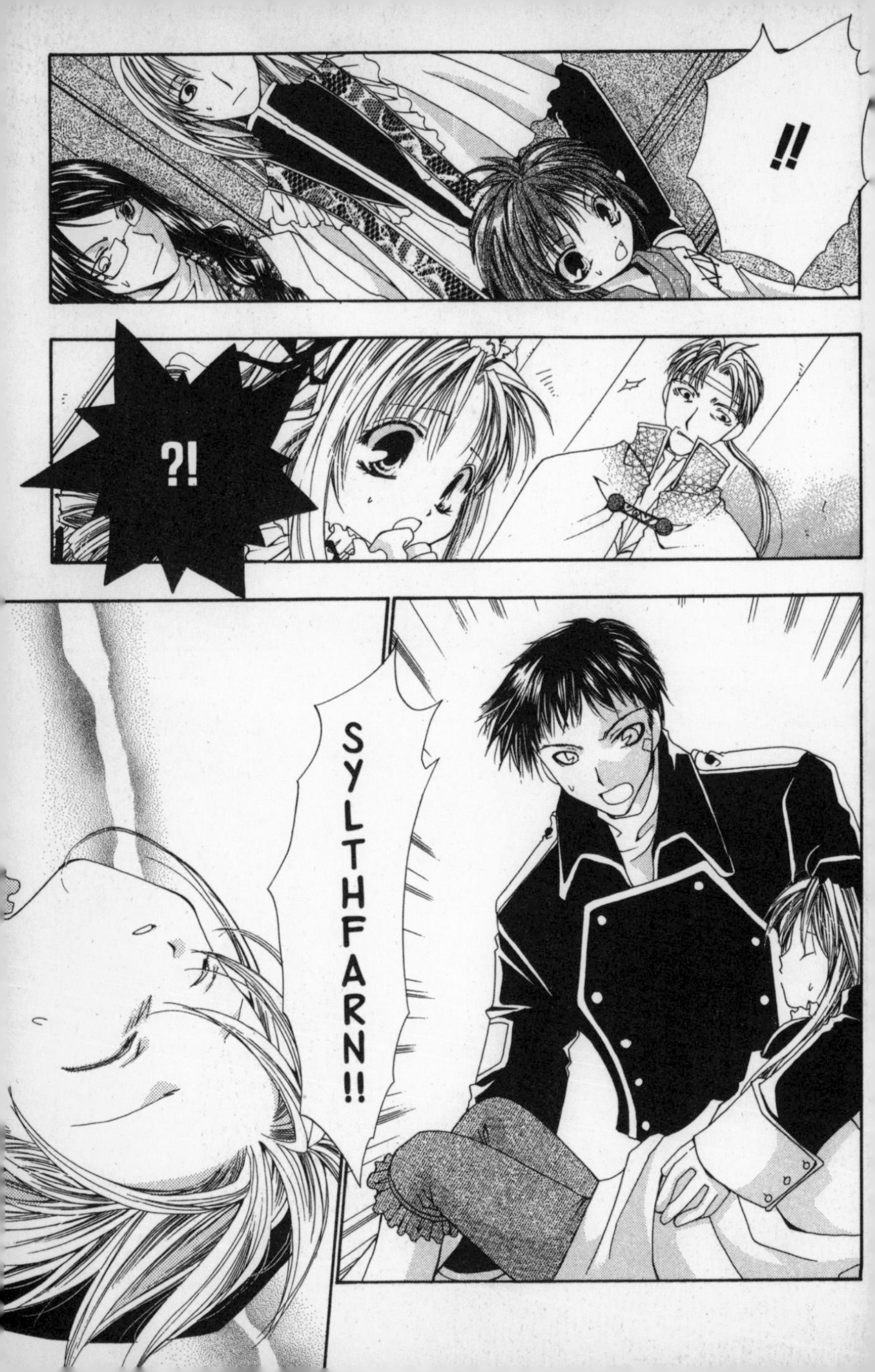
!!
?!
SYLTHFARN!!

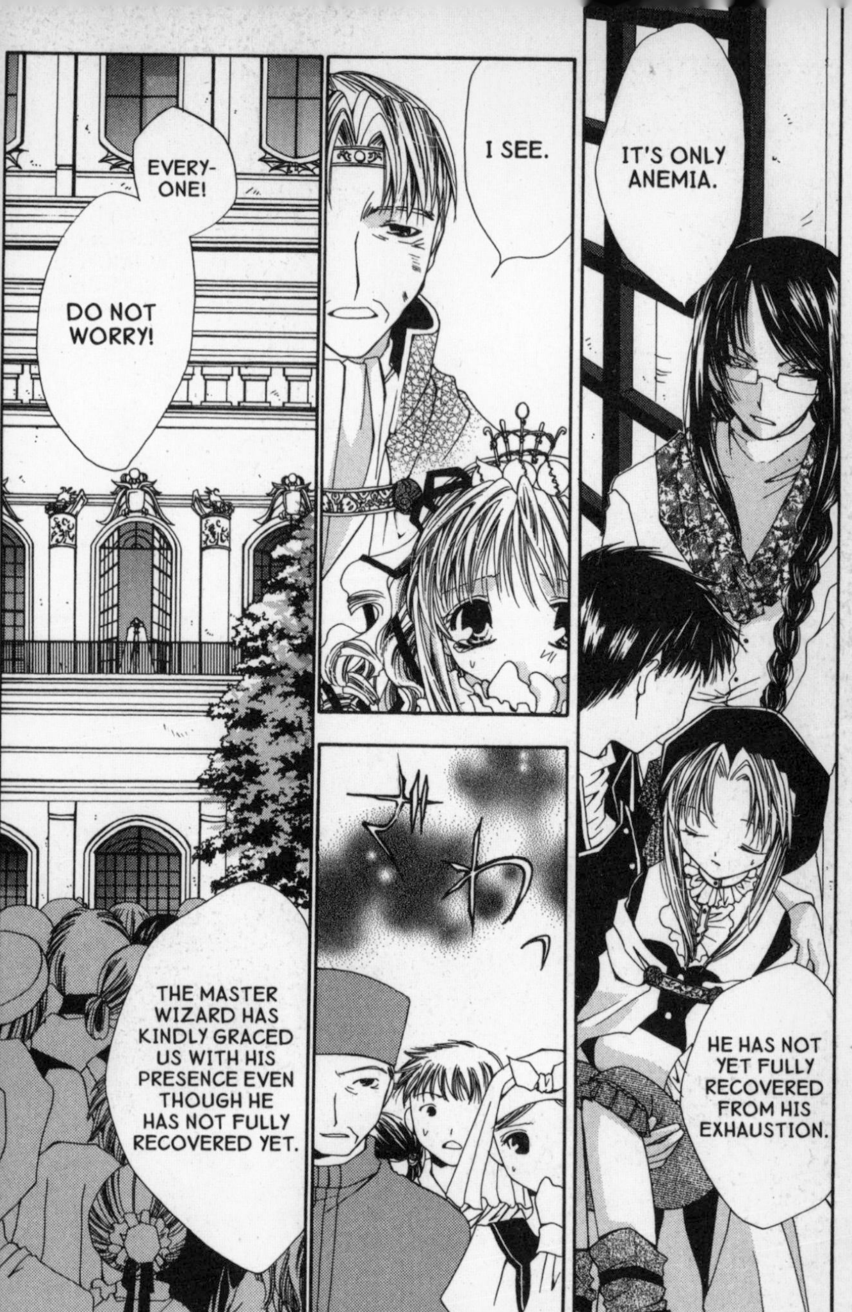
IT'S ONLY ANEMIA.
HE HAS NOT YET FULLY RECOVERED FROM HIS EXHAUSTION.
I SEE.
EVERY-ONE!
DO NOT WORRY!
THE MASTER WIZARD HAS KINDLY GRACED US WITH HIS PRESENCE EVEN THOUGH HE HAS NOT FULLY RECOVERED YET.

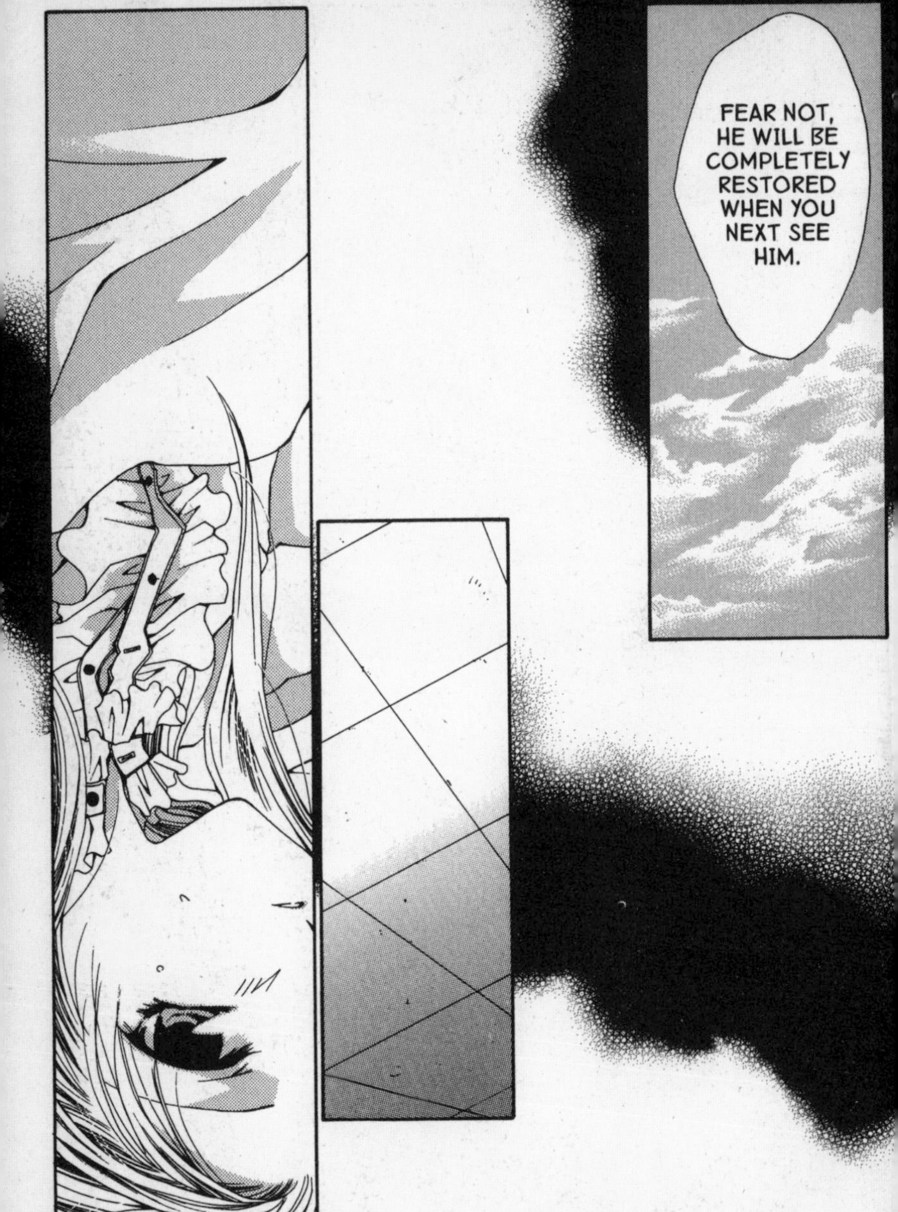
FEAR NOT, HE WILL BE COMPLETELY RESTORED WHEN YOU NEXT SEE HIM.

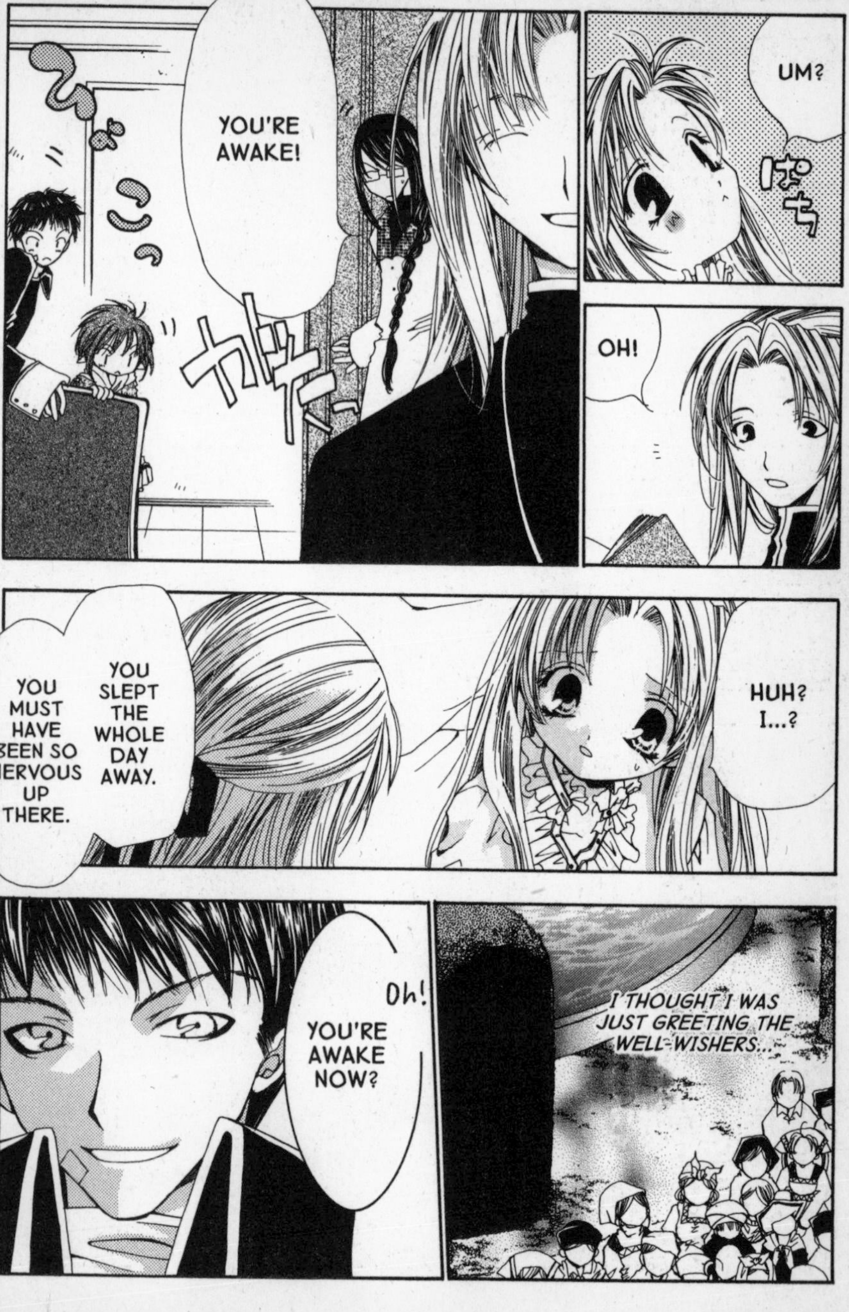
UM?
ぱち
OH!
YOU'RE AWAKE!
HUH? I...?
YOU SLEPT THE WHOLE DAY AWAY.
YOU MUST HAVE BEEN SO NERVOUS UP THERE.
I THOUGHT I WAS JUST GREETING THE WELL-WISHERS...
Oh!
YOU'RE AWAKE NOW?

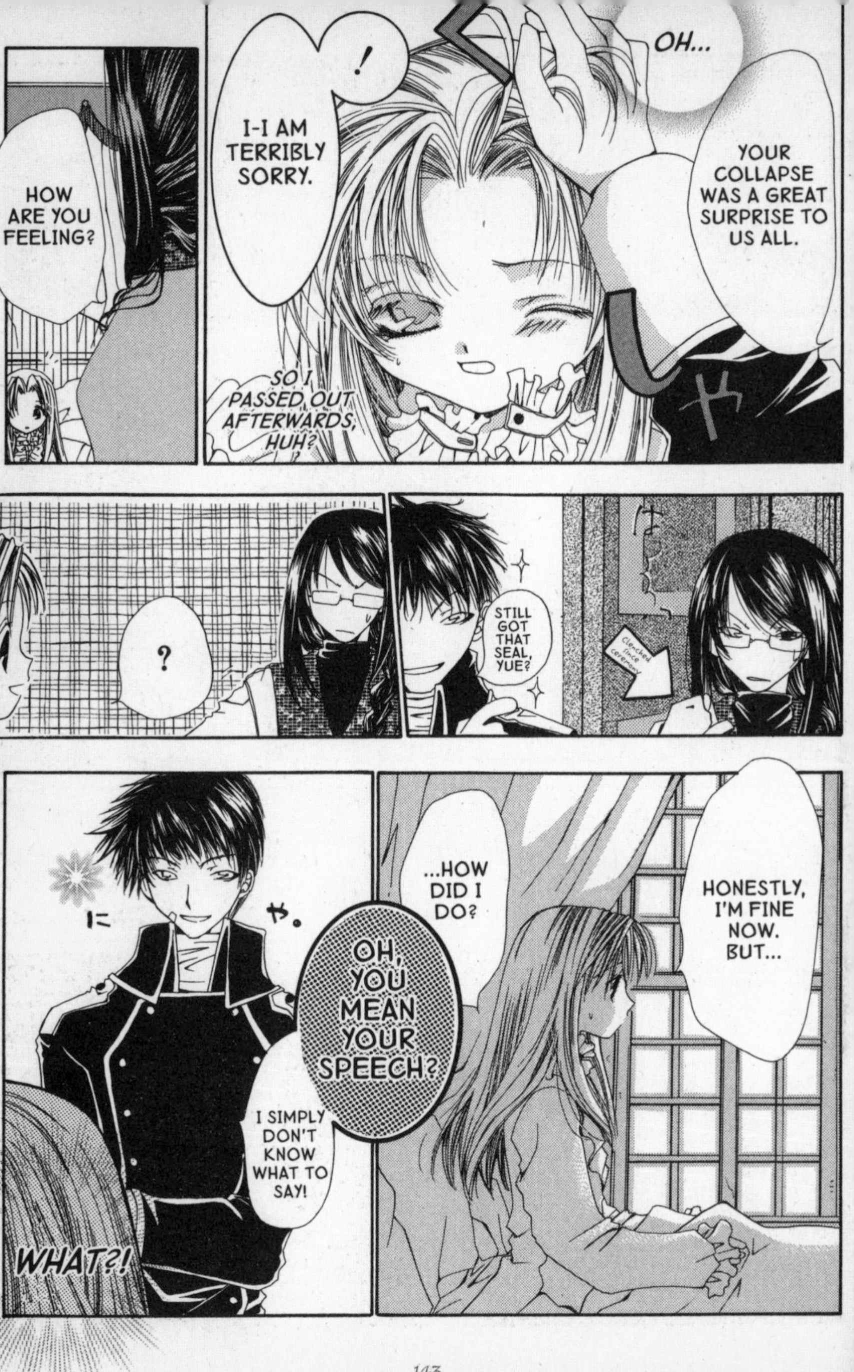
OH...
YOUR COLLAPSE WAS A GREAT SURPRISE TO US ALL.
!
I-I AM TERRIBLY SORRY.
SO I PASSED OUT AFTERWARDS, HUH?
HOW ARE YOU FEELING?
Clenched since ceremony
STILL GOT THAT SEAL, YUE?
?
HONESTLY, I'M FINE NOW. BUT...
...HOW DID I DO?
にや。
OH, YOU MEAN YOUR SPEECH?
I SIMPLY DON'T KNOW WHAT TO SAY!
WHAT?!

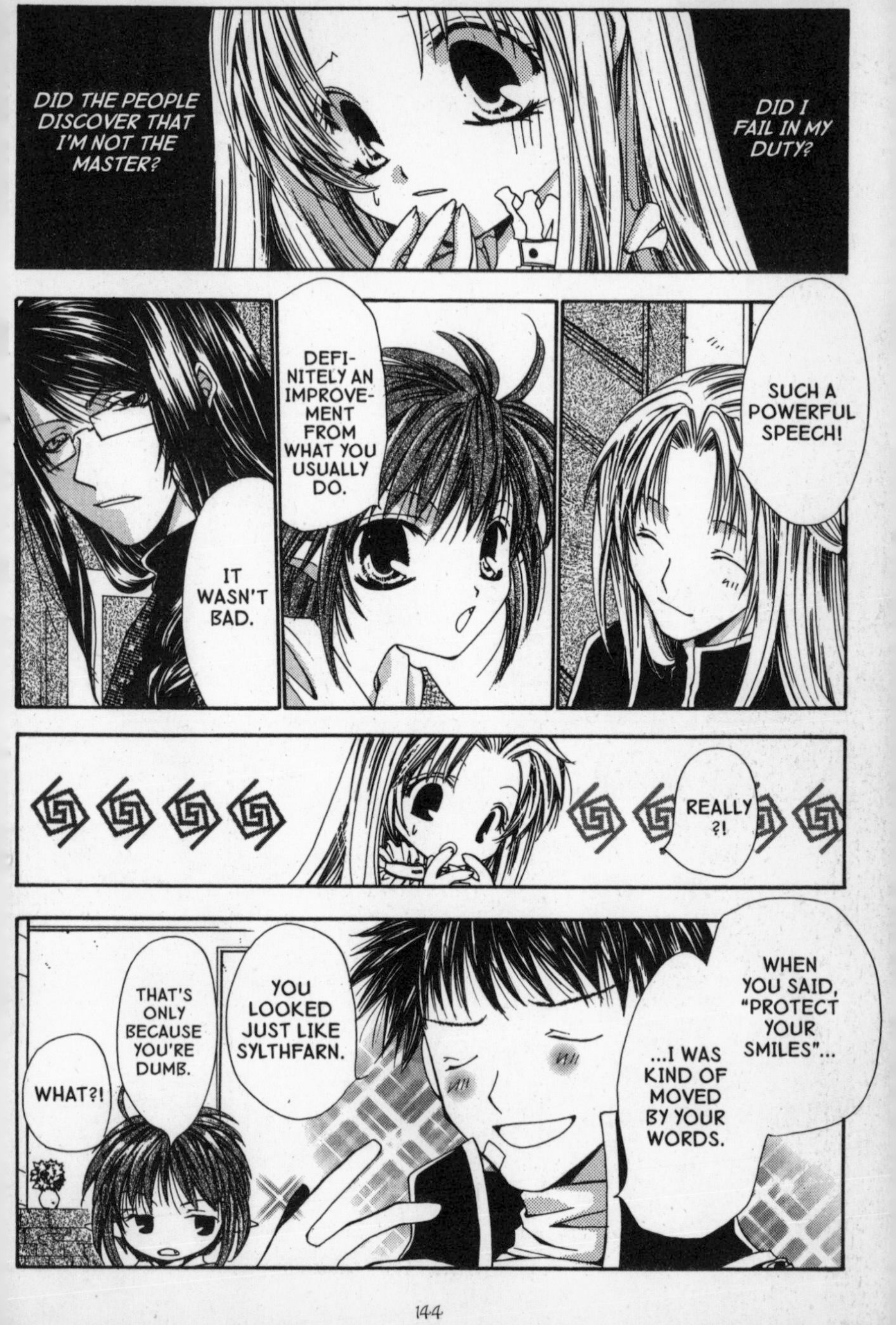
DID I FAIL IN MY DUTY?
DID THE PEOPLE DISCOVER THAT I'M NOT THE MASTER?
SUCH A POWERFUL SPEECH!
DEFINITELY AN IMPROVEMENT FROM WHAT YOU USUALLY DO.
IT WASN'T BAD.
REALLY ?!
WHEN YOU SAID, "PROTECT YOUR SMILES"...
...I WAS KIND OF MOVED BY YOUR WORDS.
YOU LOOKED JUST LIKE SYLTHFARN.
THAT'S ONLY BECAUSE YOU'RE DUMB.
WHAT?!

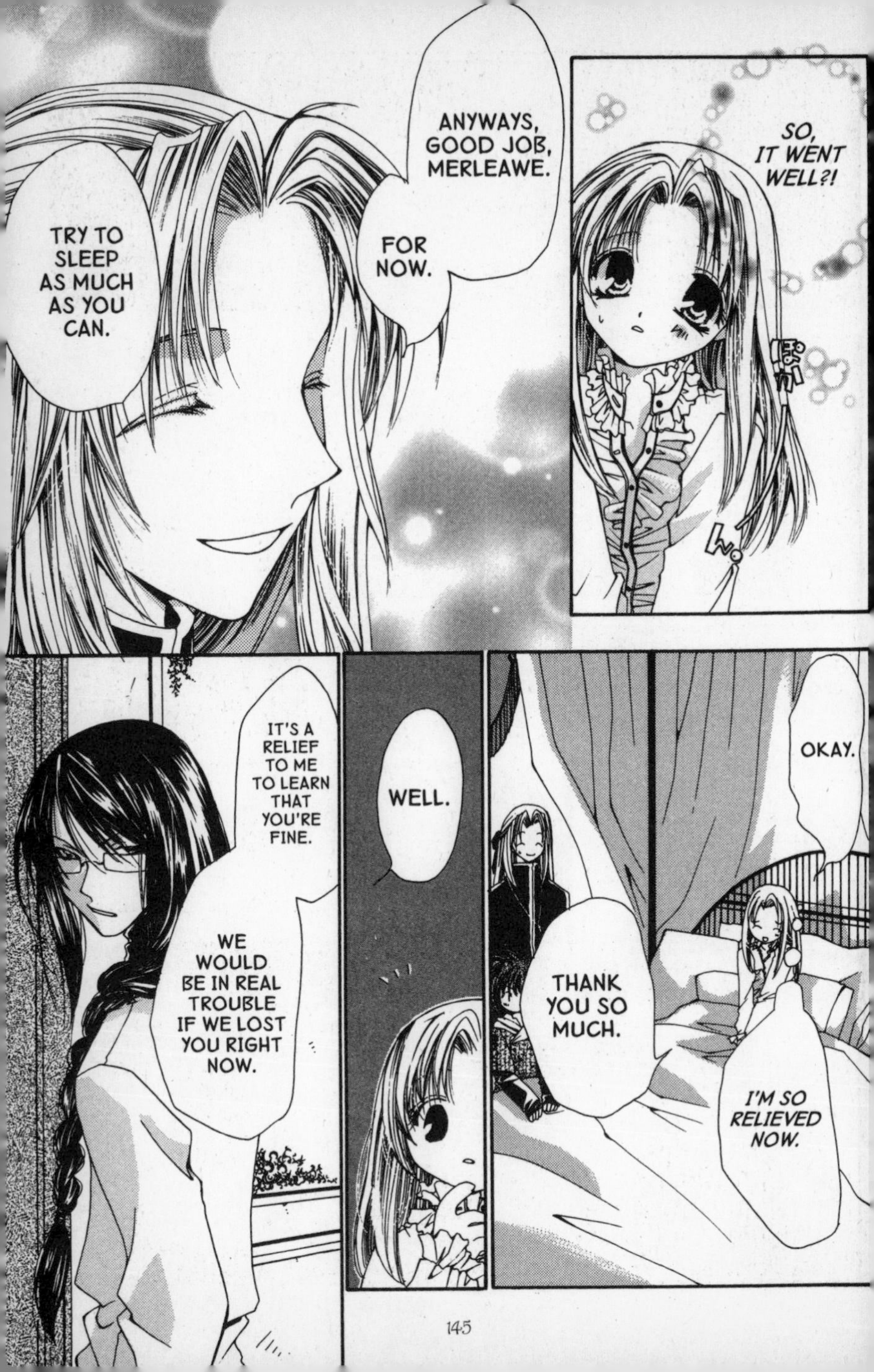
SO, IT WENT WELL?!
ANYWAYS, GOOD JOB, MERLEAWE.
FOR NOW.
TRY TO SLEEP AS MUCH AS YOU CAN.
OKAY.
I'M SO RELIEVED NOW.
THANK YOU SO MUCH.
WELL.
IT'S A RELIEF TO ME TO LEARN THAT YOU'RE FINE.
WE WOULD BE IN REAL TROUBLE IF WE LOST YOU RIGHT NOW.

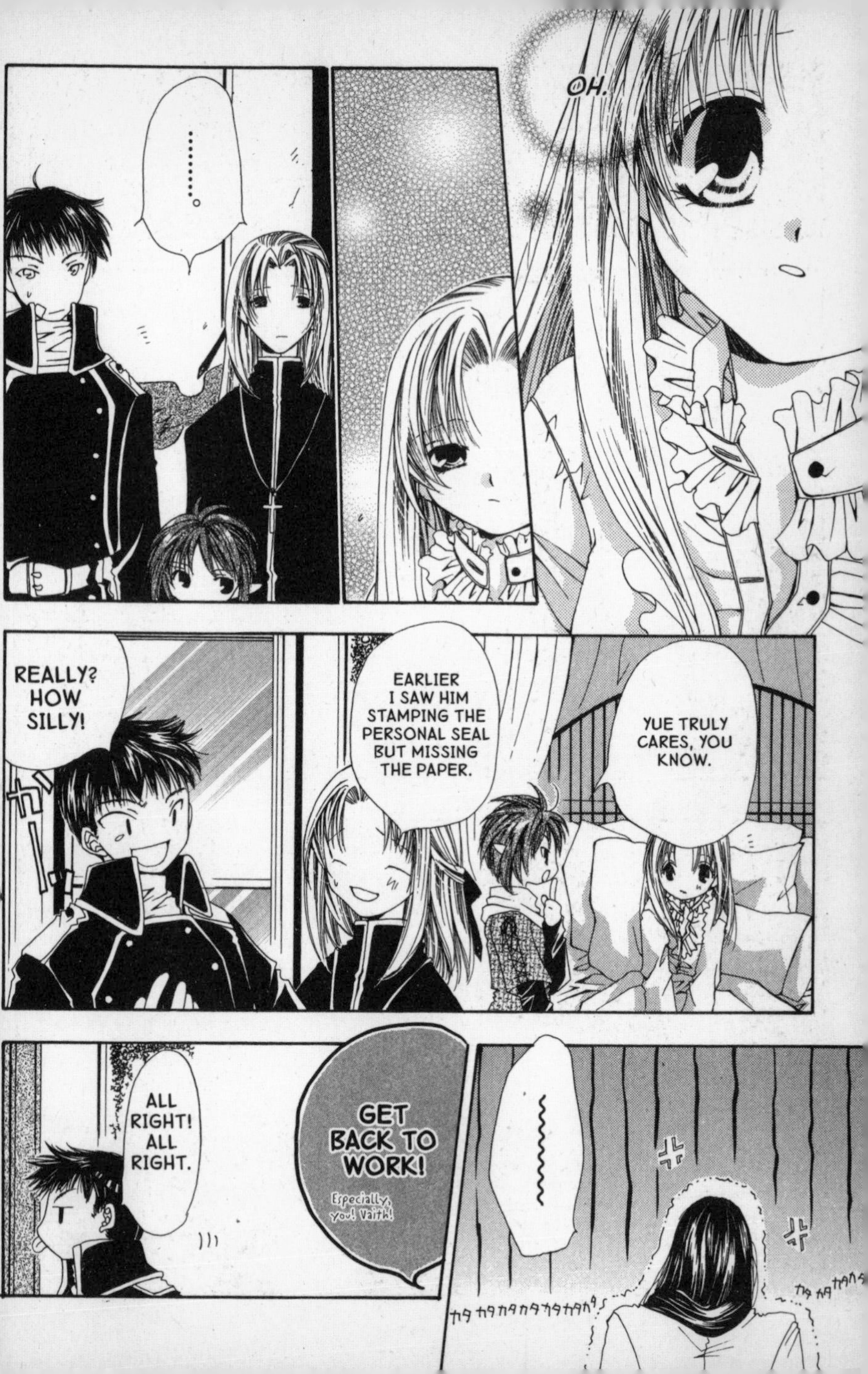
OH.
......
YUE TRULY CARES, YOU KNOW.
EARLIER I SAW HIM STAMPING THE PERSONAL SEAL BUT MISSING THE PAPER.
REALLY? HOW SILLY!
カタ カタ カタカタ
カタ カタカタカタカタカタカタ
GET BACK TO WORK!
Especially, you! Vaith!
ALL RIGHT! ALL RIGHT.

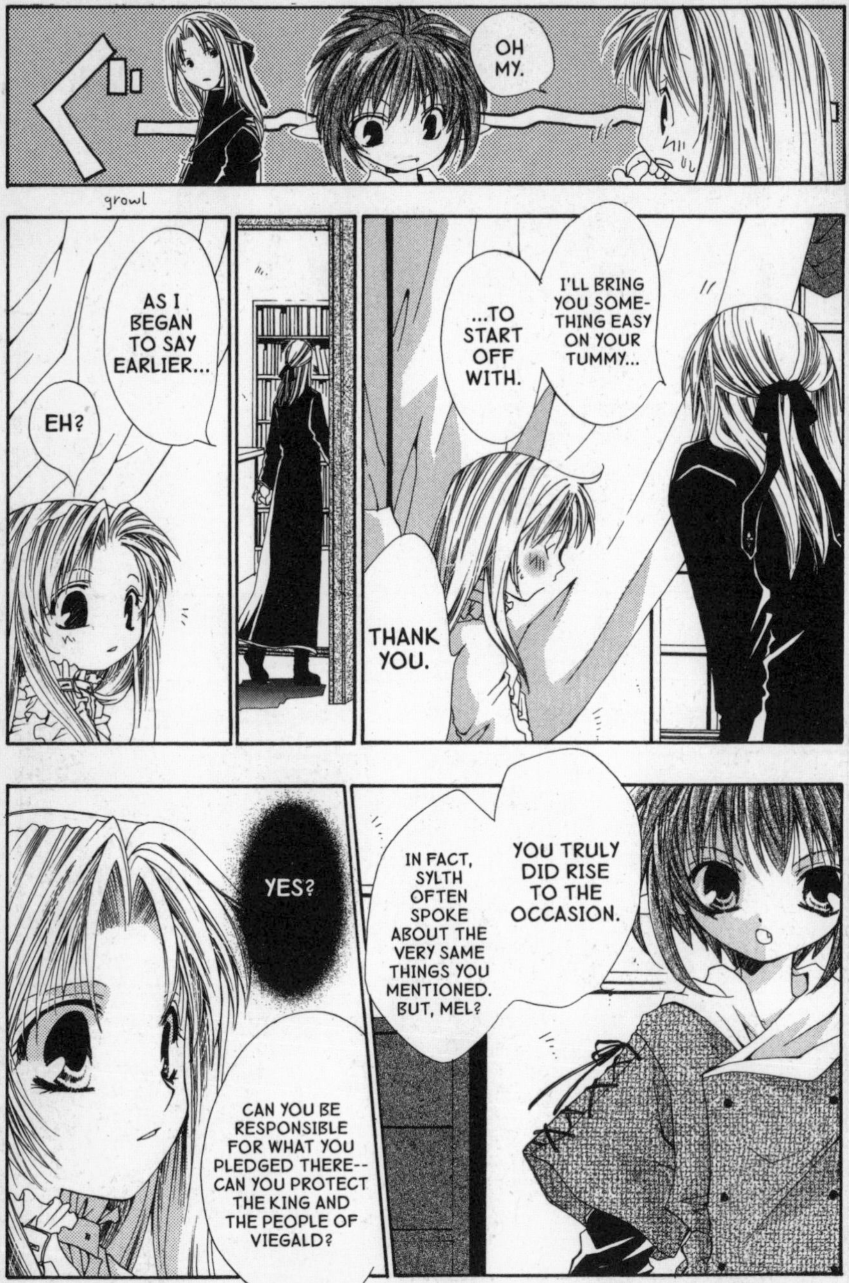
OH MY.
growl
I'LL BRING YOU SOME-THING EASY ON YOUR TUMMY...
...TO START OFF WITH.
THANK YOU.
AS I BEGAN TO SAY EARLIER...
EH?
YOU TRULY DID RISE TO THE OCCASION.
IN FACT, SYLTH OFTEN SPOKE ABOUT THE VERY SAME THINGS YOU MENTIONED. BUT, MEL?
YES?
CAN YOU BE RESPONSIBLE FOR WHAT YOU PLEDGED THERE-- CAN YOU PROTECT THE KING AND THE PEOPLE OF VIEGALD?

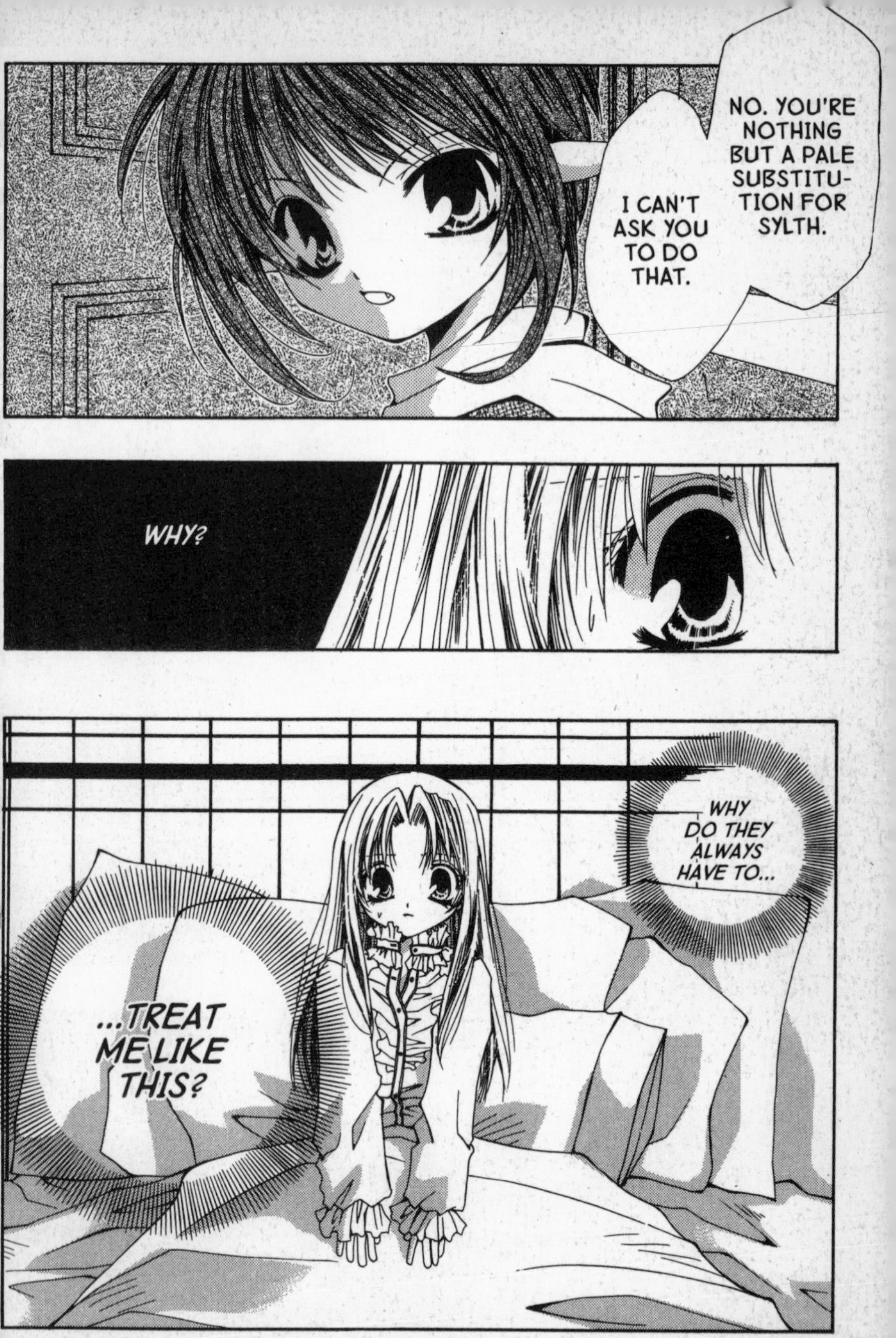
NO. YOU'RE NOTHING BUT A PALE SUBSTITU- TION FOR SYLTH.
I CAN'T ASK YOU TO DO THAT.
WHY?
WHY DO THEY ALWAYS HAVE TO...
...TREAT ME LIKE THIS?

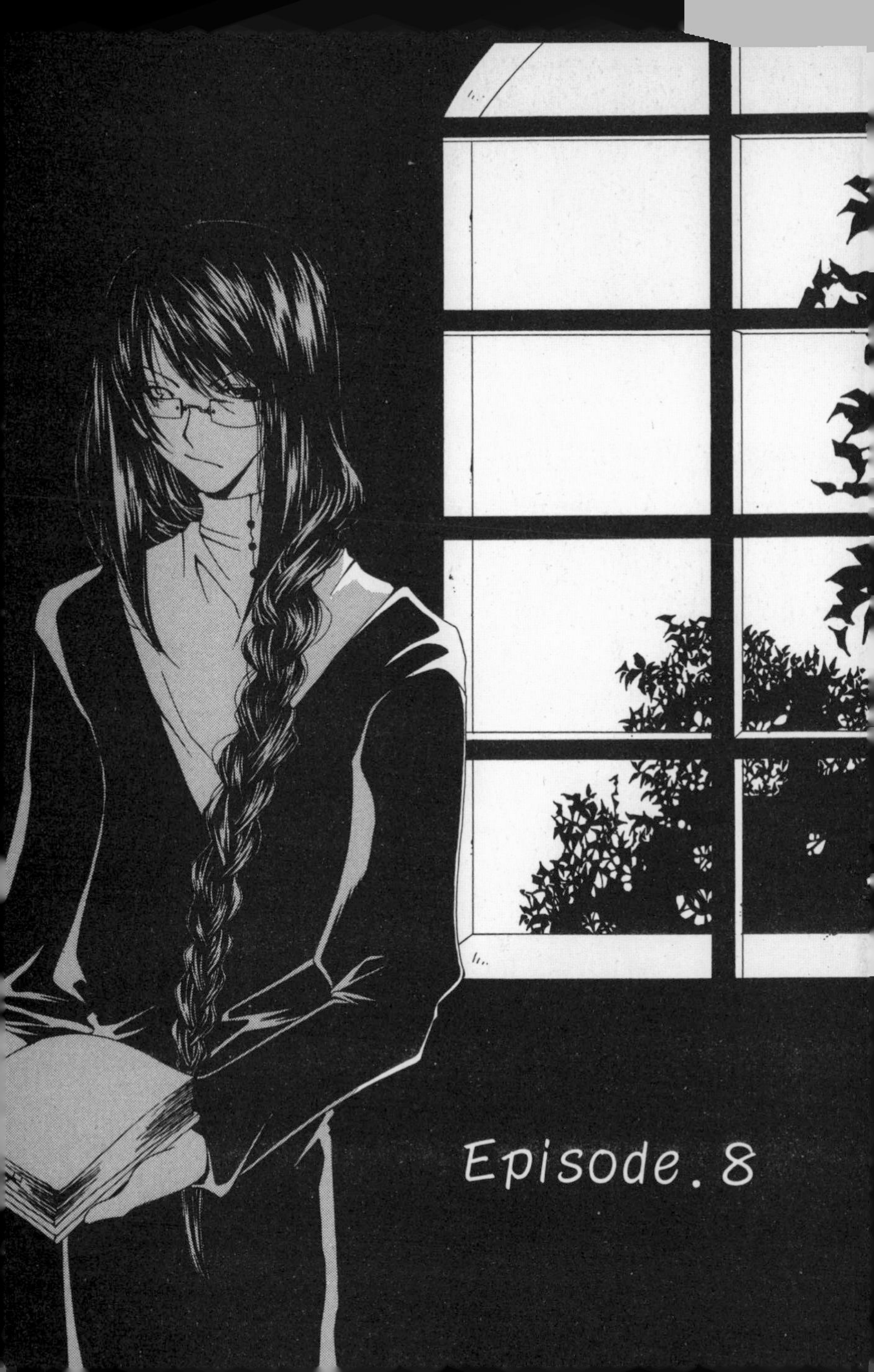
Episode.8

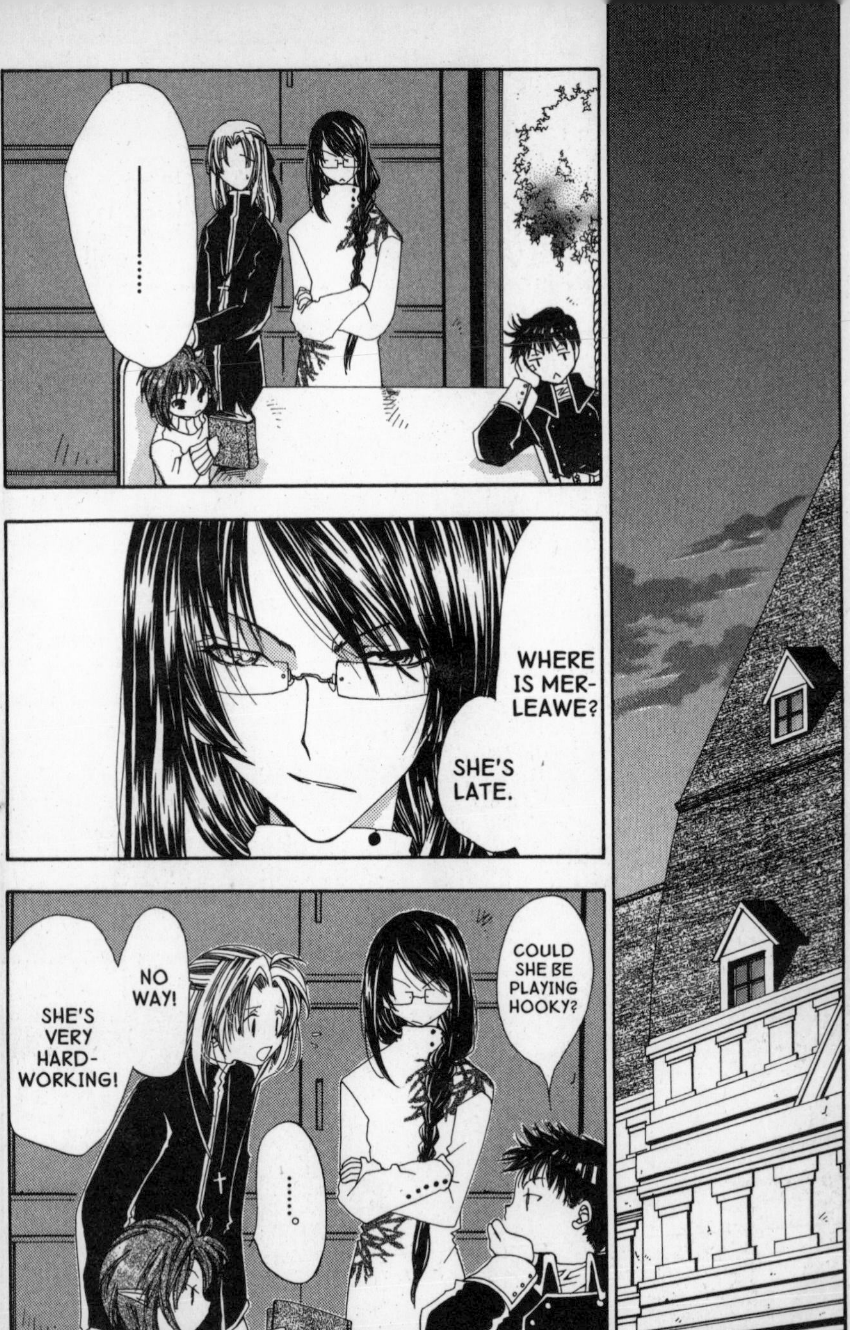
……
WHERE IS MER-LEAWE?
SHE'S LATE.
COULD SHE BE PLAYING HOOKY?
NO WAY!
SHE'S VERY HARD-WORKING!
……

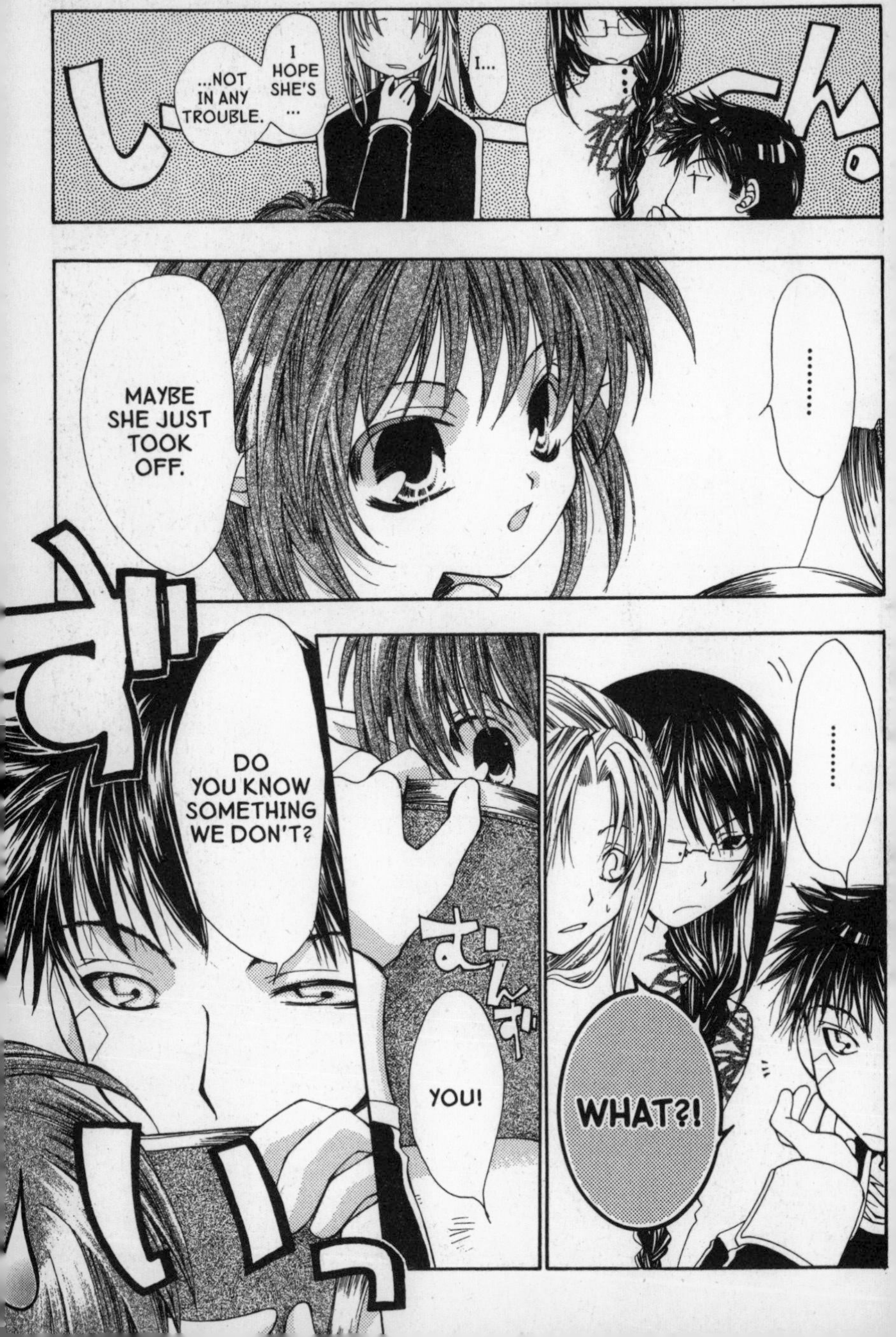
I...
I HOPE SHE'S ...
...NOT IN ANY TROUBLE.
しーん。
....
MAYBE SHE JUST TOOK OFF.
....
WHAT?!
むんず
YOU!
ずいっ
DO YOU KNOW SOMETHING WE DON'T?

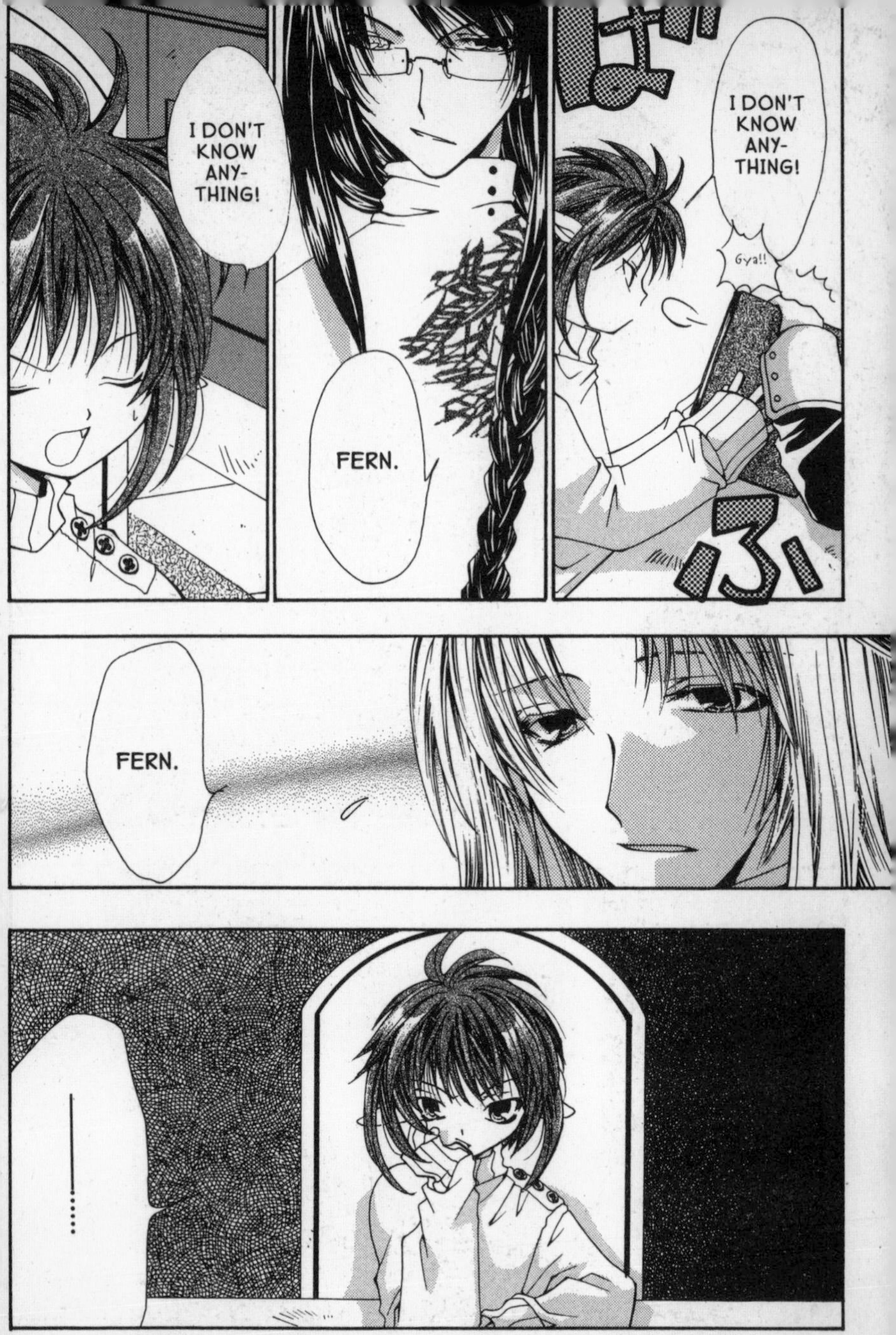
I DON'T KNOW ANYTHING!
Gya!!
ふ
FERN.
I DON'T KNOW ANYTHING!
FERN.
......

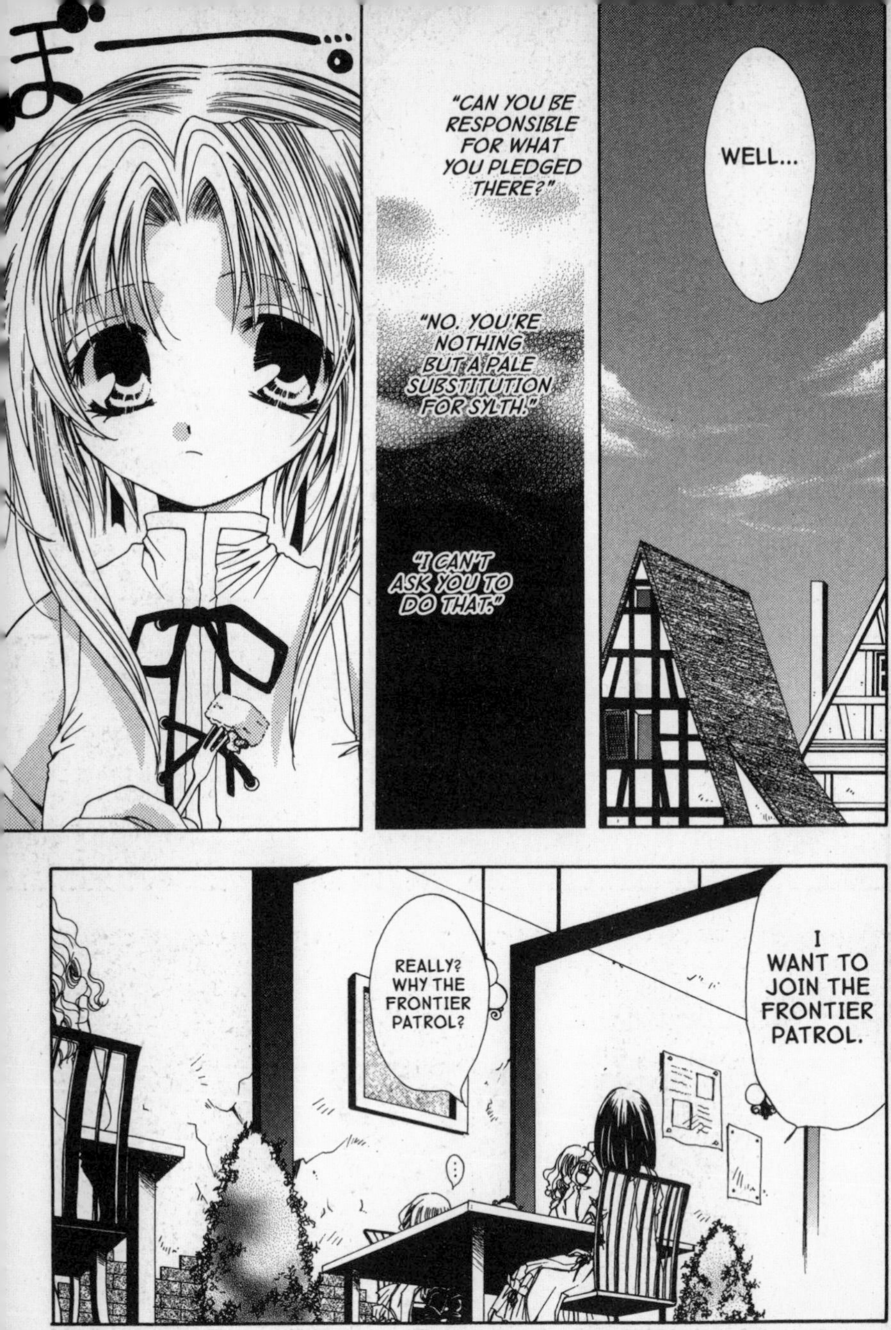
WELL...
"CAN YOU BE RESPONSIBLE FOR WHAT YOU PLEDGED THERE?"
"NO. YOU'RE NOTHING BUT A PALE SUBSTITUTION FOR SYLTH."
"I CAN'T ASK YOU TO DO THAT."
ぼー
I WANT TO JOIN THE FRONTIER PATROL.
REALLY? WHY THE FRONTIER PATROL?
...

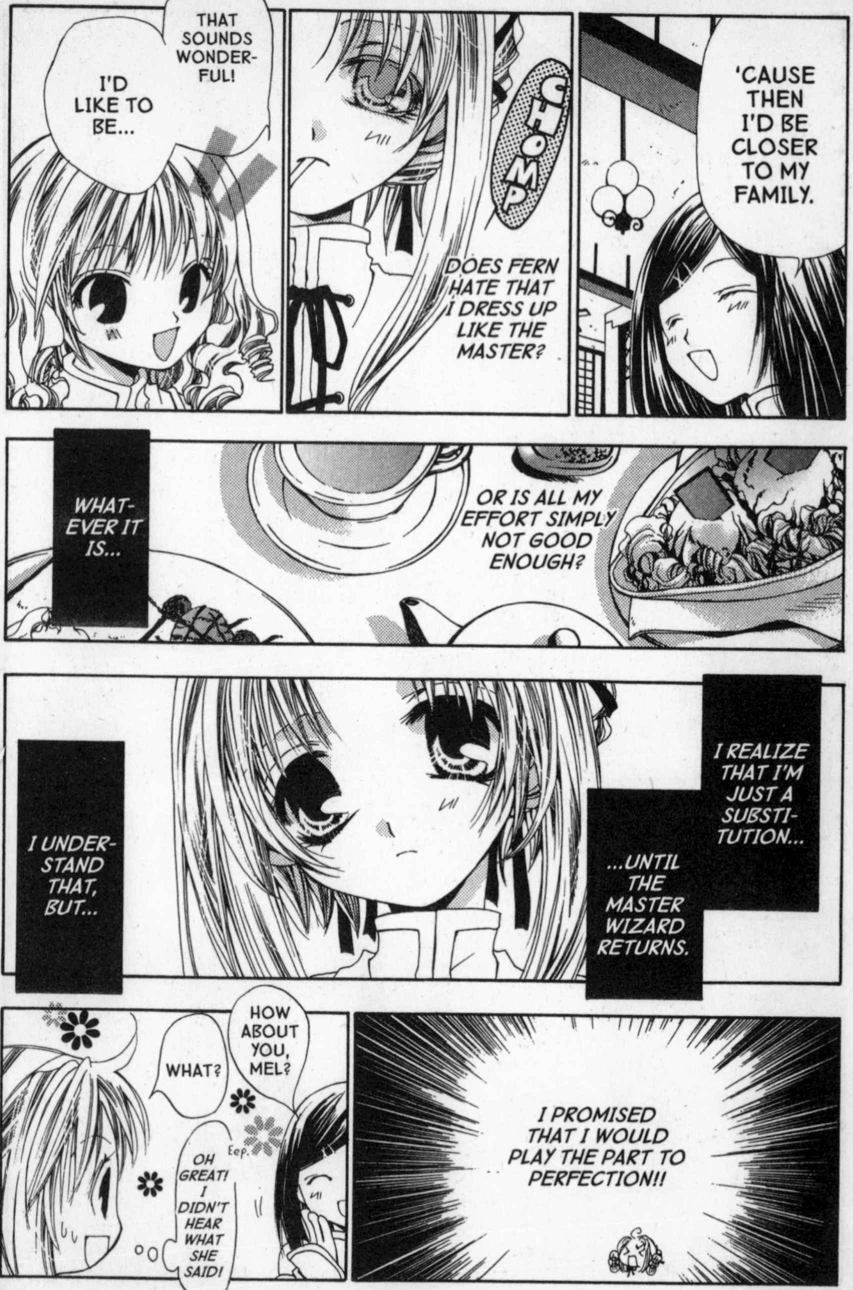

'CAUSE THEN I'D BE CLOSER TO MY FAMILY.
CHOMP
DOES FERN HATE THAT I DRESS UP LIKE THE MASTER?
THAT SOUNDS WONDERFUL!
I'D LIKE TO BE...
OR IS ALL MY EFFORT SIMPLY NOT GOOD ENOUGH?
WHATEVER IT IS...
I REALIZE THAT I'M JUST A SUBSTITUTION...
...UNTIL THE MASTER WIZARD RETURNS.
I UNDERSTAND THAT, BUT...
I PROMISED THAT I WOULD PLAY THE PART TO PERFECTION!!
HOW ABOUT YOU, MEL?
WHAT?
Eep.
OH GREAT! I DIDN'T HEAR WHAT SHE SAID!

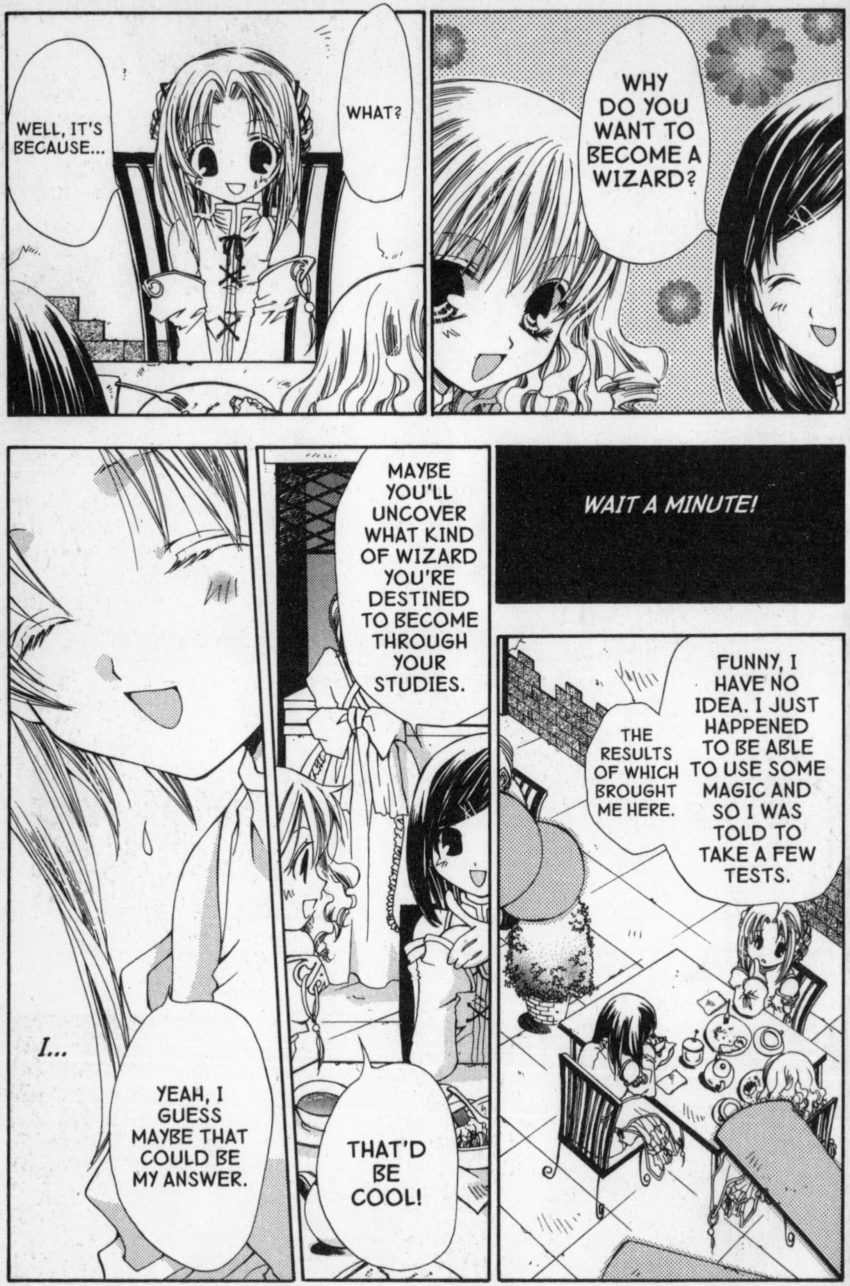
WHY DO YOU WANT TO BECOME A WIZARD?
WHAT?
WELL, IT'S BECAUSE...
WAIT A MINUTE!
FUNNY, I HAVE NO IDEA. I JUST HAPPENED TO BE ABLE TO USE SOME MAGIC AND SO I WAS TOLD TO TAKE A FEW TESTS.
THE RESULTS OF WHICH BROUGHT ME HERE.
MAYBE YOU'LL UNCOVER WHAT KIND OF WIZARD YOU'RE DESTINED TO BECOME THROUGH YOUR STUDIES.
THAT'D BE COOL!
YEAH, I GUESS MAYBE THAT COULD BE MY ANSWER.
I...

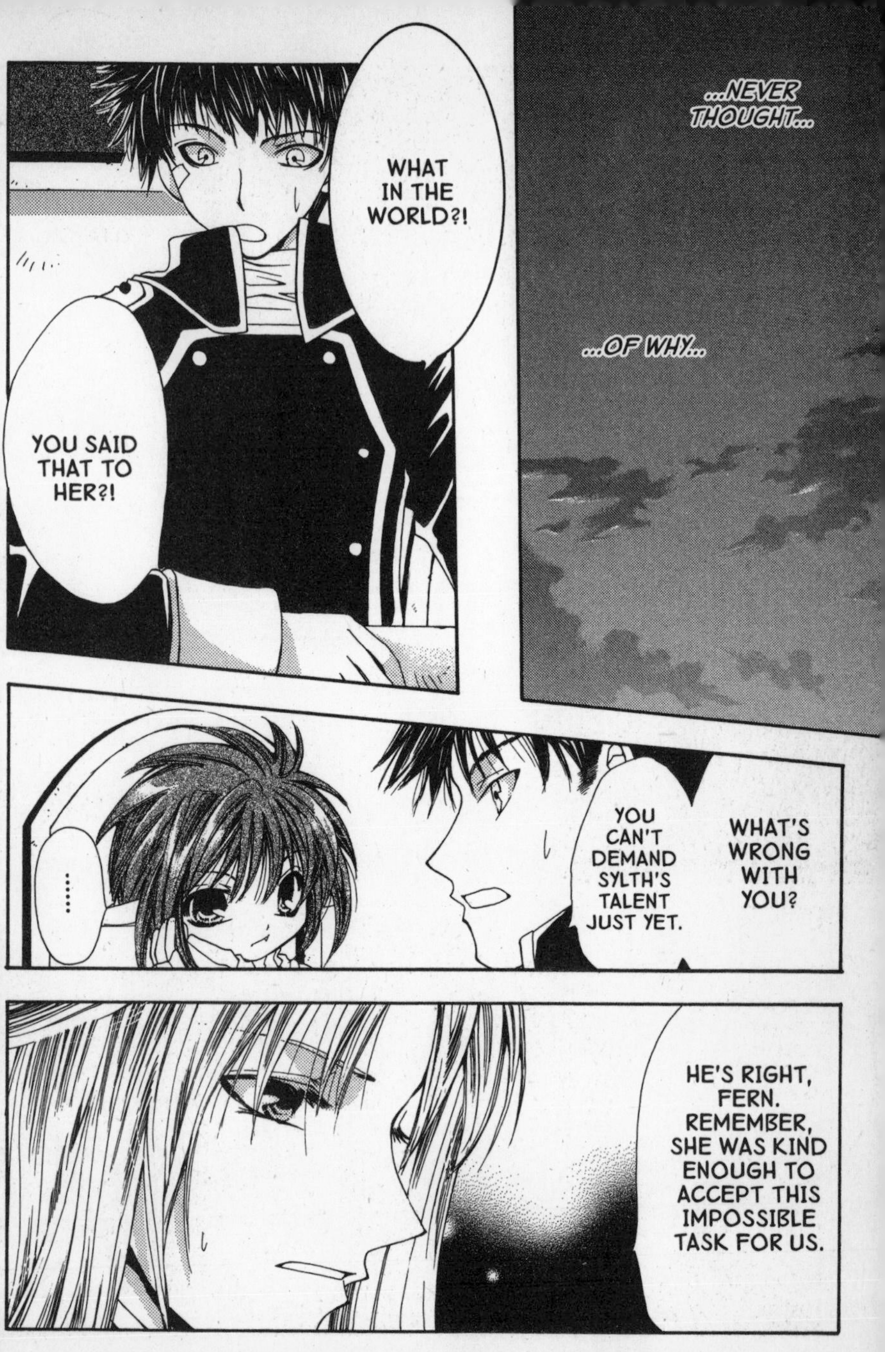
...NEVER THOUGHT...
...OF WHY...
WHAT IN THE WORLD?!
YOU SAID THAT TO HER?!
WHAT'S WRONG WITH YOU?
YOU CAN'T DEMAND SYLTH'S TALENT JUST YET.
......
HE'S RIGHT, FERN. REMEMBER, SHE WAS KIND ENOUGH TO ACCEPT THIS IMPOSSIBLE TASK FOR US.

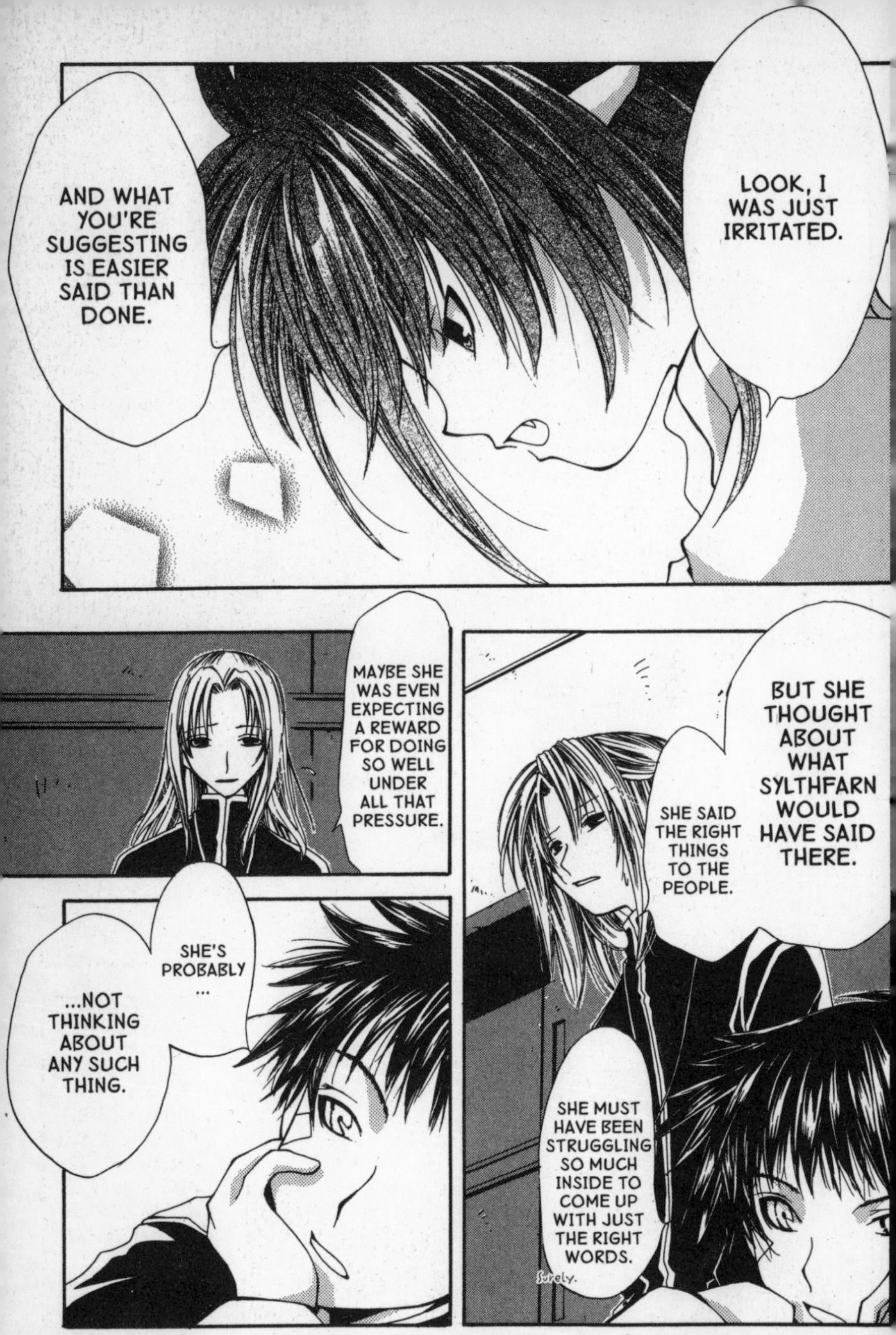
LOOK, I WAS JUST IRRITATED.
AND WHAT YOU'RE SUGGESTING IS EASIER SAID THAN DONE.
BUT SHE THOUGHT ABOUT WHAT SYLTHFARN WOULD HAVE SAID THERE.
SHE SAID THE RIGHT THINGS TO THE PEOPLE.
SHE MUST HAVE BEEN STRUGGLING SO MUCH INSIDE TO COME UP WITH JUST THE RIGHT WORDS.
Surely.
MAYBE SHE WAS EVEN EXPECTING A REWARD FOR DOING SO WELL UNDER ALL THAT PRESSURE.
SHE'S PROBABLY ...
...NOT THINKING ABOUT ANY SUCH THING.

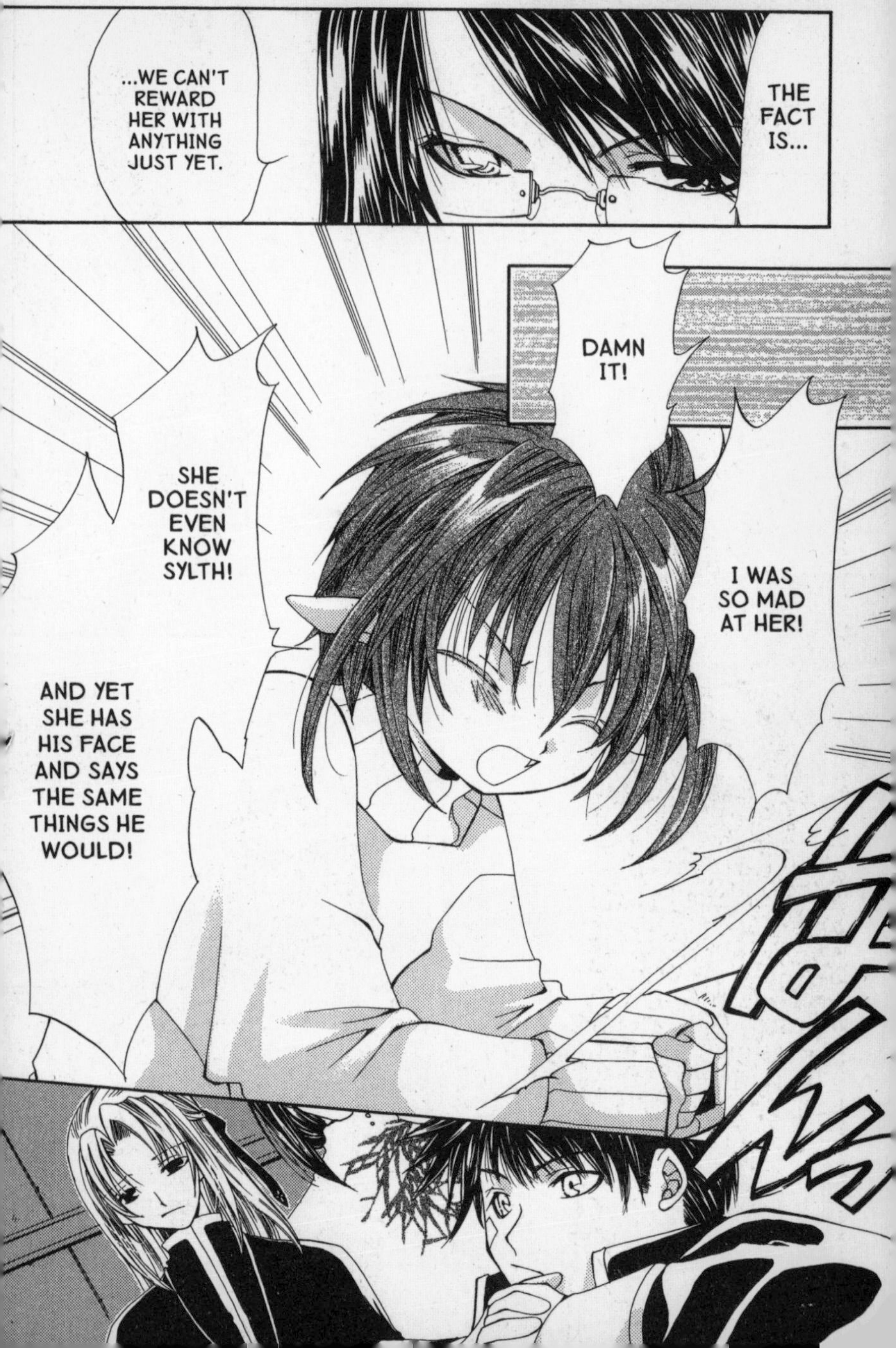
THE FACT IS...
...WE CAN'T REWARD HER WITH ANYTHING JUST YET.
DAMN IT!
I WAS SO MAD AT HER!
SHE DOESN'T EVEN KNOW SYLTH!
AND YET SHE HAS HIS FACE AND SAYS THE SAME THINGS HE WOULD!

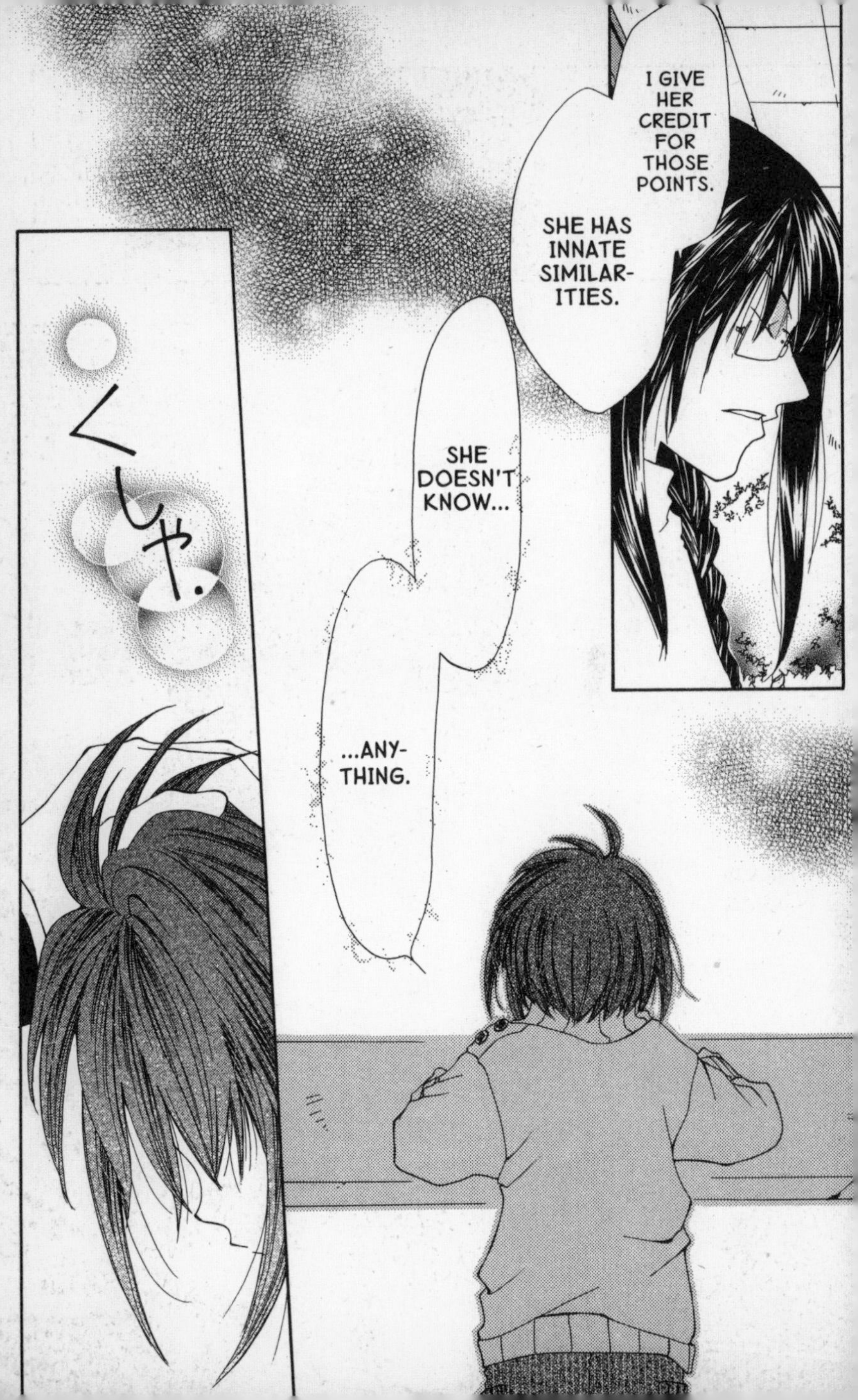
I GIVE HER CREDIT FOR THOSE POINTS.
SHE HAS INNATE SIMILAR-ITIES.
SHE DOESN'T KNOW...
...ANY-THING.
くしゃ.

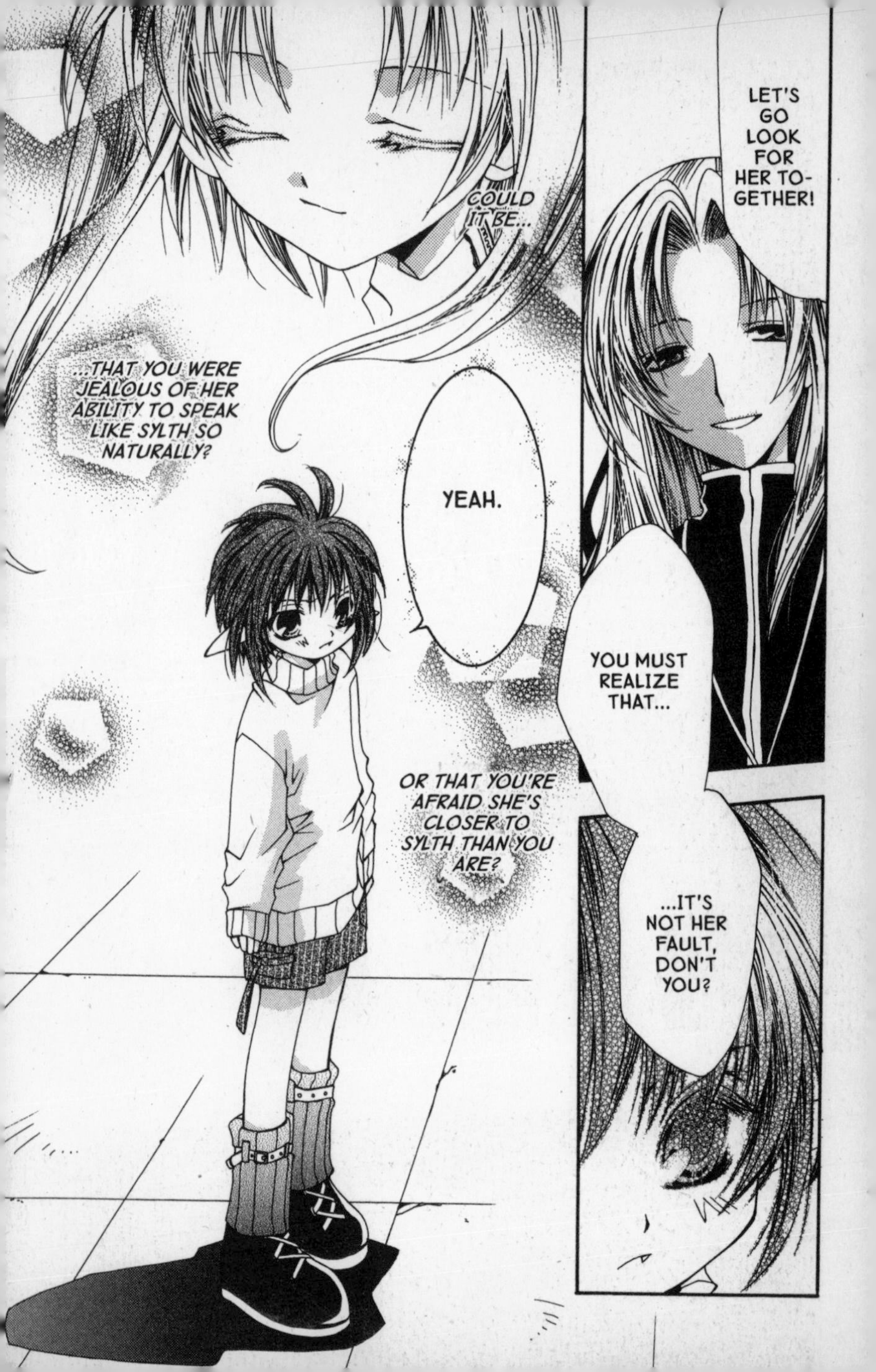
LET'S GO LOOK FOR HER TO-GETHER!
YOU MUST REALIZE THAT...
...IT'S NOT HER FAULT, DON'T YOU?
COULD IT BE...
...THAT YOU WERE JEALOUS OF HER ABILITY TO SPEAK LIKE SYLTH SO NATURALLY?
OR THAT YOU'RE AFRAID SHE'S CLOSER TO SYLTH THAN YOU ARE?
YEAH.

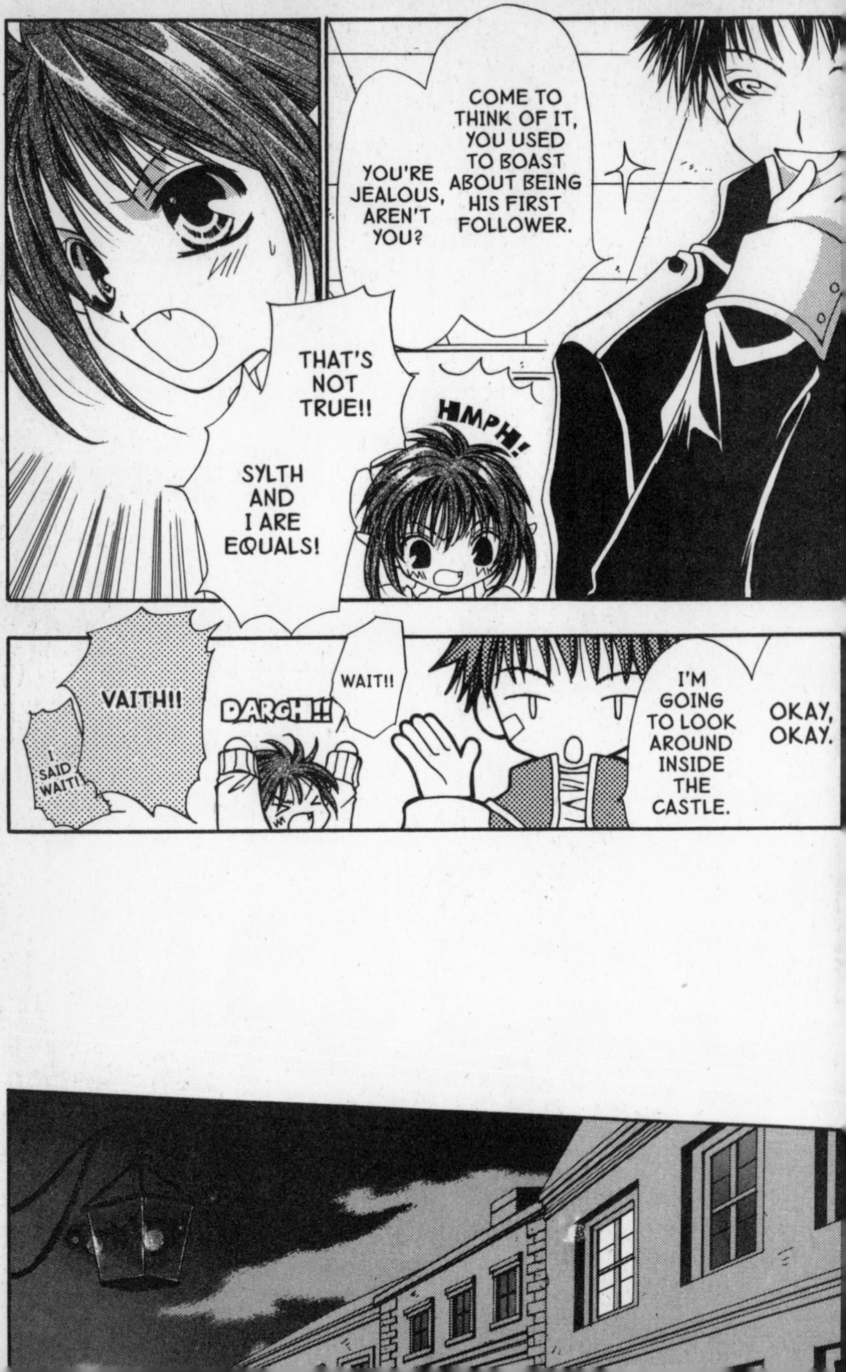
COME TO THINK OF IT, YOU USED TO BOAST ABOUT BEING HIS FIRST FOLLOWER.
YOU'RE JEALOUS, AREN'T YOU?
HMPH!
THAT'S NOT TRUE!!
SYLTH AND I ARE EQUALS!
OKAY, OKAY.
I'M GOING TO LOOK AROUND INSIDE THE CASTLE.
WAIT!!
DARGH!!
VAITH!!
I SAID WAIT!!

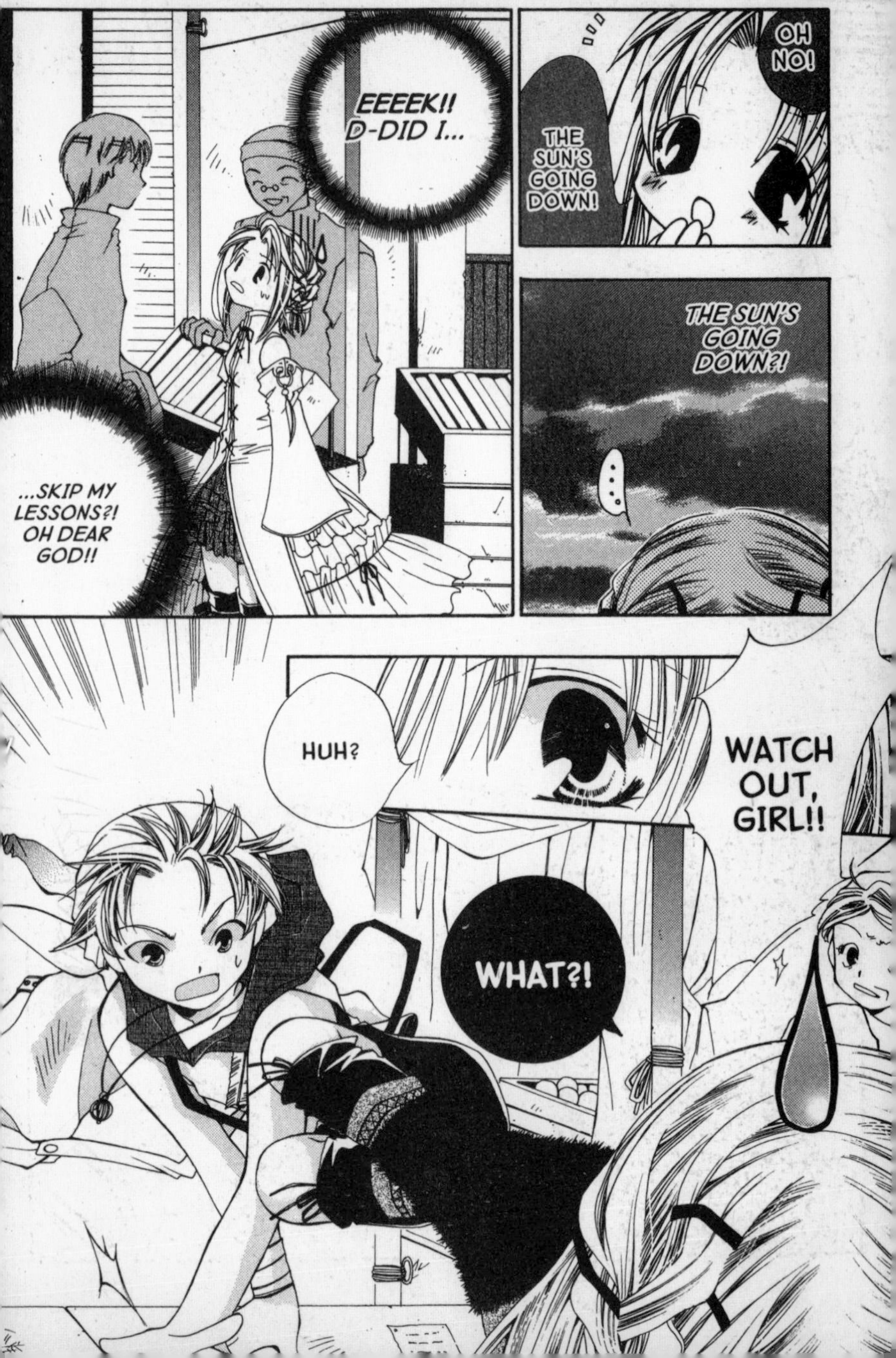
OH NO!
THE SUN'S GOING DOWN!
THE SUN'S GOING DOWN?!
...
EEEEK!! D-DID I...
...SKIP MY LESSONS?! OH DEAR GOD!!
WATCH OUT, GIRL!!
HUH?
WHAT?!

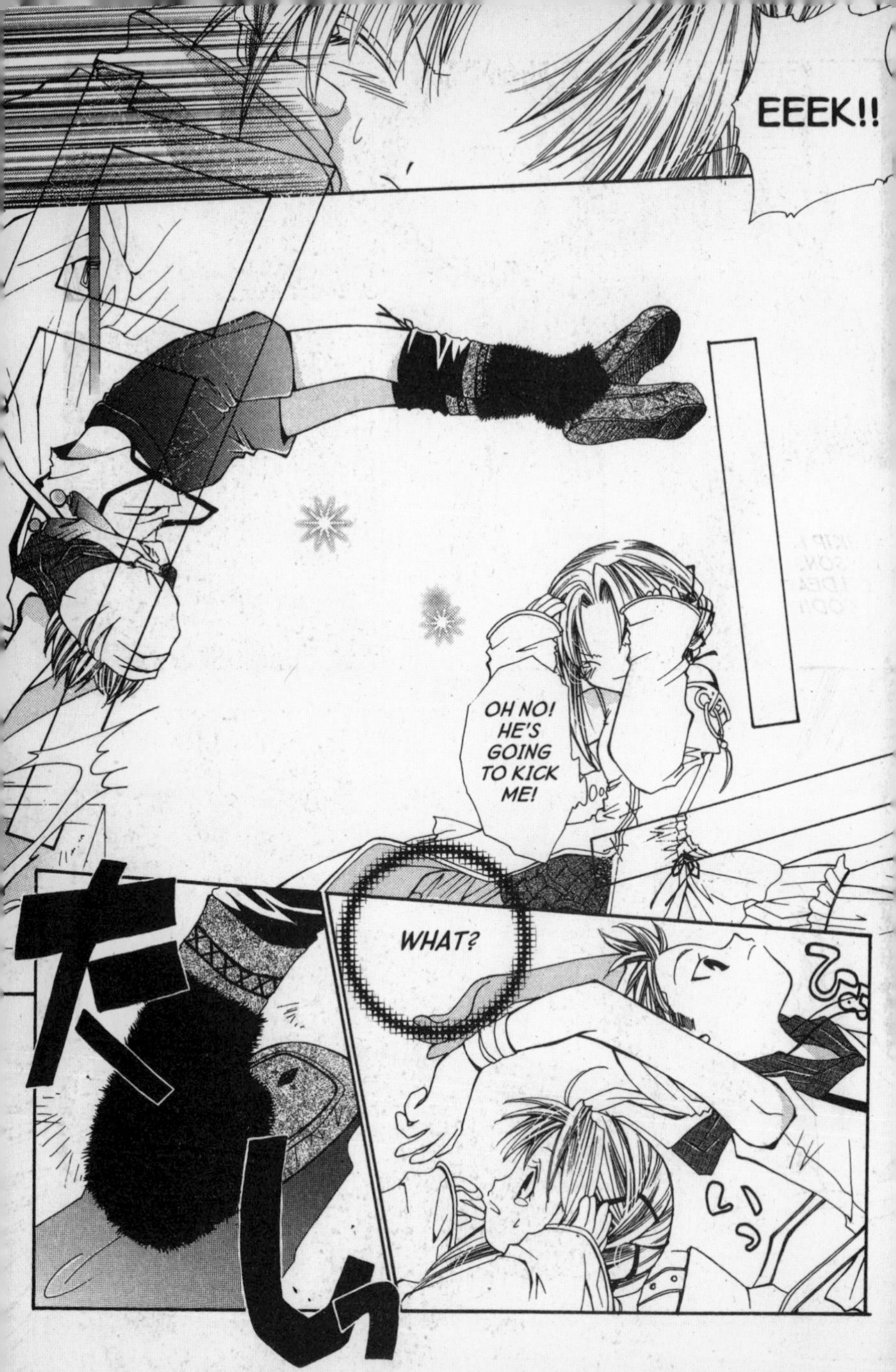
EEEK!!
OH NO! HE'S GOING TO KICK ME!
WHAT?

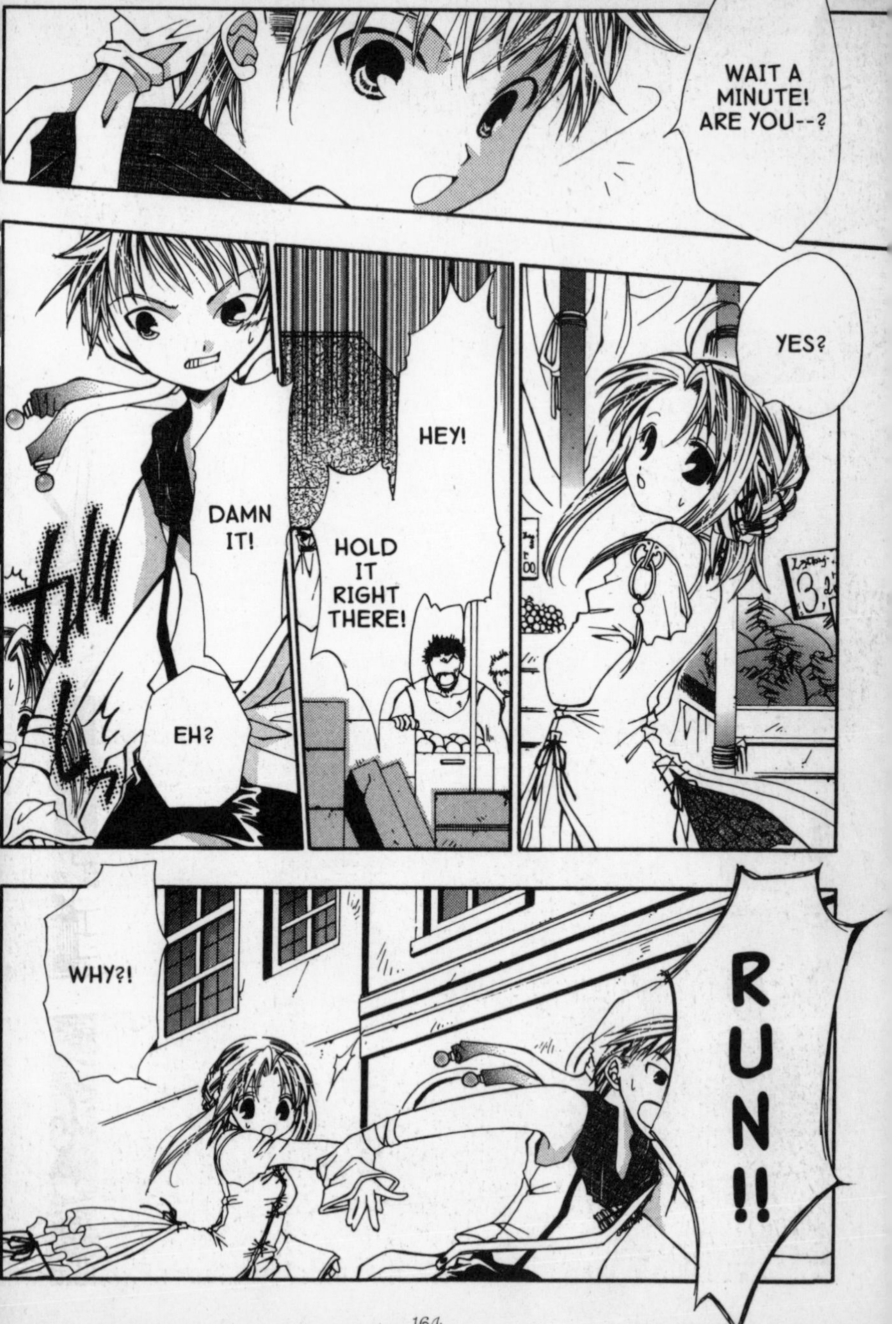
WAIT A MINUTE! ARE YOU--?
YES?
HEY!
HOLD IT RIGHT THERE!
DAMN IT!
EH?
RUN!!
WHY?!

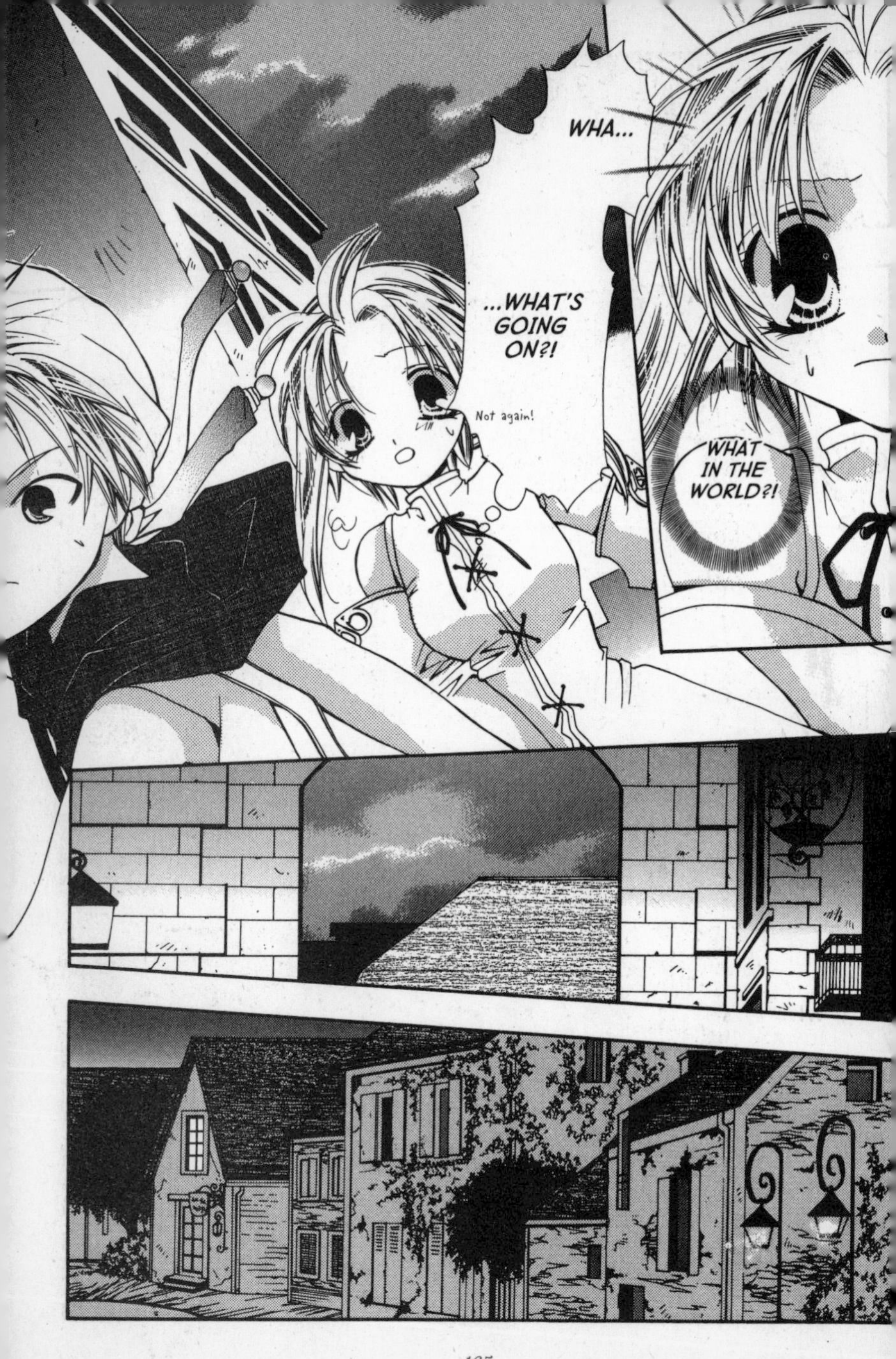
WHA...
WHAT IN THE WORLD?!
...WHAT'S GOING ON?!
Not again!

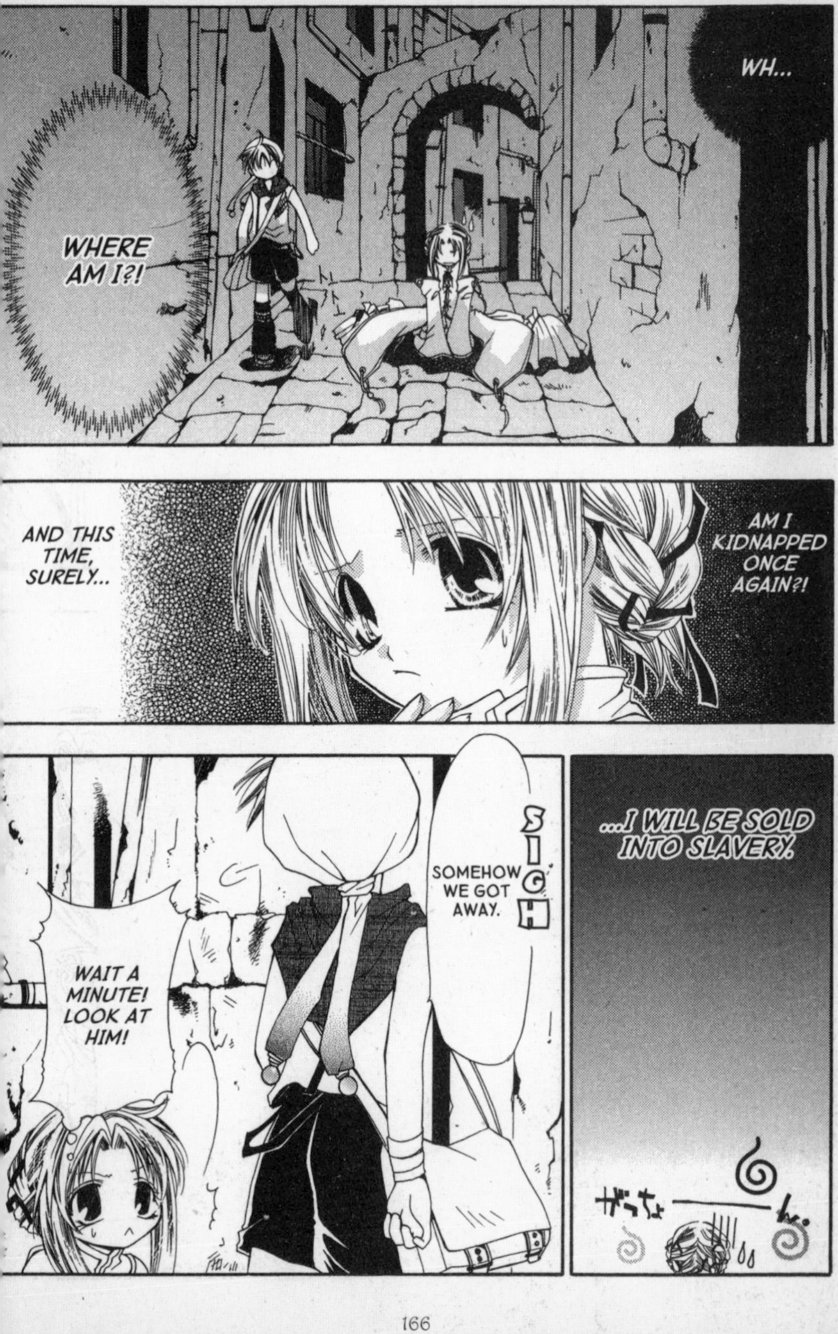
WH...
WHERE AM I?!
AM I KIDNAPPED ONCE AGAIN?!
AND THIS TIME, SURELY...
...I WILL BE SOLD INTO SLAVERY.
がっちょ——ん
SIGH
SOMEHOW WE GOT AWAY.
WAIT A MINUTE! LOOK AT HIM!

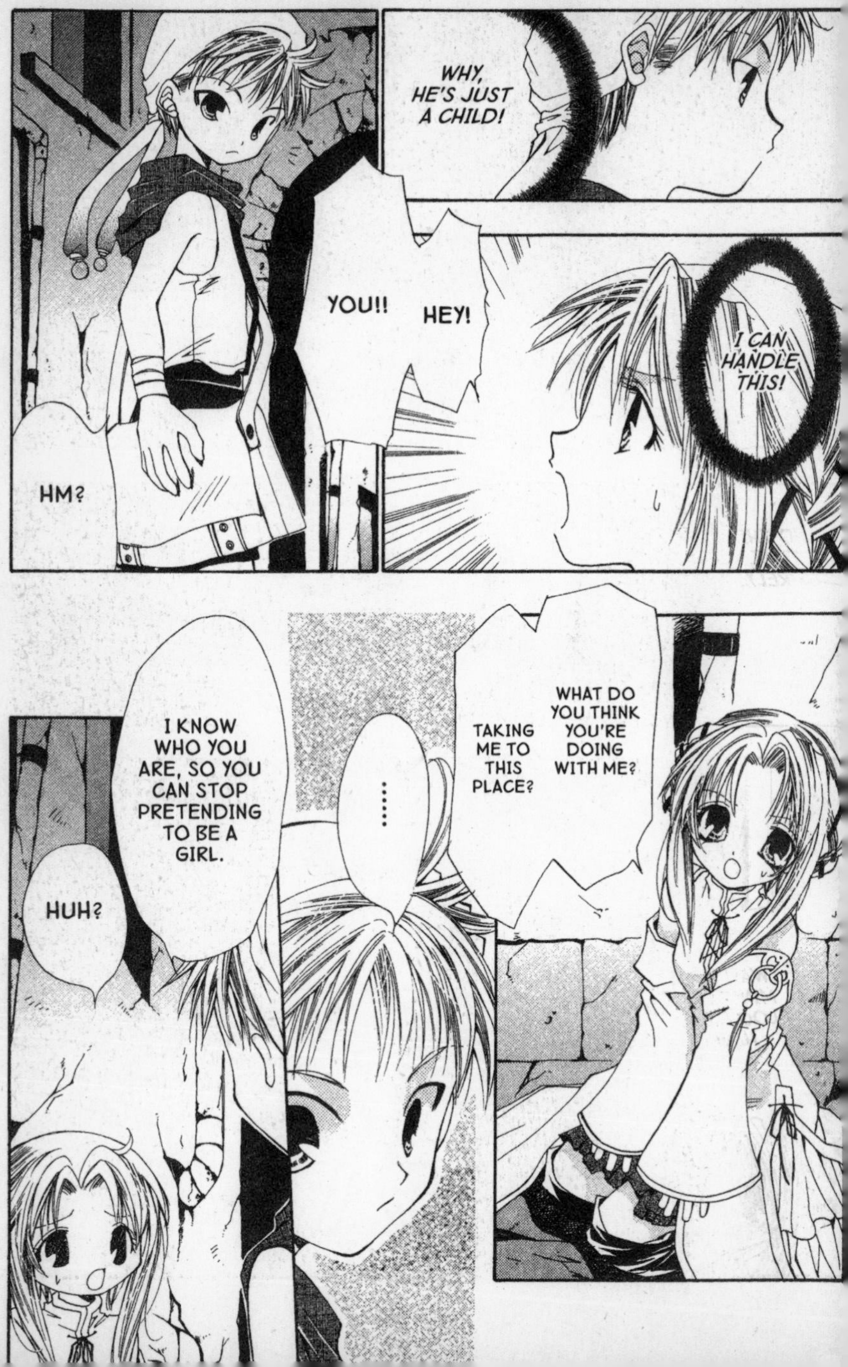
WHY, HE'S JUST A CHILD!
I CAN HANDLE THIS!
HEY! YOU!!
HM?
WHAT DO YOU THINK YOU'RE DOING WITH ME? TAKING ME TO THIS PLACE?
......
I KNOW WHO YOU ARE, SO YOU CAN STOP PRETENDING TO BE A GIRL.
HUH?

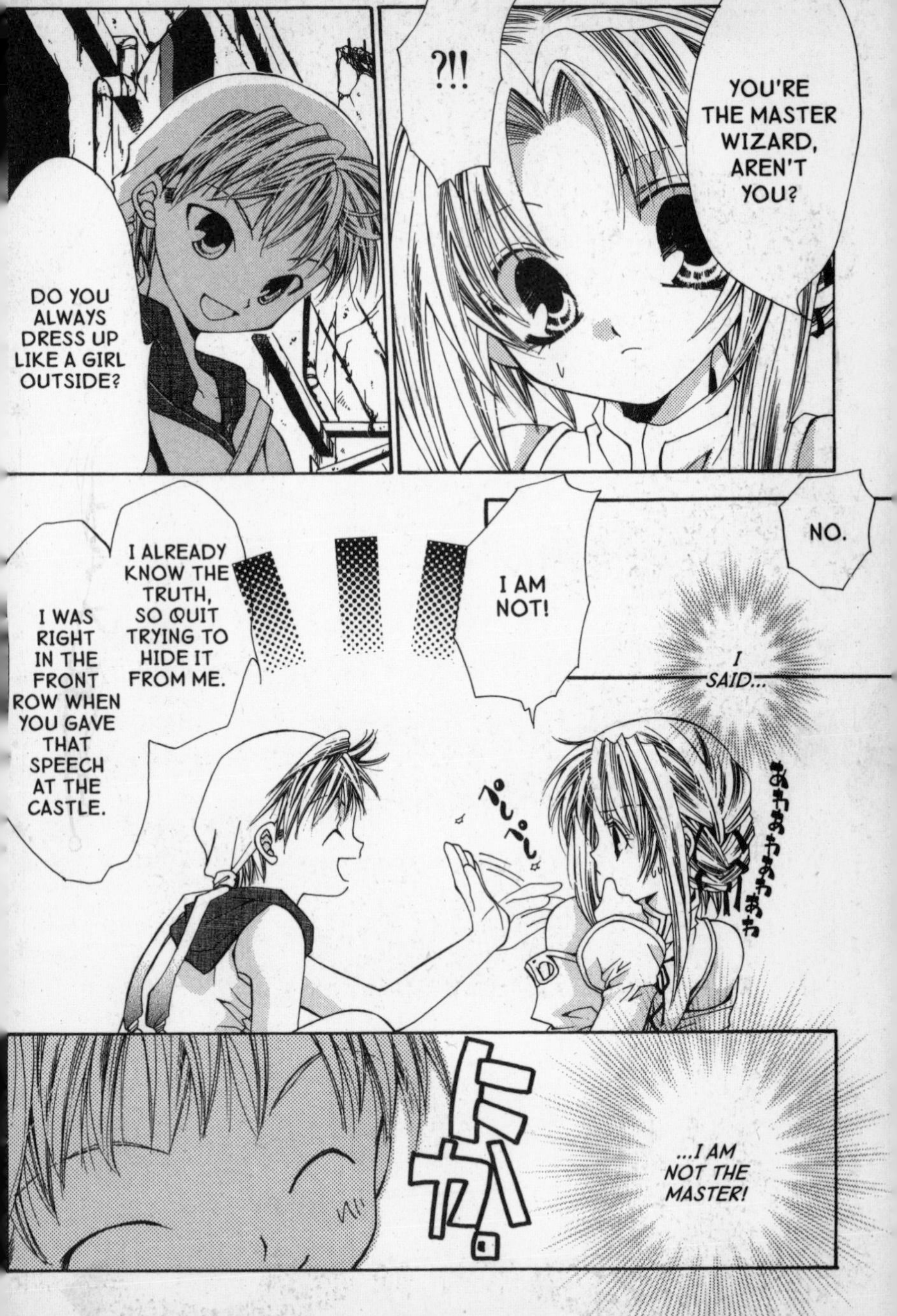
YOU'RE THE MASTER WIZARD, AREN'T YOU?
?!!
DO YOU ALWAYS DRESS UP LIKE A GIRL OUTSIDE?
NO.
I AM NOT!
I ALREADY KNOW THE TRUTH, SO QUIT TRYING TO HIDE IT FROM ME.
I WAS RIGHT IN THE FRONT ROW WHEN YOU GAVE THAT SPEECH AT THE CASTLE.
I SAID...
ぺしぺし
...I AM NOT THE MASTER!
ニヤ。

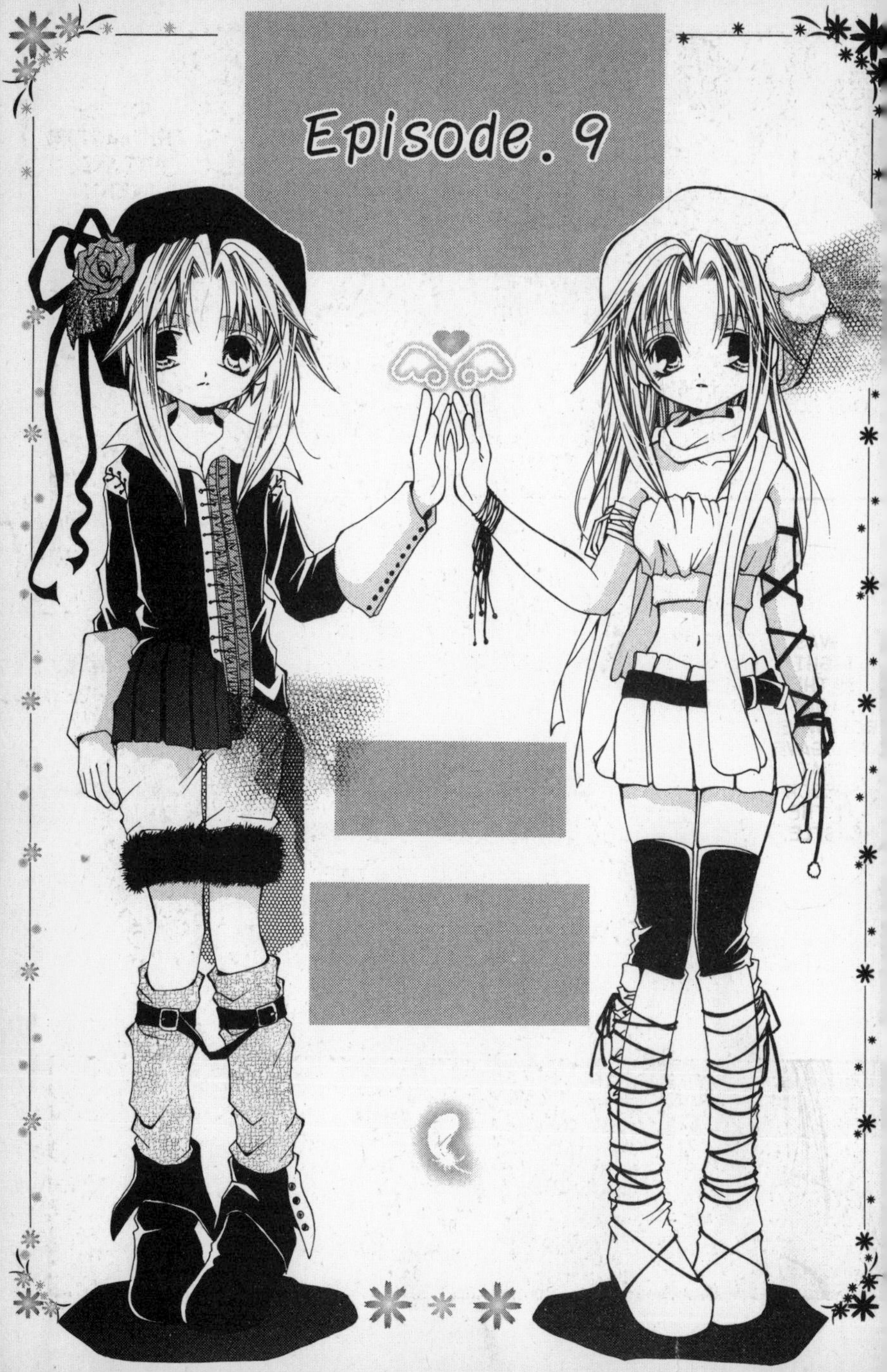
Episode. 9

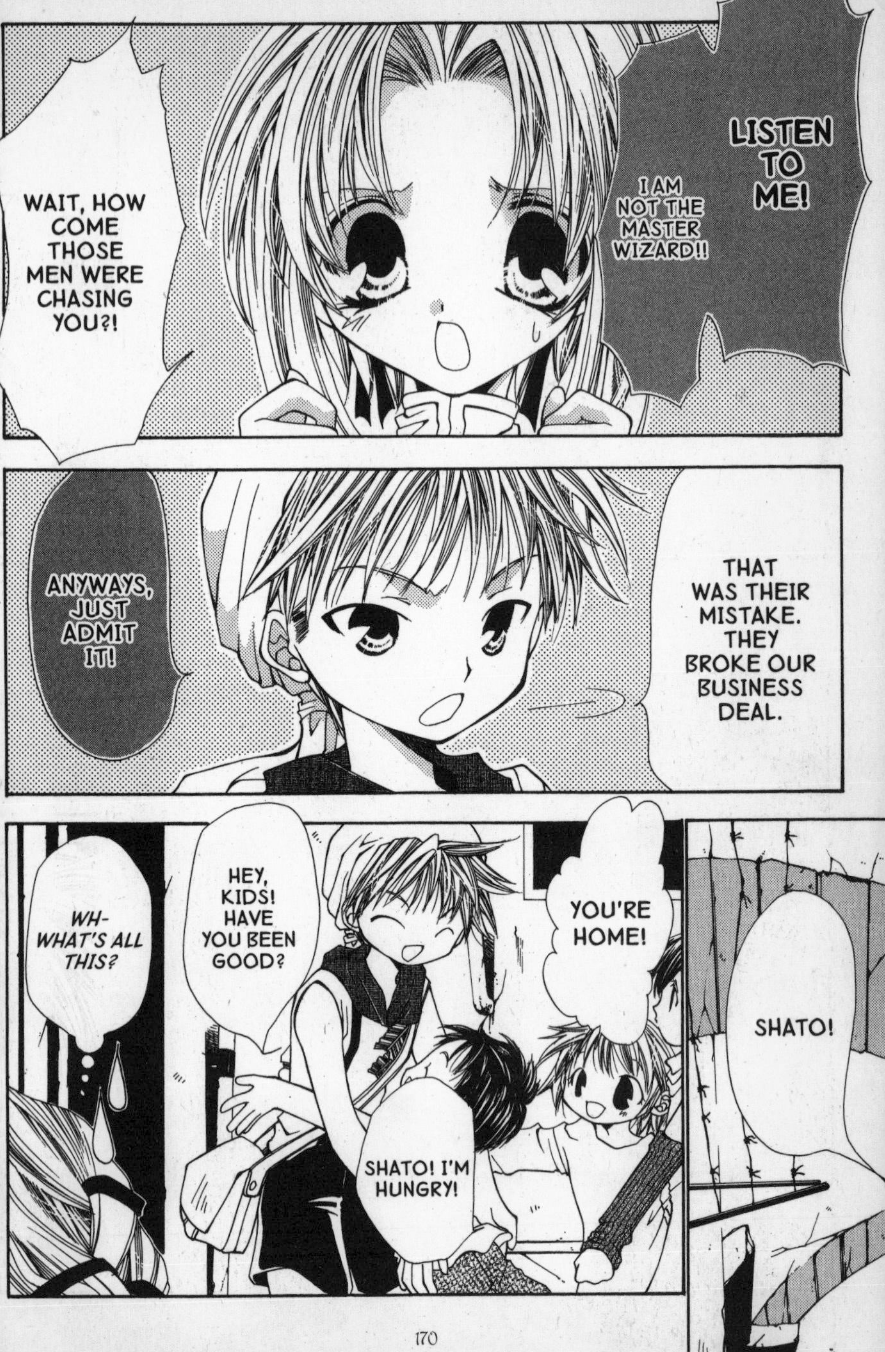
LISTEN TO ME!
I AM NOT THE MASTER WIZARD!!
WAIT, HOW COME THOSE MEN WERE CHASING YOU?!
THAT WAS THEIR MISTAKE. THEY BROKE OUR BUSINESS DEAL.
ANYWAYS, JUST ADMIT IT!
SHATO!
YOU'RE HOME!
HEY, KIDS! HAVE YOU BEEN GOOD?
SHATO! I'M HUNGRY!
WH- WHAT'S ALL THIS?

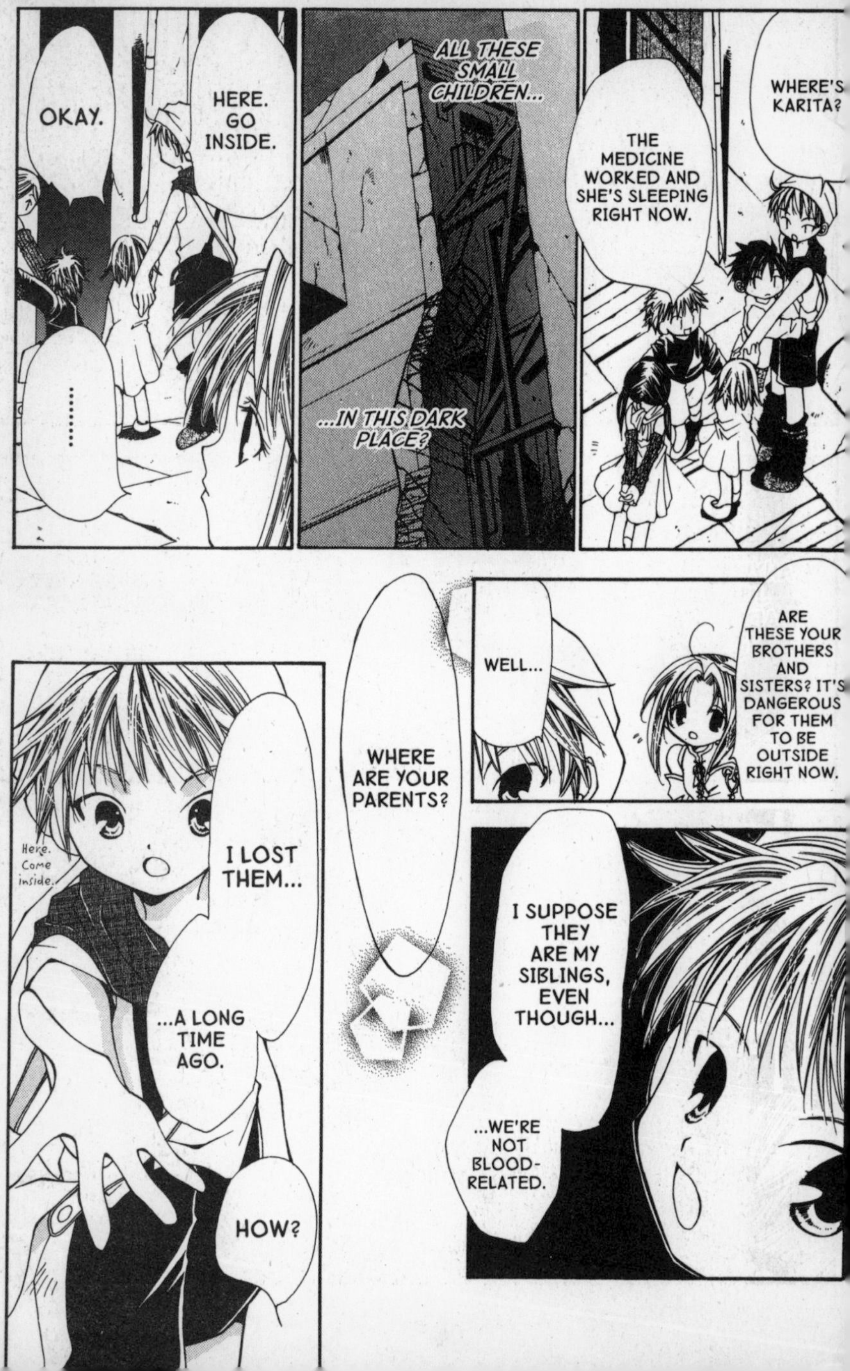
WHERE'S KARITA?
THE MEDICINE WORKED AND SHE'S SLEEPING RIGHT NOW.
ALL THESE SMALL CHILDREN...
...IN THIS DARK PLACE?
HERE. GO INSIDE.
OKAY.
......
ARE THESE YOUR BROTHERS AND SISTERS? IT'S DANGEROUS FOR THEM TO BE OUTSIDE RIGHT NOW.
WELL...
I SUPPOSE THEY ARE MY SIBLINGS, EVEN THOUGH...
...WE'RE NOT BLOOD-RELATED.
WHERE ARE YOUR PARENTS?
I LOST THEM...
...A LONG TIME AGO.
HOW?
Here. Come inside.

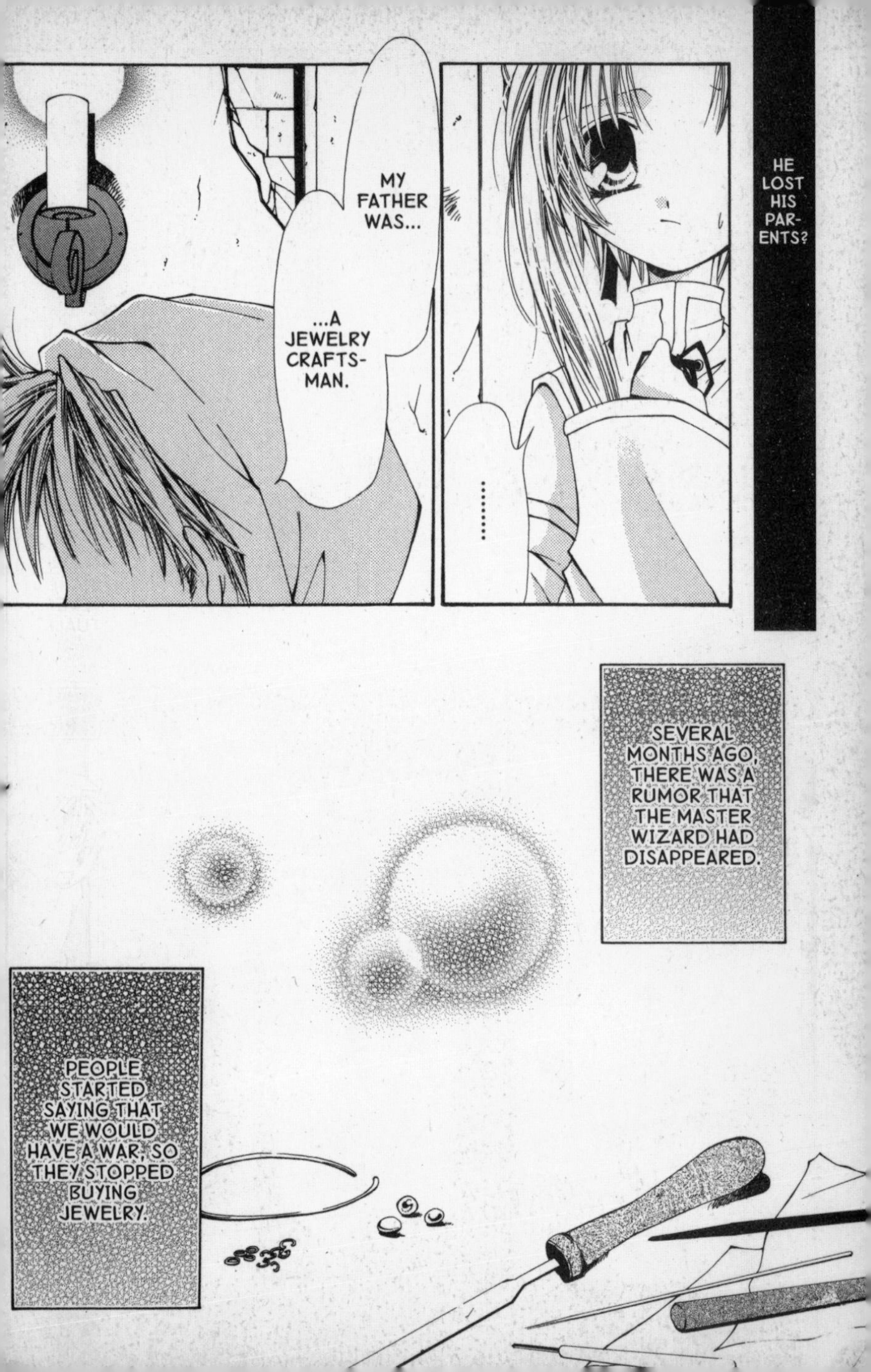
HE LOST HIS PAR-ENTS?
......
MY FATHER WAS...
...A JEWELRY CRAFTS-MAN.
SEVERAL MONTHS AGO, THERE WAS A RUMOR THAT THE MASTER WIZARD HAD DISAPPEARED.
PEOPLE STARTED SAYING THAT WE WOULD HAVE A WAR, SO THEY STOPPED BUYING JEWELRY.

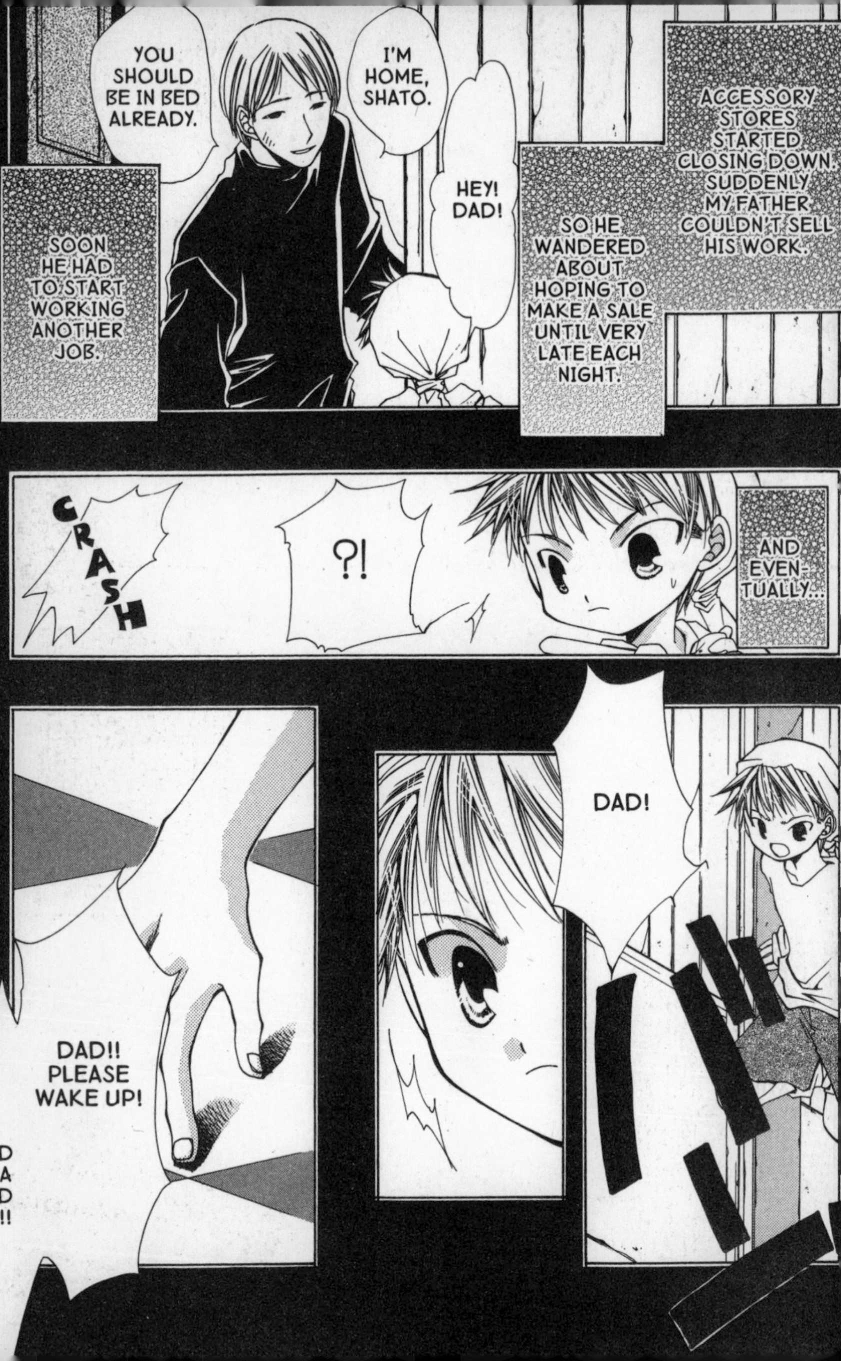
ACCESSORY STORES STARTED CLOSING DOWN. SUDDENLY MY FATHER COULDN'T SELL HIS WORK.
SO HE WANDERED ABOUT HOPING TO MAKE A SALE UNTIL VERY LATE EACH NIGHT.
HEY! DAD!
I'M HOME, SHATO.
YOU SHOULD BE IN BED ALREADY.
SOON HE HAD TO START WORKING ANOTHER JOB.
AND EVEN-TUALLY...
?!
CRASH
DAD!
DAD!! PLEASE WAKE UP!
DAD!!

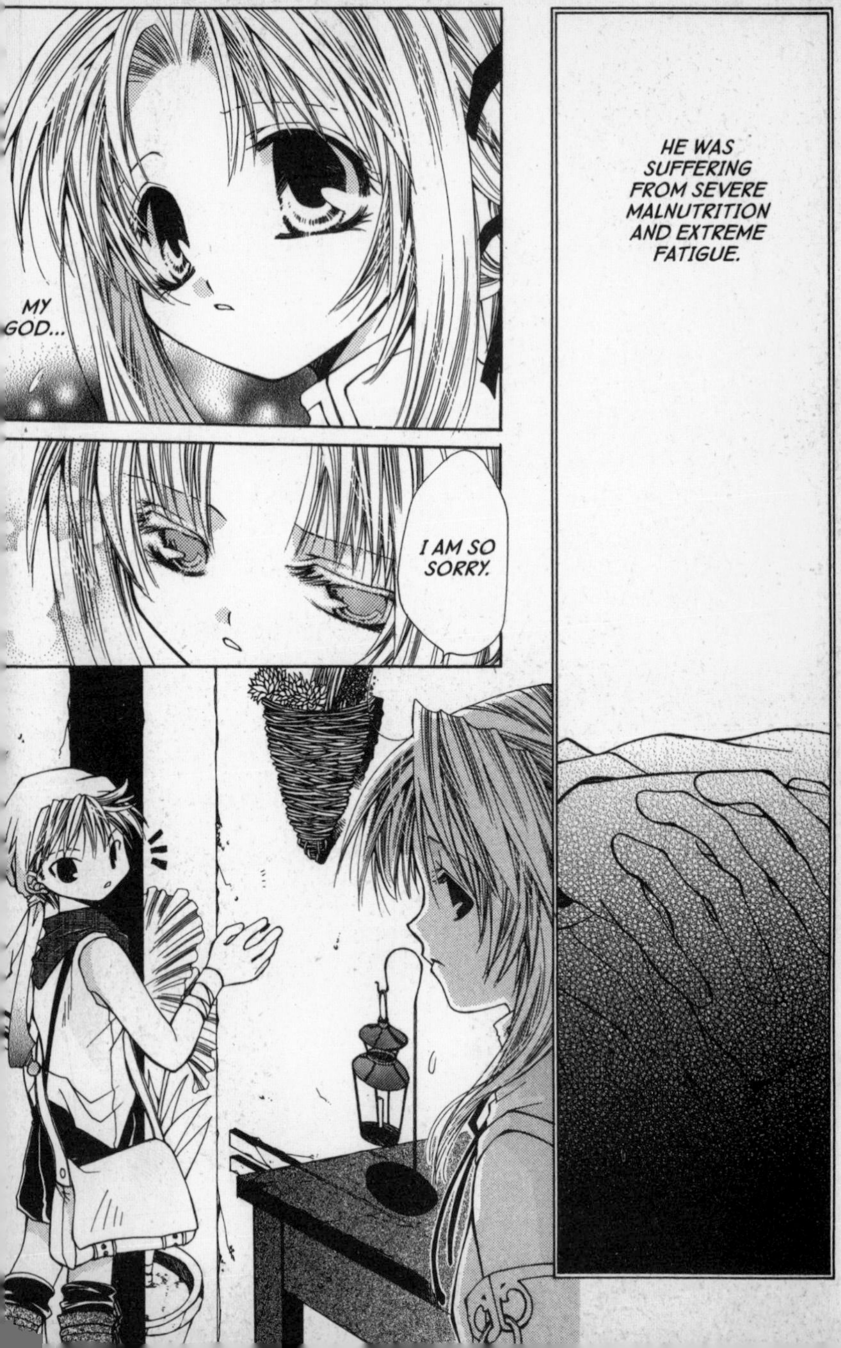
HE WAS SUFFERING FROM SEVERE MALNUTRITION AND EXTREME FATIGUE.
MY GOD...
I AM SO SORRY.

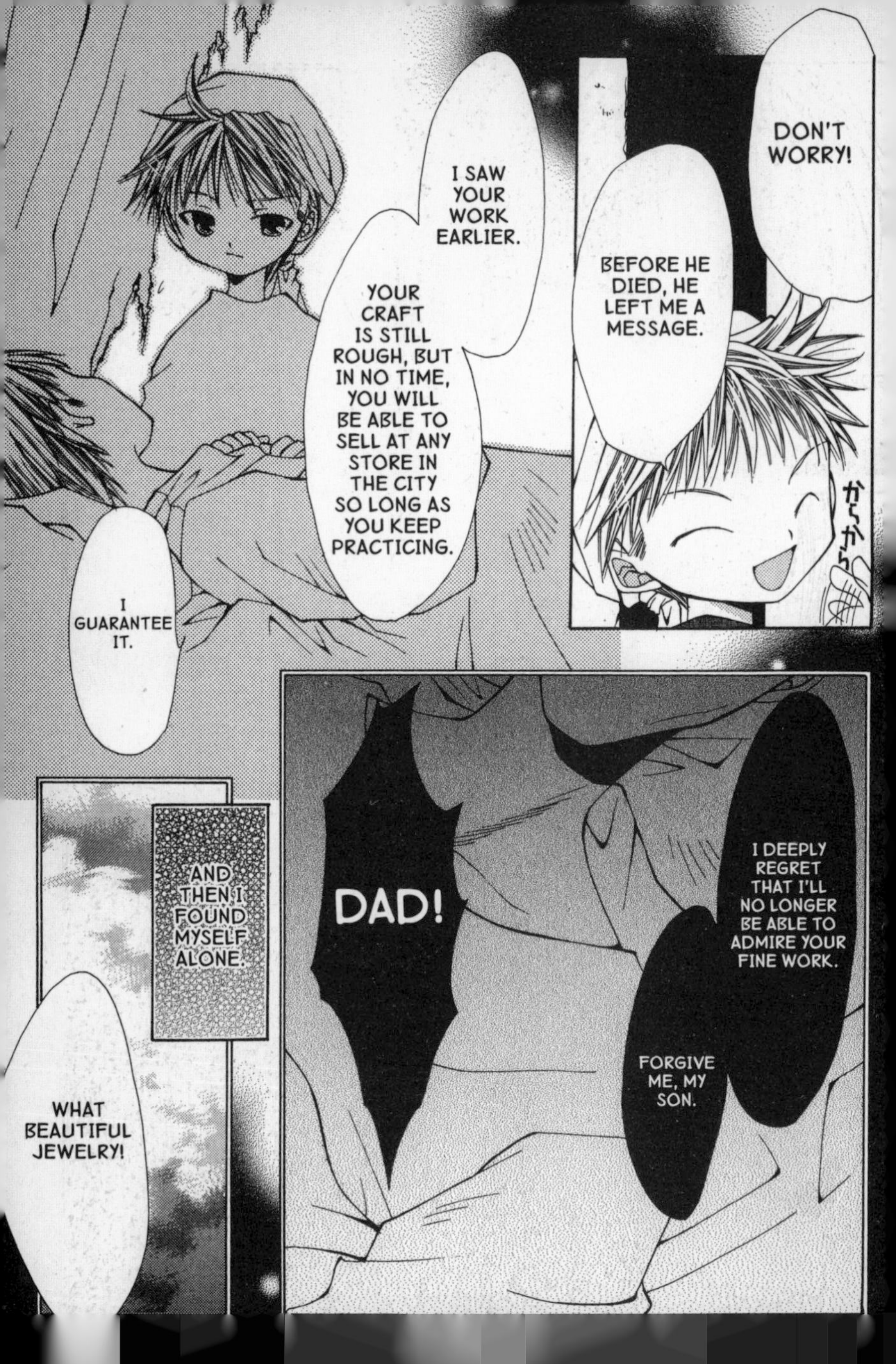
DON'T WORRY!
BEFORE HE DIED, HE LEFT ME A MESSAGE.
からから
I SAW YOUR WORK EARLIER.
YOUR CRAFT IS STILL ROUGH, BUT IN NO TIME, YOU WILL BE ABLE TO SELL AT ANY STORE IN THE CITY SO LONG AS YOU KEEP PRACTICING.
I GUARANTEE IT.
I DEEPLY REGRET THAT I'LL NO LONGER BE ABLE TO ADMIRE YOUR FINE WORK.
DAD!
FORGIVE ME, MY SON.
AND THEN I FOUND MYSELF ALONE.
WHAT BEAUTIFUL JEWELRY!

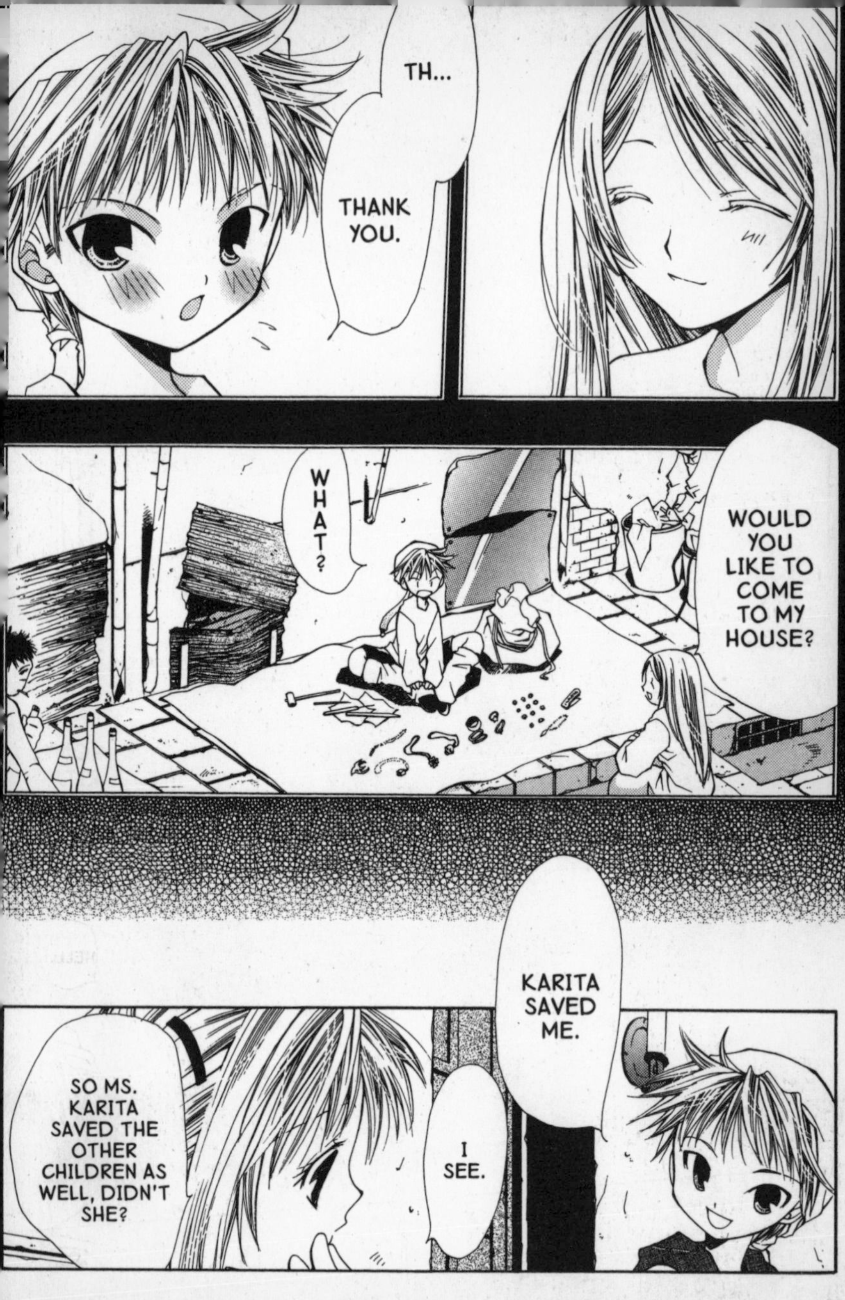
TH...
THANK YOU.
WOULD YOU LIKE TO COME TO MY HOUSE?
WHAT?
KARITA SAVED ME.
I SEE.
SO MS. KARITA SAVED THE OTHER CHILDREN AS WELL, DIDN'T SHE?

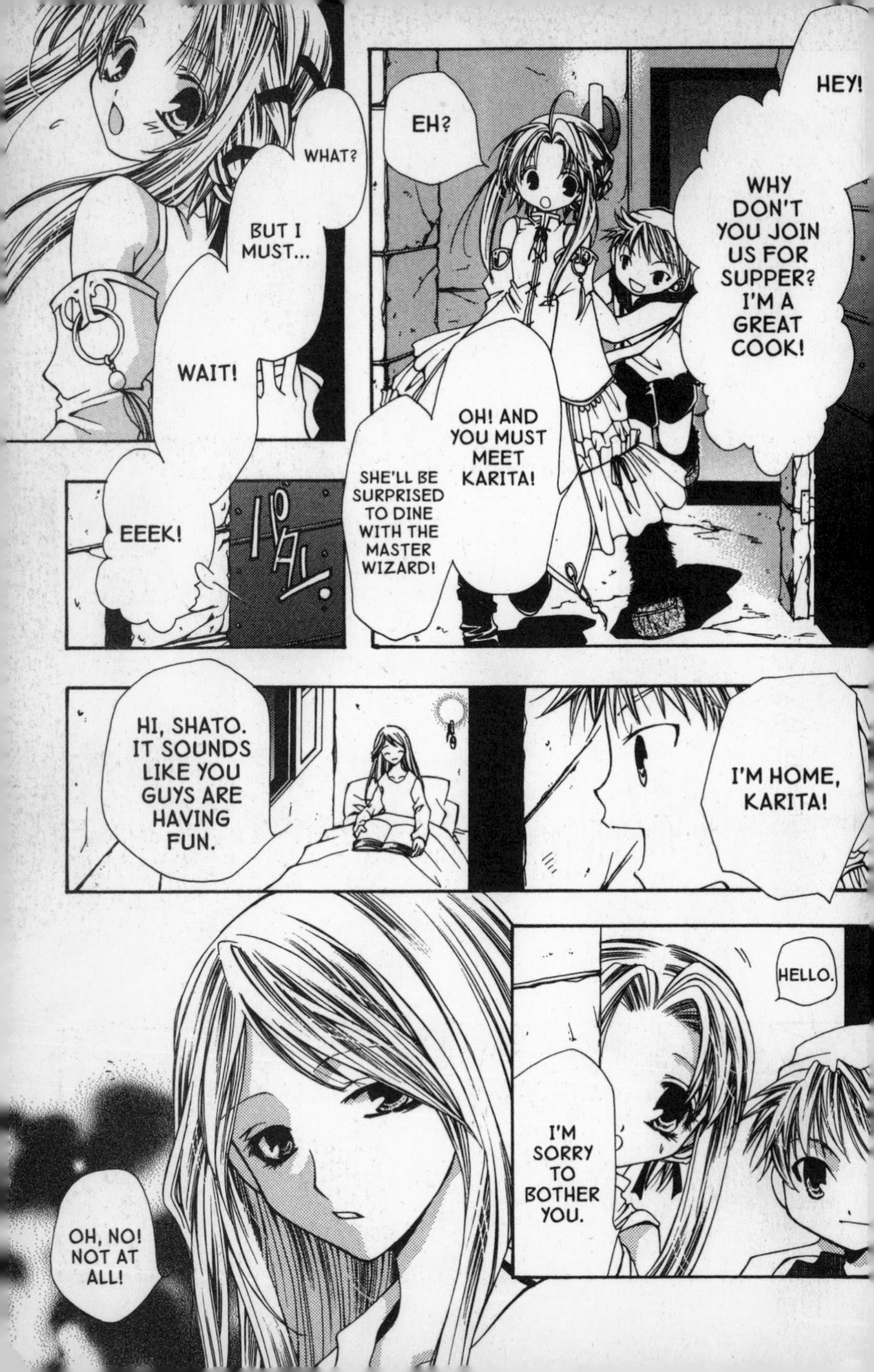
HEY!
WHY DON'T YOU JOIN US FOR SUPPER? I'M A GREAT COOK!
EH?
OH! AND YOU MUST MEET KARITA!
SHE'LL BE SURPRISED TO DINE WITH THE MASTER WIZARD!
WHAT?
BUT I MUST...
WAIT!
EEEK!
パタン!
I'M HOME, KARITA!
HI, SHATO. IT SOUNDS LIKE YOU GUYS ARE HAVING FUN.
HELLO.
I'M SORRY TO BOTHER YOU.
OH, NO! NOT AT ALL!

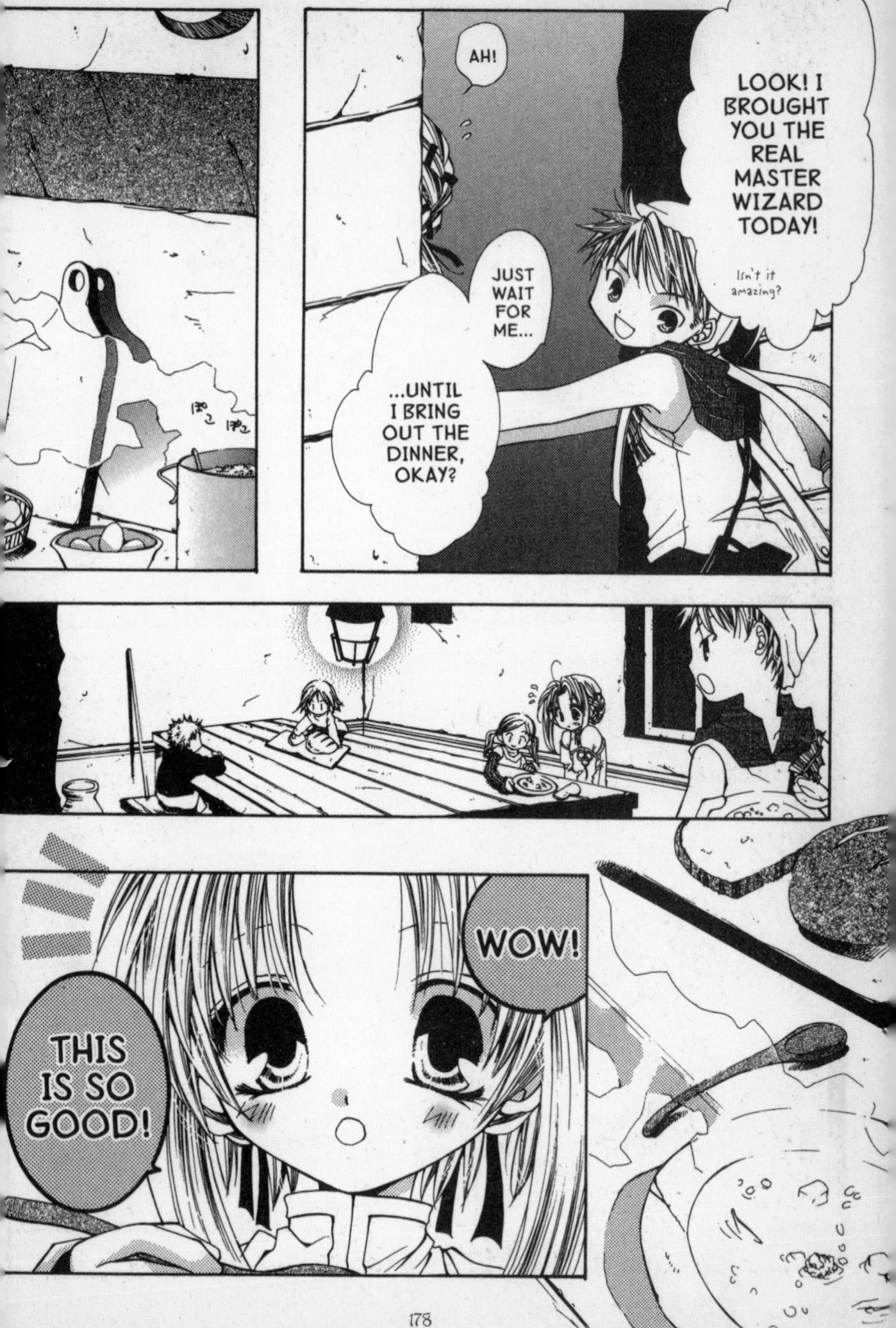
LOOK! I BROUGHT YOU THE REAL MASTER WIZARD TODAY!
Isn't it amazing?
AH!
JUST WAIT FOR ME...
...UNTIL I BRING OUT THE DINNER, OKAY?
WOW!
THIS IS SO GOOD!

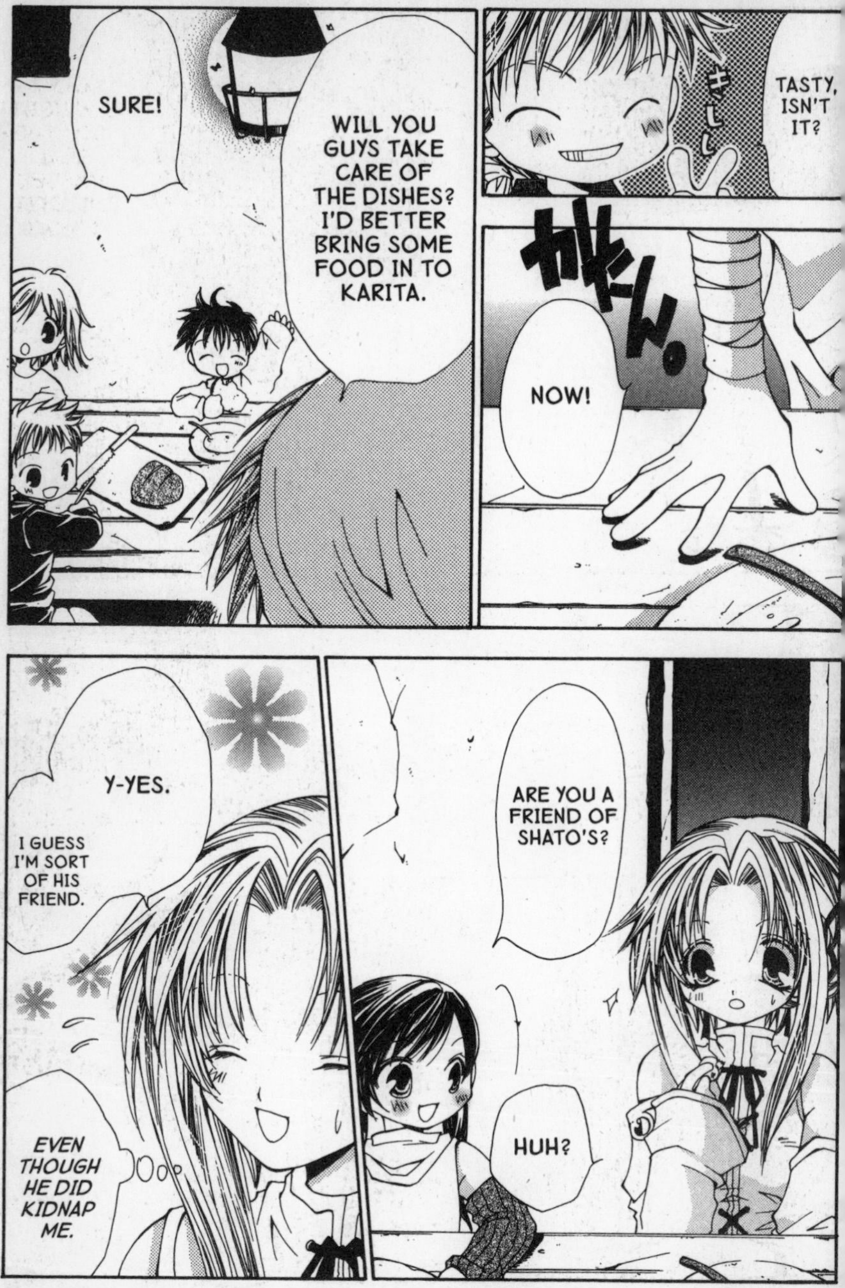
TASTY, ISN'T IT?
きしし
かたん。
NOW!
WILL YOU GUYS TAKE CARE OF THE DISHES? I'D BETTER BRING SOME FOOD IN TO KARITA.
SURE!
ARE YOU A FRIEND OF SHATO'S?
HUH?
Y-YES.
I GUESS I'M SORT OF HIS FRIEND.
EVEN THOUGH HE DID KIDNAP ME.

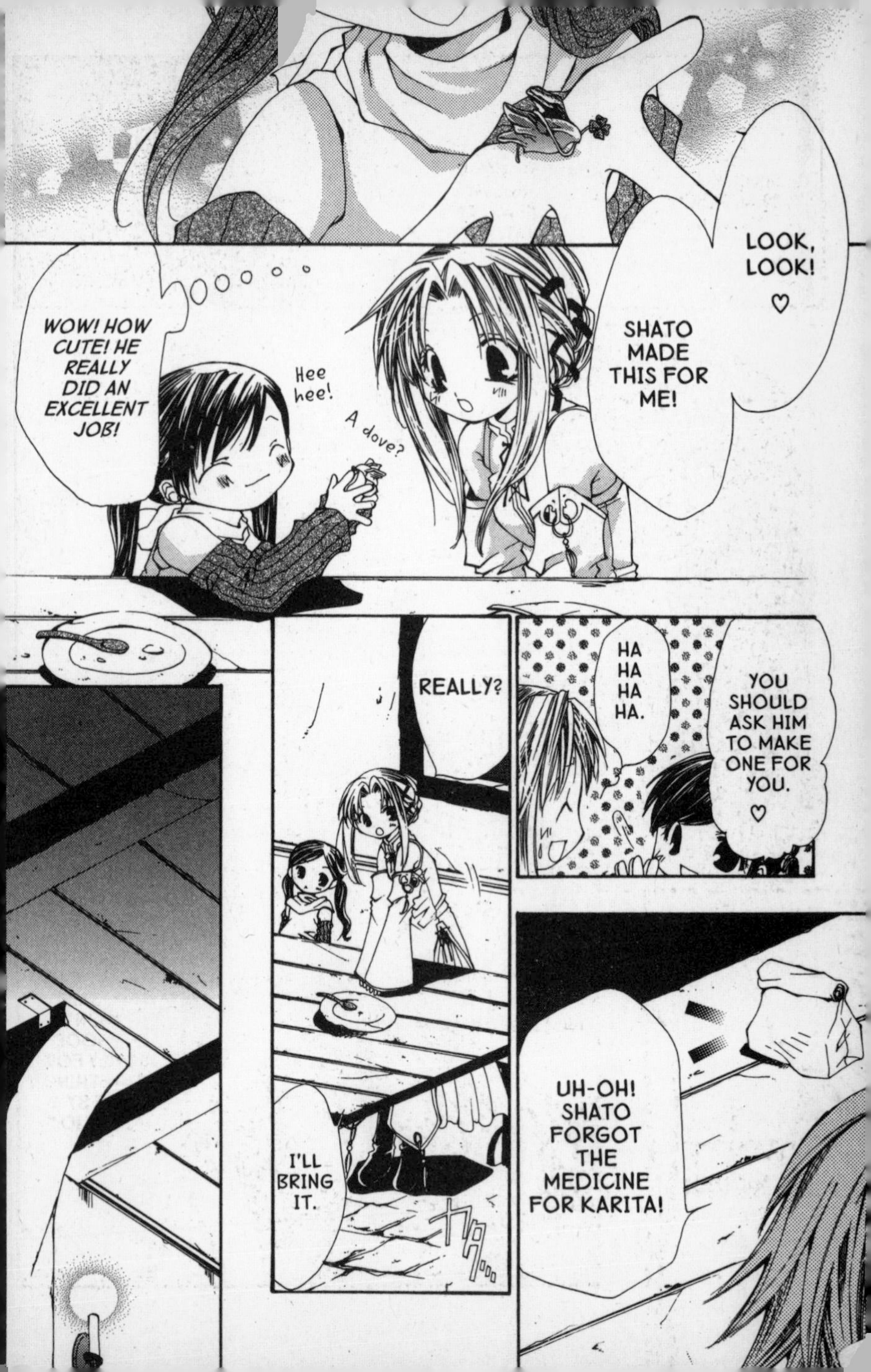
LOOK, LOOK! ♡
SHATO MADE THIS FOR ME!
A dove?
Hee hee!
WOW! HOW CUTE! HE REALLY DID AN EXCELLENT JOB!
YOU SHOULD ASK HIM TO MAKE ONE FOR YOU. ♡
HA HA HA HA.
UH-OH! SHATO FORGOT THE MEDICINE FOR KARITA!
REALLY?
I'LL BRING IT.
カタ

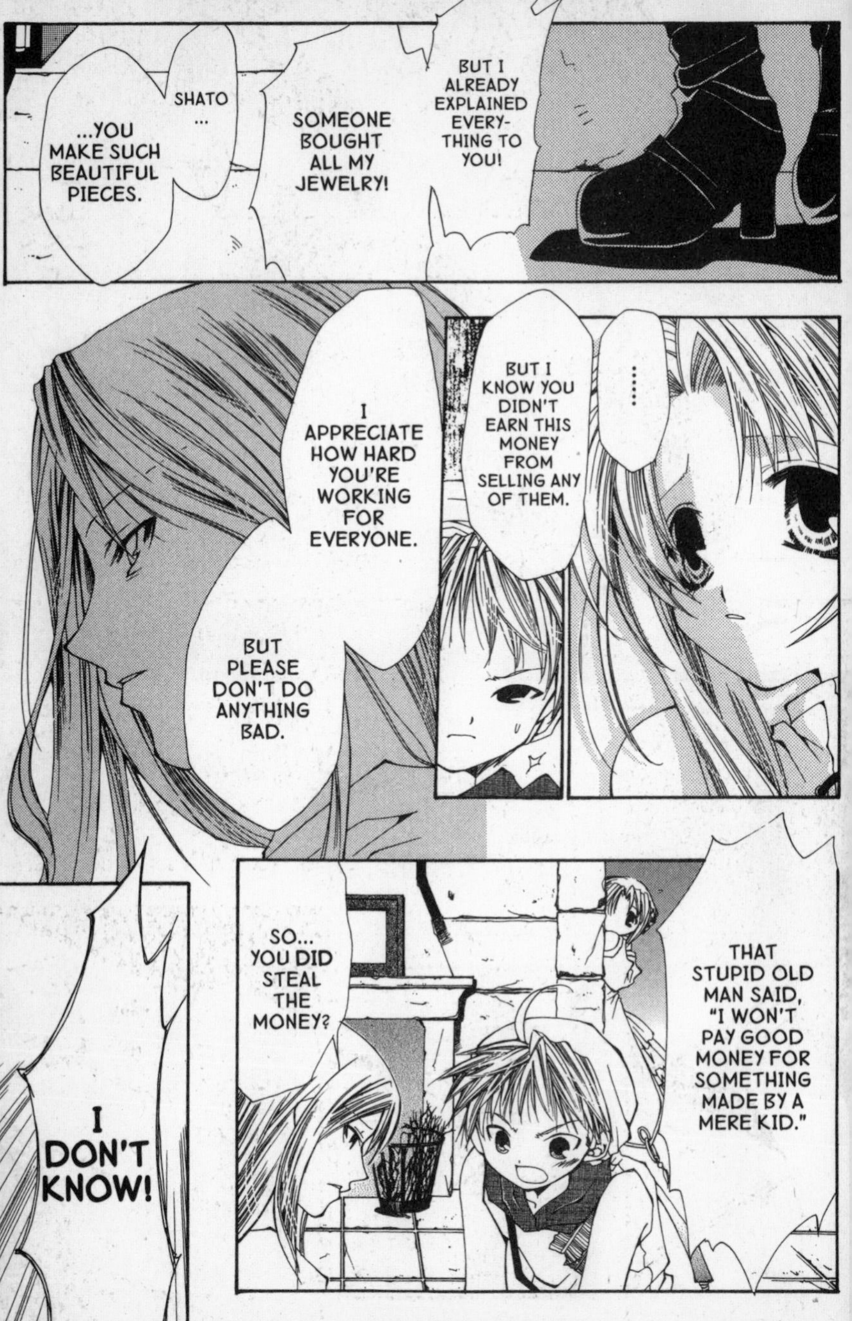
BUT I ALREADY EXPLAINED EVERY-THING TO YOU!
SOMEONE BOUGHT ALL MY JEWELRY!
SHATO ...
...YOU MAKE SUCH BEAUTIFUL PIECES.
......
BUT I KNOW YOU DIDN'T EARN THIS MONEY FROM SELLING ANY OF THEM.
I APPRECIATE HOW HARD YOU'RE WORKING FOR EVERYONE.
BUT PLEASE DON'T DO ANYTHING BAD.
THAT STUPID OLD MAN SAID, "I WON'T PAY GOOD MONEY FOR SOMETHING MADE BY A MERE KID."
SO... YOU DID STEAL THE MONEY?
I DON'T KNOW!

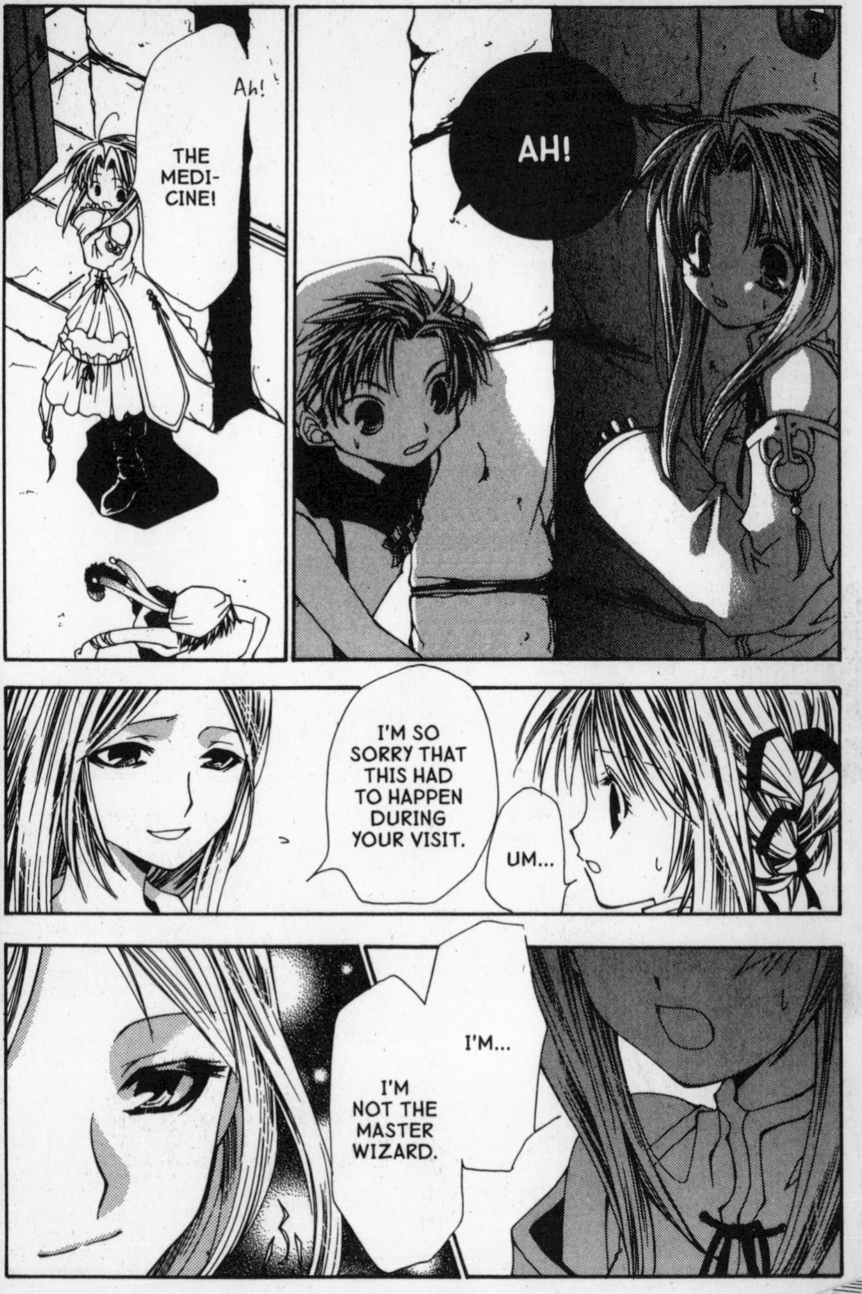
AH!
Ah!
THE MEDICINE!
I'M SO SORRY THAT THIS HAD TO HAPPEN DURING YOUR VISIT.
UM...
I'M...
I'M NOT THE MASTER WIZARD.

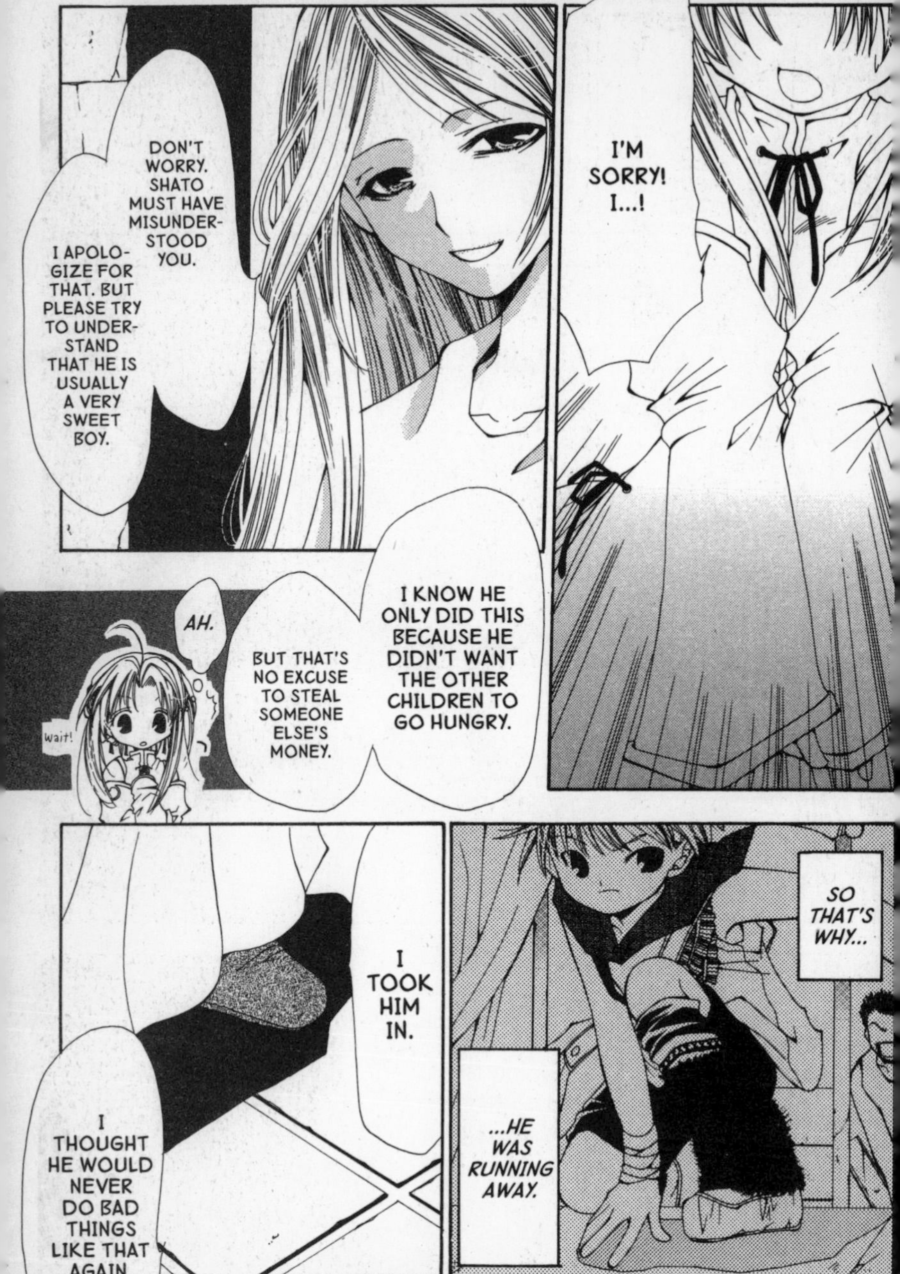
I'M SORRY! I...!
DON'T WORRY. SHATO MUST HAVE MISUNDERSTOOD YOU.
I APOLOGIZE FOR THAT. BUT PLEASE TRY TO UNDERSTAND THAT HE IS USUALLY A VERY SWEET BOY.
I KNOW HE ONLY DID THIS BECAUSE HE DIDN'T WANT THE OTHER CHILDREN TO GO HUNGRY.
BUT THAT'S NO EXCUSE TO STEAL SOMEONE ELSE'S MONEY.
AH.
wait!
SO THAT'S WHY...
...HE WAS RUNNING AWAY.
I TOOK HIM IN.
I THOUGHT HE WOULD NEVER DO BAD THINGS LIKE THAT AGAIN.

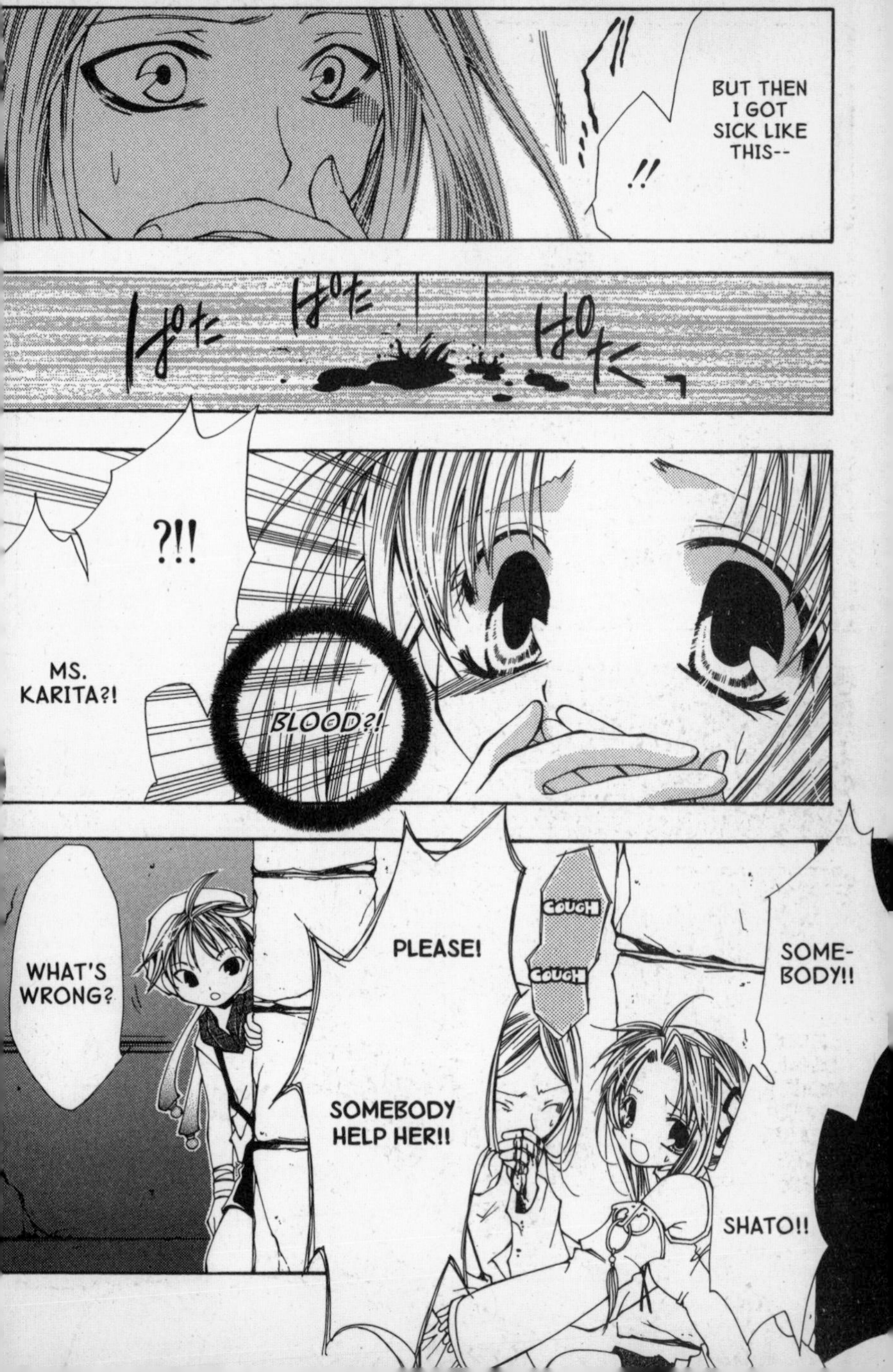

BUT THEN I GOT SICK LIKE THIS--
!!
ぱたっ
ぱた
ぱた
BLOOD?!
?!!
MS. KARITA?!
SHATO!!
SOME-BODY!!
COUGH
COUGH
PLEASE!
SOMEBODY HELP HER!!
WHAT'S WRONG?

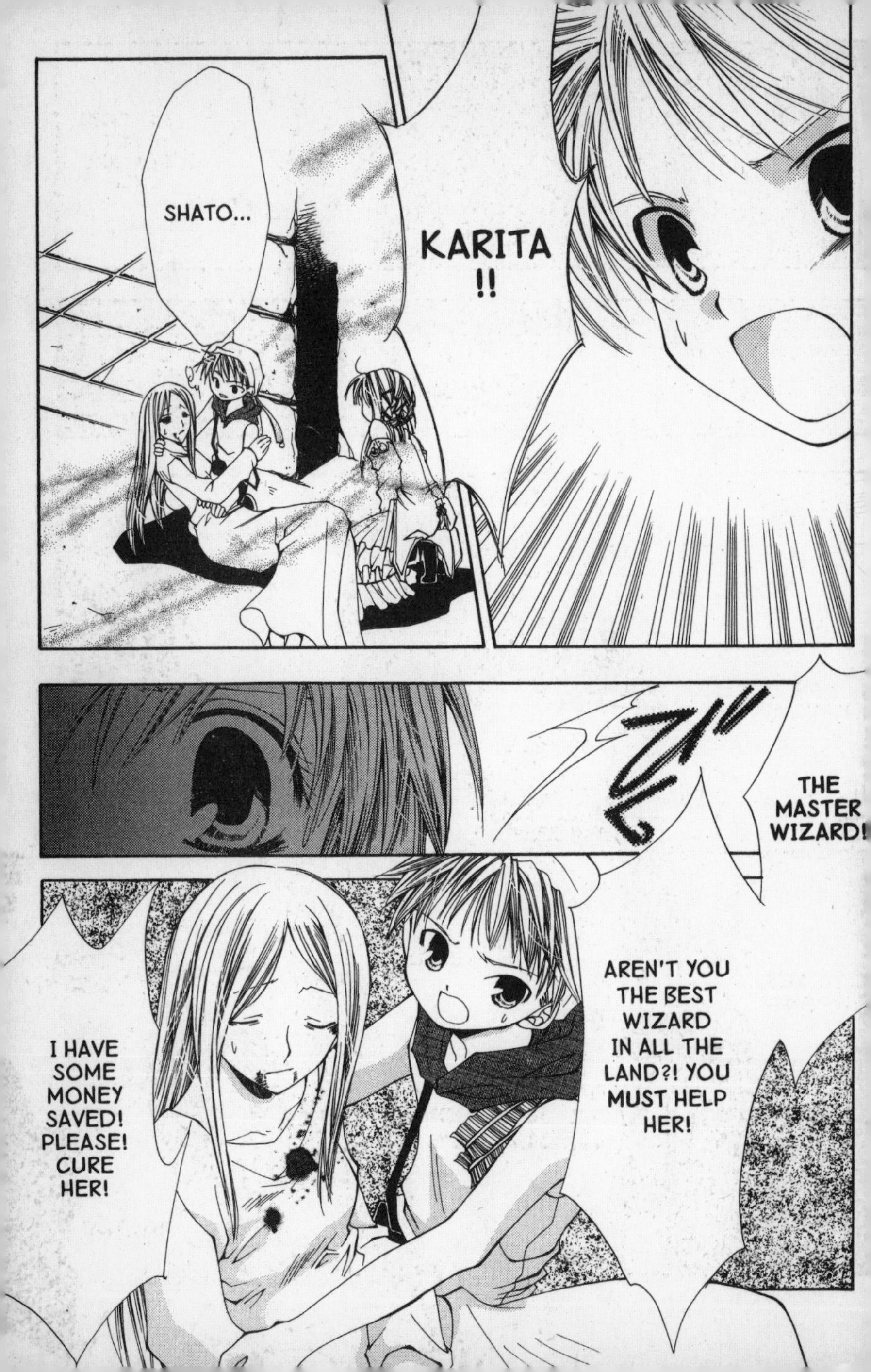

KARITA !!
SHATO...
THE MASTER WIZARD!
AREN'T YOU THE BEST WIZARD IN ALL THE LAND?! YOU MUST HELP HER!
I HAVE SOME MONEY SAVED! PLEASE! CURE HER!

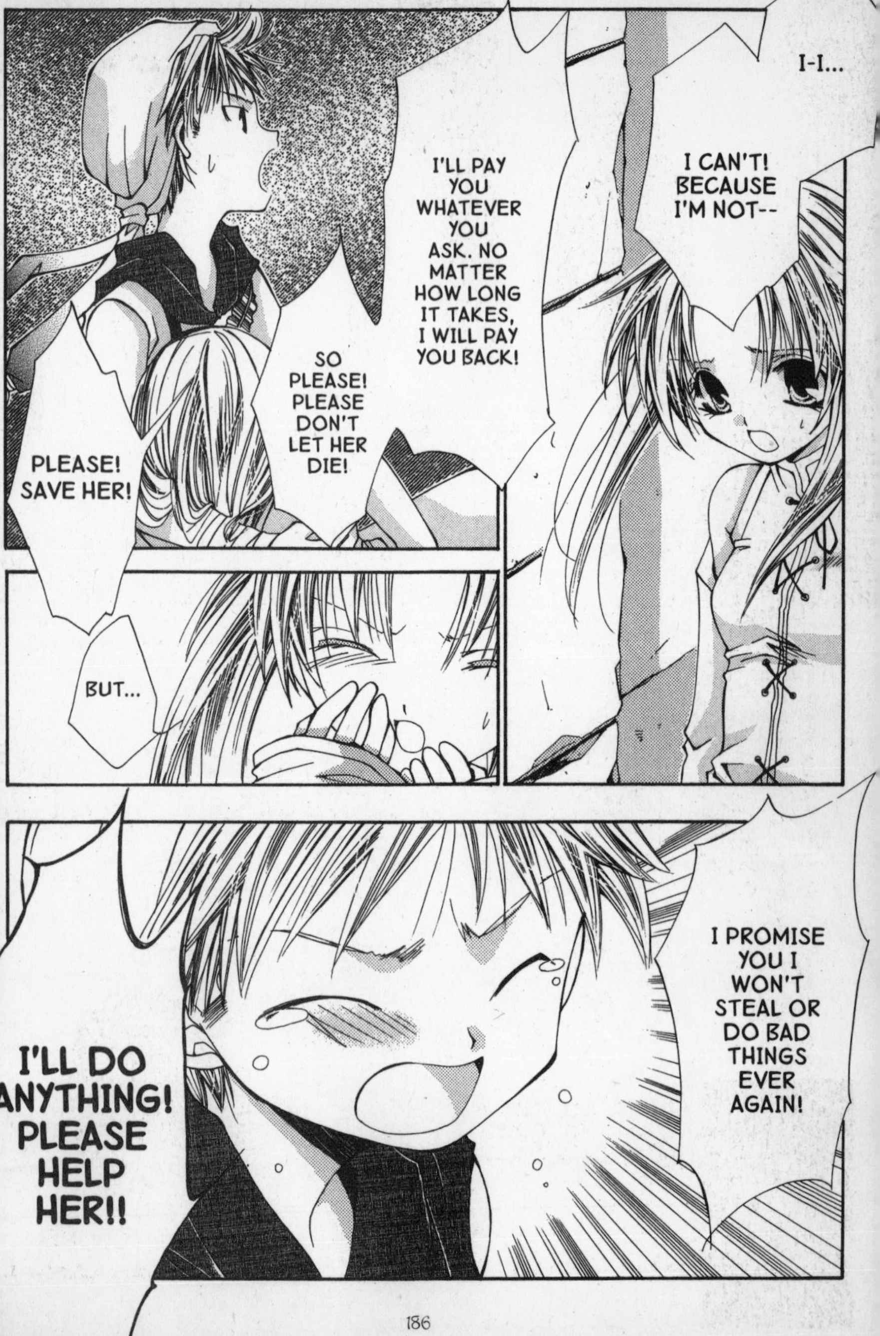
I-I...
I CAN'T! BECAUSE I'M NOT--
I'LL PAY YOU WHATEVER YOU ASK. NO MATTER HOW LONG IT TAKES, I WILL PAY YOU BACK!
SO PLEASE! PLEASE DON'T LET HER DIE!
PLEASE! SAVE HER!
BUT...
I PROMISE YOU I WON'T STEAL OR DO BAD THINGS EVER AGAIN!
I'LL DO ANYTHING! PLEASE HELP HER!!

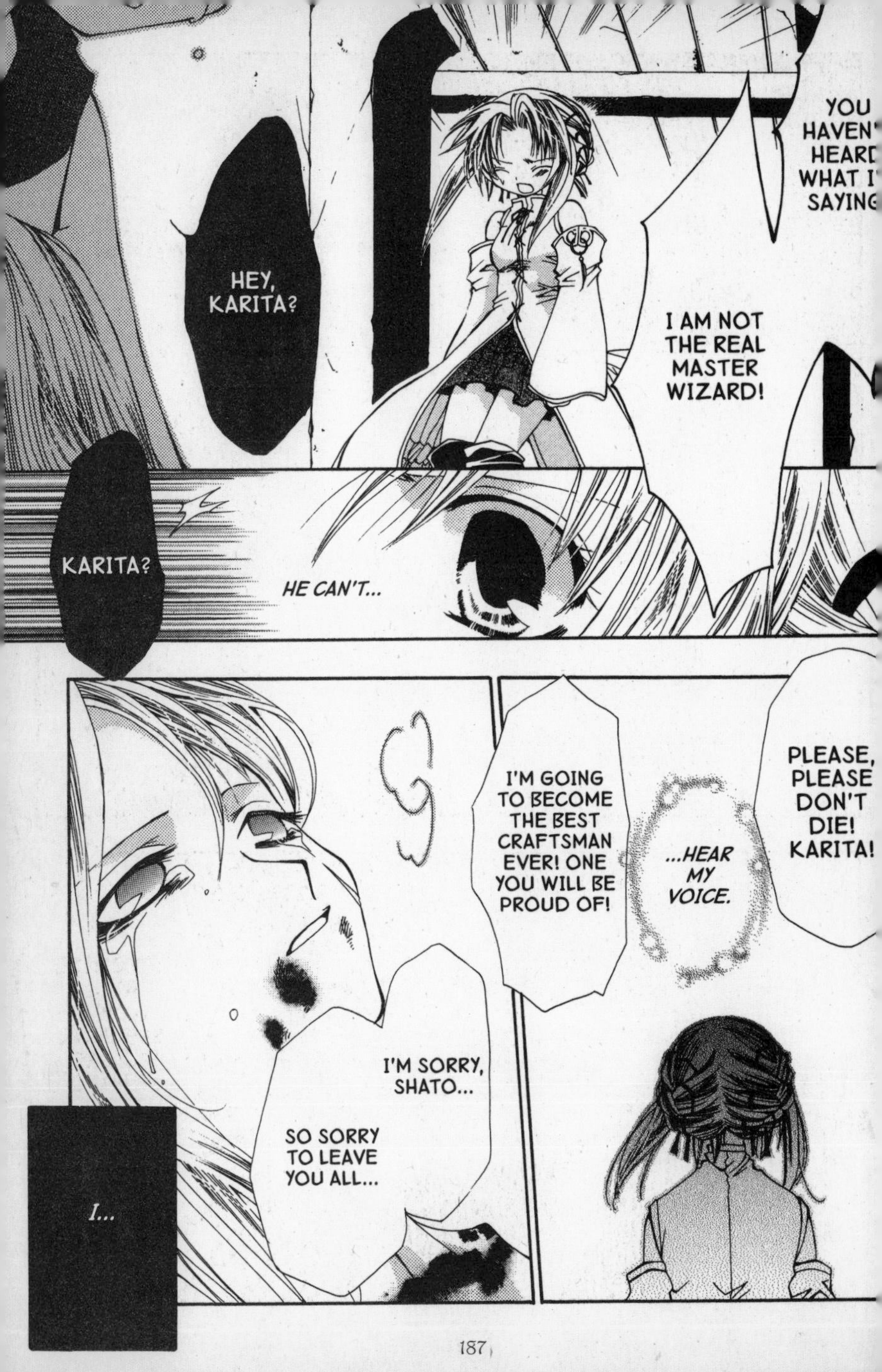
YOU HAVEN' HEARD WHAT I' SAYING
I AM NOT THE REAL MASTER WIZARD!
HEY, KARITA?
HE CAN'T...
KARITA?
PLEASE, PLEASE DON'T DIE! KARITA!
...HEAR MY VOICE.
I'M GOING TO BECOME THE BEST CRAFTSMAN EVER! ONE YOU WILL BE PROUD OF!
I'M SORRY, SHATO...
SO SORRY TO LEAVE YOU ALL...
I...

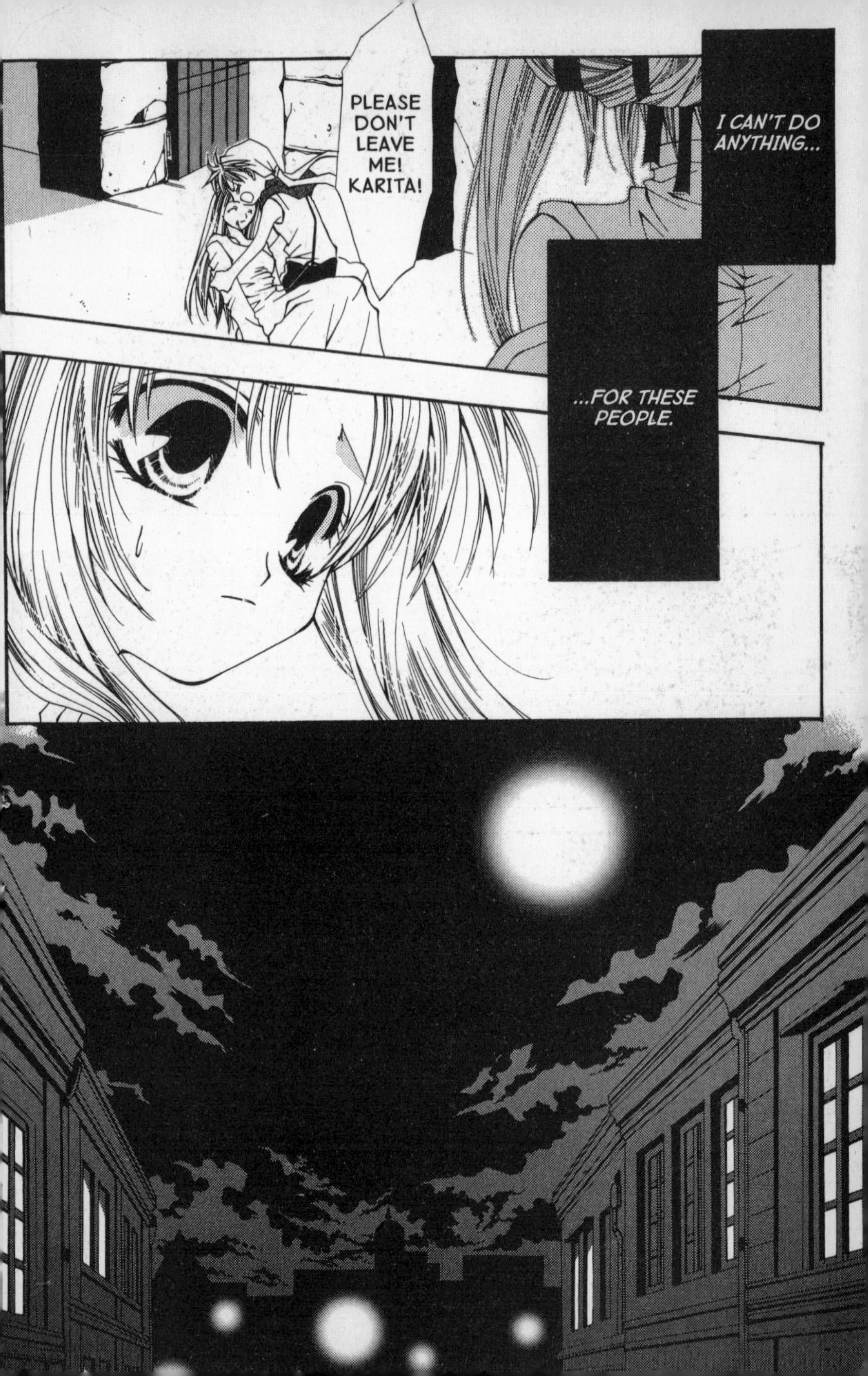
I CAN'T DO ANYTHING...
PLEASE DON'T LEAVE ME! KARITA!
...FOR THESE PEOPLE.

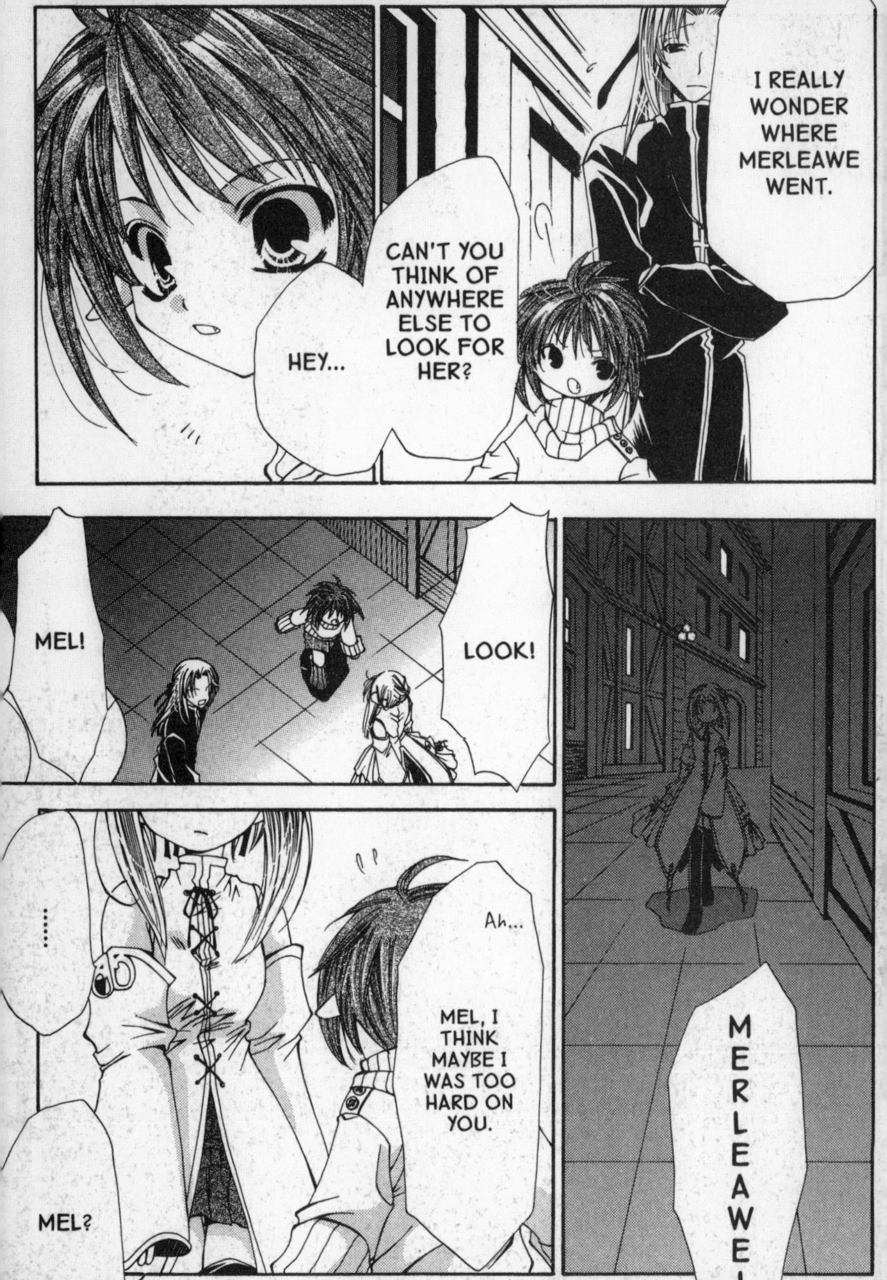
I REALLY WONDER WHERE MERLEAWE WENT.
CAN'T YOU THINK OF ANYWHERE ELSE TO LOOK FOR HER?
HEY...
MERLEAWE!
LOOK!
MEL!
Ah...
MEL, I THINK MAYBE I WAS TOO HARD ON YOU.
......
MEL?

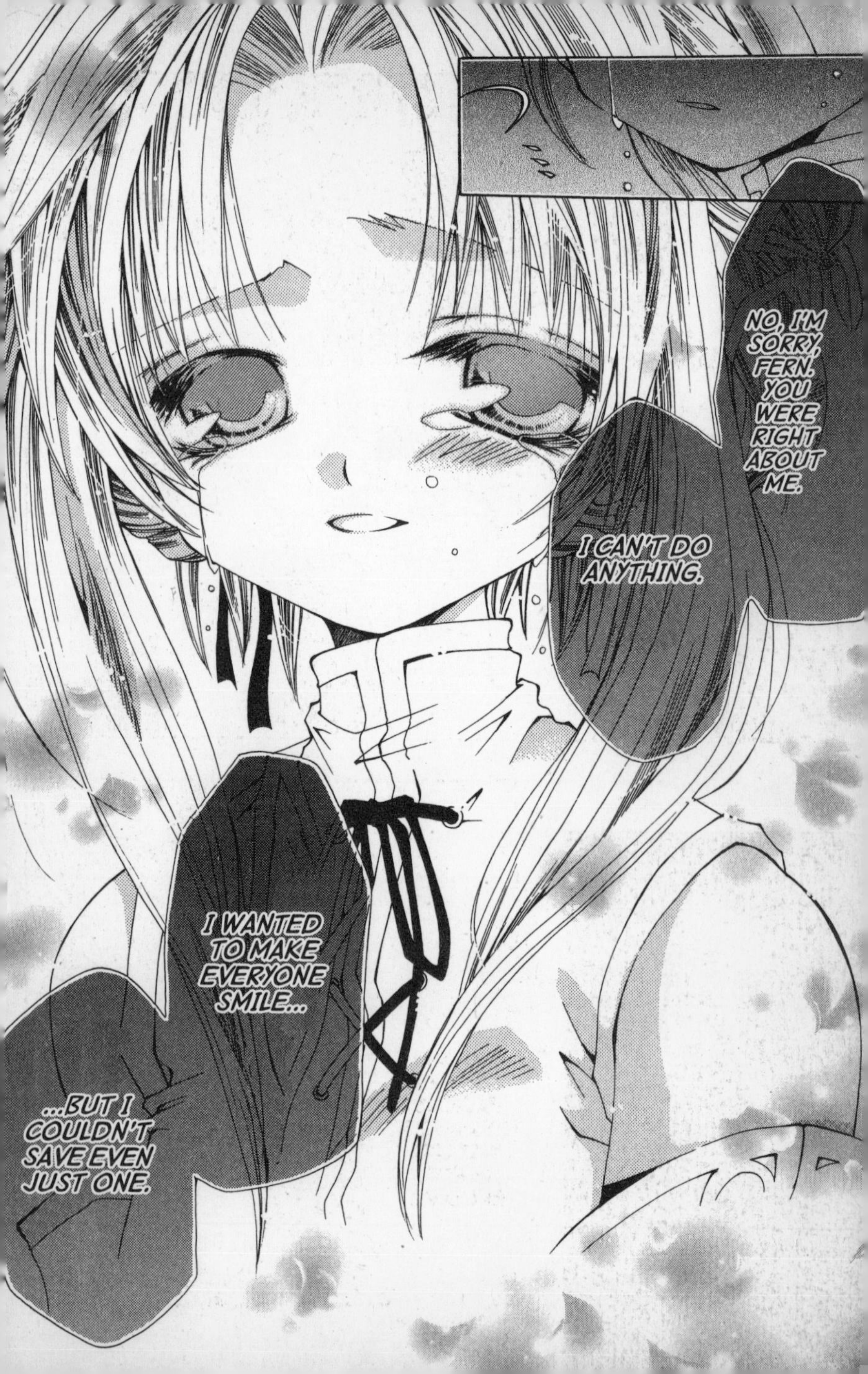
NO, I'M SORRY, FERN. YOU WERE RIGHT ABOUT ME.
I CAN'T DO ANYTHING.
I WANTED TO MAKE EVERYONE SMILE...
...BUT I COULDN'T SAVE EVEN JUST ONE.

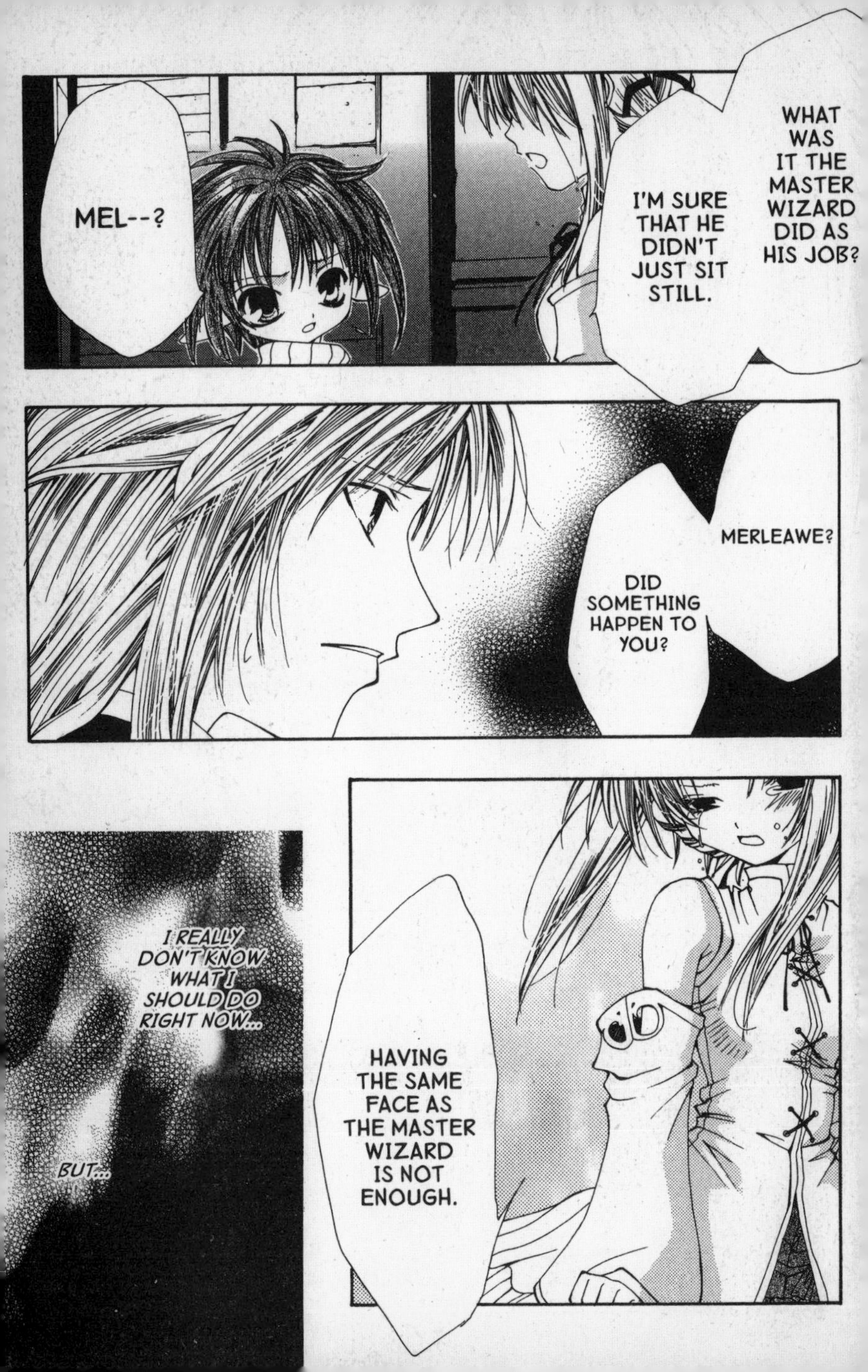
WHAT WAS IT THE MASTER WIZARD DID AS HIS JOB?
I'M SURE THAT HE DIDN'T JUST SIT STILL.
MEL--?
MERLEAWE?
DID SOMETHING HAPPEN TO YOU?
HAVING THE SAME FACE AS THE MASTER WIZARD IS NOT ENOUGH.
I REALLY DON'T KNOW WHAT I SHOULD DO RIGHT NOW...
BUT...

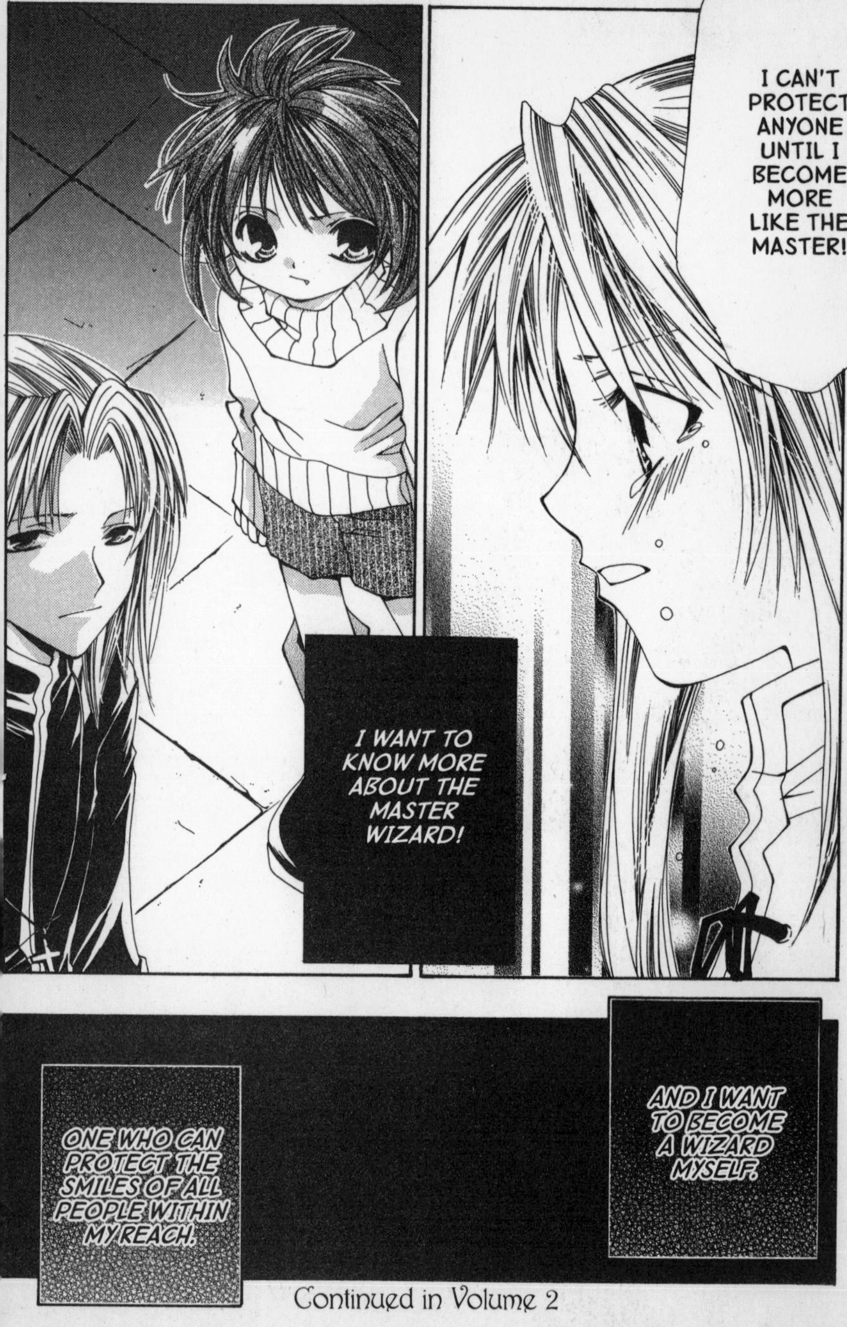
I CAN'T PROTECT ANYONE UNTIL I BECOME MORE LIKE THE MASTER!
I WANT TO KNOW MORE ABOUT THE MASTER WIZARD!
AND I WANT TO BECOME A WIZARD MYSELF.
ONE WHO CAN PROTECT THE SMILES OF ALL PEOPLE WITHIN MY REACH.

Continued in Volume 2

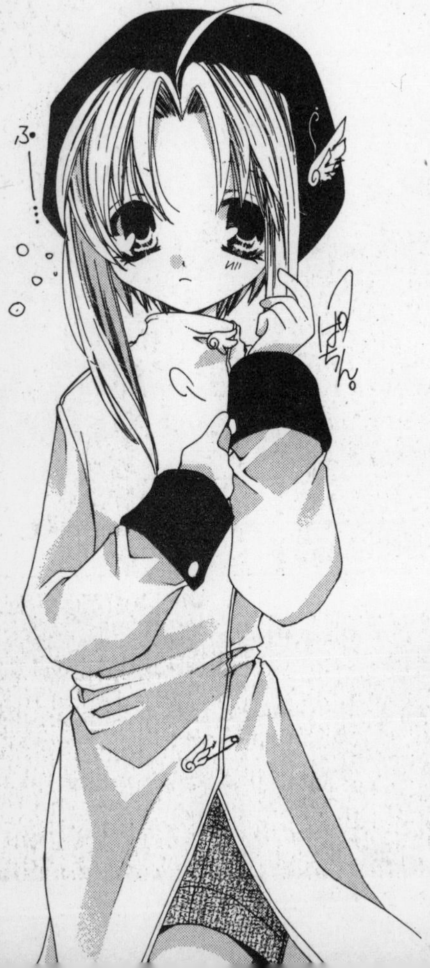
ぽわん。
ふー…

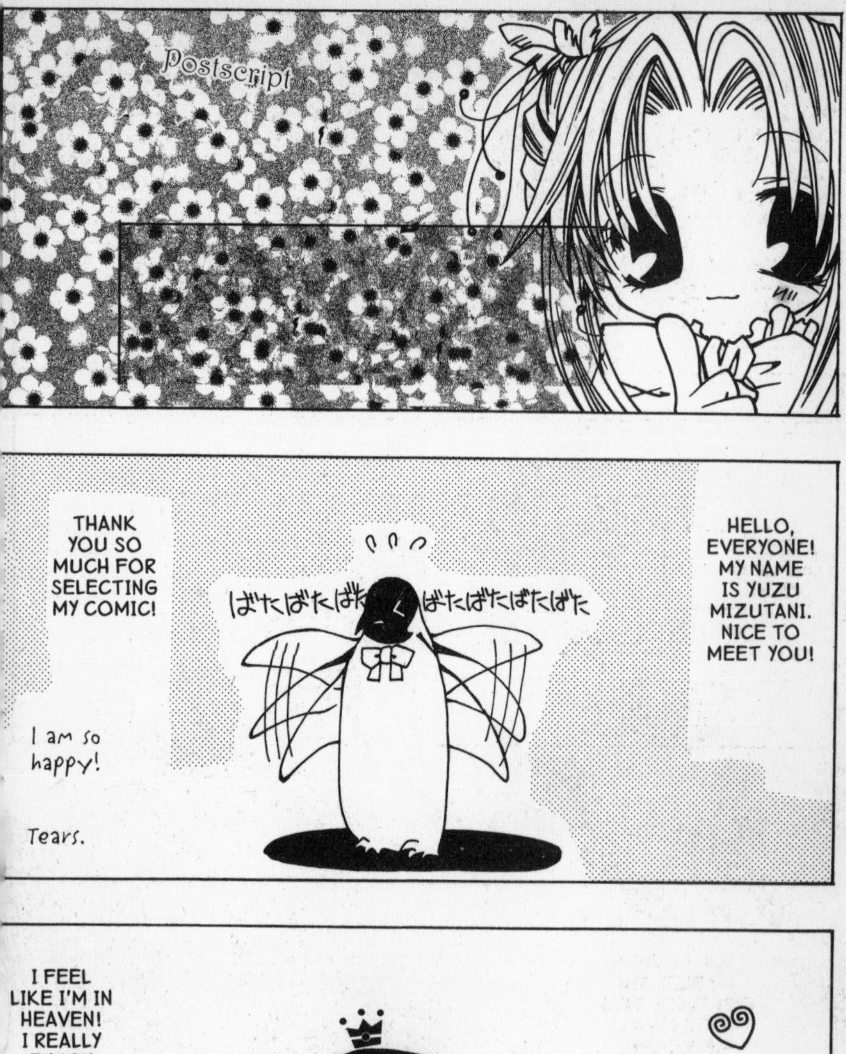
Postscript
HELLO, EVERYONE! MY NAME IS YUZU MIZUTANI. NICE TO MEET YOU!
ばたばたばたばた
ばたばたばた
THANK YOU SO MUCH FOR SELECTING MY COMIC!
I am so happy!
Tears.
THIS IS NOT ONLY MY VERY FIRST SERIES, BUT ALSO MY FIRST COMIC PUBLISHED! EVERYTHING IS MY FIRST TIME!
I usually use three kinds of pens to draw.
Please be sure to check out the extra comics at the end, too.
I FEEL LIKE I'M IN HEAVEN! I REALLY ENJOY DRAWING MANGA!

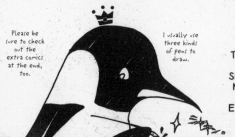

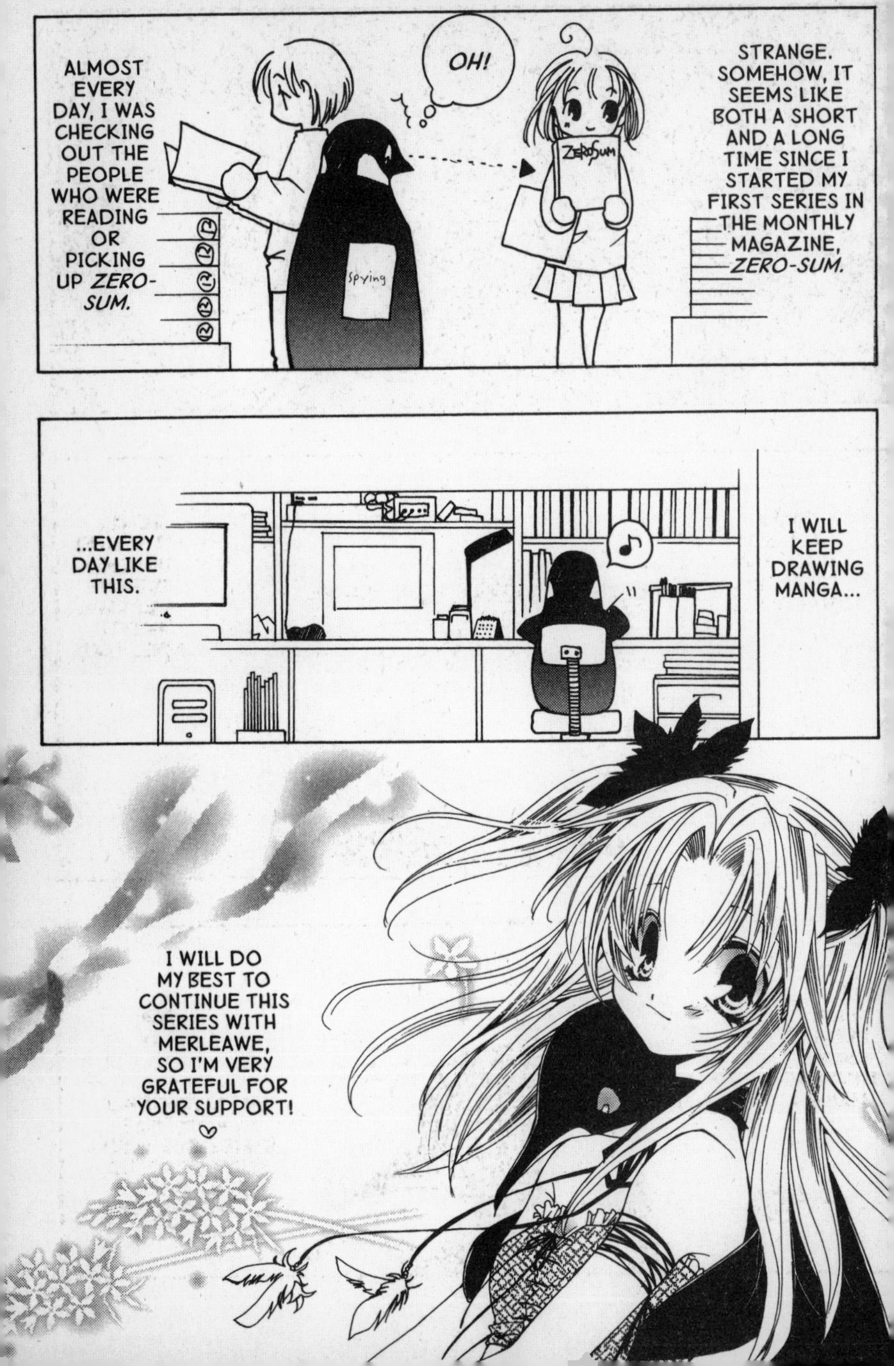
STRANGE. SOMEHOW, IT SEEMS LIKE BOTH A SHORT AND A LONG TIME SINCE I STARTED MY FIRST SERIES IN THE MONTHLY MAGAZINE, *ZERO-SUM.*
ZEROSUM
OH!
ALMOST EVERY DAY, I WAS CHECKING OUT THE PEOPLE WHO WERE READING OR PICKING UP *ZERO-SUM.*
Spying
I WILL KEEP DRAWING MANGA...
...EVERY DAY LIKE THIS.
I WILL DO MY BEST TO CONTINUE THIS SERIES WITH MERLEAWE, SO I'M VERY GRATEFUL FOR YOUR SUPPORT! ♡

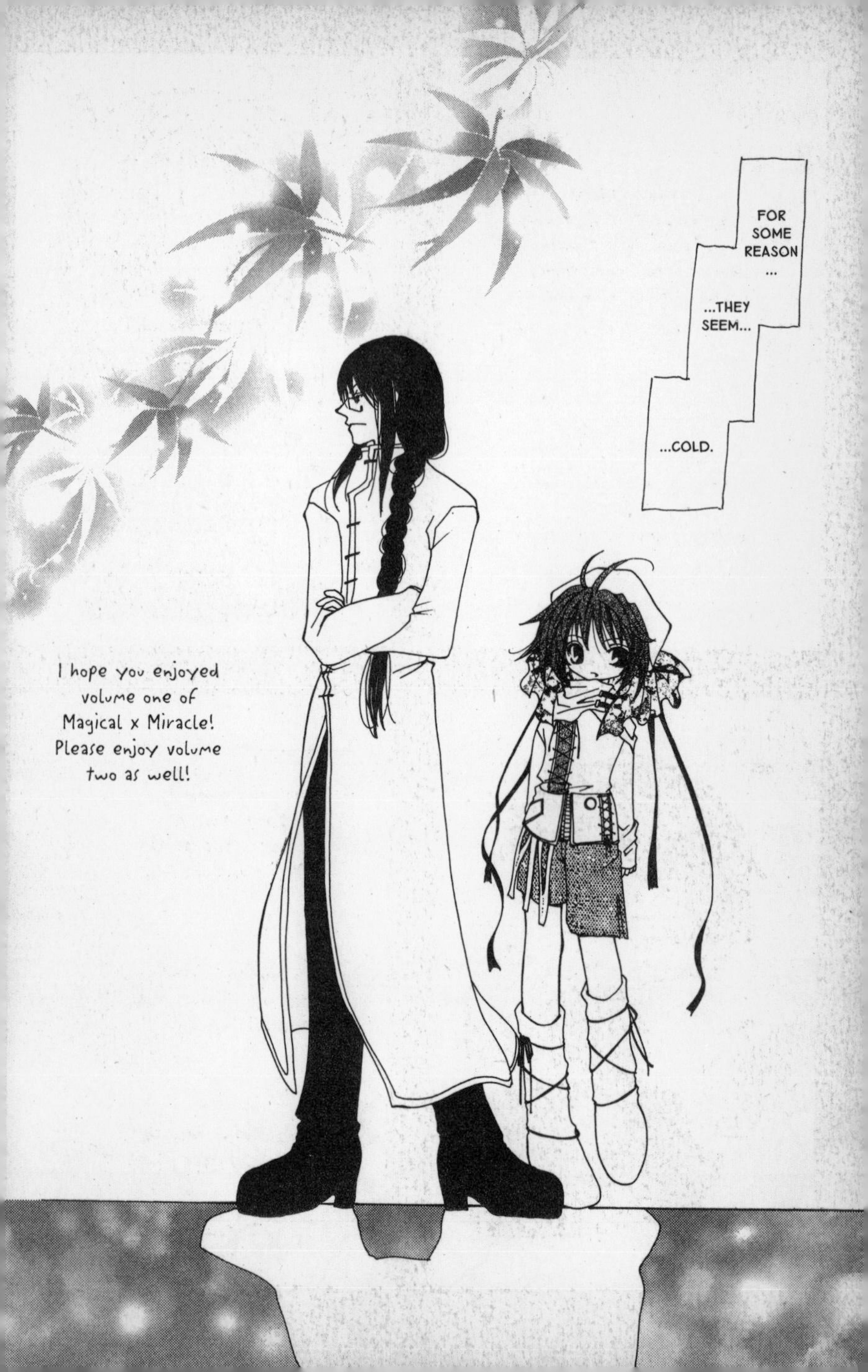
FOR SOME REASON ...
...THEY SEEM...
...COLD.
I hope you enjoyed volume one of Magical x Miracle! Please enjoy volume two as well!

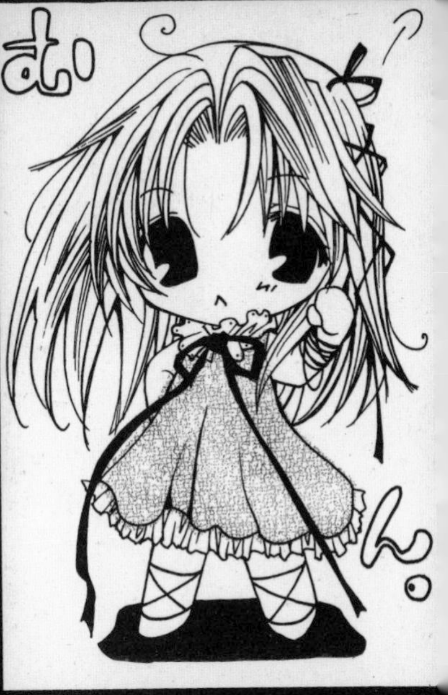
むん。

I would really appreciate it if you would write me with any of your questions, thoughts or opinions.

Please come check out my website:
http://mizyuz.cool.ne.jp

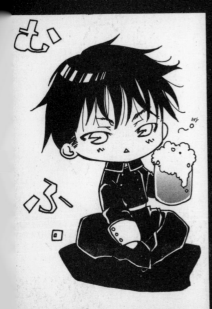

To my readers...
To my editors...
To everyone at the editorial department...

To Cherry-chan, Taocci, Seno-kun, who helped all my work...

Thank you so much, everyone!

Yuzu Mizutani

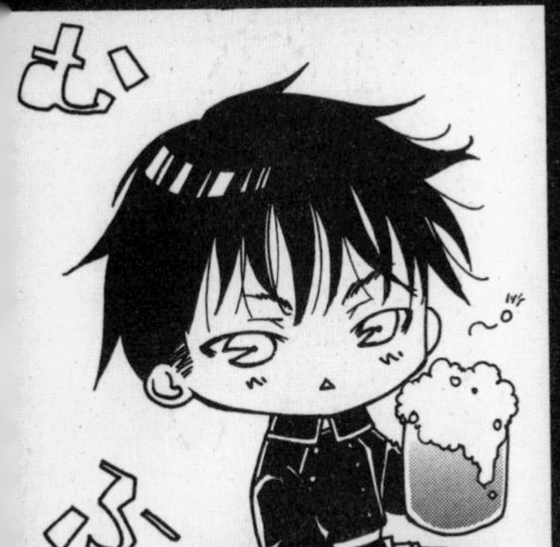
むふ。

MAGICAL×MIRACLE

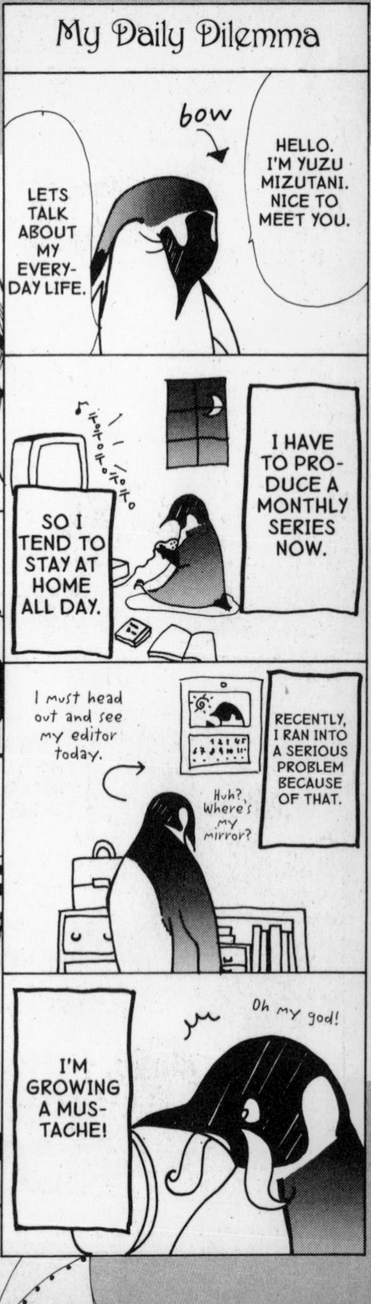
My Daily Dilemma
HELLO. I'M YUZU MIZUTANI. NICE TO MEET YOU.
bow
LETS TALK ABOUT MY EVERY-DAY LIFE.
I HAVE TO PRO-DUCE A MONTHLY SERIES NOW.
SO I TEND TO STAY AT HOME ALL DAY.
RECENTLY, I RAN INTO A SERIOUS PROBLEM BECAUSE OF THAT.
Huh? Where's my mirror?
I must head out and see my editor today.
Oh my god!
I'M GROWING A MUS-TACHE!

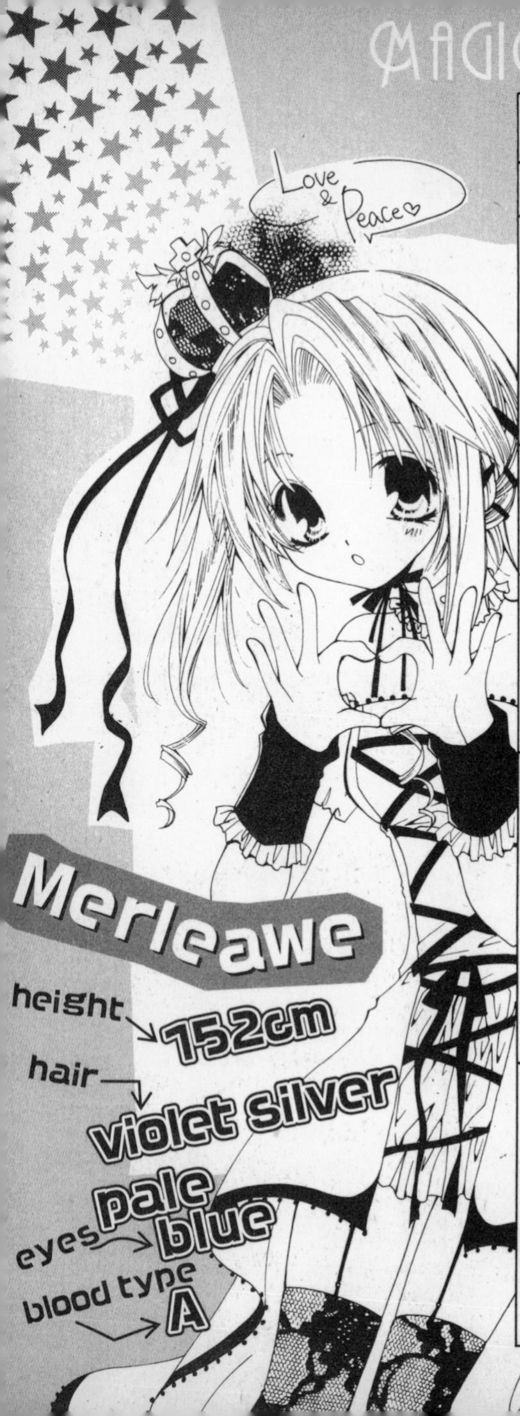
Love & Peace♡
Merleawe
height
152cm
hair
violet silver
eyes
pale blue
blood type
A

YUZU MIZUTANI

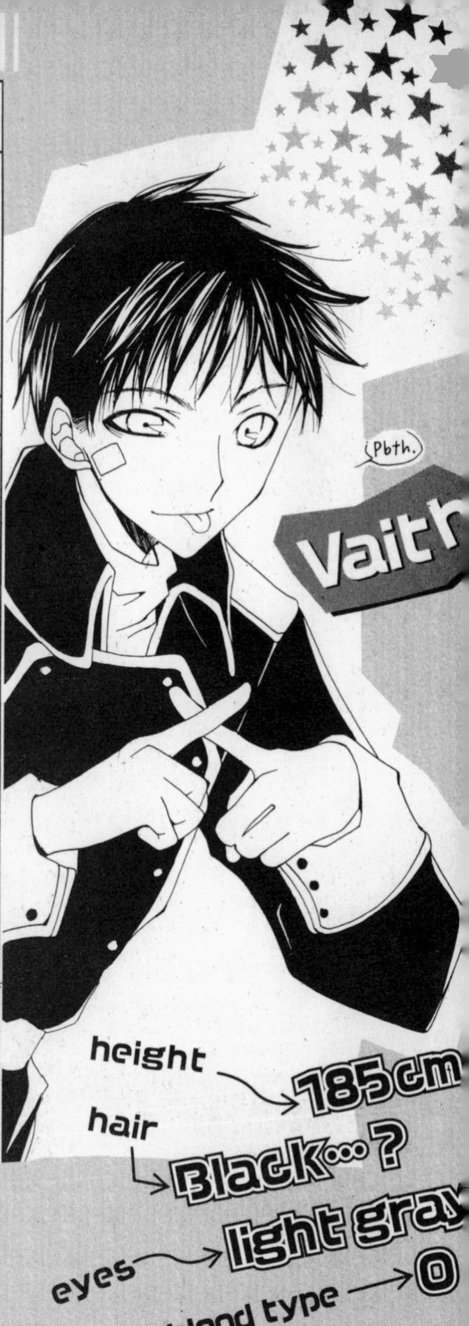
Pbth.
Vaith
height
185cm
hair
Black…?
eyes
light gray
blood type
O

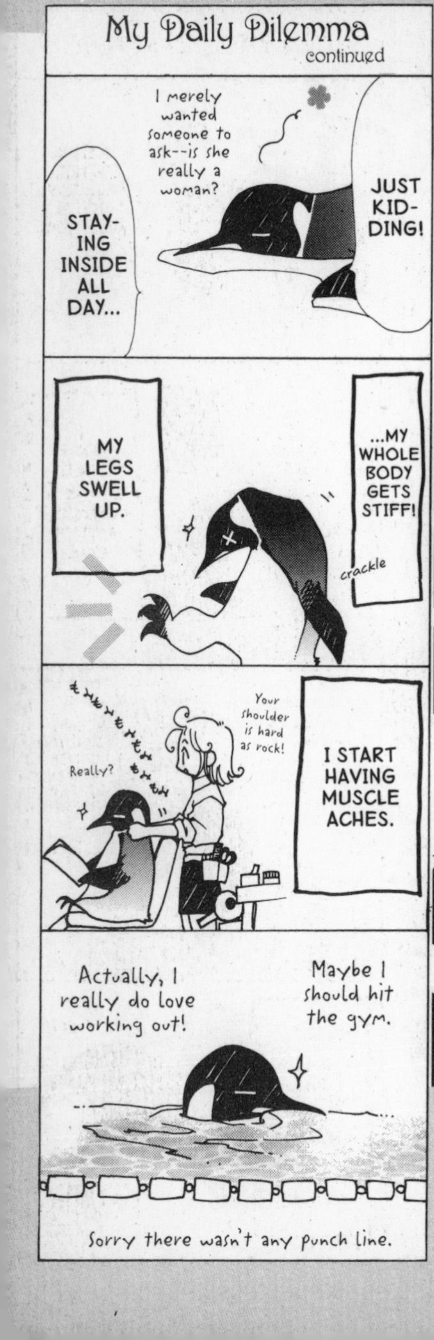
My Daily Dilemma
continued
STAYING INSIDE ALL DAY...
I merely wanted someone to ask--is she really a woman?
JUST KIDDING!
MY LEGS SWELL UP.
...MY WHOLE BODY GETS STIFF!
crackle
Your shoulder is hard as rock!
Really?
I START HAVING MUSCLE ACHES.
Actually, I really do love working out!
Maybe I should hit the gym.
Sorry there wasn't any punch line.

In the Next Volume of...

Magical Miracle

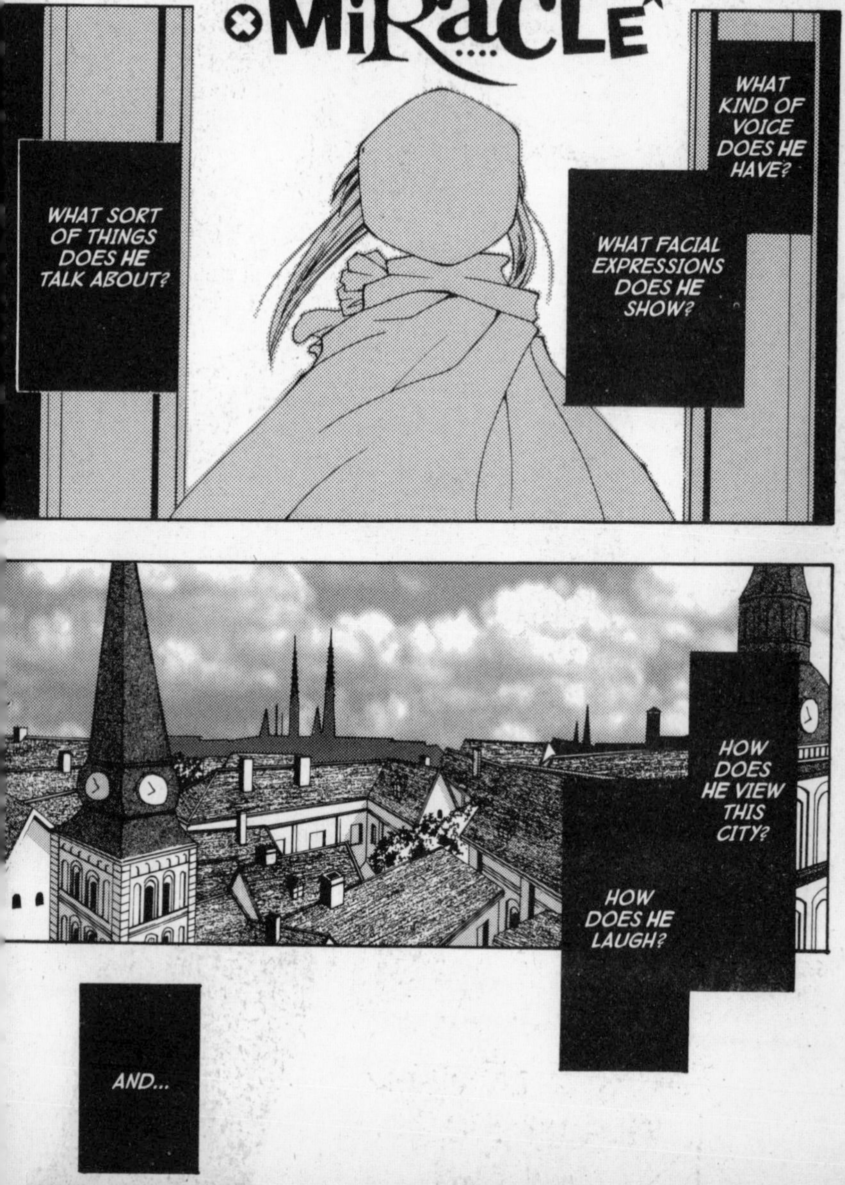
WHAT KIND OF VOICE DOES HE HAVE?
WHAT FACIAL EXPRESSIONS DOES HE SHOW?
WHAT SORT OF THINGS DOES HE TALK ABOUT?
HOW DOES HE VIEW THIS CITY?
HOW DOES HE LAUGH?
AND...

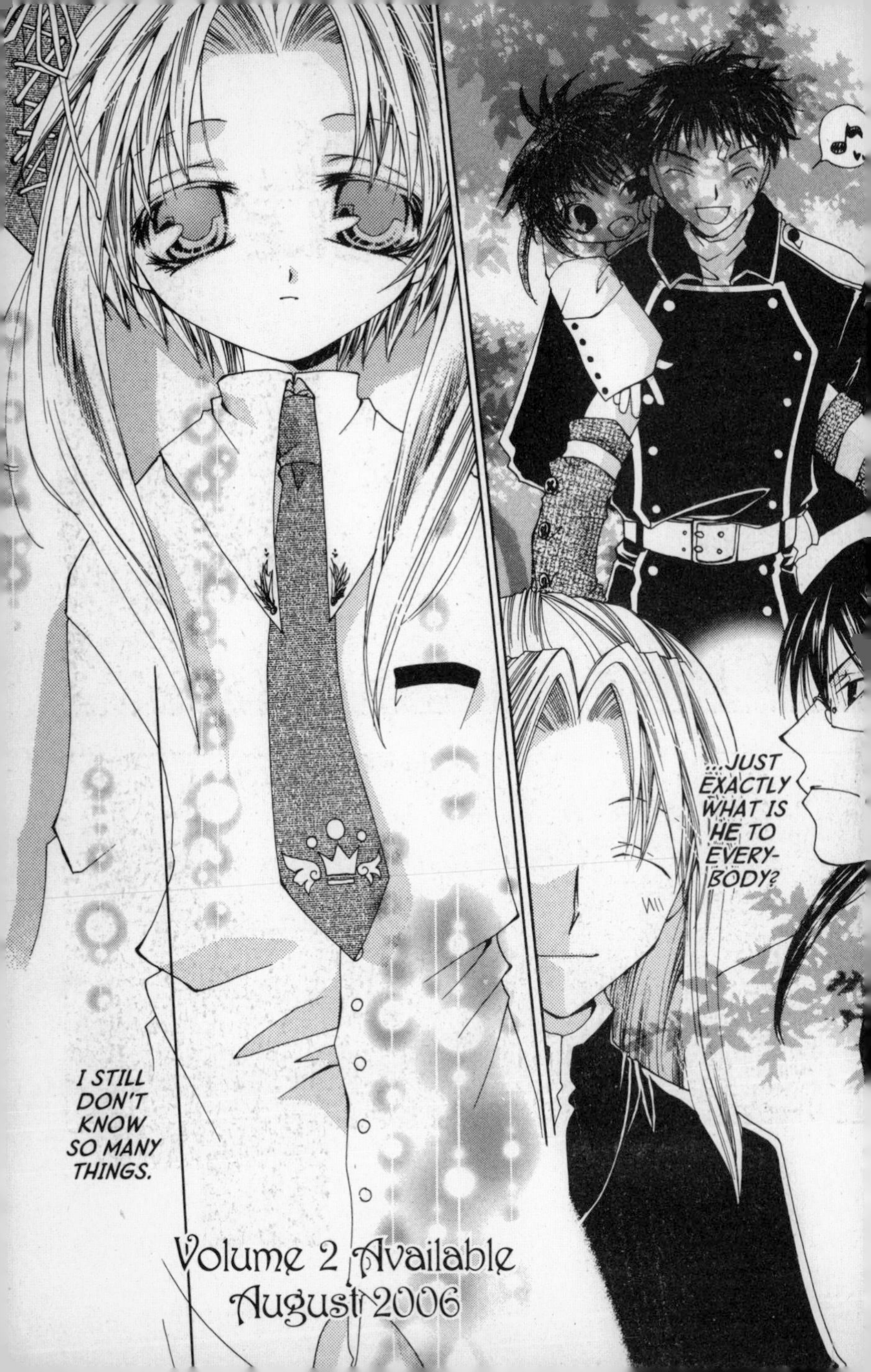
...JUST EXACTLY WHAT IS HE TO EVERY-BODY?
I STILL DON'T KNOW SO MANY THINGS.
Volume 2 Available August 2006

TOKYOPOP SHOP

Ayumu struggles with her studies, and the all-important high school entrance exams are approaching. Fortunately, she has help from her best bud Shii-chan, who is at the top of the class. But when the test results come back, the friends are surprised: Ayumu surpasses Shii-chan's scores and gets into the school of her choice—without Shii-chan! Losing her friend is so painful for Ayumu that she starts cutting herself to ease her sorrow. Finally, Ayumu seeks comfort in a new friend, Manami. But will Manami prove to be the friend that Ayumu truly needs? Or will Ayumu continue down a dark path?

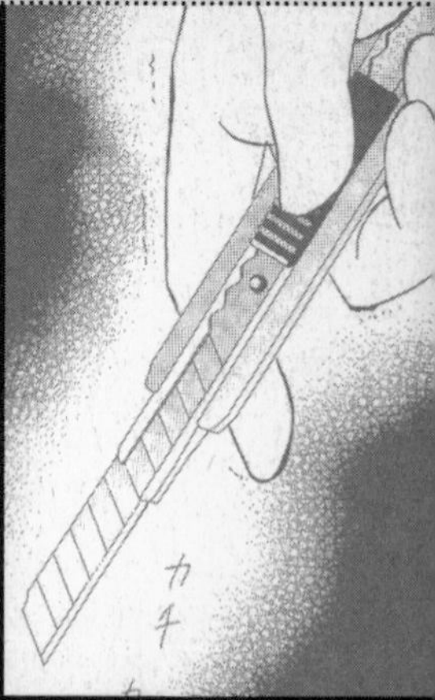

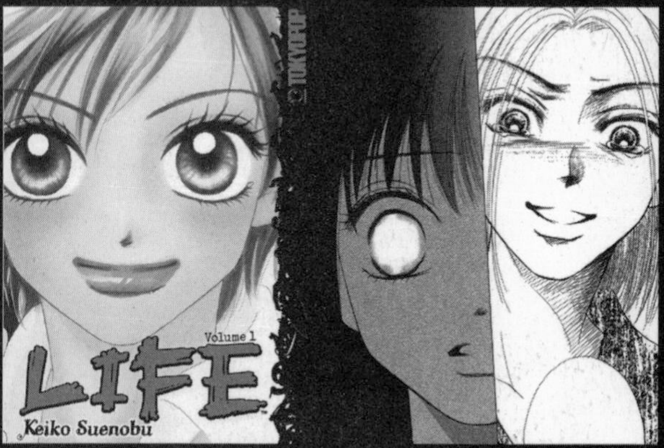
TOKYOPOP
Volume 1
LIFE
Keiko Suenobu

It's about real teenagers...

It's about real high school...

It's about real life.

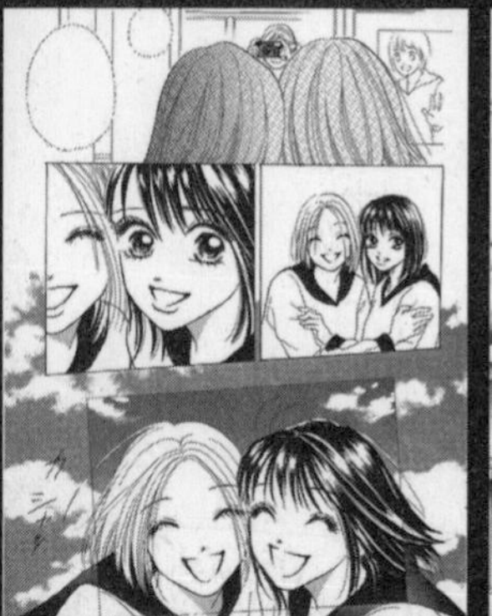

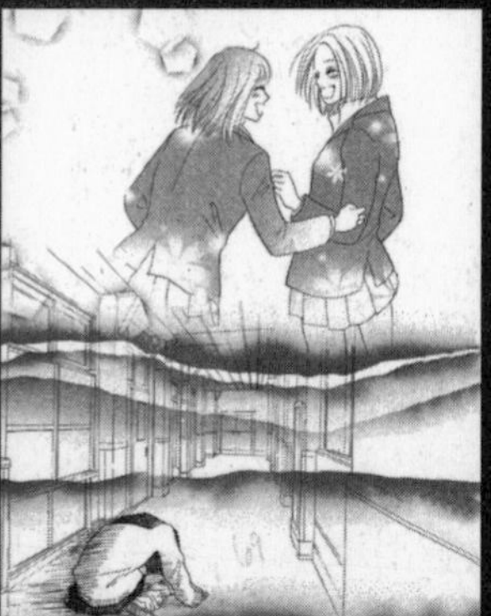

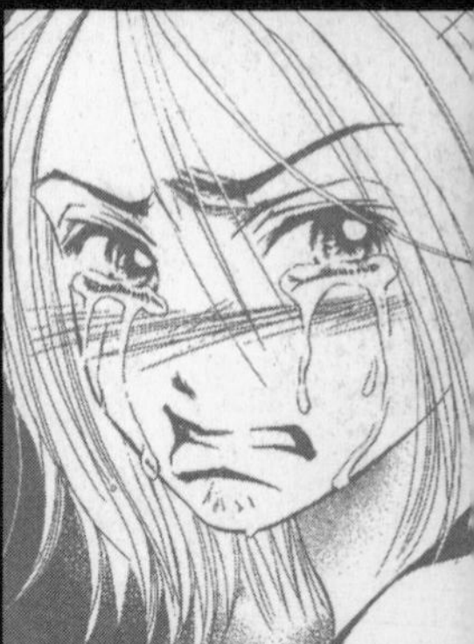

WWW.TOKYOPOP.COM/LIFE

LIFE
BY KEIKO SUENOBU

Ordinary high school teenagers...
Except that they're not.

© Keiko Suenobu

OT
OLDER TEEN
AGE 16+

READ THE ENTIRE FIRST CHAPTER ONLINE FOR FREE:

THIS FALL, TOKYOPOP CREATES A FRESH, NEW CHAPTER IN TEEN NOVELS...

For Adventurers...

Witches' Forest: The Adventures of Duan Surk

By Mishio Fukazawa

Duan Surk is a 16-year-old Level 2 fighter who embarks on the quest of a lifetime—battling mythical creatures and outwitting evil sorceresses, all in an impossible rescue mission in the spooky Witches' Forest!

BASED ON THE FAMOUS *FORTUNE QUEST* WORLD

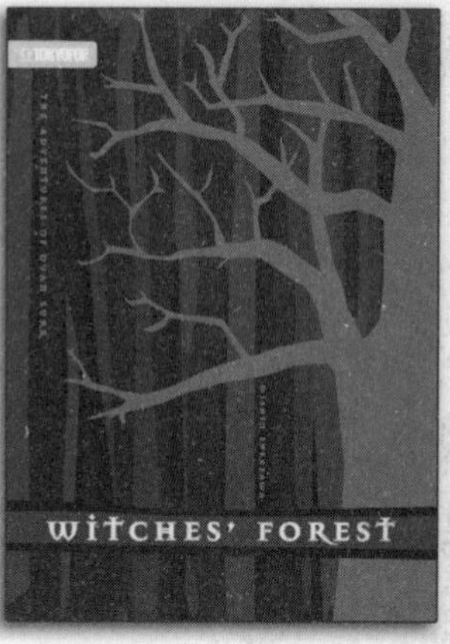
TOKYOPOP
WITCHES' FOREST

For Dreamers...

Magic Moon

By Wolfgang and Heike Hohlbein

Kim enters the engimatic realm of Magic Moon, where he battles unthinkable monsters and fantastical creatures—in order to unravel the secret that keeps his sister locked in a coma.

THE WORLDWIDE BESTSELLING FANTASY *THRILL*OGY ARRIVES IN THE U.S.!

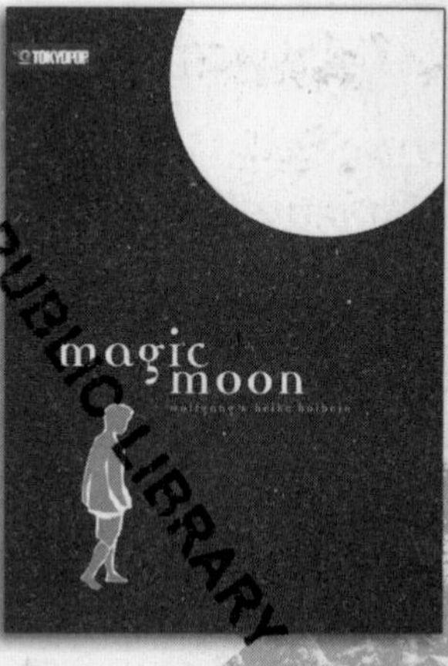
TOKYOPOP
magic moon

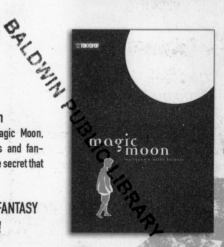

TOKYOPOP PRESENTS

POP FICTION

For Believers...

Scrapped Princess:
A Tale of Destiny

By Ichiro Sakaki
A dark prophecy reveals that the queen will give birth to a daughter who will usher in the Apocalypse. But despite all attempts to destroy the baby, the myth of the "Scrapped Princess" lingers on...

THE INSPIRATION FOR THE HIT ANIME AND MANGA SERIES!

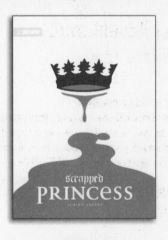

For Thinkers...

Kino no Tabi:
Book One of The Beautiful World

By Keiichi Sigsawa
Kino roams the world on the back of Hermes, her unusual motorcycle, in a journey filled with happiness and pain, decadence and violence, and magic and loss.

THE SENSATIONAL BESTSELLER IN JAPAN HAS FINALLY ARRIVED!

STOP!

This is the back of the book.
You wouldn't want to spoil a great ending!

This book is printed "manga-style," in the authentic Japanese right-to-left format. Since none of the artwork has been flipped or altered, readers get to experience the story just as the creator intended. You've been asking for it, so TOKYOPOP® delivered: authentic, hot-off-the-press, and far more fun!

DIRECTIONS

If this is your first time reading manga-style, here's a quick guide to help you understand how it works.

It's easy… just start in the top right panel and follow the numbers. Have fun, and look for more 100% authentic manga from TOKYOPOP®!